T0374240

NOTES *from a* CANCER MOM

Leslie W Jermainne

Balboa Press books may be ordered through booksellers or by contacting:

Balboa Press
A Division of Hay House
1663 Liberty Drive
Bloomington, IN 47403
www.balboapress.com
1 (877) 407-4847

Print information available on the last page.

ISBN: 978-1-5043-3852-3 (sc)
ISBN: 978-1-5043-3854-7 (hc)
ISBN: 978-1-5043-3853-0 (e)

Library of Congress Control Number: 2015912860

Balboa Press rev. date: 10/16/2015

There is only one person this book could possibly be dedicated to.

My son Brian Ross Jermainne.

He is my hero. He is my greatest teacher. He gives me love, strength, laughter and joy. Every. Single. Day.

Photo courtesy of my friend Kim Tyler www.KTPhoto.net

I would also like to remember and acknowledge other "fighters" in my life. My Mother who just lost her battle with MM on 6/12/15 and my Dad who lost his to MDS on 5/9/15 – both 83. My dear friend Anna Baldino who lost her battle in 2009 at the age of 34. My Mother-In-Law Elizabeth Jermainne who lost her battle in 2000 at the age of 75. My Maternal Grandmother, Priscilla Jordan whom I never got to meet because she lost her battle at the age of 57, 6 years before I was born. My Aunt Alberta Woodstock who is a survivor. And for everyone who faces this disease and their caregivers and supporters too, because no one fights alone.

There is only one person this book could possibly be dedicated to:

My son Ethan Ross Jermaline

Ethan is my hero. He is my greatest teacher. He gives me a
reason to [illegible] laughter and love Every Single Day

Photo courtesy of my friend [illegible] Thompson

I would also like to remember and acknowledge other fighters in my life. My Mother who just lost her battle with MM on 6/1/2015 and my Dad who lost his to MDS on 5/8/15 – both [illegible]. My dear friend Anna Baldino who lost her battle in 2008 at the age of 34. My Mother-in-Law Elizabeth [illegible] who lost her battle in 2000 at the age of 73. My Maternal Grandmother Pascha [illegible] whom I never got to meet because she lost her battle at the age of 57 years before I was born. My aunt Alberta Woodstock who is a survivor. And to everyone who faces this disease and their caregivers and supporters too because no one fights alone.

Foreword

Here is the Wikipedia definition for a Forward in a book:

"Typically written by someone other than the primary author of the work, it often tells of some interaction between the writer of the foreword and the book's primary author or the story the book tells."

I hate "forwards". I don't really know why they are there. To sell the book? I'm sure I learned in 3rd grade or something, but pretty much they annoy me - but I also have a very low guilt tolerance so I feel guilty if I skip them. Well, NOT ANY MORE! Here's the deal. If you are holding this, you're probably going to read it. If you get partially through it and are bored - stop reading. Life is short. Go do something enjoyable - or get a new book. No guilt. Seriously.

Leslie

PS - There are a few emails that have a lot of swear words in them. Sometimes cancer makes you swear. A lot. Sorry.

PPS – Any and all proceeds from my story will go to a fund set up for my son, for education or to help maybe buy a home someday. Also to Dana Farber Cancer Institute/The Jimmy Fund, Make-A-Wish and St. Baldrick's.

Here is the Wikipedia definition of a Forward in a book:

It is typically written by someone other than the primary author of the work, it often tells of some interaction between the writer of the foreword and the book's primary author or the story the book tells.

I hate forewords. I don't really know why they are there. It's [illegible] because I was taught that in 3rd grade or something but pretty much they annoy me—but I also have extremely low guilt tolerance so I feel guilty if I skip them as well. NOT ANY MORE! Here's the deal. If you are holding this, you're probably planning on reading it. If you get partially through it and are bored, stop reading. Life is short. Go do something enjoyable or [illegible] [illegible]. No guilt. Seriously.

[illegible]

P.S. There are a few chapters that have a lot of swear words in them. Sometimes cancer makes you swear. A lot. Sorry.

PPS [illegible] any and all proceeds from my story will go to a fund set up for my son, for education or to help maybe buy a house someday. Also to [illegible] [illegible] Foundation/the [illegible] Alaska [illegible] [illegible].

Why I'm writing this

I didn't sit down to write this book about my time going through my son's cancer diagnosis. I started writing an email every night while in the hospital to update our family and friends what was happening to us. Then I realized it helped me put each day away and move forward, focusing on the next day and what we had to do to fight and to win. People who read them said I should put them in a book. So I listened.

But honestly there are a couple of reasons I've put this information into book form. 1. I've always wanted to write a book, although I thought it would be a funny romance. 2. People kept telling me I should write a book after reading my emails. 3. Maybe, somehow, someone might receive some sort of help or understanding or reassurance from this. I find it hard to believe I could have that kind of impact, but who knows. Life is crazy that way.

So, from the title, I'm assuming you have a bit of an idea what you're going to read here. But here is a brief back story.

On April 18th, 2013 my only child, my 15 year old son had biopsy surgery and we were told he had Lymphoma. My world spun out of control while time came to a screeching halt. While accompanying my son through his treatment, I started writing a nightly email to our family and friends and even some people I've never met, but who wanted to know how we were doing. I think the emails helped me more than anyone. And I'm going to share them with you, along with "our story" - but it is mostly my story, since I'm not a cancer patient and I don't know what it feels like to be one. But I do know what it feels like to be a Mom, watching my only child go through this nightmare and wishing day and night it was me. So here it goes....

How We Ended Up in The Hospital and I started writing these email notes

On February 3, 1997 I found out I was pregnant. I was so thrilled. I had been married 35 days. I was in love with my wonderful husband and we had an instant family with his two daughters. On October 24, 1997 at 12:21 a.m. our son arrived. It had been a great pregnancy, uncomplicated delivery and here was my beautiful baby boy. I was so very happy. Upon taking him home and giving him his first bath on October 27th when everyone else had left the house and I was alone with my baby in his pretty nursery, I knew I had found my meaning in life. To be his mommy.

Fast forward to Sunday, March 31, 2013, my son walked into the living room and said to me, as I watched t.v. with his Dad, probably eating something unhealthy, "Mom, I have a lump under my arm, and it hurts." He said this while feeling the lump. I said, "Don't worry. It's probably just a plugged hair follicle. I get that too once in a while. Stop using deodorant for a few days and I'm sure it will go away." Satisfied, he walked back to his room.

Wednesday of that week, which would be April 3, 2013, he told me the lump felt bigger, hurt some but not terrible. I told him it takes a few days to get better, just wait. I remember just now as I type this, that way back on Wednesday, March 13, 2013 while we were at drum corps practice, I thought he looked too skinny, gaunt almost and I snapped a few photos. Oh My God. These kinds of things put my Mom guilt into overdrive.

You see, he had been working very hard to lose weight and over the course of 2012 he had lost 60lbs. He had limited his carbohydrate intake to 50grams/day and walked about 4 miles a day on our treadmill. And he did it! The only person in our overweight family to eat healthy, exercise and lose weight. And he was keeping it off. But in January or February of 2013, he started losing a bit more while upping his carb intake, trying to find the right number to hold his weight. He would up the carb amount and then in a week or so he'd say, "I lost another pound". And I'd say "okay, so up the carbs another 25 or so". This happened a few times, leveling out for a week or so before dropping more weight. He was down to around 175 I think and 6 feet tall.

On Friday April 5th, I was at a Board of Realtors breakfast meeting with my husband. I usually make sure I turn off my cell phone, as all good meeting participants should. But I didn't. While eating my breakfast and listening to the speaker, I pulled my phone out of my purse to look at it, probably to make sure it was off. It was on vibrate thankfully, and about 5 seconds after I pulled it out, up popped my son's name. Again, normally I would have ignored the call, assuming that he'd just gotten up, saw the note I had left for him, and would be asking me to bring home Dunkin' Donuts for him when I was done at the meeting. But again, I did the opposite. I got up from the table, which thankfully was in the back of the room and by the door, walked out of door and answered my phone. "Hi honey, what's up?" "Mom, I have a bump in my stomach now." Gulp. I asked him a lot of questions, did it hurt? How big is it? Where is it? When did you first feel it? I told him not to worry and I'd be home soon. And yes, I would bring him Dunkin Donuts and I would call his doctor and we'd have him looked at.

I hung up from that call and immediately called his primary care physician. I explained and they said they could see us a 3 p.m. His doctor examined him. Asked why we didn't have a blood draw done after his January physical. Because Brian didn't want to, and I didn't think it was so urgent, since he was healthy. Ugh. Mom guilt overload. So they did a blood draw there. We wouldn't get the results until Monday. The doctor said he thought the two things were unrelated. An infected lymph node under his arm, and an unrelated lipoma (fatty growth) in his abdomen. He started him on antibiotics for the underarm and off we went.

Late Monday afternoon, the doctor's office called to say his creatinine was high. "What does that mean?" I asked the nurse who called to tell me that he needed to have another test to make sure it wasn't a false reading. She didn't know. So we went to the clinic Tuesday morning to have blood drawn again. That day, Tuesday April 9th, I called the office to say the lymph node was no better and as a matter of fact, maybe worse. In we went to the office and had an exam. We decided we wanted to see a surgeon to address these two areas regardless of the blood test results. His doctor said he'd call the surgeon he would recommend and get us in to see him.

On April 11th, we met with the surgeon. He also thought what his primary care physician thought, but agreed we could have them removed. Maybe in two weeks, he was very busy. I was like 'WHAT!!!! Two weeks?' The next day, Friday the second blood test came back, creatinine still high. On Monday his primary care physician agreed to start pushing the surgeon to get this done sooner. We met with the surgeon in his office again on Tuesday, April 16th. He said he'd try to fit him in that week. I was getting perturbed. Trying not to freak. Googling lots of not good stuff. Crying myself to sleep at night. I now know that I'm sure I knew this was bad, before I knew that this was bad. But I held onto the words the doctors were saying, "unrelated", "fatty growth", infected lymph node". We finally got scheduled for surgery for Thursday, April 18th.

April 18, 2013. My son and I head to the hospital so he can have what we hope is the lipoma in his left abdominal wall removed and then drain what we hope is an infected lymph node under his right arm. What really happens is the surgeon removes a tumor from his abdominal wall and biopsies the lymph node under his right arm. The surgeon comes to find me playing solitaire on my iPad in the waiting room and tells me "it's lymphoma". I say "Okay". The conversation ensues that the surgeon has had a quick pathology done and they know it's lymphoma. They don't know if it is Large B-Cell Lymphoma or Burkitt Lymphoma, but definitely non-Hodgkin's lymphoma. The sample will be sent to another hospital pathology by express courier for confirmation. I keep nodding my head and saying 'okay, okay'. I am in utter shock and I'm holding back the tears. The surgeon asks me "Are you okay?" I nod my head up and down knowing that if I speak, the dam will open and in will surge the flood waters. He looks at me with tearing eyes and says "Well, I'm not okay. I've never had this happen with a child before, an adult yes, but not a child." I start crying. He sits with me a minute, and tells me someone will come and get me to see Brian in the recovery room. That he will come and talk with us there. He leaves and I'm alone and my son has cancer. My beautiful, funny, smart fifteen year old son has non-Hodgkin's lymphoma. The same cancer as far as I know, that killed my good friend and neighbor just a few years earlier.

They come and get me and I follow blindly trying to absorb what is happening, but I'm unable to process this information. I pass through the recovery room, where I see my husband's cousin looking at me. She must know. I plead in my head that she not talk to me, as I will seriously lose it and I have to get to my boy. I walk into recovery and meet the nurse who is taking care of Brian. He is resting and all I can do is look into his pretty blue eyes and stroke his head and love him even more. The doctor comes in and explains that it is lymphoma. It's cancer. They removed the tumor in his abdomen and biopsied under his arm. Brian says "okay", just like his mom. I don't remember much after that, but I can envision the darkened space of the quiet recovery room. The vision is one I will never forget. Once he is done in recovery, it is time for him to get dressed. As I'm helping him with his clothes, he says to me in his still somewhat groggy voice "So it's cancer, right Mom?" "Yes, Boo. It's cancer." My world is crashing down around my head. What do you say to your child when you have just learned they have cancer? I try to reassure him it will be okay, but truthfully I have no idea.

I head out to get the car to go and meet him and the nurse at the front door pickup area of the hospital. As soon as I get to a hallway and I'm walking out I call my husband. "Well?" he says. I'm crying so hard he can't understand me saying "It's cancer. He has cancer." I'm saying the words out loud and I can barely hear myself. "Oh my God" He says. I don't remember the conversation after that. He doesn't remember it either. I get in the car and try to pull myself together. I pick up Brian at the front door and get him in the car. He wants Dunkin Donuts since he hasn't eaten all day waiting for this surgery. I drive to the restaurant, park the car and go in and order coffee and food and try to not look anyone in the face. I want to shout, "I just found out my son has cancer. Like just 20 minutes ago." I am in such shock on the way home, I don't remember the conversation.

I honestly don't remember anything about getting home that evening, talking, dinner, going to be bed, nothing. My mind is a blank.

I find out later that I called my parents. I had no memory of this, until I asked my Dad how I told them the news. He said, "You called us Les. It was the worst phone call of my life. You sobbed through the whole thing." I still don't remember what I said, but I did remember one little glimpse of it after that. It was my Dad saying in a shocked and sad voice "Oh Les. I wish I could just hug you."

Friday April 19th dawned, as they always do. I feel like the sun should not have risen that day, but it does and now I understand it has to. That morning my husband and I had to go to a closing. We were buying a two family investment house in town. We had plans to work on it with Brian all summer. For him to learn about rehabbing a house. He was excited. Now, well....I didn't know if he'd be alive this summer. But off we went, cell phone clutched in my hand, waiting for someone to call me with a definite diagnosis and tell me what to do. The closing was done and when I got home the surgeon called me. Pathology confirmed non-Hodgkin's lymphoma, but still they were unable to determine what exact type. "Where do you want to be treated?" asked the surgeon. "I have no idea, I wasn't planning on needing oncology services for my son." He said he'd make some calls to his colleagues and find out. He called me back and told me the recommendation. 'Whatever you say', is pretty much my reply, since I have no clue what to do. He will call them, refer us, they will call me. So we wait. Meantime, Brian and I go to Walmart. While there he sees this giant t.v. that is deeply discounted as it is the floor model and has no remote. I buy it. This kid is going to be stuck in his room, fighting, resting, recovering. I would buy anything to give him some joy.

What must he have been thinking right then? "I have cancer. I have cancer. Will I die? Will I live? Will I be sick? Will I die? I have cancer." That is what I imagine he is thinking. Because my mind is whirling all over those thoughts, with a few others too. We get the t.v., they load it into our car. We get it home, in the house, hooked up and it all takes awhile.

I get a phone call from the pediatric oncology group we've been referred to. We go through the same million questions. Here are my answers. He is doing well. He isn't sick. No fever, no chills, no night sweats. Appetite is fine, energy is good. Pooping is good, no pain. No Nothing!!! They don't believe he isn't sick. The surgeon called me before to say they would be calling me and he told me they couldn't understand he wasn't sick.

The oncologist explains that they want to see him late that afternoon in the ER. They want to run some blood tests, have a CAT scan of his head, x-rays of his chest and abdomen. If everything is good, we will go home and come back to their office on Monday. They tell me to pack a bag for him and me, because if need be, we will be admitted.

I go into his room to tell him. He has gotten to play his video games on his giant t.v. for about 30 minutes. He wouldn't see it his t.v. again for 10 days. But we didn't know that then. We went to the E.R., Big Brian followed later and met us there. We did everything they wanted and had to wait a very long Friday night to get the last x-rays done, thanks to a very busy crazy night in the adult ER, who share the x-ray facility with the children's hospital. All tests came back good. Creatinine was high, but just drinking water would protect his kidneys, for now. Great! Could we leave then? Brian was supposed to have his friend Zack spend the night. We had already cancelled that since it was going for 11 p.m., but he was free to come the next night. Uhhhh, nope. We are going to admit you anyway. WHAT?!?! We were so sad and depressed. Why? We did what you asked. The results were good, why can't we go home? For the love of God we found out just 24 hours ago our son has cancer. Can we have a minute please!!! Nope. And the nightmare really began.

April 2013

So here start my notes, beginning Wednesday, April 17, 2013 – the day before my world stopped. I have included a few replies to my notes, and then my replies back. These are notes that I thought were the most relevant in the telling of my story. It's not all the wonderful little notes that say "we are thinking of you", "prayers being sent" - although each and every one of those were critical to my sanity and survival and were treasured scraps that were read, saved and reread too. The replies I've included help tell my story. I think so anyway.

WEDNESDAY, APRIL 17, 2013 - DAY BEFORE SURGERY

Sent: Wednesday, April 17, 2013 9:26 AM
From: Leslie Jermainne

Sorry - meant to update you yesterday. Saw the surgeon...again... who was not very diplomatic, a bit scary with his added "I'm sure it's all gonna be fine". Brian's surgery did get pushed up to tomorrow - not sure what time yet - but they are only going to deal with his arm due to risk of infection to the abdominal area. At least I think. Brian isn't going to his home school co-op today, because his teacher isn't going to be there. Hoping he will go on a walk in the woods with me somewhere today, if I can get his teenage butt moving!

I'm not sure when/who I have updated, but his creatinine levels were still really high on the second testing, and that is his doctors concern and for the surgery being moved up.

I will try to let everyone know how things go tomorrow - although I'm sure the surgery won't be any trouble. It will just be the long wait for pathology. OY!

Thanks for keeping touch - I appreciate your good vibes! Keep 'em coming!

Leslie

THURSDAY, APRIL 18, 2013 - SURGERY DAY

Conversation started April 18, 2013, 7:31pm to a few of my very closest friends, communicated through Facebook

Leslie Woodstock Jermainne

Sending an update. Incredibly bad day and I'm not up to talking, but little Brian had surgery today to biopsy/remove a lymph node in his stomach and under his arm. Lymphoma is the likely diagnosis according to the surgeon. Hoping to get pathology tomorrow as they had a special courier send the nodes to the lab to try and get results before the weekend. Exhausted, terrified, sad beyond words, but trying to hold on to a shred of hope and positive thoughts for the future. Any you can send his way are felt and appreciated. Hug and kiss your kids.

4/18, 7:44pm

Ann:

Les Honestly praying for you guys. Please let me know if you need anything!!

4/18, 10:00pm

Stacy:

Oh, my friend, I am so sorry! I am staying positive for you here and sending so much love your way!! I am here if you need anything! Love you!

FRIDAY, APRIL 19, 2013 - SENT TO HOSPITAL DAY

April 19, 2013 5:24am
Ann:

Thinking about you all night. Stay strong, Stay positive.

April 19, 2013 8:43am
Stacy:

Thinking of you here too! Positive thoughts your way.

Sent: Friday, April 19, 2013 3:53 PM
From: Leslie
To: My List
Subject: Re: not good news today

I wanted to update those people I have shared the past two weeks struggle with and today was the worst day so far. The lump in his stomach turned out to be an enlarged lymph node, which should not be like that obviously. Under his arm was also lymph nodes enlarged. The surgeon told me that in all likelihood he has lymphoma. He had the nodes sent special courier to pathology to try and get some answers today before suffering through the weekend.

I'm at the moment cried out, exhausted and frightened beyond what I can comprehend. I don't know what lies ahead of us, but I'm thankful to have friends and family I can rely on, even just for prayers and happy thoughts for us.

I will hopefully know more tomorrow and will try to update again. Talking seems to be too hard right now, as I just start crying again, but communicating with my friends via email, text and Facebook message has already made me feel better and more connected. I will try to keep it up.

Thanks for being there for us and I will let you know what we find out. I know Bri posted something on his Facebook tonight, so I'm sure Zack is probably aware. I'm sure he will need his friends, if nothing else to keep his life "normal".

Say a prayer for us and kiss and hug your children. ~Leslie

SATURDAY, APRIL 20, 2013 - FIRST FULL DAY AT HOSPITAL

Sent: Sat, April 20, 2013 7:26:25 AM
From: Leslie
To: My List
Subject: Brian Jermainne

I wanted to let a few people know that our son Brian had been diagnosed with an as yet undefined B cell lymphoma. We were surprisingly admitted to the hospital last night and Bri is now sleeping but we expect to meet with the weekend team of oncology doctors shortly. I got to charge my phone last night. CT scan last night was good and labs good. Not sure why we had to stay except that they said they wanted to complete a full work up today, and figure out what we are dealing with although I don't believe we will have full pathology until Monday or so. Brian had a biopsy on Thursday of his right axillary lymph nodes and removal of small lymphoma tumor from his left abdominal wall. It is puzzling everyone because he is so healthy besides this tumor and enlarged underarm lymph nodes. No other symptoms. We are exhausted and thankfully Bri is still asleep right now. I'm sorry to send this mass email but it is the best/easiest for me. I obviously get very upset at times and it upsets Bri so I'm doing my best to keep it under control in front of him. Talking out loud makes it hard for me to keep the crying contained so writing works better.

I hope we will be home later today and will try to update when I can. Keeping sending us love and prayers.

Leslie Jermainne

Sent: Saturday, April 20, 2013 10:01 AM
From: Paula
To: Leslie
Subject: Re: Brian Jermainne

In the absence of being able to run to you and hug you I am going to send this to you instead. Everything is going to be OK. I am crying with you and praying with you. God is with you and I am down on my knees praying that he will put his arms around Brian and help him through this. Love you and keep praying. Paula

Facebook Messages:

April 20, 2013 8:30pm
Ann:
Hang in there!! Thinking of all of you often. Only good thoughts your way.

SUNDAY, APRIL 21, 2013 - SECOND FULL DAY AT HOSPITAL

Sent: Sunday, April 21, 2013 8:28 PM
From: Leslie Jermainne
To: My List
Subject: Re: Brian Jermainne

Hi everyone,

Sunday update: it has been a long, hard, emotional day with lots of talking and no real action besides a head CT scan. After a long talk from my medically gifted sister Laurie, she re-empowered me to take control and express what my concerns are regarding our care here. This led us to talk with my father in law's doctor who helped us understand a few important things one of which is we have decided to seek care and an actual diagnosis (always good to have) from Dana Farber in Boston. We are having a bit of difficulty extracting ourselves from hospital number two, but that will be remedied tomorrow. I didn't appreciate the threat to call security if I tried to leave. Which I would never do without instructions to care for my child

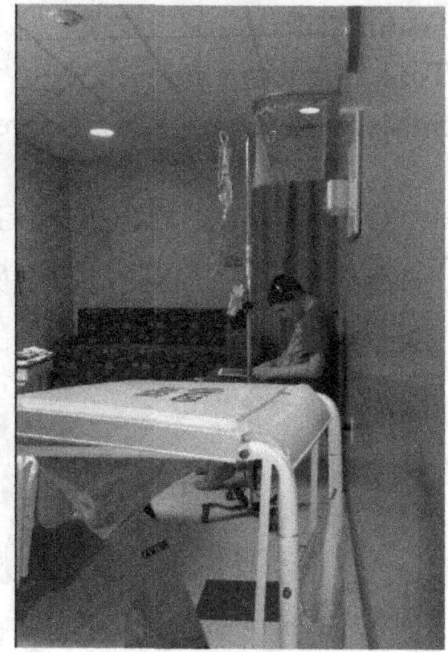

April 21, 2013 Our room at the hospital

whom by the way has shown absolutely no other results in any test or X-ray yet that indicates he has any other tumors or issues and his blood test results are all normal. Anyway...I am straying off track due to my anger of being kept here.

Tomorrow will be different and the process to move us to Boston will be started. We are finally feeling a bit in control (a tiny bit) and Brian has been able to begin to communicate what he needs and what he can and cannot handle hearing every day. Like I said, this is a learning curve, not just all the medical stuff, but what we can take ourselves. Especially for a 15 yr. old who looks like he is 18 on the outside package at 6 ft. tall and a handsome devil! (Just like his dad.)

We still have no definite diagnosis but it has been narrowed down to diffuse B cell lymphoma or Burkitt lymphoma - which is the one forcing us to be held here. Anyway, tomorrow is a new day and we will keep facing each one as it comes. Keep up the good thoughts, we are getting them and appreciate knowing all these people are out there caring about us. It truly helps!

Signing out from our room~Leslie

Sent: April 21, 2013, 9:54 PM
From: Paula
To: Leslie Jermainne
Subject: Re: Brian Ross update

Ok so hang in there girl. Good move to get to a center of excellence. We had a church full of prayers for you today.

Love & prayers,
Paula

MONDAY, APRIL 22, 2013 - 3RD FULL DAY AT HOSPITAL

Sent: Mon, April 22, 2013 6:07:59 AM
From: Leslie Jermainne
To: Paula
Subject: Re: Brian Ross update

Hi girlfriend and lead prayer getter,

Thank you from way deep down in my fractured heart. We are reaching out to other doctors in the cancer field we know and getting support and helpful, empowering advice. I don't want to complain right now but we aren't too happy with the hospital at the moment. I just want to get out of here and get to Dana Farber. I need some bedside manner for my sensitive boy and I need a damn diagnosis!!!

Anyway keep up the spiritual work for me, that will be the stuff that changes the tide for us. Love you.

Leslie

Sent: Monday, April 22, 2013 11:08 AM
From: PAULA
To: Leslie Jermainne
Subject: Re: Brian Ross update

My thought for today is that everything happens for a reason. Please just pray on this....

Sent: Monday, April 22, 2013 1:03 PM
From: Leslie Jermainne
To: Paula
Subject: Re: Brian Ross update

Thanks pal! I will do just that. I do believe there is a reason and I think I already know what it is. Once Brian is healed, we will have a new and wonderful perspective on life that most never receive. It has already started in glimpses when I am calm enough to look forward to long term. Each hour not sick is a blessing already. I know sickness and hard times are coming, but when we get to the other side it will a life full of gratitude and pleasure. Thanks for the thought - writing and voicing these things with people who love and understand me is very therapeutic for me. Any voice no matter how distant I will listen to and I'm sure each person is being brought to me that I need.

Love you!
Les

Facebook Messages:

April 22, 2013 6:47am
Ann:

Absolutely do what you have to, to take care of your family!! It doesn't matter what the healthcare people think, you know what is best. You are ALWAYS in my thoughts!!

TUESDAY, APRIL 23, 2013 - 4TH DAY AT THE HOSPITAL

Sent: Tuesday, April 23, 2013 5:05 AM
From: Leslie Jermainne
To: My List
Subject: Re: Brian Ross update

Hi again,

Monday has come and almost gone and this was a productive day for us at the hospital. Bri's head CT was fine, blood work is still no issues, vitals still no issues, kidneys no issues, abdominal ultra sound preliminary report is fine and echocardiogram is done. He is scheduled for a PET scan tomorrow which we just learned takes 2.5 hours. FUN?? NOT!!

We made great strides with our difficulties yesterday and we will be speaking with the head of pediatric oncology tomorrow at Dana Farber in

Boston for our move there on Thurs. Bri may also have further tests and surgery for a port in his chest tomorrow but not before I talk with Dana Farber.

Brian is feeling good about where things are going and is ready to move forward with chemo. Another hospital pathology has called the diagnosis as Burkitt Lymphoma, and this hospital's pathologist will look tomorrow. Then obviously Dana Farber will have their pathologists take a crack at it. By the end we will have had 3 opinions which is great.

We had an awesome visit from Auntie Al last night bringing Bri his beloved electric guitar (minus the amp!) and he spent a lot of time playing his repertoire. Also Bri's awesome friend Zack and Zack's family came for a visit and kept us very much entertained and smiling. It was a great boost for Bri - and me too! We finally turned on the TV which we had not done yet and watched one of our shows "Castle" and had chocolate cake and cheesecake for dinner at 10 pm. Many of you may know that Jan. 2012 Bri made the executive decision to lose weight and get healthy and for the next 11 months he dedicated himself to that and lost a total of 60 lbs. He did that by walking 4 miles a day on the treadmill, lots of push-ups, sit-ups, and by cutting out all the white stuff (no grains, flour, sugar, potatoes, bread, pasta (except the occasional off day or holiday) and kept his daily carb intake to approx. 50/grams a day. Lo and behold - exercising and not eating junk actually works. I tell you all this because of the chocolate cake for dinner....that was a lot of writing to justify eating dessert for dinner, but over the years I have developed the ability to justify just about anything. I'm kinda thinkin' a kid just diagnosed with cancer has some leeway to eat any damn thing he wants right now. Right Grandma?

We miss our doggies terribly and I have put us in for a pet therapy visit today, not sure it will fit in our schedule, but Bri seemed very happy by the prospect as am I. It won't be Jack and Hollie, but it will be nice to see and pet a dog in their absence.

Keep thinking about us and sending up a prayer for us. We are very quickly learning what awesome friends and family we have in our lives and we're feeling the love! Keep your eye out for big Brian, as he has the hard job of doing everything else while we are away and will continue to be away for a bit, plus he has everything else to do and takes care of us. He's doing an amazing, outstanding job, as he always does.

Namaste from our room. (Trying out new phrases every day!)

Leslie

Sent: April 23, 2013, 6:42 AM
From: Frank
To: Leslie Jermainne
Subject: RE: Brian Ross update

Oh my God! Leslie & Brian, This is the first I'm hearing of this. We're traveling today and I will write more, but please know that our thoughts and prayers are going out to all of you. Give little Bri my best and know that we are here for you whatever you may need -please don't hesitate to reach out. Good, bad, or otherwise I have walked this road and maybe I can offer some perspective... and a hug if nothing else. Trust your instincts and the information you are given - the professionals you are dealing with want nothing more than the best for you.

Tell Brian to stay strong.
Love - Frank & Family

Sent: April 23, 2013 11:26 PM
From: Leslie Jermainne
To: My List
Subject: RE: Brian Ross update

Hi Again,

I've added a few names to the list, so I'm not sure who has gotten all my updates and who has not, but I'm sure you will quickly see what is going on. Today was a very good day, but ending with a lot of stress. We started the day with a PET scan, which had a little IV problem when he got up to go the bathroom, after being injected with radioactive sugar. The IV wasn't handled correctly and he dripped blood all the way to the bathroom before the attendant noticed. She told him to go into the bathroom anyway, not knowing this kid doesn't like to say the word blood, let alone see it dripping out of his arm onto the floor. As she left, to get clean up stuff, I got to the door of the bathroom and was concerned he would faint on the tile floor in there by himself, so I pestered him so much that he couldn't "go". We got him back to his bed where he was pale and nauseous thanks to the blood viewing and blood on his shirt and pants. Then out came the Geiger counter to go over all the blood drops and cleaning clothes to check for radiation. Really helps a Mom to think they just pumped him full of that stuff. Then came meetings, phone calls and at a surprise announcement that surgery is cancelled and pack your stuff you're going to Dana Farber in Boston today. We were/are so elated to have accomplished what we wanted. We packed, made calls, Brian rushed to pick up our extra "stuff" and then later rescue my car with Alison. Meanwhile Bri and I were loaded into the ambulance for a very long ride to Boston. Only 2 u-turns, a bit of traffic, the smallest ambulance bay you have ever seen, especially for a huge inner city hospital and then we had arrived. Another good note is the slides from pathology, tissue sample and all reports arrived at the hospital and came directly here with us. That will help the second opinion here get started and confirm if the diagnosis of Burkitt Lymphoma is accurate and then narrow down the sub type of Burkitt and get therapy designed.

The good news is we are getting settled. Brian lost his IV line on the way up, but it wasn't a problem. He just had two IV lines placed and managed to not faint. We got some food, answered lots of questions. Got a tour of our new home away from home for the next week, and are awaiting a blood draw for labs. We are feeling like two tiny sheltered country mice plopped into the middle of the big city. A little culture shock. Our big spacious private room and private bathroom at the other hospital is gone and we are missing that. Our roommates don't speak English very well, but as we are in the same boat, I'm sure the gap will be bridged this week. My new folding chair for me to sleep on and a total of about 12x10 isn't looking so hot right now. But, we are adjusting and keep telling ourselves it is short term. We had a major scare when we thought we couldn't use our cell phones, but the crisis was averted and all technology is a go.

There are cool lights in the ceiling that change color and we are enjoying a little light show while Bri listens to music and is furiously texting friends. Brian said he needs to have them in his room and I figure I have a new bargaining tool with God. If God helps him recover, I will install any lights the boy wants. I think I have a new book idea from this - Bargaining with God. I've received 3 huge packets of info, but I don't think the brain can handle it tonight. I can no longer use the bathroom in the room, so I have to go find the one I can use, get cleaned up and attempt some sleep. Nursing rounds start at 7:15 and I think I better be ready. I've got a huge new learning curve again tomorrow.

We feel a bit like we are back to about Saturday as far as progress goes, but once we meet our team, nurses, oncologist and whoever else we need to know we will be fine I'm sure. We are concerned about getting a pic line vs. a port, but I guess I need something to worry about all night, so that fits the bill.

Hoping, hoping, hoping poor Big Bri will make it here tomorrow rather than Thurs. He has so much to do at home, and we can certainly wait until Thurs. which was the day we thought we'd be coming here with Big Bri. But little Bri really wants his guitar back that Auntie Al brought him last night and well, I just need Big Brian.

Ok - include us in your prayers tonight. We have big strides to make tomorrow to get things moving towards therapy starting and getting us sprung from here and back safe on our street.

Love to You All from our new room at Boston Children's Hospital Room 618. (That is where pediatric cancer patients of Dana Farber are treated, see I'm learning already!)

Leslie

STORY ADDED FOR CLARITY:

Here is the story to relay what transpired at the other hospital since we arrived, but particularly the day we left, because that day someone or something was watching out for us, but I didn't include it in my update that night. Here is what happened.

After being admitted late on Friday night 4/19/13, I ordered food from an outside delivery place since no one had offered us anything and it was now midnight and my son had not eaten since lunch. The next day on Saturday nothing happened. My son received one bag of fluid that day. That was it. We had a meeting with one of the pediatric oncologist who overwhelmed us with a lot of information and no encouragement. We were scared, sad, deflated and exhausted. They wouldn't let us go home and we felt at their mercy. Hospitals and doctors know best, right? And you have to trust them. You do. But something wasn't feeling right. If it was so urgent we stay at the hospital, why was nothing being done?

Sunday came and this was the worst day of our entire treatment. Yes, looking back this was the worst day. Brian had a head CT, but that was all that was done medically besides the ever present one bag of fluid a day. We had another visit with the same oncologist and this time it was overwhelming. Panic was setting in for us both, after an hour or more of telling us all scary stuff and making us feel like a diagnosis of Burkitt was what we ***didn't*** want, she finally left and Brian had a real breakdown. I was trying to be as strong as I could for him, but I felt like we had just been beaten - physically and emotionally and spiritually for that matter - by the place and the people that were supposed to save us. When my son asks me with tears streaming down his face, "Mom, am I going to die? If I die will you be okay?" Well, that was the worst moment of my life. I think it was worse than the doctor telling me he had cancer, because this was pain and fear in my own baby and I couldn't take it away. "No Brian, I won't be okay. I will never be okay again." I couldn't lie. But then I did my best to reassure him it would be okay. And it took a little while, but the tide started to change right then. I didn't know it. I really thought at that moment, we were drowning.

I talked with my sister Laurie on the phone and relayed what was happening and what I was feeling, especially about what was not happening. I felt we were locked away on the pediatric oncology floor with people telling us too scary things, with no words of hope and no one really caring. I know now that Burkitt Lymphoma is rare. My feelings in retrospect about that time makes me feel like the hospital, the practice, the doctor wanted a Burkitt case. I don't feel they really saw us as people. I don't think they once looked as my son and saw a boy, a person. I feel like they saw a case, a case of Burkitt and nothing more.

After Brian's PET scan debacle, (you read about that on April 23rd update) he was wheeled back up to his room. He was free to get up, use the bathroom, etc. While I was talking with a nurse about the timing for his port placement surgery which was to happen in about 2 hours, Brian was shuffling around behind me. The nurse walked out of the room and I turned around and Brian was eating a Sour Patch Kid. I said "What are you doing!?!?!" Of course his reaction is one of, 'eating a sour patch kid, duh!' followed by a scared look of 'why, what horrible thing will happen to me now?!?!?' You see, he had spent all morning not being able to eat for the PET scan. You can't eat before surgery either, but this is all new to him and nobody, myself included, thought to remind him that once the PET scan was over, he still couldn't eat because surgery was next. I quickly told him not to worry, it was no big deal. He assured me he ate one, maybe two that was it. I told him I had to tell the doctor, but it was fine. If the port had to be done tomorrow, so be it. We had been here for four full days now with what seemed to be no big rush on their part to get anything done and they would just have to deal with it.

I met with the new doctor who we were dealing with now. That was another part of the story that I avoided telling to all the people who were worried enough already about us. After the Sunday visit with the first doctor and Brian breaking down and getting so emotional and so upset - which of course you would expect - he said he couldn't stand her and didn't want her in his room again. He explained how she didn't say one encouraging thing. How she scared him and he thought he was going to die. Even now I am just skimming over the worst of it. After my phone call with her on Sunday where she threatened to call security, DCF and the police should I decide to remove Brian from the hospital, I told her that I would meet with another doctor from her practice but that she was no longer welcome in my son's room. I would meet with her outside of the room, but that was it. I never saw her again.

Back to the Sour Patch kid...I asked to see the new oncologist working with us from the same practice. I met with her in a small meeting room and explained the sour patch kid. She was obviously disappointed with us, and said she would have to check with anesthesiology but was sure that the surgery would need to be rescheduled. She seemed quite disappointed with us at first, but after a bit decided to reassure me it would be fine. How nice (said in a sarcastic tone). I understand that oncologists deal with this stuff every single day. And I am thankful they do. However, this is day six for us. Six days of uncertainty. Six days of being in a foreign land, not speaking the language. Six days of being scared that my son will die and my son being scared that his life will be over, soon. No one gave us a friendly little reminder "hey - don't eat anything, surgery is next!" But honestly, it is all good, and here's why.

After doctor number two came back and said surgery would be rescheduled for the following day, Brian was able to eat a real meal. Just after that, about two hours after being told that there would be no surgery, doctor number two comes and gets me. She is excited, and wants to talk to me in the hall. This is the first time I feel that someone at this place cares about what WE want. She tells me that Boston has just called they have a bed for us!!!! We are going - the ambulance has been called, they should be here within the hour. I am so excited at this point, I can't even tell you. We are getting out of this hospital and going to Dana Farber Cancer Institute. (There is one more piece to this story about the Port that gets placed vs. the Port that would have been done at the first hospital, but that is coming up in an update.) Brian would have been in surgery at that point and we would have had to refuse the bed, but thankfully some force had him eat a sour patch kid and it was the best thing that could have happened. The rest of the story I told in the update, but I learned three things from being at the second of three hospitals.

1) Someone or Something was watching out for us and had been for some time - even when we thought we were all alone.
2) I learned that sometimes bad things happen (doctors who aren't a good match for us, eating when you aren't supposed to) to bring you to better things that you need.
3) Trust your instincts, even when you think you don't have any - especially then - and reach out to people even if you don't know who the right person is - they will show up and help you reconnect with your inner voice and then listen to it. Be strong and don't take no for an answer. You are your child's and your own best advocate, even when you feel like you don't know what in the hell is happening. You know your child and you know you. That is all it takes.

APRIL 24, 2013 - FIRST FULL DAY AT DFCI/BCH

Sent: Wednesday, April 24, 2013 8:21 PM
From: Leslie Jermainne
To: My List
Subject: RE: Brian Ross update

What day is today??? Oh Ya, Wednesday - time sure does disappear when you're in the hospital. The late post last night was an issue with my iPad and apparently some email addresses got missed and some new ones have been added so I've left last night's update attached just in case.

Today started out a bit of a shock, just waking up in my fold out chair after about 4 hrs. of sleep, but things steadily improved from there. After early morning encouraging texts from Toni and words from Laurie I overcame the sleep headache and we moved forward. Bri enjoyed his chocolate chip pancakes for breakfast (and again at dinner), we had a quick meeting together with his new WONDERFUL oncologist, then I met with him again to go over Brian's surgery tomorrow and one more meeting with him together later in the afternoon to hear that Pathology has confirmed his diagnosis of Burkitt Lymphoma. We however got a much better explanation of Burkitt vs. Diffuse B Cell Lymphoma (which was the diagnosis we thought we had wanted, when the two options were very scarily laid out for us at the other hospital.) Now, we feel much better with a calm, less frightening explanation of the very little difference of the two and some of the positives of the one we have. Nice to hear something positive when you get these explanations. Still waiting on the scans to come from the first hospital, but things are moving forward.

Tomorrow Brian will have surgery to do 2 bone marrow tests, a lumbar puncture and administer chemo into the spinal column and then have his port placed in his chest. Say prayers for an easy outcome of surgery. It should go smoothly and Brian will be a bit sore, but shouldn't remember anything as he will be under general for all of these. That will be it for tomorrow, quite enough I think.

Friday might bring the first dose of chemo, but it may be Saturday. We don't have a real timeline yet, as those scans and final tests aren't done, but hopefully late tomorrow or Friday morning all that will be reviewed and a protocol will be developed for him and ready to get going. However, the first dose of chemo will be somewhat mild, and then we have to see how he does (3-5 days) then 2-3 days off and then the first 'real' dose of chemo, then 3-5 days to see how he does. If all goes well, we'll get to go home for a few weeks, before round 3.

The other great thing that happened today was our roommate got moved to another room, and we got his half of our room, which is much bigger, I have a window seat/bench to sleep on (not a fold out chair) we have two windows we can see out, we are next to the bathroom door, we have two cabinets to store our things in and so far no new roommate, although I doubt that will last. All those things might seem pretty little, but it is amazing what you start to be truly, deeply grateful for when you are here. We have had several visits from all the great resource people here and are feeling so well cared for.

The last and best thing was Brian got to visit with us today. It took him forever to get here and find the wrong parking garage. Bri brought us all the things we needed - it was too hard to carry an electric guitar in the ambulance ride up here, and we got to have dinner together and big hugs and kisses before he had to turn around and get home to run the whole show there. Thanks for my BFF's bringing the guy food - thanks to my Dad for mowing the lawn, thanks to my Mom for helping with our doggies, thanks to Al for helping get my car rescued, thanks to Laur for being my medical sounding board, thanks to Toni for sending me constant text messages with reassurance and info that keeps me positive and moving forward every minute - plus I know she is thinking of us with all those texts and helping us get through this.

We are missing Drum Corps practice tonight, but Bri now has his sticks to practice - on a pillow - so it might/or might not be something he can do.

Thank you again for all your email notes, just to say a quick hi and send us well wishes and throwing prayers up to be caught by the unseen, but felt up here in room 618 Boston Children's Hospital under the care of Dana Farber Cancer Institute. Mom, you wanted to know our mailing address here it is:

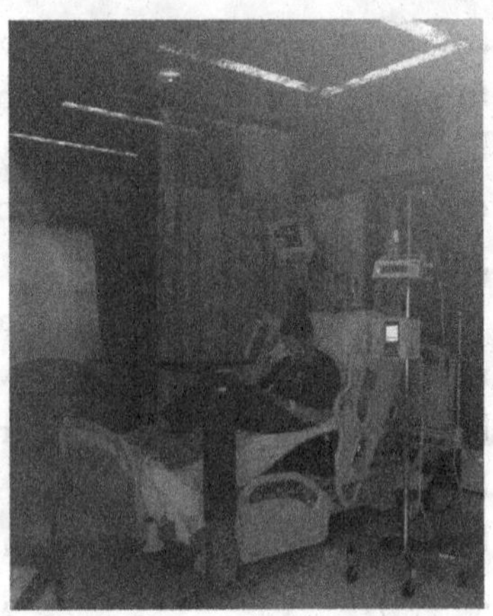

Brian Jermainne
6 North, Room 618
Children's Hospital Boston
300 Longwood Ave.
Boston, MA 02115

Sending along an attached photo of Bri in his bed, playing his guitar, which you can't really see. The cool colored lights changing colors for a little light show too!

Thanks everyone! Leslie

Sent: Wednesday, April 24, 2013 9:10 PM
From: Frank
To: Leslie Jermainne
Subject: RE: Brian Ross update

Hey Leslie,

My God, I read your emails and I can recall every feeling I had sitting in your place. (Not comparing at all - I couldn't imagine being there with [my son] - just saying I 'get it') I'm happy to hear you finally feel like you're in good hands - that means everything. We had complete and total confidence in the guidance and direction we received from the doctors at Dana Farber. If I had a similar experience as you I would have left the other hospital too!!! I have lots of advice if you need it - like wake up early wash up, go for a quick walk, and grab a bite to eat before the doctors round in the morning so you're 'fresh' and refueled to wait around for the docs and not miss anything. Try to get out and get some fresh air every once in-a-while to keep your sanity - usually after the doctors swing through. Also, get in with the nurses - kindness goes a long way (so do bagels or donuts :) They will know exactly when you can expect the doctors - they will call or text you if you're out and the docs are rounding - and they know where to get the best food around.

I don't want to burry or burden you with emails - but I'm here if you need me. Tell Brian the hard work will be over soon and we'll be planning the next fire night (we'll just have more to talk about). The chemo may suck for a short time, but that will definitely pass.

Plenty of prayers, strength, and (((HUGS))) going out to you in Boston.

Love,
Frank & Estelle

APRIL 25, 2013

Sent: Thursday, April 25, 2013 12:34 AM
From: Leslie Jermainne
To: Frank
Subject: RE: Brian Ross update

Hi Frank,

I have thought of you and Anna so many times over the past days...I was so heartbroken for you both back during your fight, but let me tell you as I know only you will understand, I had no idea of your struggle. I listened, I cared, I prayed for you both time and time again, I sympathized and empathized, but I had no idea....

I want to apologize for not getting it back then, but then again, you and I both know, you can't understand this no matter how many times you might try to imagine what it must feel like for the other person/people. I have such a new appreciation for what you went through, the highs, the lows, the anger, the fear, I mean the sheer terror, the hopes, the dreams, the plans, the caution not to make plans. Oh my God this is horrible.

Every moment becomes endless, but the days seem to fly by. There is so much to learn, think about, try not to think about and to do. And imagine, we are just the caregivers. What are our loved ones going through that even you and I can't imagine.

I know you aren't comparing our struggles, and neither am I when I say I know it is such a fear to even think about losing your spouse, your best friend, your partner for life but the thought of losing my only child, who is my life is beyond comprehension, which I know you will understand. The thought as his mother that I'm allowing the doctors to pump him full of poison that will make him sick, and exhausted and is basically trying to kill him, but not quite as much as the cancer is, is just so disturbing when I think about how I've spent these last 15 years trying to keep him safe and healthy and growing. And now his own cells are trying to kill him. It is absurd.

I hope my ranting isn't too much for you. But reading your letter, your suggestions, just the words - doctors, rounds, nurses - soon it will be chemo and meds, fevers and sickness, names of drugs I can't yet pronounce but will soon become simple words like cat or dog. The hum of the IV pump has become a welcome sound in the dark at night, because it means he is lying there asleep and having some peace for a few moments. The look of fear in his eyes, the need for hugs, the "I love you's" said when you are just going to the lobby to get a cup of coffee, the tears....the exhaustion, the constant "please God, please God, please God" that runs through your mind whenever it can slow down for a second, the bargaining with God that I will do anything I am ever asked, I will take the cancer gladly and make it my burden, if my son gets to live to have a drivers license, a first kiss, a true love, a first job, his first house, a wife, a child. What if he never gets those things...what if this, what if that - it just gets to be too much to bear and then you have no choice but to make it just about the next hour, the next decision, I can only handle the next meal, or snack, the next vital sign taking, the next bag of fluid. Purell, wash your hands, don't touch stuff outside of this environment, keeping people away, cringing when you hear a nurse, or patient or visitor cough. Looking into each other's eyes for long, long durations when there is nothing else you can say. But you search each other's face in hopes it holds an answer. You apologize over and over in hopes it will take their pain away and they apologize for being sick, and needy and a burden and you can't believe they would ever think such a thing. You replay all your favorite memories, like if you don't keep them fresh you might forget. Then you have these odd moments when you are so busy just being in the hospital, you kind of forget that cancer is lurking. It just seems you live here and you're on some sick, twisted little adventure that if you do everything and read everything and get linens, and food and water and listen to reports and ask questions you might just get off the ride and continue on with life.

But then again life will never, ever, ever be the same no matter the outcome and I am full of hope and will not allow myself to imagine anything but success at this point, as I spent the first few days imaging everything but success and the fear of that is paralyzing, and one thing we can't be is paralyzed. When my mind takes a quick trip back to that horror, I whip it back to the present because it is too terrible to imagine. I don't know how you've done it. I thank God you had Anthony. You have that piece of Anna, that person who needed you, that little soul that is her legacy and your legacy together. I am tempted to erase that last few sentences as even just writing the thought makes me ill. And if we beat the cancer, what about all the other stuff that could get him. Infections, heart problems, kidney issues, liver failure. Jesus Christ! How much can you take? And again, we are "just the caregivers". Red blood cells, White blood cells, transfusions, plasma, Neutropenia, hemoglobin, less than 10,000, normal range, call the clinic, do this, do that. I swear I will take his temperature every hour on the hour for the rest of his life if I have to.

I wish you could tell me it gets better, but in some cases it only gets worse. In an attempt to lighten up the tone of my letter, to which I've not talked this way to anyone, I so appreciate your advice. I've figured out the up early before rounds thing. The first day of rounds in my pajamas wasn't a great idea. Maybe that is what set off the first hospital and I not getting along very well. The leaving for a walk, well...I just can't yet. Not with my child being there "helpless". Being a minor, and all that implies. The thought of my child not knowing who might be coming into his room to listen to his lungs, press all over his stomach, ask him the same questions, what did you eat, drink, poop and pee. Any night sweats, itching, vomiting, diarrhea, pain. I just can't leave him to face all that alone. I can't even imagine the parents I watch with their little babies in strollers roaming the halls with patchy heads of hair, and tear streaked faces. Those little guys can't even voice what hurts and where, and ask for help. But in some bent sort of way I almost envy those babies because they don't know what lies ahead every minute and what lurks around the next corner. They play with toys and get held and rocked. I just can't decide who has it worse, then I think it is <u>all</u> the worst - just equally terrifying forms of worse. Well I failed at lightening it up, and frankly a lot of this is in fear from my last meeting tonight about his first chemo into his spinal column tomorrow, the port going in, the bone marrow tests and lumbar puncture. I really am feeling hopeful and positive overall, I'm just frightened and exhausted and the print is starting to wiggle on the page. Please forgive me if I've taken you down an old road that might be best if not traveled any longer, but know that your words were the first I have felt that someone out there really, truly understands the turmoil that has taken hold. And it is a relief. I have arranged to talk with the social worker tomorrow while he is in surgery. Obviously I need it. I'm also going to try to find out about some relaxation techniques and I think I can arrange a chair massage or something for some time. I'm starting to see I have to do a better job with me, so I can do the best job for him.

Thanks for listening and again I apologize if this has caught you off guard. -Leslie

Sent: Thursday, April 25, 2013 8:10 AM
From: Leslie Jermainne
To: Frank
Subject: cancer typing

Hi Frank,

Feeling bad like I drunk texted you last night, so I'm calling it cancer typing. I apologize. I'm sure you understand and you are going to tell me you are there for us, and believe me I know you are. It's just that I finally feel someone understands. So, to that end, that long crazy email helped me, I just hope it didn't hurt you.

Send any tips my way - nurses are awesome, but your right - treats never hurt...gonna put that into motion today!

Thank you. Thank you. Thank you.

Say hi to Estelle for me, and apologize to her for me if needed, for my craziness. Do we get chemo brain too?

Leslie

Sent: Thursday, April 25, 2013 9:13 AM
From: Frank
To: Leslie Jermainne
Subject: RE: cancer typing

Leslie,

No. no. no. That's what I was hoping to get out of you – you CAN count on me for venting, worrying, yelling, and being an overall sounding board. (I was starting an email when this one came in. :)

First – you cannot stir up bad or traumatic memories. I only have good memories, and the knowledge that I was able to do everything within my powers for Anna. It actually helps to share and help others. So please, please, please feel free to vent – I had one or two people that I would lean on as well that 'got it' – and for some reason it is therapeutic to do so and helps slightly.

Second – know that you and the Brian's were a tremendous part of our support system. Knowing that you were there for us meant more than you know. You did support us even if you didn't fully understand or if we didn't share all the worrisome details at the time. You touched our lives forever and will always be good friends.

Third – I cannot imagine being in your place. Your situation is undeniably different. But I do understand the roller coaster ride, the fears, the confusion, the worries, the tiredness, the showering in a public bathroom sink, eating crap, the fact that you are incredibly smart and resourceful, but are helpless at the same time. What's right, what's wrong, putting on a strong supportive face and not showing any fear while you're falling apart inside. Argh!!!

I will write more later when I can, but know that I'm here for you guys – and that's not just 'cause it's the right thing to say – it's because I am! Good luck with all the procedures today. In my mind, the port is the right decision – it will make it soo much easier and painless for Brian.

Hang in there,
Frank

APRIL 26, 2013

Sent: Friday, April 26, 2013 8:34 AM
From: Leslie Jermainne
To: My List
Subject: Brian Ross Update

News update from Room 618...

First I wanted to let anyone know they are free to "opt out" of daily updates. Just because this is our focus every waking minute (and many sleeping minutes also) doesn't mean it has to be yours. Most of you didn't ask to be on this list, so if you want to let me know, it is not problem to remove your email address. We won't be offended and we know that you still love and care about our family and will send us prayers and well wishes. You just might like to get a break from us for a bit.

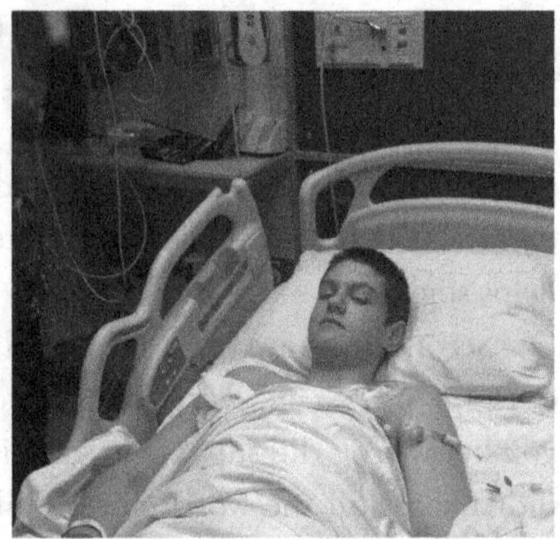
Brian after port placement surgery

Today started with good news that surgery was moved up from 1pm to 10 am, only to be pushed back to 4 pm. Oh well, such is hospital life. I spent the time after he left talking with the social worker, figuring out what might be good for Brian, things that might help him and me while we are here, cried a bit and then moved on. Passed the time. Finally got a bit of food, picked up snacks for later if he's hungry (hasn't eaten since midnight last night). Before I knew it they called me from anesthesia as I was on my way back down and he was done. Things went well and he received a "power port". I'm learning what that is, but the nurses sure seem excited about it. So far I've learned not only can he get meds and fluids in the port but he can get contrast die for future scans in his port, so no need for further IV lines in his arm. Now if we just avoid infection we'll be all set. Brian got back the room, hooked up to fluids, received an adorable little gift which he is sleeping with - thanks Johnsons!!! It isn't his real puppy dogs, but the next best thing. He had 2 cups of water

Other good news was that after calling our insurance and finding out where we stand, we are in good shape considering we have major medical only. After we reach our $6,000 deductible - which believe me we are already well past, just haven't received the bills yet, then 100% coverage will take over. YAAA!! Thanks Hoyt - you're the best! We finally will be getting all our money over these many, many years back and probably then some. It is just such a relief to know that we are covered. One less thing to worry about right now.

Looking forward to a visit from Abby and Britt tomorrow and maybe Auntie Al this weekend. I can't believe I'm getting to type this out at only 8:26, maybe I'll get to sleep early tonight. We did have a roommate join us, but haven't really met yet. Tomorrow we can make friends. Also just trekked halfway across two building to the family laundry to wash some clothes. On the way back I see a lady come out of a door by our elevators which are about 60 steps from me, and I think to myself, I wonder what is in there? I read the sign outside the door and guess what....it's laundry for this floor because this is an oncology floor so we don't have to leave to do laundry. UGH! Oh well, next load will be done there.

Brian has just woken up, had some water and is working on yogurt while video chatting with friends under his red lights in the ceiling. This is a good night. So good night!

Leslie
PS. Thanks Frank!!

Sent: Friday, April 26, 2013 12:19 PM
From: Frank
To: Leslie Jermainne
Subject: RE: Brian Ross Update

Leslie – I'm finally back in the office. Coming home from vacation always causes a bottleneck for work.

Sounds like Brian is doing great. Procedures going well and making progress – you can't ask for more than that. More importantly – it sounds like he is rolling with the punches well and finding ways to express himself with the video chats and keep himself busy. The port will spare him many, many needle/IV pricks for the months that follow (not to mention that it's more sanitary and less prone to infections than the PIC). I'm sure the port will be painful for a week or so, but after that tell him that he won't even know it's there.

So how is Leslie holding up? It sounds like you're learning the ropes (like with the laundry). You are an incredibly smart and resourceful woman – I don't doubt that you will know more than some of the nurses soon. Just a little warning – nothing will stop the plan but progress always seems to slow on the weekends. Don't get discouraged or feel like you're losing momentum – you just need to have patience. Unfortunately this has become the new 'normal' for you. Just remember that what you are doing is very important. I know you wouldn't or couldn't be anywhere else. So if it takes a few extra days or weeks to get Brian healthy, happy, and moving forward – so be it.

I'm glad the girls may come up and visit. If they do – try to use that time to visit for a bit and then get out and get a walk in or something. Believe me, I didn't do enough of this and not only did it take a toll on me – I would get so burned out I was of no benefit to Anna – yes, I would even find myself arguing with her. Not proud of that, how could I argue, even if provoked sometimes, with someone fighting an epic battle – the answer is because I was stressed out and had nothing left at times. I learned (after talking with social workers & therapists) to take care of myself, find time to regroup, distress and breathe. When Nick or Eleanor came to visit Anna – that was when I would get out to clear my head or maybe even go visit Anthony.

Gotta run for now, but will check in soon… Frank

Sent: Friday, April 26, 2013 10:05 PM
From: Leslie Jermainne
To: My List
Subject: RE: Brian Ross Update

Hi Everyone,

It's been one week since this nightmare started. Just to recap quickly, since we have several new emails readers, here is what the last 8 days have dropped on us like a bomb. Last Thursday, Brian had surgery which we hoped was going to be an infected lymph node under his arm, or even better a cyst. Also to have a lipoma removed from his left abdomen. Only that isn't what the surgeon found. We left there and went home, me on the verge of hysteria. Friday came confirmation of Non-Hodgkin's lymphoma, but definite diagnosis of Diffuse B-Cell or Burkitt Lymphoma was not determined. We were sent to another hospital's ER to "have a chest x-ray, cat scan and blood test. If everything is good, you can go home and then come back to meet with Pediatric Oncology on Monday. If there is an issue we will admit Brian, so pack a bag just in case." We go there, have blood test ánd x-ray w/in 1/2 hour. Spend 4 hours waiting for CAT scan, and then get all the results. Nothing scary, kidneys are fine (which was the real concern, because Burkitt can grow and break down very quickly and flood his kidneys - and Burkitt was how the pathologist was leaning) so.... "no you can't go home, we're going to admit you anyway". BOOM! We have not been back home since.

To try to shorten our nightmare story, we were in the hospital pediatric oncology wing where Brian was unable to leave the floor, the oncologist repeatedly scared us with these huge discussions when we had no final diagnosis, we met with no support staff, but we had wonderful visitors - Big Brian bringing us tons of stuff to make our stay tolerable, especially Brian's electric guitar which isn't the easiest thing to drag around - right Bri? Christi and Toni were a big help to Brian and especially to me, thanks for all the support. And of course the Gomez family who made us laugh and pass the time. Nothing like having your best buddy to make you laugh. And of course Auntie Al making a couple of visits to keep our spirits up. By Sunday we'd had it...and wanted to be released. Remember, Brian's blood counts were all normal. The tests that he had done were normal, his kidney tests were normal, but despite wanting to be released for just the night - the oncologist said no, and threatened to call security if we tried to leave, which we would never do. So...we decided to get the H-E-double hockey sticks out of there and go where the best of the best are - Dana Farber Cancer Institute in Boston. A very long ambulance ride on Tuesday brought us here and we settled in a mouse-size side of our shared room and hunkered down for the night.

Wednesday brought me fear that we'd made the wrong decision, based solely on our accommodations, but once I talked with our oncologist - the real reason we were here - I knew this was the best place to be. Later that day, our roomy moved to his own room and we got to move to his side of the room - we like to refer to our new digs as the Ritz - because compared to the other side of the room, this side is amazing. Windows, bathroom is on this side, although only for patient use. There are 2 closets for our stuff - I KNOW! - 2 closets. And my bed doesn't fold out of a chair - it's a window bench and I love it (not really, but it is better than night 1).

Yesterday was surgery to have bone marrow aspiration and biopsy, lumbar puncture, chemo administered into his spinal column and have his Power Port placed in his chest. All went well, although it was a long day because surgery was pushed back 6 hours, 1 hour at a time, but still...it got done. And that is where I left off last night. Unfortunately we capped off the night with Brian discovering a new lump in his right abdominal wall. He didn't seem too upset - but I could have crumbled to the floor once again. Held it in though, after a trip to the bathroom to cry for a few minutes, beg God some more, but apparently we must have a bad connection. Also after our one night of having the big side of the room and the rest of the room empty for a peaceful night, we got a roommate. A young boy, in quite a bit of pain who we feel very sorry for, but the crying just makes you cringe and panic slightly, and think...what if that is us. He was doing better off and on today and just about 20 minutes ago he was moved to a new room, which should be better for him and selfishly us. Will try to get to bed early tonight and do some major sleep catch up if possible.

Today brought lots and lots of good things, and I think we will end it on a positive note. I hate to tempt fate by saying those words. Today was fairly easy - 2 blood draws for labs for Brian, a great visit from Brittany and Abby who brought us tons of food, some magazines for me, and a iTunes Gift card, card and poster from all the great families at our home school co-op that Brian attends (or attended) on Wednesdays. During their time here visiting with Brian, I got to go out for a walk and get some things we need. The sun seemed blinding, and the flowering trees are all in bloom and petals are already falling...missed that happening. Besides a long talk with the oncologist where I got our plan, which I'll talk about in a minute, we also had a great surprise in that Auntie Al fought her way through terrible traffic and arrive at about 7:30, has a room in the city tonight and will be back to visit tomorrow. YAAAA!!! Also Brian decided to shave his head today, as short as we can go, so he is prepared to say goodbye to his hair. The other good news if you can call it good news, is his first chemo drugs have been administered and the last one is infusing right now. We are on our way. Also found out results for PET scan which showed the right underarm lymph nodes, a small spot right where he is feeling it in his abdomen, and an even smaller spot in right gluteus area. Two bone marrow tests and lumbar test came back with early results of not finding cancer cells there, and final results should be in by the morning, but the doctor felt confident it wouldn't change. WOOHOO!!!!

So here is the "plan"- Brian will receive chemo tonight. We may possibly get to come home next week for one or two nights, but Bri had a good point tonight - we could lose the Ritz if we leave - we'll make that decision when the time comes. But...we will definitely be back next Thurs. afternoon for readmission for round 2. That's when the big guns come out. We will be in for 7 days for round 2 and if all goes well go home for 9-14 days before readmission for 7 days for round 3, then home for 9-14 days then 7 days in the hospital for round 4, then home for 14-21 days, then back in for 7 days for round 5 and then guess what??? We'll be done!!! Of course if all goes well, which we are sure it will. So the next 4 months or so, will be all about treatment. But we are on our way, and for today, that is all that is important. The pages and pages of scary side effects, long term effects are all filed away somewhere in a part of my brain I hope not to have to access, but they are there.

It is amazing how this changes your life. How such simple things become amazing. How minutes can last forever and days fly by. Both Brian and I agreed it seems that his biopsy last Thursday feels like a month ago. Yet every night I look at the clock and think at home I'd be in bed reading right now, the book falling on my face, exhausted. In here, I'm still writing, reading, dressed and haven't made up my bed yet. And yet,

I might get lucky to be invited to lay on his bed with him, watch a movie on his iPad with our newly purchased double earphone jack, so we don't have to share pair like last night, and feel the warmth of my child's body and maybe his head occasionally on my shoulder. In a strange way that is sort of a gift for a mother of a 15 year old boy. Usually you get not much talking, a lot of eye rolls, and certainly no cuddling. Now I get asked for hugs, even more I love you's than before, smiles and long stares in the eyes as we each look at the face we've been staring at for the past 15 years, but seeing it in a new way. Looking for reassurance, answers, trying to detect fear or a need that I can meet before it is even asked for.

Tomorrow is a new day - one I hope won't be filled with sickness, mouth sores, hair loss, nerve irritation, crankiness, and the start of chemo brain. There are a lot more things I pray won't happen, but they are locked away, not to be discussed. I am still bargaining with God. If anyone knows how to transfer cancer from your child to yourself - let me know. I want that. I can't seem to come up with the right words, or God isn't listening. I'm reduced to working with "God, help us through this day". So, I think you are all doing an amazing job sending up the prayers for us. Little things are happening that make our moments better. I can't say days yet... but hours are getting better.

Thanks for listening...from Room 618
Leslie

Sent: Friday, April 26, 2013 11:11 PM
From: Sheila
To: Leslie Jermainne
Subject: Re: Brian Ross Update

God bless, Leslie. I gotta go give my child a hug and kiss. You are reminding me what I take for granted. You are an amazing, strong and inspiring Mom and Brian is lucky to have you.

Praying for Brian, and you and your family. Get some rest.

Love,
Sheila

APRIL 27, 2013

Sent: Saturday, April 27, 2013 9:28 AM
From: Frank
To: Leslie Jermainne
Subject: RE: Brian Ross Update

Again, great news Leslie. Minute by Minute; Hour by Hour; Day by Day…

Tell Brian he's a trooper! Another thought – he's only as sick as he feels. If he feels good – he is good. Just because he gets chemo doesn't mean he will have any side effects. There were only a few chemos (and Anna pretty much had them all) that affected Anna. Yes the hair loss for some specific ones, but only one gave her headaches and/or chemo brain (and that was only when it was infusing). They are great at controlling the nausea and believe me when I tell you that getting chemo is sort of anti-climactic. It is a big deal, but based on my experiences – I really believe Brian will do well with the actual infusions. More often than not, we were probably getting chemo in the morning and drinking a glass of wine or beer with you guys at night.

OK – trying for re-assurance here – Anna did not die from the cancer, chemo, infections, low blood counts, side effects from any treatment, medication, or radiation. She died because of the donor transplant and graft vs. host disease. The donor cells did kill all the cancer in the end but also caused scleroderma which in the end was the culprit.

Anna had a ZERO white blood count for months at a time with a small child in the house and never got any infection. She would go grocery shopping, on vacation, and everything else normal families do. You just have to be cautious with what you eat and expose yourself too. She never had mouth sores or any of the potential scary stuff they talk about – keep in mind that Brian is strong and healthy despite this – it is not the same as a weak 70 year old getting chemo.

Also, not to scare – but some of the chemo's can cause constipation – just make sure Brian is going – if you recall Anna had issues with this right at the start. Nobody ever warned us to be cautious of constipation – so just keep it in mind to have him stay regular.

Again, listen to Brian – if he's telling you he's fine – he probably is! I was always waiting for the ball to drop or something to happen because I was paranoid due to everything I read and was learning – but other than some isolated things – it never did with chemotherapy.

Hang in,
Frank

Sent: Saturday, April 27, 2013 9:43 PM
From: Leslie Jermainne
To: Frank
Subject: RE: Brian Ross Update

Hi Frank,

This was all so helpful and encouraging, thank you once again my friend. After going over his plan, and discussing thoroughly with his Doctor I think chemo is likely to be a bit rough, but it will be short. 4 months should do it. That is the plan anyway. I hope he has little side effects - but as long as he gets through them all with the best outcome, that is all I can ask.

As far as the re-assurance Frank - you hit the nail on the head. It was enlightening and re-assuring that we can do this. That he's going to be okay and enjoy all those life milestones that I talked of the other night. Especially the mouth sores - that one scared me yesterday. My Mom had that just after she started chemo. But within 7-10 days she was better and it never came back. We definitely have been warned a lot about the constipation. I can't believe you weren't warned. They check with him that he has gone every day and are ready to give him Myralax if he doesn't stool one day. Thanks for the advice though. I want to hear anything you can tell me. I feel like someone knows what I'm going through and is telling me things I really need, even more than prayers at times. I have a lot of well wishes which is amazing and wonderful, but I need the experience and wisdom you are offering me. I will always be grateful.

I hear you on the ball dropping. I don't dare let my guard down, or be to at peace or stop moving, picking up stuff, buying water, food, treats, making the bed, Purelling my hands, etc, etc. If I let my guard down, something might get in. UGH!

Keep the advice coming - whatever you think of - it is so nice to have practical stuff coming my way.

Thank you. Thank you. Thank you.
Leslie

Sent: Saturday, April 27, 2013 10:10 PM
From: Leslie Jermainne
To: My List
Subject: RE: Brian Ross Update

Hello Outside World:

It is Saturday (not Sunday as my mind would have me believe all day today) and we had a good day. I mean all day a good day. Really a great day, all things considered. Brian has felt no real side effects as of today, just a bit tired. He had breakfast, prednisone, a nap, a long visit with Auntie Al and then a surprise visit from Christi, Anna and Christi's Mom and my newest BFF Toni. These are just some of our new Junior Colonial Fife & Drum Corps family who after a parade today (which we were sad we missed) jumped in their car and drove all the way up here to Boston to surprise Brian. He was so thrilled, as was I. And they stayed 4 hours, got Brian out of his room several times, down to the lobby and all around, face mask and all. It was so uplifting for us. Thank you guys!!!

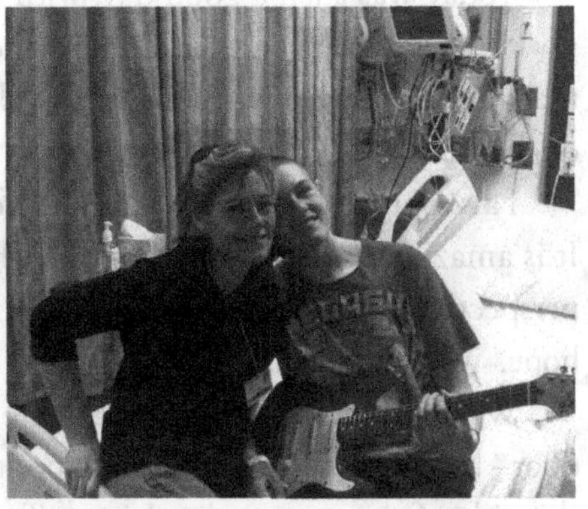

While Brian napped this morning, Alison came over to visit, I got to run out and get Dunkin Donuts, call my Mom and Dad who are taking great care of our dogs, the lawn and laundry. Big Brian couldn't be doing it without them! Al and I had coffee in the lobby for a while so Bri could sleep and it was great to get to talk, and to realize I can talk - at least for now - without dissolving into a mass of tears. I've got control again and I'm not going to let it go. Then while Al and Brian visited, got crazy silly as they always do and laughed and laughed, I walked about the hospital a bit to find out where more things are. Monday we will visit Dana Farber gift shop and check out all the "cancer stuff". Exciting huh?

Tomorrow I hope will be a day of rest for us - maybe an ear plug filled nap if possible. You know you're tired when you are getting ready for bed and already planning a nap for the next day. Brian was going to come for a visit tomorrow, but we are holding off to see what the doctor is thinking about going home a bit next week. He will need to come and pick us up. When we come back I will drive us up so we will be free to move about on our own. We miss him terribly, but I'm so relived and blessed to be able to have such a strong partner in life who supports me fully and makes it possible for me to concentrate solely on Brian Ross. I love you Bri!

Today was such a good day, with so many smiles crossing the face of my child that my heart feels a bit mended. Scared, sure - still large cracks that need to heal, yes - but just one day that was really, really good can do wonders.

I also want to thank Frank again - for not just one, but two great emails. It is amazing to have someone share their experience and knowledge and perspective with me. To give me encouragement and practical advice and hope. What a blessing to me.

We have another new roommate - ours seems to be the revolving door - but I am stills so grateful to be at this wonderful facility and to have this side of the room - that I just offer them all the blessings and prayers I can spare.

Goodnight from room 618.

Leslie

APRIL 28, 2013

Sent: Sunday, April 28, 2013 11:46 PM
From: Sally
To: Leslie Jermainne
Subject: Re: Brian Ross Update

Yes, you absolutely can do this, Leslie. Not only that, you are doing this very well! Someday, things will feel "normal" again. They may never be "like they were" but they will regain a place that is sustainable. Normal enough. Until then, I wish for peace, comfort, and healing, for you and all of Brian's family & loved ones. Look how far you've already come!

Sleep well.
~ Sally

Sent: Sunday, April 28, 2013 11:12 PM
From: Leslie Jermainne
To: My List
Subject: Re: Brian Ross Update

Hi People:

Sunday is almost done. Today was pretty uneventful. Didn't think I would ever say those words again. We met with doctor at rounds, all blood counts are good and if things continue that way we may get a small break this week and go home Mon. or Tues. until we are due back here Thurs. I must admit, I'm a little scared or maybe alotta scared to go home. What if something happens, what if I miss something? We have 24 hour care here from people who actually know what they are doing, what to look for. I certainly want to be with my husband in my own house and for God's sake in a human size (by human I mean 5'10" or above - sorry short people) bed and eating food that doesn't put me in a carb coma. But, but, but what if....

Ugh! I have one of those minds that doesn't ever shut up. My parents always said (as have many, many others) that I talk a lot. I only say out loud a fraction of what goes on in there, so just imagine that. And my baby having cancer?!?! That is just a crazy brain Buffett of worry.

I have to keep telling myself I can do this. It will be okay. I am capable and so is Brian Ross. He can tell me how he feels, what hurts, if he is hot, or sick or hungry. Those parents who are going through this will little babies and small children without that ability, my God. How frightening that must be. I guess I've learned to be grateful for what is in your life, because it could be worse. What is that saying...if everyone put their problems in a pile, you would probably grab your own ones back. I don't know...I'm tired.

To that end, since I don't have too much to report, I'm going to call it a night. Kiss your babies if you can, and appreciate every single second with them. I know I do.

Goodnight y'all from room 618.

Leslie

APRIL 29, 2013

Sent: Monday, April 29, 2013 9:07 PM
From: Leslie Jermainne
To: My List
Subject: RE: Brian Ross Update

WE ARE HOME!!! Do I really need to say anything else? Probably not, but I will anyway. So...at rounds today Brian's counts are still awesome, no nausea (I finally learned to spell this yucky word), no nothing. So, we get sprung out of the big house! At about 2:45 we piled in Brian's car with ten tons of "stuff". And hit the road. After several pit stops (Bri has to drink lots and lots fluids) we got home to have a little love fest with our doggies. Brian took a shower, got to play a video game on his new big screen t.v., and then went straight to bed. Poor guy is exhausted. And I'll be hitting my big, luxurious, clean sheeted bed for at least 8 hours, but I'm hoping for even a bit more.

I got to visit with my Mom and Dad, ate a yummy meal from pasta vita from my BFF Liz - thanks! I don't have to cook tomorrow or the next day either. The other bad thing is that Brian is already dreading going back. We have to be back in Boston @ 10 on Thursday for 8-9 days. I hope he can enjoy the 48 hours we get to have here. He's going to have a friend over tomorrow, be at drum corps Wed. night and get a bunch of sleep and probably some extra showers. I'm going to get a haircut (something shorter to make it easy for the next 4-5 months), and then start reorganizing for the return trip and for any future emergency trips. Gotta pay bills and try to think of anything that needs to be done ahead of time.

Thank you to my brother Andy and his family for the yummy Edible Arrangements that held us over while waiting to leave. Yummy stuff! Thank you all for the words of encouragement, prayers and love. It really does help as I've said.

Gotta go wake the boy up for a minute and give him meds. Wish me luck!

Leslie

Story of rounds that morning, which I did not relay in my update:

So that morning at rounds when they told me his counts were good and they felt fine about sending us home for two days to rest, I panicked. I cried, standing there in the hallway, showered and dressed but in slippers, wet hair from my shower and hyperventilating just a little. I was so scared. I asked them not to send us home. "What if I made a mistake? What if something goes wrong? I don't know what I'm doing!" I cried. And they all (there is like 5-7 people at rounds every day - your nurse, the doctor on the floor that day, the NP on the floor, the pharmacist, a student and usually a visiting doctor from another country, and sometimes a fellow - its crowded) are comforting me and telling me it will be okay. They understand I'm scared. It is a normal reaction they tell me, someone is rubbing my shoulder. And I feel that they really do care, but it is hard, when you are so broken to stand in this circle and beg like a child not to be sent away. Not to venture out on your own in the big scary world. I had just gotten comfy there. I trusted these people to save my son and now they were trusting me and I thought they might be a bit crazy. I knew Brian wanted to go home. Badly. But he didn't have to know I was losing it. I guess I thought that if I missed something I would kill him.

We had a plan in place. If he was to get a fever, I call and run it by them. They would call our local hospital which was the closest hospital with a cancer center, even though they don't have a pediatric cancer center they would be able to get things started and get us transferred back to Boston via ambulance. They would draw blood, start cultures, start IV antibiotics and get us moved. I certainly wasn't going to go back to the first hospital, but that is even farther away, especially if it was during traffic time. And the other one was too far away. That's about an hour. Do you understand what that means? One hour is TOO LONG for my son to not receive treatment. Do you know how scary that is? It feels like, "In one hour he could be dead". Now that isn't what they are saying, but it is what my brain is thinking. See why I didn't want to go home?

They talked and reassured me that I could do this, as I cried my quiet tears so Brian wouldn't hear me. I knew what to do and they were there to help. I could call as many times a day as I needed to feel okay. We had a plan. Go home, repack your bag to be ready to go if need be and then try to rest. It will be fine. After I regrouped, we all went in the room for rounds with Brian, upbeat and happy - we we're going home!!! Yay!!!! Oy.

May 2013 Notes

MAY 1, 2013

Sent: Wednesday, May 01, 2013 6:31 AM
From: Leslie Jermainne
To: My List
Subject: RE: Brian Ross Update 4/30

Hi Friends:

What a wonderful day. Up with the birds at 4:30 (actually I think I beat the birds by a bit) but got to hear them sing which I love. You don't hear that in the hospital. As soon as I wake up my crazy brain starts working and lists all the things I need to do this day, so I figure I might as well shut the monster up and get stuff done. Did all the mail, paid bills, straightened my desk. Made lists, which is a favorite activity of mine.

Brian Ross got up a happy boy today a little before 9. He went to bed about 8 the night before, although I think he was still texting with friends, but still he looked refreshed and had a big smile on his face. That makes my heart the most happy. Got his meds, breakfast and dressed and went for a visit to my parent's house. His great friend Anna came over about 12 for the entire afternoon and again it was such a lift of his spirits. They walked down to Main Street which was awesome for Bri - what a beautiful day - and just got to be teenagers. He wasn't a cancer patient today. What a wonderful day.

Auntie Al and Carl came for a visit after supper, which is always fun. And Brian got to say hi for a bit. He was tired and off to his room he went. We made a last minute run to Dunkin Donuts for him for a donut for dessert and to take his night time dose of prednisone. And then got to watch Castle on t.v. with Big Brian which was relaxing. Could barely keep my eyes open, but it was good to sit on my own couch with a cup of tea, my dogs and my husband with my son happy, playing video games and chatting with friends in his room. What a wonderful day.

I did manage during the day to go have a pedicure and relax for 30 min. I think the guy thought I was a bit strange when I was falling asleep at the end. I also did a few errands and got us some stuff for our next trip. New slippers, PJ pants, a few snacks, an iPad case in Lime Green (the color associated with Non-Hodgkin's Lymphoma - like the wrist bands) for Bri and an extension for his charging cord. Not many plugs in a hospital room. And they all seem to be behind the patient bed. In this day and age, we are charging two phones, two iPads and my computer on a daily basis. It's a whole other job just keeping us charged and connected. I also got to lie in the sun for about an hour in my hammock which I find very relaxing. I may have even dozed for a bit. Talked on the phone with a good friend, and then got another quick visit in with my parents. What a wonderful day.

Had many emails sent again in support, and each one is like a hug from a friend. Actual hugs from friends and family that I saw. I got a message through the grapevine that someone who hasn't been in my direct life for many, many years was happy to be added to the email list. My hope when this is over, that we reconnect again. That is Big Brian's wish too.

Thank you again to Liz and Paula for all the food for Brian (and us!) And all the other offers of food - you may be hearing from me, as I don't think Brian will reach out, but it is helpful for him to not have to worry about that every day when we are away. Thank you to two special friends who want to organize a blood drive in Brian's name. WOW - that just blows me away, and is such an honor. If I can help - maybe get the word out to all the people in our lives, let me know. Thank you to all the people who have added Brian to prayers at their churches, synagogues, and daily rituals. Again, we are in awe of such faith and willingness to extend it to us.

We had a piece of great news today. Our amazing doctor - for this past week at Dana Farber is going to be our assigned oncologist and along with his team is going to see us through this process. You may not understand what a comfort this is to us, but we have made such a connection with him. He took us out of a very bad place after leaving the other hospital and has shown us that this do-able. He is easy to talk to, kind, understanding and just the best! The way things work at DFCI/CH is that you get whoever is "on the floor" for the week, when you first arrive. Then later when you are scheduled your first "clinic" visit (which for us will be tomorrow, and that is how we get back in the system, and readmitted) you are assigned a team based on that day of the week. That team will then be your oncologist for the whole big ride. Dr. S.'s "normal" day is Tuesday. We are going on Thursday. Some little miracle must have happened, but we got him and his team!!! It may have been the begging when we talked, but hey - you gotta do what you gotta do for your child. That being said, all the oncology attending physicians we have met so far have been out of this world wonderful, so any team I'm sure would be great. But a big thank you to the universe for whipping up this little miracle for us.

Tomorrow will bring repacking, a haircut, drum corps practice (can't wait to see everyone) and hopefully a nap and a few more quick errands. We'll see how much gets into the day. Have to get a call into the clinic to find out about getting his port accessed before the CT scan, but that's about it. Being home is such a joy. Trying not to concentrate on going back for over a week, but we have to do what we have to do and a positive outcome is all I can focus on.

Goodnight everyone!
Leslie

PS - just got up and realized I never pushed "send" last night...so here it goes!

MAY 2, 2013

Sent: Thursday, May 02, 2013 8:02 AM
From: Brenda
To: Leslie Jermainne
Subject: Re: Brian Ross Update 4/30

Hi Leslie - I literally was crying as I read your email. You must feel so much better being home close to your family, friends and dogs! I can't imagine going through this nightmare over the past couple of weeks. Remain strong and know that Mark and I are praying for you, Brian and "little Brian" every day. I got your first email at the airport flying out to Las Vegas to meet my girlfriends. They all remember you and Brian and have also kept your family in their prayers as well. The power of prayer from all those who love you guys has brought you where you are today. Please continue to keep me on your update list and know that we love you guys and will continue to pray for you all. This goes without saying, but if you or Brian need anything - if there is anything we can do for you - please let us know.

Love you all
Mark and Brenda

Sent: Thursday, May 02, 2013 9:09 PM
From: Leslie Jermainne
To: My List
Subject: RE: Brian Ross Update 5/2

Hello Everyone:

Didn't write anything last night as I fell fast asleep with my head on Brian's lap at about 7:30. Just so exhausted by the end of the day. But the day was certainly a good one. The weather was beautiful and got to enjoy some of it while I had a nice visit from Paula and Luca! Can't believe how big he is. Also had a nice visit time with my parents. Did some more errands, packing, dinner and fun visit with Laurie and Jess who brought

Brian a beautiful book on guitars - his current favorite subject. Also got my hair cut - thanks for getting me in Dawne, I love it and it will be easy to deal with in the hospital.

This morning we were up bright and early and headed out the door at 6:30 to make a 10:00 CAT scan appt. at Boston Children's Hospital. We made it to valet parking at about 9:52. Yikes! Plus I freaked out a bit, since I didn't know how to really get there, and I'm always convinced the lady in my GPS has no clue what she is doing! I promptly called Brian who turned around and went back home to look at MapQuest, and basically quell my fears. He was a big help, by making me feel like someone was helping me, but in the end it was my son on his cell phone map reassuring me that GPS lady knows her stuff.

We get into CAT scan on time, however apparently the nurses there are not quite familiar with the power port. After two attempts to access Bri's port, a nurse from 6 north (the oncology floor) was called down and Rachel saved the day! First try!! CAT scan happened quickly, but due to the delay accessing the port, we missed our appointment at the Jimmy Fund clinic. They got us in at 1:00 instead of 11:30, but still it was all good. While we were at home, I had gotten info that we would stay with the same oncologist (although I said I felt unsure the person who told me this was correct) and sure enough, it will not be the same. We have a new oncologist. We are a bit sad about that, as we LOVE the first doctor, but we know that we are still getting the best care and protocol. Our original oncologist did stop in to examine Brian and turn us over to our new doctor, and when he felt the lymph nodes under Brian's arm he said they were remarkably reduced in size. WOOHOO!!! We should get CAT scan results tomorrow, probably at rounds and I can't wait to hear what they see. Brian has been staged at Stage III Acute Burkitt Lymphoma. We aren't even phased by this at this point, as we are moving forward and this information changes nothing.

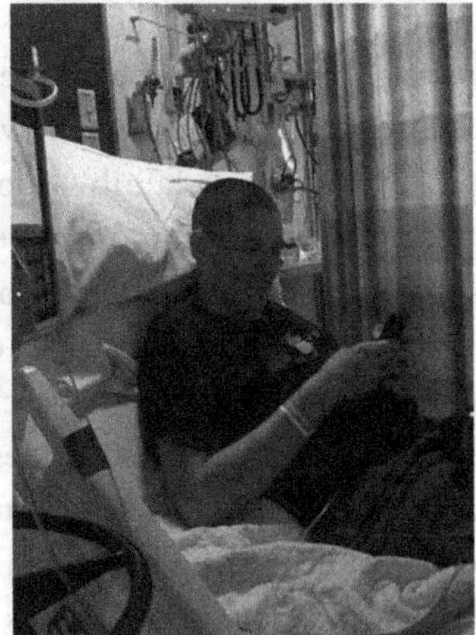

After meeting with our oncologist and her fellow, Brian was taken to the infusion rooms at Jimmy Fund Clinic and started on IV fluids to rapidly hydrate him to get ready for chemo. Although he drank way more fluids than was required at home, the contrast die has to get pushed through and out and also be really ready for chemo. By 7pm he was cleared to get chemo - which has now been started. We didn't think we'd start until tomorrow, so this pushes up a day - great news!

We have settled into the small side of room 631 - although it seems a bit bigger than the small side of our first room. Our roommate is a 17 yr. old boy, which is good, however he isn't feeling very well right now. Hopefully he will feel better soon and maybe he and Brian can talk a bit. It scares me to see this other very big guy sick. It is hard when you know this is what your child will be facing in the coming days. I'm trying very hard to just appreciate every minute he feels well, and steel myself for the times he will be sick. I just hope they are as few as possible. This is a new chapter in our story, and it brings up all the feelings of dread, fear, worry that were the first days - although I guess not quite so bad. Every little bump, change in the road brings new worries and old fears right back to the surface, for about a split second, before I have to say "NO!" and shove them back down. "You have no use here" has become my mantra to those bad thoughts, and so far keeps them at bay.

We have seen our favorite nurse today, and we felt like Laura was waiting for us, which was a comfort. She got us settled in, asked how great was home? And listened to our stories of visits and sunshine, green grass and flowers. And our doggies! Nice to have a friendly face waiting for you. What a job these nurses have. What amazing, comforting, brave people. I never appreciated the nurses who are in my personal life, family and friends, the way I do now. Thank you for all you do for your scared patients and their family. I doubt you truly understand what you bring to us. You are like a mother, best friend and nice boss all rolled into one.

The moodiness of prednisone visits us daily in different and surprising times of day. Like a teenager doesn't already have enough of that going on naturally, we now have chemically enhanced crabbiness, followed sometimes by regret and sadness (that part takes awhile though) and I feel as bad for him in those moments when he regrets being crabby to me, as I do when he is being harsh. I'm learning, slowly the best thing to do is just leave him alone, which means to not even look at him, once I figure out that is where we are in the cycle. Looking at him, especially with concern, is apparently one of the most offensive things I can do. Noted. Also noted, he is not a baby...his legs still work...and he can handle it! Until 30 min. later when he can't lift the tray off his lap and doesn't know where his PJ's are. Uh oh...I just looked at him, and he looked at me, and I averted my eyes just fast enough to avoid a scolding. See...I'm learning!

The last note of the day is that his pump is about the noisiest thing I've heard yet. I think it is the oldest one in the hospital. Apparently it is so noisy, a nurse just stopped in who was walking by and said "What is that noise!" "We're going to have to get you a new pump". Ya, that would be great but they just started a 3 hour infusion of methotrexate, so that ain't happenin'! Nice thought though. I bought Brian a pair of noise cancelling ear phones used for shooting guns (thanks for the idea Al) so when he has those on, with earplugs in his ears, apparently he couldn't care less. Lucky guy - what a nice Mom he has! ;-)

Well...as you can see, once in the hospital the words start flowing. So I better cut this off and go get linens to make my bed, find a place to wash my face and change and maybe watch a show on my iPad or read until I might get some sleep. Wish me luck - oh, and pray for Bri - we need that too!!!

G-NIGHT (says Bri) currently from room 631.

Leslie

MAY 4, 2013

Sent: Saturday, May 04, 2013 7:54 PM
From: Leslie Jermainne
To: My List
Subject: RE: Brian Ross Update 5/3

Hi, Hi, Hi

Today started early, as usual...and included a hunt for a shower. There is one nice bathroom with a shower on the 6th floor that everyone shares, however it was not available due to a need for a child on precautions. So...I got to go up to 8 and get a "shower card", then go across the lobby in my PJs to the other building and start searching floors 4, 5, 6 for a shower room. Found one on 5, thanks to a helpful worker who saw me wandering in my slippers, teddy bear covered pink pants, with a change of clothes, a plastic bag of toiletries and a towel in my hand.

Once back, it was a quick cup of coffee and then transport Brian to have spinal tap and put chemo into spinal column again. I stayed in the room for that one...proud of myself. It went easy, and it was quick. Back up to the room just in time for rounds. Good news! His CAT scan yesterday results showed that the tumors are responding to the meds. This is a good thing! So we are now full steam ahead. The next round has just started at 8:15 after making sure he has cleared the meds from last night. I got to see his actual PET scan at rounds which was interesting. If all goes perfectly we are hearing we might be out late Tues. but Wednesday is more realistic, and of course if anything goes on...fever, or anything we'll be here longer. Hoping for the best outcome. Today went well and he was feeling no side effects yet. He seemed to have a bit more energy than normal this morning, which was nice and we went to the teen room and played Call of Duty Nazi Zombies - my favorite. Then he played a skate boarding game while I laid down on my side of the couch and put my head on his leg and fell asleep in an instant. So tired!

Bri had a good nap this afternoon with his earplugs, eye mask and sound reducing ear muff thingy's. He played his guitar a couple of times today, texted with friends and perused guitar center website in search of guitars. I just don't know where this guitar thing came from - but he loves it.

I spent some time dealing with discharge info, meds, visiting nurse and supplies. Scares me again. I just don't want to miss anything when we get home. I found out we have been assigned a case manager at Aetna, our insurance company which is great. I haven't made contact yet, but she left a message and seems aware of what is going on with us. I have to pick up Brian's meds at CVS down in the lobby before we get home and I'm hoping the anti-nausea meds get approved for more, because right now they are only approving 12, and 90 were ordered. To pay for the remainder out of pocket is just under $400. The nurse practitioner said she'd get working on pre authorization to get that approved.

Phoebe our social worker visited us today, which was great and we talked about working with Brian with Reiki, massage and guided imagery to help him through this. I hope to get more info on Monday, and Phoebe is going to work with him on the guided imagery part. I did take a Reiki class over a year ago - so I'm hoping to brush up my skills and be able to help Brian relax both here and at home when he is feeling good and when he is feeling poorly.

I feel like I'm in this false sense of security because so far the side effects have been basically non-existent, but I'm walking around waiting for the sky to fall in and he will suddenly be so sick. Our roommate is sick and it scares me all day long.

I am also realizing that when we get home, I've got to be a gatekeeper to keep Brian feeling safe and secure in his environment - no matter what if his blood counts are up or down. Mentally he is a bit of a worrier, like me, and just the fear of catching stuff I think could harm his overall outlook. So...I'll be requesting that any visitors call first. And don't be offended if I say no, not today - or meet you outside, or sit outside for a visit. Glad we're going into nice weather! I'm sure he will adjust as we go and feel more comfortable with judging these things, and knowing his counts and such - but for now, he needs to feel safe in his home. And so do I. Sorry Abby, but there probably won't be a lot of friends visiting for a while, until he gets more comfortable and secure. I'm sure you can all appreciate how scary this is, although as I have said to Frank - who understands what we're going through completely - no one really understands until it happens. I know I didn't get it before this. I tried, as so many people are trying and giving their all to us - which means so very, very much. But the severity of what we are dealing with becomes a bit overwhelming at moments, even now - and we've only just begun.

Anyway...I feel like those bad thoughts are creeping in, so I have to shut them down. Some other news is that I have submitted Brian for Make-A-Wish and also found a program for cancer patients to talk with a mentor/survivor of the same type of cancer. Not sure how that will go as of yet, but I thought it might be good to talk with someone who fought this fight and won. If anyone knows of other resources that might be helpful, let me know...again the more the better.

So for Tonight - we are done. Med #2 is being added to the infusion as I type these words, he is trying to sleep, but feeling restless and I'm looking at the clock and can't believe it is 9:00 p.m. already. Hoping for some real sleep on my hunk of cement bed. Might try lining the whole thing with pillows and see how that goes. Wish me luck, and sleep.

Over and Out from Room 631.

Leslie

MAY 5, 2013

Sent: Sunday, May 05, 2013 7:13 AM
From: Leslie Jermainne
To: My List
Subject: RE: Brian Ross Update 5/4

Sorry Folks,

For some reason last night's email never left my outbox. I didn't know this until my Dad called looking for an update. Sorry Dad. On top of it, when I called him, I was walking through the entire hospital to use the far away laundry, since the one on our floor was full and Bri had no t-shirts left, and then my phone lost its signal.

So how was today? Well it was really a great day until about 7:30 or so. First we had Auntie Al up for a visit which was a lot of fun, silliness, and laughter. Then we had Toni, Christi and Anna stop to see us after the Lexington Muster. Bri was so happy to have so many visitors, get out of his room, and be a teenager. Then the effects started to hit. Toni noticed him zone out during the conversation, and we decided to end the visit and get him into bed. After goodbyes, Bri tried to lie down, but he complained of nausea, headache and his legs were aching. He was given anti-nausea meds (more of them), and a small dose of pain meds. We took a walk, because his legs were so restless, got a few saltines into him, since he hadn't eaten since lunch, and then back to bed to start the next dose of chemo. Poor boy has finally closed his eyes, and is going to sleep. I'm praying for a restful night for him. I think I won't get a winks sleep worrying he will be sick, or in pain and waiting for any noise or sign of that happening.

We knew this was coming, but it hit suddenly. And scared him, and me. Thankfully with medication and 1.5 hours, he seems to be resting now. Mental note - one visitor a day, if that.

Our roomy is feeling a tiny bit better and I heard his prednisone kick in today. Interesting how it sounds the same....

Thanks Al for bringing our extra xBox controller, Bri's favorite flip flops and the exercise mat that I'm attempting to cushion my chair/bed with.

I don't have much else to say tonight - my mind is too busy with worry of sickness to come. I have to go back across the hospital to get our laundry and fold it. And then I hope to get ready for bed and get into it, and stare at the ceiling and wait.

Goodnight from 631

Leslie

Sent: Sunday, May 05, 2013 7:36 PM
From: Leslie Jermainne
To: My List
Subject: RE: Brian Ross Update 5/5

Sunday News....

We made it through the night, uninterrupted from any sickness. Today went well, very mild bouts of nausea, but that was it. We played Call of Duty again, and got a chance to talk with our roommate and his Mom for a bit which was nice. Brian spent most of his day on his phone texting. I had a nice long phone call with Laurie, picked up Brian's meds from CVS in the lobby, actually took about a 30 min. nap - and all is good.

Brian's Methotrexate level is already at acceptable levels to go home - he is still receiving cyclophosphamide. Tonight and tomorrow and has to have a spinal tap and more methotrexate put into his spinal column on Tuesday, and then start an injection for recovery that he will need to have at home.

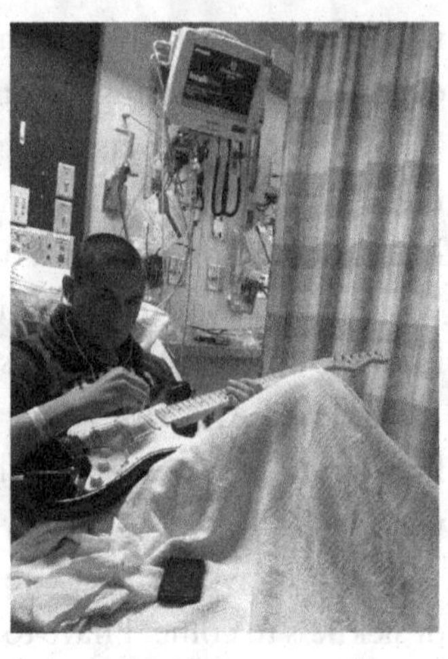

We made an interesting discovery this evening. Brian received Reglan last night and again tonight at the same time. Guess what? That is what made him feel so crappy last night, because it's back!!! The nurse was great, came and explained what it is used for (anti-nausea) that it can be given with Benadryl if side effects are bad, but then he has to lose the anti-nausea patch behind his ear. So...we are going to switch to Ativan and dump the Reglan. The nurse has put in for that to happen, and I will bring it up at rounds tomorrow.

It is a strange reaction, first he feels a bit queasy, then he starts shaking - like his hands shake. Then he gets really jumpy and jittery, his legs hurt and he says he can't describe how he feels but he certainly doesn't like it. He has gone to the teen room to try to take his mind off of it until the Adavan kicks in to override this reaction. He was a little crazy. At least we have figured this out before going home and can fix it before getting home.

I'm hoping to get good details at rounds tomorrow about maybe going home on Tuesday - or Wednesday. Keep your fingers crossed. Going home into our own beds, surroundings, foods etc. will be so wonderful.

Over and Out from room 631.

Leslie

Sent: Sunday, May 05, 2013 9:10 PM
From: Frank
To: Leslie Jermainne
Subject: RE: Brian Ross Update 5/4

Hi Leslie,

Thanks for the updates - Estelle and I get nervous when we don't hear anything. Glad things are moving forward.

As I read your emails - I remember more and more about the stresses of a caregiver and life in the hospital.

I remembered that I would get up at 4:30 or 5:00 in the morning just to get the good shower. I know it sounds early but, I'm sure you were like me - yes you sleep, but you're never really out as you're constantly on guard and hearing things. So I would shower, get a coffee and get back to the room before rounds, and before Anna woke up. I would then rest again for a bit but knowing that I was ready to meet the day.

...just got your new email. Reglan did not work for Anna either - her side effects weren't as bad - but she definitely had cramps with it. She used Zofran successfully for nausea and Ativan for helping to sleep.

Try not to stress and wait for the bad stuff to happen - I have a lot of grey hair because of this and as you are finding out - it's not so bad. It's crappy with the potential for something but don't harp on it. When it's good and he's good - just enjoy the good. Give him space when he needs it - he will tell you when he needs you. Getting back to one of your previous emails where he was snappy at you - just remember he is coping/trying to cope and make sense of this all while still trying to be himself and also a teen. You are 100% there for him and deep down he knows it. I guess I'm saying to have tough skin and remember it's not your little boy frustrated with YOU - it's your little boy processing and fighting to beat this thing. He may have a short fuse due to the chemo - (part of the chemo brain), but also just part of feeling crappy and stuck somewhere he really doesn't want to be.

Sorry - I'm dozing off, but wanted to get a few words out to you. You are doing a WONDERFUL JOB !!!!

Frank

MAY 6, 2013

Sent: Monday, May 06, 2013 7:12 AM
From: Leslie Jermainne
To: Frank
Subject: Re: Brian Ross Update 5/4

Hi Frank,

Yes, something was going on with my computer for 2 days. Once again your note is just the things I needed to hear today. Here it is 6:42 a.m. And I have already put a load of laundry through the washer and now into the dryer, taken a shower, put my bed away, gone downstairs to get Bri a muffin, made some coffee and I'm sitting back in my chair listening to my constant and reassuring companion, his pump. A day or two when I slept past 6 were like "oh, no...I bet someone is in the shower. I won't be ready for rounds."

Although the last two nights were a bit scary when he got the Reglan, I'm so happy we figured out somewhat quickly what was causing this stuff before going home, or before another dose even. He does get Zofran via IV, and that is what we'll go home with, I think the patch will come back today since it just had to be removed so he could get some Benadryl to calm down the Reglan, and then I think the plan is to add in some Ativan, but we'll get that ironed out today.

So the part I really, really needed to hear is when you said "try not to stress and wait for the bad stuff to happen." You are so right and for the most part I try, but one little thing that he feels off brings on the "here we go..." thoughts. The other crazy thing that I realize started lurking in my brain yesterday and I finally formulated into a real thought in the shower today is - 'he isn't so sick, maybe it's not working enough?' - How crazy is that one? I'm hoping you're going to say normal, but don't lie to me. It's not that I want him sick, it's just that sick is what I expect to cure this thing.

The other thing is yesterday I went back to reading info about Burkitt Lymphoma, especially cure rates. On the websites where it was high, I was happy. Where not quite so high I was crying. I finally put it away and said who cares? It really doesn't matter what they report because we are here, we are in it and the only way out is to fight through treatment. Should I stay away from that stuff? I feel a little like I'm neglecting info if I don't keep reading.

Also I'm afraid to look on any support group sites, because of reading about people dying. I'm trying to only look for survivors, but it is tough. Did you or Anna do any support group type of stuff while fighting?

Once we got our plan, and have been moving forward, I don't feel as scared. We have stuff to concentrate on. We a have a job to do. And I try so hard not to let the thought of him dying in my mind. But sometimes I want to yell at people, "THIS IS REALLY SERIOUS!!! HE COULD DIE!!!" Again, it's an absurd thought, but because he is doing so well, I feel like people are forgetting how serious this is, even me at moments, but I feel like I'm the only one who snaps back into reality and remembers...I could lose my baby.

I also find that when I'm out in the "outside world" and anybody who looks at me for anything, I say in my head "my son has cancer", like everyone in the world should know and understand. UGH! It is so overwhelming at moments.

I know the snappy stuff is normal, drug induced and frustration amplified. And giving him his space protects us both. It's a tightrope us caregivers have to walk. Be there to give just what they need, try to anticipate when they need it, but don't overstep or go too fast or try to do too much. I am learning, and I do think I'm doing a good job. But hearing that I'm doing a wonderful job from someone who worked the job before, is very uplifting. Thank you. I'm ready for the day. I hope you enjoy yours.

Leslie Jermainne

Sent: Monday, May 06, 2013 8:43 AM
From: Frank
To: Leslie Jermainne
Subject: RE: Brian Ross Update 5/4

Hey Leslie,

You are NORMAL. Everything you mentioned about thoughts - I have, and I'm sure anyone in the situation would run through in their mind.

Ditto, ditto, ditto. Thought all those things you listed.

- I definitely thought things weren't working if Anna wasn't feeling well. Keep in mind that you know the worst potential side effects - cancer treatments and symptom control have come a long way - bear in mind they are only treating the cancer - not a massive assault on his entire body like 20 years ago. Plus - look at the warnings and side effects for Advil or Tylenol. Also, don't underestimate the strength of Brian and his will to fight. Remember he is only as sick as he feels.
- Group sites - Anna never used one. I did - and it helped me. When I first emailed - I mentioned I had a few people that I would chat with to keep my sanity. These were cyber friends (caregivers of young spouses with cancer). You need to keep your perspective though - there are a lot of people in a 'bad place' or desperate situations that can scare you. Not to mention the sick people that prey on others for fun. But overall you may just find another Mom or Dad out there. You will know as every word they write you will feel as if you already thought it. (PS - this is how I met Estelle) Just be careful!
- The thoughts of death are a normal part of the job. You wouldn't be normal if your brain didn't cover all the bases as far-fetched or as scary as they are. You know all too well the seriousness of this (as do all your friends and family). Just like you, I would want to shake people and say 'THIS IS SERIOUS!!! and you're bringing over a cake and telling jokes???' Just keep in mind most people are putting up a strong front - not letting on that they don't fully

understand - but can fully grasp what it would be like if it were their child was going through this. Their job is not to stress like you are - their job is to help out where they can, be compassionate, and maybe try to make Brian feel like all is normal despite this ordeal. (If you're like me - your brain will also wish someone else was going through this instead of you - and maybe even resent people for not having to go through this. All normal.)

Hang in there,
Frank

Sent: Monday, May 06, 2013 6:47 PM
From: Leslie Jermainne
To: My List
Subject: RE: Brian Ross Update 5/6

Hi There Family and Friends,

What a day this has been. It started out not my best...things have slowed down a bit in the "getting stuff done" department, which gives my overactive Mom brain too much time to think. In the wee morning hours when I am able to get the shower, I finally realized I had been mulling around the thought "he hasn't been sick, is this stuff really working?" This thought leads to the "If this stuff isn't working, the outcome will be horrible." I spiraled down into tears quickly before being able to shake it back and realize it was crazy thoughts.

As if by magic I get an email from the person who keeps giving me the best advice, who I can tell the crazy thoughts too, and who has the best tips and understand living in a hospital as a caregiver. I got just the answers I needed to hear, and just the advice I needed to get to keep moving forward. The day really has turned around from there. I guess I'm entitled to those moments still, when the fear of my child not making it out of this mess is instantly overwhelming and debilitating, but I need to keep them few and far between.

So the good stuff...At rounds we got confirmation that Reglan has been marked as a drug Brian is not to receive ever again. We asked other good questions, like "if his counts are so good, should we just go to round 3?" Nothing like the patients trying to manage the protocol, huh? Of course we learned why his counts haven't dropped yet (it's too early), we got lots of good talks about how things will work at home, what to do if he gets a fever (call the Jimmy Fund clinic and head to our local hospital), the likelihood of that happening (very likely), how he's going to feel when his counts are very low this coming weekend and start of next week (really exhausted and crappy), reviewed all his meds (one of which I still need to go get), dealt with a paper cut (yes, that requires a doctor's visit, gloves and all), a pain in his head, which he decided he didn't need anything for, I've done more laundry, so as to pack all clean stuff tomorrow, he got a nice Red Sox baseball hat from family day yesterday (sorry Big Bri, they don't give out Yankee hats in Boston), and a new shirt for the pajamas they gave him (they gave him an adult small at first...really?) I met with the nice lady to arrange for visiting nurse to come on Thurs to access his port and draw labs, we're still working on one med that needs to be refrigerated and delivered to home, and both Brian and I had a great talk with our social worker, who told me that I have been one of the most involved and best advocator parents she has ever worked with, so GO ME!!! Laurie has been telling me this on the phone, but she knows and loves me anyway, so although her words were what encouraged me in the first place, hearing it from Phoebe here, was an added boost.

Then we got the good news that we are 99.9999% sure we'll be home by dinner tomorrow. The only hold up would be any reaction to the GSCF shot tomorrow, which I will be learning how to administer for our days at home. But that is not expected to happen, so we should be on the road by midafternoon. And to top off a day that just kept getting better, I got a call from a place called Imerman Angels that I contacted last Friday. They match up children in treatment with survivors of the same diagnosis to talk and mentor. We got a match!!! I was crying talking on the phone with The Imerman people and Brian's match has already made contact! He had the same diagnosis of stage 3 Burkitt lymphoma and is 3 years out from diagnosis. I feel so happy for Brian to have this new person in his life that can understand what he might be thinking, feeling, worrying over and enjoying. What a blessing for him! I hope it will be a great mentor and outlet for Brian.

There have been other people today who have reached out to us in amazing and generous ways, of which I'm sure in the future we will be taking them up on their offers. I am so touched everyday by the people who are caring for us from afar.

So...I need to go call my hubby and tell him all this great news that he will soon read. I want to thank you all for reading and caring and sending well wishes to us and prayers out into universe.

Goodnight from room 631 (hopefully for the last time in this room)

Leslie

Sent: Monday, May 06, 2013 11:31 PM
From: Sheila
To: Leslie Jermainne
Subject: Re: Brian Ross Update 5/6

God bless, Leslie. I wouldn't ever doubt that you would be one of the best if not the best advocate for your child -- something you have been all his life! Xoxo

MAY 7, 2013

Sent: Tuesday, May 7, 2013 8:55:58 PM
From: Leslie Jermainne
To: My List
Subject: Re: Brian Ross Update 5/6

We are home. I will write about our day today, tomorrow. Too tired. Love to you all!

Leslie

MAY 8, 2013

Sent: Wednesday, May 08, 2013 7:52 AM
From: Leslie Jermainne
To: My List
Subject: RE: Brian Ross Update 5/7

Hi! I'm Awake! (Thanks to Jack the dog at 5:45, his usual time)

So here is our update from 5/7/2013. Our night was terrible. Our poor roommate was not well which means a barrage of nurses, doctors and anyone else needed come in and out of the room repeatedly. We of course feel bad for our roomy and want him to get better, however Bri needs his sleep too (not to mention me, but I'm not battling cancer) and he was scheduled for a spinal tap at 9 a.m. At 3:00 a.m. I finally got him moved into the treatment room which has a gurney. They made it up for him, put a sign on the door and he was able to get a few hours sleep. I slept in his bed which was like heaven, and managed to get about 2 hours of sleep. I did get about 3 hours earlier in the evening before all the people in the room.

Brian's spinal tap and chemo infusion into his spinal column went well, and we were back up to the room by 10:00 and having breakfast. I started packing and getting organized and about 12:00 he got his GCFS shot in his leg which went easy. I will have no problem doing this, as I inject myself with B12 every three weeks with a much bigger needle into my muscle, rather than the tiny one he gets. We will have visiting nurse here to observe me give the first shot and check his blood pressure which was a little high.

After his shot, and being observed for an hour, reviewing all his meds, getting our instructions, we practically ran to the car and got out of there! We were free! We hit the highway, made one pit stop and were home by 4:30. So nice. Our doggies were very excited, the weather is beautiful, the grass so green, the flowers so pretty. Everything just seems wonderful. And so quiet! It strikes me the lack of people here at home as opposed to Boston. And it is lovely.

After pizza and salad from Pizza Works (my choice) a glass of wine with my husband and our favorite show "Castle" which I fell asleep at the end, it was off to my wonderful, comfy, room and bed with amazing sheets (they aren't really special, they just feel that way). As I tried to lie on my side, I realize that both of my hips are bruised and sore from sleeping on that chair with no cushioning. Sheila - I gotta get that blow up mattress from you today!

So that was our day! Now we should be home until readmit on 5/17/2013. We will have visiting nurse once a week and will be driving to the Jimmy Fund clinic in Boston once a week for checkup. Our things to watch for at this point are his counts going way down and having to go to Boston to get a blood transfusion. Watching for fever which will send us to the hospital to get evaluated and most likely transferred to Boston via ambulance. His counts are really good right now, and we are hopeful to not have either situation happen until we go back on the 17th for round 3.

We aren't having visitors now, unless Brian says it's ok. It is important he feels safe, healthy and comfortable to recuperate in his own home. As he starts to feel more comfortable and we know how his counts are dropping and how he feels, he may adjust his thoughts. The lowest his counts should get will be over this weekend and start of next week and then start climbing. If his counts don't climb back enough by the 17th, then we will stay home until they are high enough and then go again!

Keep us in your thoughts and prayers. They are working!

Have a great day!

Leslie

Sent: Wednesday, May 08, 2013 8:57 AM
From: Paula
To: Leslie Jermainne
Subject: Re: Brian Ross Update 5/7

Wow you are amazing. Do I see nursing in your future? I do have a quilt that our church has made for Brian. I will await your word on how to get this over to you, completely understanding the no visitor policy. Please just know it's here.

Love ya kiddo, & praying hard,

Paula

Sent: Wednesday, May 08, 2013 5:29 PM
From: Leslie Jermainne
To: My List
Subject: RE: Brian Ross Update 5/8

Hi!

Writing early today, as we plan to go to drum corps Tonight and I'll probably be too tired afterwards to send out an update so...

Today has been great! We both had a good night's sleep. I unpacked and repacked our bag so we are ready to go at a moment's notice if needed or next week when it's time to go back in. We had a visit from the visiting nurse today who watched me give Bri his GCSF shot - I passed! It was actually not bad at all, plus he has numbing cream put on beforehand, so it went well. His blood pressure was back to normal today and his temp was great. All good signs and a big relief!

Brian had ordered a new laptop computer just before all this started. He had saved up for this computer and had it custom built. It arrived today and we have one very happy computer nerd! It is awesome and I must admit I'm slightly jealous. This will be great for when we go back, as it is powerful enough to run his video games. Most laptops are not able to handle video games very well.

Brian went to visit his grandparents today, and had a very nice visit he told me when he got home.

I made a trip to the grocery store for lots of bottled water (he must drink at least 3 liters a day) so to make it easy to track. Drove up to Haddam to get him his favorite sandwich for lunch at the Cooking Company, and spent an hour or two going over my cancer notebook, adding new pages, making a chart for the fridge on who we call and why we call if we have a problem. The visiting nurse was impressed with my organization. She doesn't know it's the only way for me to get through this. I showed big Brian the list, on the off chance I wouldn't be home at some point. He said "holy crap!" Ya, exactly! But I have it under control.

So it's time to get some dinner in me - Brian already had some yummy mac and cheese, and get ready for drum corps. Very excited to see everyone.

All these wonderful families who have become our good friends over the past year, have been so supportive of us.

Tomorrow will be a visit with the nurse from another company that will access his port, draw blood for labs, and de-access, plus check his blood pressure and temp again. After we get those results, and they are good, we will be set for the weekend and then visit the Jimmy Fund clinic on Monday for checkup, blood draw, etc. Hopefully to return that same day (see why I need a bag packed at all times). Once that goes well, we will be back home for another 4 days. Think of all the good sleep I'm gonna get. YEE HAW!

Good Evening!
Leslie

MAY 9, 2013

From: Leslie Jermainne
To: My List
Subject: Re: Brian Ross Update 5/9
Date: Thursday, May 09, 2013 8:44:25 PM

So here we are at day whatever. Overall a good day. Visiting nurse came today and accessed Brian's port, took blood and de-accessed his port. Took his blood pressure which was back to normal. All went well and I expect good results tomorrow a.m. Bri is counting on a sleep over visit with his BFF tomorrow which will be great, and very much needed. I am reminded of my girlfriends who often spent overnights with me or I with them looking back on my teenage retrospective. What amazingly good times we had. Talking about boys, and clothes, and boys, and makeup, music and boys. It is all so crucial, I now understand. The simple things you take for granted until they are no longer a right but a privilege. Oh my God, if I could have saved him the effort or the pain.

I worry that I won't be able to hold onto this micro perspective when this is all over. The joy in the simplest things has become amazing. There was a practice I was trying before this all happened to "be in the moment". I will try it here to remember why being home is amazing.

1) My bed is amazing. It is king size with so much soft room.
2) The sheets feel wonderful and soft and inviting when I lay down
3) My house that holds my bedroom is wonderful. I am lucky to have such a house to keep me warm and sheltered and loved.
4) My husband is such an amazing partner to me. One for all and all for one. The gift he gives me by caring for me, and making my ability to care for our ill son is amazing.
5) My dogs, who also provide unconditional love to us all are amazing parts of our life.
6) My family being near, supporting us, seeing my aunts and uncles today, even just for a moment, reinforces our family connection.
7) Being home is amazing because it is warm, nurturing and restoring.
8) Our bathroom is clean and private and clean, and private.
9) My son can sleep in peace to restore his health
10) The street we live on is so beautiful and clean and unpopulated
11) The trees are so green and the flowers are so pretty.

I was just watching a recorded Ellen show and the dogs were annoying and barking and being noisy, prednisone boy came out and yelled at all of us for being "too noisy," The poor dogs just don't get it.

Time to call it a good night, talk to you all tomorrow.

Leslie

MAY 10, 2013

Sent: Friday, May 10, 2013 3:07 PM
From: Estelle
To: Leslie Jermainne
Subject: (((((((hugs)))))))

Hi Leslie,

I hope this email finds you rested and less stressed. I feel like I have talked to you recently but I have only been listening. I read your updates and think of you and Brian every day. I have had many conversations in my own head (: I can't imagine what you are experiencing (as did Frank with Anna) but I am truly happy that Frank is able to give you some support and understanding. I know from personal experience that when life deals you hardships it is more endurable when you are able to talk, yell or cry with someone who really gets it. (It took me 2 1/2 years to figure that one out!!)

When you talk about being in the moment and appreciation for the small stuff…THAT I TOTALLY GET!! When you said that life would never be the same for you…I understand. How can this experience not change you?? I still have those feelings all the time. Sometimes I have to remind myself to not stress over things but I still gawk in wonder when I cross the causeway and see the water and beautiful nature all around me because it's something I always wanted and here it is!!! It's a blessing. I also like to give the kids lectures about how they don't realize just how lucky they are to be here in O.S. blah blah blah (I'm sure that is how it sounds to them lol)…….You may also realize that you have less tolerance for crap! Any or all inconsequential stupid stuff! There are people in this world who still take everything for granted or don't understand how something can happen to turn your whole world upside down and change who you are. I let go of many people in my life due to the way I changed but it opened up the door to my new life here with a man who gets me! You found a good outlet for your thoughts and a way to stay connected to all your friends and family by writing each day. I admire your strength. Thank you for allowing us to be in your circle of friends. I hope you will also trust that we are willing and able to help you if you need us.

Love and Prayers and positive energy (Ii really believe that positive attracts positive- it's a law of the universe!) Stay strong!

MORE (((((HUGS)))))
Estelle

Sent: Friday, May 10, 2013 4:33 PM
From: Leslie Jermainne
To: Estelle
Subject: RE: (((((((hugs)))))))

Thanks Estelle, I am so lucky to have such amazing friends old and new who have shown up to support us. I can only look for the positive these days, as the negative is too scary to allow in my mind. I have those moments, but try to stop them before they take over. Hearing from Frank - the hospital lingo, the understanding of rounds and all the medications and the living day in and day out in the hospital is so very helpful. Big Brian is home doing all the things we need done to survive, run our business, keep our home, etc. while I'm away. As is our way and why we complement each other so well is I do one thing and he does the other and we make it happen together. Because of that, he hasn't experienced what I have being in the hospital, the beeping machines, the loss of privacy, the confusion, the need to take charge and advocate for your patient. Frank is the only person I know who has been where I have been and his willingness to maybe revisit some of those times in order to help me is extraordinary to me. I am forever grateful, and I hope someday, if needed I will be that person for someone who might need me.

There have been so many positives to this negative situation, and I try every day to remember them. I feel weird when I'm talking to someone and say "we are lucky" and they look at me like I'm crazy, but we are. We caught this early, we are at the best hospital, Brian isn't "sick", the doctors know what to do, we have each other and amazing friends and family who reach out to us on a daily basis. We really, truly, are lucky people overall.

Thank you for keeping in touch, and we are looking forward to reconnecting in person this summer when possible at fire nights. It will be nice for Bri too, as he can visit outside as much as he feels up to it. I will stay strong for my son, my husband, myself and all our friends providing us with strength.

Hope to see you all soon!
Leslie

Sent: Friday, May 10, 2013 8:01 PM
From: Leslie Jermainne
To: My List
Subject: RE: Brian Ross Update 5/10

HI Again!

Today has been such a great day. We got Brian's counts back from Jimmy Fund Clinic - all are still high and he is doing well. No need to worry through the weekend, just watch for signs of fever or any other issues, and be ready for our trip to the Jimmy Fund Clinic in Boston @ 12 on Monday. The weather was/is spectacular today, so that was an added bonus. I got outside a bit to pull a few weeds, try to start the mosquito machine (failed, but will work on it tomorrow), our BFF Carlo came and took away a bunch of metal stuff that needed to be recycled and had been sitting out back since just before this all happened. So nice to have that cleaned up. Thanks Dude!

I got to talk with Paula, and also arranged to have breakfast with my girlies Liz & Ann tomorrow, can't wait for that! Made a stop at the dump to drop some stuff while out delivering a check for Brian. It was nice to be able to help him out a bit for a change. I worked on cleaning up the house a bit - not that much was needed when we got home, Bri has kept it very nice, but little Brian and I are like a tornado coming through with all our stuff. I also picked up some camping cot mattress pad thingy's yesterday, and today was able to rearrange our giant suitcase and fit them. The Jermainne family members are all professional over-packers!

Brian has his best buddy Zack over for a sleepover, which almost didn't happen, and is having a great time being a teenager. The sound of my child's laughter is more valuable to me at this point than anything else I can imagine. So thank you to Zack and his Mom for making this happen for him. Hanging with your friend is like a booster shot. You gotta have it to feel good.

I had some very nice emails today from people reaching out to me once again providing encouragement and love and support. You are all so awesome. I had an interesting thing happen after reading and responding to an email today, thanks Estelle. I picked up a magazine (Good Housekeeping) which my Mom had given me. I flipped it open and the title of the article I landed on is "How to Be a Friend to a Friend Who's Sick". Seriously. So I start to read just the first little bit and it is written by a woman battling breast cancer. After the big bold type that happens at the beginning of every magazine article to suck you in to reading it, the real story starts. By the way this is really for Frank and Toni to understand how they have helped me. And here is what is says: "I worried about asking my friends, years beyond their own diagnoses, to revisit that period in their lives, but they made themselves available to me in every way. As another cancer survivor told me, when someone who has experienced a serious illness or tragedy reaches out to you when you're in comparable circumstance, it's as if that person is going into a cave and sitting with you in the darkness while everyone else is standing outside, trying to coax you to come out." I stopped reading at that point, because I knew I had read what I needed that day. And I knew that I needed to share that with the people who have crawled into the darkness with me and are waiting it out by my side. Everyone is amazing, and the people standing outside encouraging us to come into the light are very, very important and needed too. But the experienced people, offering their wisdom, friendship and comfort are the most special of all.

I also had a real revelation at dinner tonight while talking to my hubby. There is one singular person I have to thank, and probably need to meet in person, as I've never met him and only had one solitary conversation with him, but he turned the entire tide in 30 minutes with his words of wisdom, his understanding and his encouragement. Dr. D., my father-in-laws doctor is our angel of sorts. If it weren't for him, taking time on a long ago Sunday, to reach me while suffering at the hospital, listen to what I had to say and for the first time I was heard and encouraged and given advice from a true patient advocate that changed our lives. I will meet him someday and give him a tear soaked hug I'm sure, for saving us. For saving my son, my husband and me. Without him, I fear we would still be at the first hospital, not knowing any better than what we were told in the first 3 days of this horror. Because of him, we went to Dana Farber and our whole world and our outlook on the future was changed after a 3 hour ambulance ride. An ambulance ride we paid for out of pocket and it was the best $3,000 I have ever spent.

So...last night's email ended on a weird note, when I reread it this morning. Here is my excuse: I was typing it on my iPad, which was difficult because if the message is more than a few lines, the text goes behind the keyboard and it is impossible to fix your mistakes. And....I had a big glass of wine and that wasn't helping me in the typing dept.

So Tonight I want to end my email with thanks and gratitude for all of you who reach out to us hourly, daily, weekly or even just the one time, like Dr. D., who changed everything for us. Each person we are grateful for what they have brought to us in our time of need. We are lucky.

GOODnight!
Leslie

Sent: Friday, May 10, 2013 9:47 PM
From: Sheila
To: Leslie Jermainne
Subject: Re: Brian Ross Update 5/10

Leslie,

I love reading your emails, you are so real and I look forward to your updates now. And last night, I just figured you had a glass of wine - lol! God knows, you deserved it and I was thinking, 'thank goodness she is relaxing.' You are such a good mom and wife and doggie mom.

I am having a cold beer as I type this, it has been a long week. At school, I hear some whining and complaining (not from the kids, but the adults!) about really dumb, petty little issues. And I am just thinking, 'really?! Do you realize how lucky you are to have this job?!!' Because, I couldn't be more grateful to have my job; I feel incredibly fortunate to have a job I love where I feel I am doing something good. And for you to say, with all you are going through, that you feel lucky is just a confirmation for me of the power of faith and positive thinking. And so, I will resist the whiners and negative energy people, and thank God I have good people like you and Brian in our lives. So, thank you, Leslie for being there for us.

Have a wonderful Mother's Day! xoxo Sheila

Sent: Friday, May 10, 2013 10:43 PM
From: Frank
To: Leslie Jermainne
Subject: RE: Brian Ross Update 5/9

...sorry Leslie - started this email this morning and ran out of time.

I love getting these emails and good news. You guys collectively are strong and are doing all the right things. Brian is doing great and you and big Bri are both great advocates for him.

Like you mentioned - I can also attest that you will always be able to carry your new found perspective and 'living in the moment'. What's important is what's around you. Way too many people in the world today just don't understand that.

I loved the analogy in your email tonight that describes people that have had similar experiences to you that have the ability to come into your cave and offer something - even if only that they have been in a similar environment. I did some thinking about it - as I mentioned - I enjoy being able to help you. I look back on my journey and it brings back nothing but good feelings. It makes me feel good to know that I was there for Anna. In some way I think it was my mission in life to be there for her - and I know in my heart that I did all I could and that it made some difference.

Here's a good tip though I may have said it before but - don't be afraid to take people up on an offer to help. You definitely have a good support system of people both in the cave and on the outside. I know the people on the outside feel helpless and would gladly help out in any small way. I will drag Big Brian out for a beer or something soon - but I've been working Brian hours ever since we got back from vacation.

I think of so many things on the fly at work but sometimes come up short in emails. I may need to keep a journal for you. LOL. One day soon we'll have to chat and I'm sure they'll all roll right out. We would love to see you guys at some point -but I definitely understand minimizing visitors. I'm glad Brian is getting time to be with his best friends.

Keep up the good work,
Frank

MAY 11, 2013

Sent: Saturday, May 11, 2013 7:23 PM
From: Leslie Jermainne
To: My List
Subject: RE: Brian Ross Update 5/11

Hello Peeps!

What another fantastic day. It is amazing to live the simple days in techno-color. Brian's sleepover visit was awesome, fun filled, much needed teenager time. Love that kid! (His friend, and him too!) We are so lucky that years ago Sarah tracked us down through a home school list, and we were blessed with amazing friends. Feeling so very lucky. After Zack went home, Brian had a little bit of time to rest and to let me inject him again... poor kid, yesterday I sort of "missed" the numbed spot in his leg. I did much better today - he is my hero!

I had a wonderful breakfast with two very important, supportive friends (sorry Paula couldn't make it) who have seen me through so many rough times (this being the worst by far) but also so many good times, and many I hope that are yet to come. My family is very much more than my "blood" relatives. My family includes so many friends, both old (very old) and new. I'm sometimes a bit sad that I didn't always live with this sense of gratitude for the people in my life. The people who show up. The people who text, and email and call and send cards and just say "hey!" when they think of me. The girls that watch me cry and listen to my fears, the ones that stand by my side and say "I've got you", the ones who say "I understand where you are, because I've been there too." The ones who say "give me a job, I want to help". The ones who amazingly thank me for being strong, because somehow it makes them stronger and more appreciative, which in turn enriches me. I am a lucky girl once again today.

Then we had an awesome visit with Toni, Christi, Dillon and Bria for an afternoon filled with fun, talking, listening, a drive, a walk, food, coffee, Wii, ping pong and laughter, and much needed friendship! Thank you to you guys who continually go out of your way (way out of your way to Boston, twice!) to comfort us, entertain us, and make us feel like normal people without cancer invading our lives. I have recently read that the right people show up in your life at the right time, and that has been proven to me over and over in the past month.

Brian is feeling well, tired and a few headaches, but is doing all he is supposed to do (drink 2-3 liters a day, rest and be a teenager). We hope to have a visit with Auntie Al tomorrow and have my Mom and Dad down for a grinder dinner for mother's day. Brian and I have just both finished work (Brian more work than me, as usual) and will have a nice dinner, a glass of wine and a movie before probably falling asleep on the couch and then shuffling off to bed, exhausted but happy, another day has finished, and it was a good one.

I drove past the two family house we purchased on the day after Brian was diagnosed. We had such hopes for a fun summer renovating the house (I know, but we like that stuff), but since 4/19 I have barely thought about it. Today I drove by to take a minute to think about the future and what we need to do there. The best thing I saw was a huge lilac bush in full bloom. Tomorrow there will be a large vase full of lilac blooms when I visit there again tomorrow. I can hardly wait to have their scent perfume our home. It will be delicious.

I hope you all enjoy your Saturday night. Instead of praying for us tonight, send one out to our very special friends Mark and Brenda, who have not left my mind in the past two days. Right now they need some love too, and I have such an abundance, I'm asking you all to share for me.

Thanks -

Leslie

Sent: Saturday, May 11, 2013 11:28 PM
From: Sally
To: Leslie Jermainne
Subject: Re: Brian Ross Update 5/11

I know exactly what you mean about 'technicolor days', Leslie. Recently, you were wondering if you will be able to hold on to the appreciation you have for life. I think you will. For a while, I rode the high of that feeling... the sparkling clarity that happens when suddenly the important things in life are so obvious and everything else just disappears. Eight years out, it's still with me. I had a very difficult time the past several years, and yes, I lost my way for a while. But I was brought back to that place abruptly, by life's circumstances. As difficult as those circumstances have been, I am so very grateful for the reminder, and now, I do take the time to acknowledge, mindfully, like a mantra or prayer. Each morning before my feet hit the ground and each evening before I fall asleep, and again whenever I realize I'm being pulled or pushed away from that joy/love/appreciation/optimism/clarity, I actually say the words (sometimes out loud), "I am grateful for all of the love & good stuff I do have and I am letting go of this difficulty". I could never have imagined the effect that would have on my life! It saves me, every day. Matty is definitely my hero. Not only because of what she deals with and the beautiful person it has helped her become, but also because of the gift she gave me... a Technicolor life. I'm not sure our kids can grasp that at this stage of their lives, but Matty and I often talk about the gifts that have come from her illness. I have the feeling Brian will also understand that concept. What an amazing thing, at their age, to have that perspective, you know?

Enough of my rambling.

I really appreciate your update emails, Leslie. We think of you all every day and celebrate the path to health that you are all traveling. Rock on! And a very happy Mother's Day to you! ~ Sally

MAY 12, 2013

Sent: Sunday, May 12, 2013 6:14 AM
From: Leslie Jermainne
To: Sally
Subject: RE: Brian Ross Update 5/11

Sally,

I knew you would understand this all from all your great notes. I was saying last night that I believe Brian will have a gift for the rest of his life from this experience. The gift of gratitude. One that I'm sure he will need to keep polished, but one he may not have to work as hard as some to appreciate. Your words that the feeling is a "high" is so very accurate. It is also striking that the 'everyday' tries so desperately hard to try to win back control. In my case it isn't even close to taking over again, but like I said I do worry it will win out again someday. Your thoughts that even if it does creep in with difficult times or just the passing of time, it is much easier to revisit and remember and restart, so that is so very encouraging.

Thank you for keeping in touch so much. It really means the world to me. A shared path is such much easier to travel.

Happy Mother's Day! Enjoy the high!

Leslie

Sent: Sunday, May 12, 2013 7:09 PM
From: Leslie Jermainne
To: My List
Subject: RE: Brian Ross Update 5/12

Happy Mother's Day!

What a nice day again today. Coffee with my hubby, french toast breakfast with my baby boy who gave me a nice gift certificate for a pedicure! Gonna use that soon! Had an hour nap, nice visit with Auntie

Alison, and dinner of grinders with my parents and strawberry shortcake for my Mom (old family tradition).

Brian has been having back pain today. He awoke me at about 5:45 with pain, and again this afternoon a bit of pain. We are attributing it to the filgrastim shots which help his white blood cells recover. Muscle and bone pain is a common side effect. I'm looking forward to our Jimmy Fund clinic appointment tomorrow. We will get his counts checked and have him looked over. We will get to ask some new questions we have (like about the back pain) and figure out some stuff for our trip back on Friday. Didn't think I'd really be looking forward to going back so soon for a clinic visit, but I am. It will make me feel reassured.

So was this an extra special Mother's Day for me? No, it wasn't. I liked Mother's Day last year and the year before when my son took me out to breakfast. We always had a nice breakfast and that is all I would ever want. Those two mother's days, just him and I, were my favorite. There was no worry. No fear. No cancer. Was today nice? Very. But my baby boy doesn't feel the best and we now have this worry. Anyway, if I had to pick the day every year that means the most to me in regards to being his Mom, it's his birthday. October 24th. That is really Mother's Day for me. That is the day I officially became a Mommy. That was the day my little soul mate was born and as I tell him now, it was the day I knew what my Dharma was. It was - and still is - to care for him and be his Mom. So on his birthday I always remember what a great day it was when I became a Mom to my only child. That is the day I think of to celebrate being a Mom. At least for me.

I hope everyone enjoyed Mother's Day, whether they are a Mother or with their Mother. I know I certainly appreciate my Mom and all she has ever done for me and my family. I wouldn't be half the Mom I am today without her as my role model offering guidance, support and love. She's the best!

So wish us luck for a good Jimmy Fund Clinic visit tomorrow.

Goodnight (from home, once again. *smile*)

Leslie

Sent: Sunday, May 12, 2013 9:48 PM
From: Brian W.
To: Leslie Jermainne
Subject: Re: Brian Ross Update 5/12

Happy Mother's Day Leslie...although it's not the true Mother's Day for you. I get that. YOUR Mother's Day is the day you became a mother. So sweet. I think of you all every day. You are so strong, as are Brian and Brian.

Sleep well...

Brian W.

MAY 13, 2013

Sent: Monday, May 13, 2013 11:22 AM
From: Frank
To: Leslie Jermainne
Subject: RE: Brian Ross Update 5/12

Hey Leslie,

Glad you had a nice day. I read your email this morning with coffee and was remembering how I felt. Yes, your day was nice - coming home was nice - being with loved ones was nice - seeing Brian get some 'normal' time with his friend was great I'm sure. But.... I'm sure your brain never stopped worrying for one instant. I just remembered vividly the feeling of always being on high alert and worrying about blood counts,...infections,... who's coming over and potentially bringing germs,...is he eating, drinking, or pooping enough, did you take the right meds,...what does the pain mean? ARGH !!!! Everyone takes little symptoms like headaches or minor pains or issues for what they are - little symptoms, but I know in your mind your running through everything you've ever read about side effects and what to look out for. Talk about nonstop stress!

My point being - I also remember a big feeling of safety going to the hospital to be checked out by the pros - I would actually look forward to them. It really gave me a huge sigh of relief to know that I could somehow stand down, let my guard down slightly, or breathe a little easier because they were protecting Anna better than I could. They know what was going on inside vs. my mind running away with every little symptom coming down the pike. They would give me honest answers to all of my questions and concerns. For me the reassurance was worth every miserable minute being stuck there.

I can feel the weight on your shoulders, and while I can't take it away, I can say that you are very strong and that you are doing all the right things. Good luck with your appointment.

Talk soon,
Frank

PS - Anna would also get bone pain with the shots to boost white blood cells. She would get it in her legs/thigh bones, and chest/sternum.

Sent: Monday, May 13, 2013, at 9:11 PM
From: Leslie Jermainne
To: My List
Subject: FW: Brian Ross Update 5/13

This is a quickie note - I'm exhausted and already in bed, but didn't want to leave you all hanging, as I've heard that is worrisome for some, and secretly I love that, since again it shows me how much you care. So today was a deep down good day. We went to our Jimmy Fund clinic appt., and had an easy drive up there. 12:00 seems to be the magic appointment time. After port access and blood draw we met with our oncologist and reviewed the last week (almost) that we've been home. Besides some back pain and some headaches, the only other issue has been some numbness today for his waist to mid-thigh. Something else to keep an eye on. His blood counts were still "good" although the white cells are down quite a bit. Expected? Yes. Worrisome? Uh, Ya. Need a transfusion? Nope (obviously you can't transfuse white cells, but he doesn't need platelets or plasma or red cells) so that's good news. Just have to be super careful in watching for a fever, keeping germs at bay, resting, drinking fluids, all that fun stuff.

Our trip back home was good, despite my GPS app lady wanting desperately for me to drive home via her route. I keep telling her "NO, our route is this way!!!", but she keeps trying! Once home Big Brian and I used up the last little bit of gift certificate we had to Liv's on Main Street and had some time to catch up with each other over dinner. A nice visit with my Mom and Dad, and now off to bed. I got up at 4:00 a.m. with a list of things to do, so I had no choice, thanks to my crazy brain but to get up and do them, now it's sleep time.

Good night from a happy home.

Leslie

Sent: Monday, May 13, 2013 10:01 PM
From: Sheila
To: Leslie Jermainne
Subject: Re: Brian Ross Update 5/13

Please save ALL of these Leslie, print them, and make a book. I look forward to your updates. Love to you all, and especially prayers for Brian that he stays strong and wins this fight.

MAY 14, 2013

Sent: Tuesday, May 14, 2013 6:33 AM
From: Leslie Jermainne
To: Frank
Subject: RE: Brian Ross Update 5/12

Hi Frank!

Again, such words of wisdom and complete understanding. Thank you. My brain won't shut up about any of it. The minute it takes a breath from the onslaught of "why does his back hurt?", "Is his face clearing up now that he's off the prednisone?", "I wonder what his counts are now.", "He looks tired.", "I wonder if I should take his temperature just for the fun of it?", "I wonder what his counts are NOW." "Did he poop today?" "Was it soft or hard?" "Did he drink enough water, did he pee enough pee?" "What if he dies?" Of course that last one is the one that sneaks in when I'm busy trying to get the other ones to quiet down.

So, yes, yesterday's clinic visit was good for me. He is doing well. They are pleased and unconcerned by anything they are seeing, even his WB counts down. "That is expected," my mind reassures me. "But what if they drop more?", "They will, we know he isn't at the bottom yet, it doesn't mean he'll get sick or get a fever". "How do you know?!?!" It's like living with Jekyll and Hyde in there.

So what helps with this stuff? You telling me I'm normal. That you thought the same things. That it's okay to carry around his world on my shoulders and that I'm strong enough to do it. And I finally believe that I am strong enough to do this, to get us through, all of us, with flying colors. As long as that last bad thought doesn't come true, I can do this. If that bad thought happens, I feel like I am done. The end. I don't think I can go on one minute of one day without my baby boy. I'm sure those are normal thoughts too - but they are the worst, and I do my best to not even think them. But they lurk around like the boogey-man and jump out and scare me, probably at least once a day.

However, we trudge on, and I try to realize I have to do some real, normal life stuff and that he is o.k., right now, this minute, for the next few hours, he is o.k. and I need to get on with life. So, today I'm off to do some yard work at the 2 family we bought. It will be good to be outside. However, I plan to listen to my iPod, otherwise, those mundane jobs have in the past been the time my mind likes to take off on a wild jaunt. Well, not up in here! NOT UP IN HERE! (a little Hangover reference for ya!)

Thanks for continuing to talk me down. It really, really, really helps me.

Leslie

Sent: Tuesday, May 14, 2013 8:40 AM
From: Frank
To: Leslie Jermainne
Subject: RE: Brian Ross Update 5/12

Leslie,

Do you know that even now - you are helping me too! It helps to know that I (and anyone in our positions) are thinking and processing 'normal' thoughts. Sometimes I envied the people I saw that didn't understand what they were going through - it's the curse of somewhat intelligent or 'common sensical' (my own word) type of people to try to justify, fix, or analyze everything. I've learned that talking about this stuff and what you're thinking helps immensely.

People would ask me how I could work and deal with the things I was dealing with. The short answer was because we needed medical insurance and without work - I ran the risk of not having good medical coverage - and we just couldn't afford that possibility. The real answer is that other than chatting/emailing with others in the same boat - it was the only thing that kept my mind busy. Not that doing a mundane task can stop the wheels from turning upstairs, but it certainly helps to avoid the dangerous side of dwelling, stressing, and maybe even going a little crazy. What's the saying - an idle mind is the devil's playground. I don't know how much that applies - but I do know that if you're paralyzed mentally and wallow in the bad stuff consistently - you will not be able to provide the support you need to. But please don't worry - you are not this person - you are smart and strong, reasoning, venting, and talking things through.

Gotta run, but keep up the good work!!! You guys are going to have to tell me all about the 2-family.

Frank

Sent: Tuesday, May 14, 2013 8:40 PM
From: Leslie Jermainne
To: My List
Subject: RE: Brian Ross Update 5/14

Hi There,

We had a nice day today at home. Brian is feeling well, except the numbness in his waist to mid-thigh area. Not really sure what that is about. We had several good things happen today. We found out that our insurance will pay for our ambulance ride to Dana Farber is being covered so we will get $2,376.00 back that we had to charge to our credit card. YA! Also - we will be going to Boston on Thurs. afternoon and staying overnight at a hotel that was arranged by the hospital for a very reduced rate. Our appt. for Friday is now 8:30 and that is a tough ride from home. Friday will entail getting his port accessed at 8:30 and have blood drawn, then an ultrasound of his right underarm, then a PET scan, then a clinic appointment to review and see if his counts are good enough to start Chemo on Saturday. If not, we'll be coming home and going back for clinic visit on Monday to test counts and see if he's ready for chemo then. I'm hoping, as is he, that he's good to go Friday. We both just want to get this over with and move on.

It was such a nice day today, I got to do some work outside. I hooked up the outdoor shower and after done with yard work, took the first outdoor shower which was great until I tried to adjust the angle of the shower head and instead it snapped off. Nothing like a plastic shower head made for interior use, being used in an exterior setting. Tomorrow, new shower head will get installed as well as new bushings, or some such thing, on my car. I will be walking to do some errands tomorrow, but it will do my lazy ass some good.

Ready to go watch Castle with the hubs and fall fast, fast asleep. Up at 5:00 again today. Where are those days as a teenager when I slept until 11:00 regularly??? I even tried taking melatonin at 3:00 a.m. Nothing!!! I am beyond tired, and can't seem to find my way back.

I want to give a shout out to my biggest understander (my word) Frank for again allaying my fears and crazy thoughts. Also to Sheila for our nice but somewhat quick talk. So nice to touch base in person (Sheila has been a great e-mailer for me) to my friend and neighbor. I realized again how lucky I am to have such support and friendship. Also - Brian got a great gift from his Aunt Candy & Uncle Doug. Lots of Yankee stuff that Big Brian is eyeing being the real hard core Yankee's fan in the house. Thank you both of you! It was a nice treat. Hoping to see you both later this year.

Lots of other great emails and contacts and phone calls that made me laugh - thanks Liz!!! No one gets me or makes me laugh like Lizzy Brown McCall. Love you chica!

So - off we go. One more full day at home to relish and roll around in delight. I'm planning to appreciate it and maybe even with my eyes closed some time mid-afternoon. Oh how I love to nap. I also plan to use my Mother's day gift certificate for a pedicure. Heaven! The best part of the pedicure is the massage chair and warm water. Lovely.

Peace Out from home.

Leslie

MAY 15, 2013

Sent: Wednesday, May 15, 2013 7:43 PM
From: Leslie Jermainne
To: My List
Subject: RE: Brian Ross Update 5/15

Last night at home-

Tomorrow night I will be writing to you from our hotel room - arranged by Dana Farber - where we will stay since Brian's first Friday appointment is at 8:30 with a busy day ahead of us on Friday. But what did today bring us?

Overall Brian was feeling pretty good today. He slept pretty late (I got 7.5 hours last night - WOOHOO!!). The numbness in his leg/waist seems to be just on one side now and maybe a small improvement he thought. I see him squinting a lot and he says it is just the "spring air or allergies", which he has never really had - and eye issues can happen, so I will be

bringing that up. He gets mad when I ask about any little thing, so I have to be careful a bit. So pretty much just tired and numb, but no nausea, hair is still intact for now, all else seems good.

The awesome folks at our favorite garage fixed my car and gave it a once over so we know we are safe and sound for all our future Boston Trips. I got to meet with an awesome friend, Charlie who met us (Bri had to leave for an appointment) at our 2 family house and went over the massive landscaping job. Plus we got to catch up a bit - he and I are both good talkers. I then gave Brian his meds and shot, got to pick up my car, run an errand or two and then have a pedicure compliments of my son for Mother's Day - boy I love those massage chairs much more than the pedicure. Once back home did some work at my desk, got to see my girlfriend and neighbor Sheila for a nice talk and catch up with the happenings of the 'hood and beyond. Then visited one last time with my parents, took a few phone calls from Boston and our visiting nurse for tomorrow and had a nice dinner.

I had a very nice note from an old/new friend who has reached out to us repeatedly since hearing our devastating news. It still amazes me who shows up, who shows up and stays and who doesn't really show up at all when you need to know people care. I hope, although if I'm honest I'm not sure, I would have been the best example of show up and stay before this time in my life. I have learned a great deal from the people who have shown up for us, and now that the original "rush" is over, have stayed. I know that I will be that person from here on out. I am in awe of their support and I want them to know I will pay it forward. Thank you to them.

I've also realize more and more that Brian and I are "get-it-doners" and we sometimes are missing out in the joy of just being here. I hope that will change in our future, at least a little bit, when we get through this ordeal. Brian and I are both very focused and I think determined people, which is good most of the time. But I think we often miss out on the just-beingness of it all. I listen to country music and a song struck me today when I was in the car. It's a song called "motor-boating" - stay focused here people - and really it seems to be a little story of being out on the water in your little pontoon boat, relaxing with friends, in the sun and water and doing a whole lot of nothing. To me...to imagine taking a Sunday or God Forbid a Saturday off, to do nothing but lounge around on a boat, or what have you, just doesn't ever really exist in our vocabulary. And it should. And how many of those days have we let slip by.

When talking with Sheila today, I was commenting that even though I home school Brian (really he does it himself these days), and even though we spend pretty much 24/7 together, the love I feel for this kid still makes me wish I had spent more time with him. More time doing nothing - but lounging around on a pontoon boat, going for a walk or bike ride, playing a game, watching a movie he wanted to watch. Anything. If I could go back, and have life just as I wanted it, I would change only one thing. I would do nothing a whole lot more. As long as I got to do it with the people I love. So I guess my goal now, is to do nothing - much more often. To stop worry about being a "get-it-doner". I don't have to get all the laundry done. Or get the house work done. Or get this listing done (well, not this second anyway). Get the mowing done, the cooking done, the shopping done. I have to get nothing done, with my boy, and my hubby and my friends and my family. How sweet that picture looks in my head. I hope I have all the time I'm due with them, to do just that. I hope I haven't squandered too much precious time. Nothing brings life into crystal clear focus as a life threatening diagnosis. Especially for my child. Especially for me. Please God, give me another chance, and I'll do nothing....I swear it.

I hope this coming weekend, you might all do a little nothing but be with your most loved ones. Even though we will be in the hospital having massive doses of poison voluntarily injected into my baby's body, he and I will be doing nothing together. And frankly, I'm looking forward to it, just a little bit. I could do without the medicine, but as long as it gives me years more to do nothing with him and maybe his family someday, I'm all in.

A hug and a kiss from home.

Leslie

Sent: Wednesday, May 15, 2013 8:57 PM
From: Sarah J.
To: Leslie Jermainne
Subject: RE: Brian Ross Update 5/15

((((((((((Leslie)))))))))):-) :-) :-) :-) You make me smile-you are so honest and brave and even though you have been dealt this horrible thing you are reaching up to grow through it. Good luck with it all tomorrow.

Sarah

MAY 16, 2013

Sent: Thursday, May 16, 2013 7:49 AM
From: Laurie
To: Leslie Jermainne
Subject: RE: Brian Ross Update 5/15

Les...this was so powerful, I had to respond (now that I have stopped sobbing)...you are and have always been a wise and powerful woman and I am so proud of you. Brian's illness has brought up a lot of stuff for me, guilt for all of my faults, my "troubles", not enjoying life to the fullest every moment. Thank you for making us all aware of our precious gift of life and providing us with a "conscience jab" to stop and feel the moment. I am going to be one of those people in the background that you should know will be there at a moment's notice, any time of the day or night, no matter where you are...as I've told you before, I feel like you were my first child, and it's killing me that I can't take this heartbreak away for you...I don't know why the universe had this experience in store for you, but I have to believe good will come of it...you are influencing the course of many people's lives with these messages and I for one, appreciate what you're doing...I love you and you are never far from my thoughts...

Sent: Thursday, May 16, 2013, at 8:42 PM
From: Leslie Jermainne
To: My List

Subject: RE: Brian Ross Update 5/16

Hi Out There!

Brian and I are currently both entranced on our laptops as we sit in our hotel at the Longwood Inn in the Longwood Medical Complex in Boston. Tomorrow will start early and DFCI got us this room to stay in for the night. It took us 4 hours, even with only one quick pit stop. The traffic starting just outside the city was miserable. But I got my MASS driver on, and blended right in - cutting people off, keeping within an inch of the bumper in front of me.

Today Brian's visiting nurse came to the house to do a blood draw, I had a Doctors Appt. to see why I'm still having heart palpations...can you say stress? I will be doing a holter monitor when we get back home and see if we can catch any of these buggers. If we don't, it will be a miracle since it is going on frequently throughout the day.

Then it was home to have some lunch, go to the bank to open a tenant security deposit account for a property we manage for a client and get the last few things packed and in the car. 3pm we took off and at 7:00 we checked in. WHEW!

One of the first things I seem to do every day since this has all happened and I have started writing these notes is to check my email and see what people thought about what I had to say. It seems many people are being affected by what I write and that makes me joyful. I am really writing this stuff to A) keep everyone informed so I don't have to answer a million phone calls, texts and emails individually throughout the day; B) so people don't forget that my son is battling for his life and in turn my life and C) because it is therapeutic for me to put away the day and have a record of what went on. I already think back to the first few days, and I can't even remember how I told my family that Brian had cancer. It seems a blur of tears and fears and gut wrenching agony. What a far way we have come already.

When I check my email and Facebook messages, I'm always happy to see some response and when my writing has touched someone else that is even better. Last night's email, struck a chord with several people. I was surprised as I thought it wasn't some of my deepest work. But then I realized that a lot of my deepest "writing" never makes it to the page. It gets talked out in my head and I allow some of it to make it to paper. I still censor myself a lot, when sharing my thoughts and feelings (and language). But, anyway...I'm glad that my thoughts on wishing to do less may inspire people if even for just an hour to not do something they think they "have to get done" and spend it with a loved one, even if that loved one is yourself.

Another great note from yesterday was from Ann, explaining why the hardship we are going through, has "changed her for the better". It was a nice reminder to me and I shared with her some of my thoughts that might affect some of you all. Before all this happened, I was working on gratitude in my life. One of the things I was concentrating on was being grateful for the mundane chores of everyday life. My son changes his clothes...a lot. There is always laundry to do. Everything that touches his body or God Forbid the floor goes into the wash. Years ago I had tried just folding and putting back some of things that really weren't "dirty". First of all, kids are paying attention and he would often catch me, and secondly, I realized it wasn't fair to him. He had an issue with those clothes being back on his body or in his room, and I was taking that away from him and not supporting him. We all have our weirdness things that we do, or don't do. I always think of a line from the movie Dirty Dancing which goes like this "If you love me, you have to love all the things about me". So in order to work on gratitude while doing mountains of laundry I started to think that when he doesn't live here anymore, I will have almost no laundry to do, and I will miss it. And since I do have a lot of laundry to do, I'm so lucky I can afford to run extra loads. I have a beautiful front loading Bosch washer and dryer that is wicked efficient and saves time and money. I have a beautiful home to keep these appliances in. I use nice detergent that is free of all the bad cleaning stuff. We have plenty of clothes to keep us warm, and dressed and even on occasion looking pretty darn good. Ann was telling me of her kids' texting her repeatedly asking for things to be done for them, and instead of being annoyed, she chose to appreciate the fact that they come to her. I reminded her that someday, they won't. They will be off running their own lives, and probably she and I will be checking our phones hoping for a text or message that lets us do something, anything for our kids. Plus I can always throw in the shock value of "I hope my son will be here to text me to do some inane thing for me. Nothing will make me happier."

I did the same exercise with garbage. If I can be grateful for garbage, then pretty much anyone can be grateful for anything. I won't give you the rundown of my "how lucky I am to have garbage" speech, but believe me, if you take something you really dislike, and turn it around and find just one little thing about it that is good, that one little thing easily reaches out to ten other good things and pretty soon that thing you dislike starts to look like a blessing. Try it, I dare you.

So, that is enough thoughts for tonight. I'm getting tired and I need to be up by 6:00 in order to get Brian some breakfast (hopefully the Dunkin Donut downstairs will be open) since he can't eat past 7 a.m. for his PET scan at 11:00. EMLA cream to numb the skin over his port has to go on by 7:30 and then we have to get ready and get our bag back to the car and be up to the Jimmy Fund Clinic for 8:30 port access. Wish us luck. We are hoping for good blood counts so that we get admitted to the hospital and start round 3. "Once that round is done, we'll be past half way!" said Brian. God I love that kid. He is so brave and so strong. He's my rock - and I hope I'm his.

Good night from room 638 @ Longwood Inn.

Leslie

Sent: Thursday, May 16, 2013 9:13 PM
From: Paula
To: Leslie Jermainne
Subject: Re: Brian Ross Update 5/16

Ok so I need to tell you that I planned an "hour of nothing" this weekend with the family. They are all excited for this - we are thinking of going outside to stare up at the clouds. How ironic that we have to schedule this into our lives? I must tell you that you have been inspiring me with your emails from day one, so this is now turning into our blessing too!

We are thinking and praying for Brian and you in this next step you are taking. Please take care and talk soon!

Paula

Sent: Thursday, May 16, 2013 11:37 PM
From: Toni
To: Leslie Jermainne
Subject: Re: Brian Ross Update 5/16

You amaze me each and every day. I will be thinking of both of you tomorrow and sending positive thoughts and love and strength. Give that amazing guy a big hug for us!

Toni

Sent: Thursday, May 16, 2013 6:16 PM
From: Rebecca
To: Leslie Jermainne
Subject: Re: Brian Ross Update 5/15

You are an incredible woman, and I have so much respect and admiration for you. Your honesty...ability to cut to the chase is just amazing. That, I believe, is one of the blessings behind this sorrow...there are so many more too. As always, thank you for sharing.

My prayers are right here, and G-d is too.

Bless you and yours,
Rebecca

MAY 17, 2013

Sent: Friday, May 17, 2013 8:52 AM
From: Frank
To: Leslie Jermainne
Subject: RE: Brian Ross Update 5/16

Oh Leslie - I feel bad I missed two emails, but I am caught up now.

Please know that when you speak of who shows up and stays (friends & family) - for support over the long haul - that is the Jermainne's for me. You guys were/are always there (even if you don't know it). So you can look back and know that you guys are in fact some of the 'good ones' and were such positive support for us then and now.

I remember Anna getting mad at me (just like Brian is doing with you) when you ask the doctors questions. It got to the point where I would have them ask about "insurance" and that was my cue to go outside the room and ask any questions I may have had. I think from the patient point of view - they may be feeling OK and don't see the need to ask the questions, but they definitely don't know the 3 ring circus that is going on in the caregivers brain. (The large amounts of stress that cause heart palpitations) So if you have to, go outside and ask questions - some that you may not want to ask in front of Brian - outside of his earshot. You know that they are more than willing to answer questions and give you support/answers.

I can also relate to your 'doing nothing more'. I am a doer too! Just last year I've learned to let things go. I am proud of myself for implementing this last summer. I went to the beach with the kids instead of working on the house, went to the aquarium instead of working on the yard, I come home instead of going the extra mile at work - yes, it's impacting growth and $$$ but it's worth it!!! Though because I didn't do anything last year with the landscaping - I'm buried now - who cares - I guess?

Frank

I hope all goes well and you can keep moving forward this weekend.
Don't forget to take care of Leslie in all this

Sent: Friday, May 17, 2013 8:52 PM
From: Leslie Jermainne
To: Frank
Subject: RE: Brian Ross Update 5/16

Hi Frank,

No worries on missing two emails. I know where you are. The happiest part of this email is that you implemented the letting go of things. Your family is so much the richer for it. I will be trying to do the same thing. I'd like to get my hubby on board, but I'm unsure if he will. He talks a good game of it though, so I'm hopeful.

I did implement the talking to the doctors first, before Brian hears the info due to him demanding it be that way after getting so overwhelmed and scared at the other hospital. I will continue to do that, and ask all the questions I need to feel comfortable. There sure are a lot of them aren't there?

Thanks Frank - gonna go write my update now

Good night!

Leslie

Sent: Friday, May 17, 2013 8:06 AM
From: Lorna
To: Leslie Jermainne
Subject: Re: Brian Ross Update 5/16

Hi Leslie

Thanks for all your updates. It has helped keep me sane as we go through a tough time with my Dad. He was told before Easter that he had 2 inoperable lesions on his pancreas, probably mets from his stomach cancer. Chemo was an option, but dad had decided this was not for him, and wanted to spend what time he had left reasonably fit. However fast forward ten days and the hospital changed its mind and decided they didn't know what they were dealing with so referred dad to the Royal Infirmary in Edinburgh.

These guys are HPB specialists, and agreed that they didn't know what they were dealing with but were prepared to operate. Dad underwent a 6 hr. op last Wednesday (a Whipple procedure) and is making a great recovery. Unfortunately they have found abnormal tissue in the pancreas, but it may still be benign. I'm not going to worry about this until we have the path results.

Obviously you are having a tougher time, as it is so unfair for someone of Brian's age to have to go through the cancer journey, but I find your thoughts echoing mine, as I'm taking time to stop and appreciate the smallest thing, as time is such a precious thing that we so often overlook.

So here I am, sitting on the bench we got in memory of my mum (13 years ago today), enjoying the sunshine and loving the gorgeous roses I bought for her.

I'm then going to go home and play with the cats and catch up on Castle (I laughed out loud when you wrote about that) and just have some me time.

I wish I could ease some of your burden, but all I can do is pray for you and the family and let you know that I'm thinking of you every day,

Take care, Lorna

Sent: Friday, May 17, 2013 1:11 PM
From: Sarah S.
To: Leslie Jermainne
Subject: RE: Brian Ross Update 5/16

Your e-mail last night helped me through a lot of darkness and brought some tears. If you can be thankful for all of life's chores so can I. I'm very thankful for my children and although every time I clean their room it only ever lasts one day, I'm thankful that they're so creative when they play and enjoy life. There was a short time ago where I didn't. You kinda inspire me to seize the day because you don't know what obstacles are around the next bend in the road. I'm so happy that God granted me two children at such a young age because I'm able to enjoy them longer. I pray for you and

Brian every night. God only gives you what you can handle so obviously your superwoman. Love you.

Sarah

Sent: Friday, May 17, 2013 9:26 PM
From: Leslie Jermainne
To: Sarah S.
Subject: RE: Brian Ross Update 5/16

Hi Sarah,

I'm happy you have two beautiful, bright and healthy boys. It is hard being a Mom, but I'm sure you would agree it is the best job around. I had only ever wanted one child. I wanted to be devoted to one little soul, and frankly I wasn't sure I would be able to create and build this one human being. I was definitely designed to be the Mom to one. When I see other parents here in the hospital with their sick child, but another child in tow, I think - "if I had another child to love, I wouldn't be so frightened to lose my only baby" - isn't that crazy! But I also think to myself now, that maybe it is good I only had one, because of this cancer, I can be totally devoted to Brian and his care and not be 'neglecting' another child. Oh, the crazy demented things that go on in the brain.

All I can say, like you said, is God only gives you what you can handle. I think you're pretty much in the Superwoman category too. I know that I wouldn't not have been able to be so strong in my convictions and determined in my decisions at such a young age to do all you have done. I am so happy that you and Tom have made such a complete and happy family. You are very lucky to have such wonderful boys and I'm glad that you are appreciating them so much. I hate when I overhear Moms say stuff like "I can't wait for summer vacation to be over so the kids will go back to school". I always hated when vacation was over. I guess that explains homeschooling. I had this baby boy to spend every possible minute raising him, enjoying him, knowing him. The thought that could be taken away from me after only 15 years just shatters my heart into little pieces just by the thought of it. But, for today, I am grateful. He is here. He loves me and I love him and I get to accompany him every day no matter what that brings us.

I had been working on gratitude for the last year. I find I sometimes have to write it down on paper to find the gratitude for the mundane jobs we Mothers due out of love, yet earn so little appreciation for. If there is something you hate to do - like my laundry story - just start with one thing that makes it worthwhile. For me, it was that I want Brian to be in my home. Then I think about what a nice home it is. It is nice because we take care of it, and fix it. We fix it with money we earn. We are lucky to have jobs that make us enough money to have a nice home and to have a nice washer and dryer and nice clothes, etc, etc. I think you will find you can look at anything that you dislike and turn it around to something to be grateful for. Sometimes I have to reread what I wrote, but a reminder is a good thing.

Thank you for the bracelets for us, the nice notes, the gift card for Brian and all your thoughts and prayers. Mostly thank you for sharing this note with me. Sharing a piece of your story with me is something special.

Now kiss those boys and that husband and say a prayer of gratitude for them, as I'm sure you often do.

Love you too!
Leslie

Sent: Friday, May 17, 2013 9:11 PM
From: Leslie Jermainne
To: Lorna
Subject: RE: Brian Ross Update 5/16

Hi Lorna,

Wow - I don't think I'm having a tougher time, at least not for today. What a day this is for you. I loved the photo of your Mom, and I can hardly believe it has been 13 years. Brian was only 2 then! I'm glad that you took some time today for yourself and to sit and appreciate your Mom - as I'm sure you do really every day.

I'm sad to hear the difficult time your Dad is having and I'm hoping for benign results and a speedy recovery. Cancer is a horrible beast at any age. My Mom is 81, and dealing with Multiple Myeloma, my Dad has prostate cancer at 81 also (although it started earlier), I lost a good friend almost 3 years ago who was 35 - it is just terrible. It is unfair for my son and any other young person to have to deal with this. I worry that he won't experience so many wonderful things. Getting his driver's license and having that freedom to go where he wants by himself. A first kiss. His first job outside of our business. His own place to live. A wife, maybe a baby (although that may not happen now anyway - but there is always adoption). But then I think of all the other children who have never had those firsts or those experiences. Those kids who didn't learn how to walk or talk or become a teenager or go to school. Then I have to be a little grateful we have come this far. UGH! It gets to be too much to think about at times.

Hearing from the people who are supporting and loving us, everyday, really make things so much easier - at least for me. I think for Brian too - although most of the contact is to me.

I will be sending prayers out to your Dad and you and your family too - keep me up to date on his progress.

Leslie

Sent: Friday, May 17, 2013 10:09 PM
From: Leslie Jermainne
To: My List
Subject: RE: Brian Ross Update 5/17

WHAT A DAY!!!

It has been a very good and very long day. Starting at 6:00 getting Brian some food before he wasn't allowed to eat anymore - get us ready and packed up and stuff out to the car and then over to the Jimmy Fund Clinic to get his port accessed and blood drawn. Then it was 9:30 at ultrasound to look at his right underarm

This is me watching him at ultrasound

and left abdominal site. Everything looked good! Nothing to see there, except some scar tissue. Then to Nuclear Medicine where he has his PET scan - had to wait awhile there and he was very tired and cranky. I finally left him to go to the lobby to get cell phone service so I could find out his counts. Counts were very good so I knew at that point we'd be in for round 3.

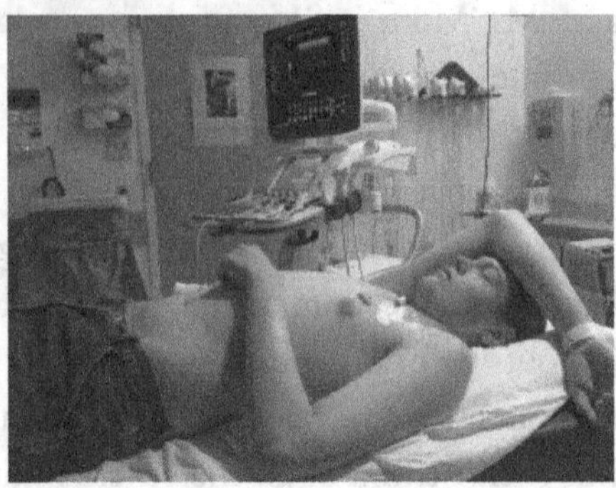
Brian waiting for ultrasound

Back up to wait for PET scan. First you sit in a warm room so your "brown fat" can warm up. Nice, huh? Then they inject him with the radioactive isotope, and then you have to lie still for an hour - luckily he got to sleep during this time, while I sat in the dark room with him. The PET scanned showed that things are shrinking which is exactly what we want. I secretly was hoping to hear they were all gone, but we are moving in the right direction anyway. After that we got a quick bite to eat in the cafeteria at the Yawkey Cancer Center then on to the Jimmy Fund Clinic again to start hydration to get rid of the stuff from the PET scan.

We finally got a room very late afternoon and it is good 'ole room 618 - our first home here at Boston Children's Hospital. We got put in the tiny side of the room, but were told the roommate was leaving shortly, which he did and we got to move over to the Ritz side of the room.

Getting settled in our room –
Brian texting with friends

We are unpacked, fed dinner, guitar has been brought in, water and snacks purchased and chemo has officially started. Guess what else has started...hair loss. This morning I noticed about a 1" bald spot on the top of his head. He seems fine with it, which is good.

I know I keep mentioning all these different hospitals so here is how it works. Dana Farber Cancer Institute runs all the cancer programs. That is where the doctors are affiliated. Adults get treated inpatient at Brigham and Woman's and outpatient at the Yawkey Center, which is a very nice new building. The Jimmy fund Clinic is where children are treated on an outpatient basis. However, whenever we come in either for a clinic day or to get admitted, that is our place of first contact. Boston Children's Hospital is where children are treated inpatient for cancer treatment and the Dana Farber doctors come here. The Jimmy Fund clinic is undergoing rehab work, so part of that clinic has been moved to the Yawkey Center, and that is why we go there too. Hope that explains it. It took me awhile to figure it all out.

I had so many great emails today. So many people who have reached out to me, not just in support but to share stories from their lives too. That is very touching to me - that by me sharing our troubles and our simple joys, has caused people to share with me. You should have gotten an email from me earlier today because I was so touched by one of my BFF's Stacy. Stacy lives in Ohio now, although I met her in 6th grade in Old Lyme. Today I got an amazing message on Facebook.

Stacy is going to ride in a 25 mile bike ride to raise money for cancer research. She is riding for Brian. I am still crying every time I read this, which I have done about 8 times today. It just touches me so much that she is doing this for us. Here is what her profile says:

"I ride for Brian

On 4/19/13, Leslie, one of my best friend's in the world found out her son Brian has Stage 3 Burkitt Lymphoma. In that instant their lives changed forever! I live 680 miles from Leslie and her family and I feel completely helpless. I can't hug her every day, can't help out bringing her family meals, can't help her drive Brian to Boston, MA every few days for treatments. Those are among the many things I can't do.

What I CAN do, is RIDE FOR BRIAN. I will be riding 25 miles! in the Pelatonia Bike Ride. ALL of the money raised will go to Cancer research. 100% of it!! I am nervous I won't be able to do it and I even hesitated signing up for this amazing ride. I am not in shape, I don't exercise regularly and I haven't been on a bike in more years than I care to count. Then, I thought about Brian. Brian is 15 years old. He is kind, funny, smart and rips it up on the electric guitar. Brian is in the fight of his life and facing it head on.

So, that's what I'm going to do. I am going to face this ride head on and raise money in hopes to someday find a cure for Brian and so many others. I also ride for my mother in law Lucy, Beth, Dana, Sue, Priscilla, and Lesa. In looking at my list of family and friends affected by Cancer, I realize everyone's list is too long. I can make a difference in some small way. No more feeling helpless for me! I will ride!

If you can find it in your hearts to give even a little, I will be forever grateful. For every person you have lost and for everyone we can save, let's cure Cancer together!"

I read this the first time while in the waiting room for the PET scan. Tears slid silently down my cheeks as I tried to keep it quiet and not embarrass my son, but it was hard. He looked at me like I was crazy, and then I showed him the profile, so he could read it too. His eyes said it all to me, when he looked back up in amazement. It is astounding the way people have reached out to us. To ride 25 miles and raise money to help us and everyone dealing with cancer in their lives and the lives of their loved ones both lost, present and those that will be diagnosed in the future, is just so powerful to me. I am touched so deeply by her courage to rise above her fear of doing this, her ability to put us and others above her own comfort, her thoughtfulness and bravery, I don't think she will ever understand that this gesture is more than I could ever hope would be done for my son. Thank you Stacy. I love you.

Well, I think that is enough from me tonight. I'm tired and ready to make up my luxurious bed (not the hard chair of last visit), and try to get some sleep while we have a private room - which is already scheduled for a roommate tomorrow. Thank you all for your love and support, whether riding a 25 mile bike ride, delivering food to my husband, sending cards to my son, or emailing words I need to hear to keep us going - you are all so appreciated - and you will never know the impact you are making in our lives. I am a grateful girl.

Peace from room 618 - B.

Leslie

STORY: So my husband and I are Realtors and have our own tiny company in our little home town. The company consists of him and me. That's it. The whole time our son is being treated in Boston, I am with him. My husband is home, holding down the fort, running the business, earning money to pay for our health insurance which I will never take for granted again. He is doing the work of us both, letting me focus on our son. I felt such an outpouring of love and support from people emailing and messaging me during this time. Brian had none of that. Or very little. So I contacted our local board of Realtors to let them know what was going on. My thought was two-fold. As you just read, one of my BFF's had committed to doing a bike ride to raise money for cancer research. She too is a Realtor, but lives in Ohio now. I thought this would be a great way to raise money and to let our local Realtor community know what we were going through. Maybe these people who work in conjunction with Brian every day would give him some support or at least acknowledge what we were going through, since they probably didn't know. Like I said before, I had this strange compulsion to tell every person I made eye contact with, "my son has cancer". It is such an unbelievable thing that it feels like everyone should know about it. So here is my note to the board of Realtors, that I had sent while waiting in the dark room while Brian slept awaiting his PET Scan. We received amazing support. People are nice.

Sent: Friday, May 17, 2013 11:35am
From: Leslie Jermainne
To: Rachel
Subject: Our son Brian/cancer fight

Hi Rachel,

I'm not sure if you know, but our son Brian, age 15, was diagnosed with stage 3 acute Burkitt Lymphoma on April 18, 2013. This is a rare and very aggressive form of Non-Hodgkin's Lymphoma. As I type this on my phone, I'm watching him try to get some sleep on the too small gurney for his 6' frame. We are in the nuclear medicine clinic at Boston Children's Hospital awaiting his 2nd PET scan. Later we will be admitted for a minimum of 7 days while he receives round 3 of his chemo treatment.

This is what we have been doing for the past month. In the hospital for 7-11 days, then home for a bit before returning.

Anyway, I'm writing because my exceptionally good friend who grew up with me in Old Lyme and now lives in Ohio, where she too is a Realtor, is doing something awesome for cancer research and for my son. She is participating in a 25 mile bike ride to raise funds for cancer research. I want to support her like she is supporting my son, so I'm asking - if this is appropriate - if maybe this link and our story might be shared with the membership who in turn might support another Realtor who is supporting us. If not, no worries...it was just a thought. If you would like any more details from me, just let me know. Thank you for your time.

"I ride for Brian

On 4/19/13, Leslie, one of my best friend's in the world found out her son Brian has Stage 3 Burkitt Lymphoma. In that instant their lives changed forever! I live 680 miles from Leslie and her family and I feel completely helpless. I can't hug her every day, can't help out bringing her family meals, can't help her drive Brian to Boston, MA every few days for treatments. Those are among the many things I can't do.

What I CAN do, is RIDE FOR BRIAN. I will be riding 25 miles! in the Pelatonia Bike Ride. ALL of the money raised will go to Cancer research. 100% of it!! I am nervous I won't be able to do it and I even hesitated signing up for this amazing ride. I am not in shape, I don't exercise regularly and I haven't been on a bike in more years than I care to count. Then, I thought about Brian. Brian is 15 years old. He is kind, funny, smart and rips it up on the electric guitar. Brian is in the fight of his life and facing it head on.

So, that's what I'm going to do. I am going to face this ride head on and raise money in hopes to someday find a cure for Brian and so many others. I also ride for my mother in law Lucy, Beth, Dana, Sue, Priscilla, and Lesa. In looking at my list of family and friends affected by Cancer, I realize everyone's list is too long. I can make a difference in some small way. No more feeling helpless for me! I will ride!

If you can find it in your hearts to give even a little, I will be forever grateful. For every person you have lost and for everyone we can save, let's cure Cancer together!"

MAY 18, 2013

Sent: Saturday, May 18, 2013 8:31 AM
From: Lisa
To: Leslie Jermainne
Subject: Re: Brian Ross Update 5/17

Hi Leslie,

Your emails are always touching and often inspirational, but Wednesday's message particularly resonated with me, as it did for many others based on the responses you received. After I managed to stop crying, my next thought was: I hope you are saving all of your daily emails. If you are willing to share them (or a selection of them) with a broader audience, I think they should be published. Given that your words touch those of us who are not facing cancer in our immediate families, can you imagine how deeply meaningful they would be to parents in your situation?

Lisa

MAY 19, 2013

Update was from 5/18

Sent: Sunday, May 19, 2013 7:38 AM
From: Leslie Jermainne
To: My List
Subject: RE: Brian Ross Update 5/18

Good Evening!

Well day 2 is almost done. It wasn't the best of days, but it wasn't the worst. The worst was exactly one month ago today on April 18th. By this time that day, we knew Brian had some sort of lymphoma. That was all we knew, and it was the worst day of my life. One month later we have come a long way, but we have a long, long way to go.

Kind of bad night's sleep, although our room was relatively quiet with no roommate, which we also still have no roommate, so tonight should be pretty good. It just takes some time to get used to sleeping here again with people coming in during the night to check his vitals, change his fluids, etc. They did get him a bed extender (wish we had known about that the last two times we were here), so all 6 feet long of him is a bit more comfy. Plus this visit we have his new laptop computer that he can play games on so that is good for him - and of course the beloved guitar.

The morning started off with him being awoken to go to surgery suite for his lumbar puncture and intrathecal methotrexate and hydrocortisone. Woo - look at me saying intrathecal, if you are like me and had no idea what that means (it means spinal) or what afebrile means (having no fever) now you know. I had to ask during rounds a few weeks ago. I'm just showing off my new vocabulary. So this is his fourth L.P. The first was done during surgery to test his spinal fluid for cancer cells (there were none), place his port and do his bone marrow aspirate and biopsy. He was under general for that one. Second was done in the GPAC unit (I don't know what GPAC stands for) but I get to be in the room with him. That first time I was kind of scared to go in, but on the other hand I wanted to be there. The oncologist who did the procedure and the anesthesiologist were awesome. I couldn't believe how quick it went, and my fears were allayed.

In case you are wondering what those fears were/are here it goes. Of course they explain to you all the horrible things that can happen. Stopping breathing was the biggest thing for me, especially when I saw the metal thingy-ma-bobbers that I know they use to intubate you - after all I used to watch E.R. on t.v. What if I was sitting there three feet from his face and he stops breathing? What if I have to watch them intubate him? What if it fails? What if I sit there hysterical and watch him die? I'm sorry for the downer here, but this is what goes through my mind, as I would guess it would for most parents at that moment. I think I shouldn't be in here because I can't handle that. But then I think, if that ever did happen and I wasn't there when I had the chance, I wouldn't be able to live with myself knowing that I could have been with him every step of the way, but chose not to be out of selfish fear. So I sat there smiling at his droopy eyed faced so that he would know everything was okay while I bit the inside of my cheek to keep the tears at bay. But like I said, that one was a breeze. I was so impressed.

Number 3 wasn't quite so good. I learned a bit about the hierarchy that goes on in a hospital setting between doctors, nurses, receptionist, different units, etc. Everything is very "PC", but still, if you are an observer of people you can see it go on. Everyone, every department has a way of doing things "the right way". So that was apparent in the room that day between the oncologist and the same anesthesiologist that we had for number 2, who I loved. By the way, you happen to get whatever oncologist is on that day - that is just how it works. Well, number 3 was a little more difficult, took a little longer and although I couldn't see his back, I would say it took two tries to do what they needed to do.

Then comes today. It's Saturday so the GPAC unit isn't open. L.P.'s happen in surgery instead. We are lucky we are told, that they squeezed us in early - which they are right because he can't eat before this. We go over anesthesia the night before and they seem to want to do general, which we say he has done great the last two times with just twilight and why put him under if it isn't needed? They agree and we head down to surgery. I'm not allowed to go in with him in this unit. It is a new oncologist to us who is doing the procedure. Off he goes, being wheeled away in his bed, which never seems to unnerve me any less. I have to go wait in the waiting room. It takes what seems like forever, about an hour. Finally the oncologist comes to see me, and says it was difficult and they had to stick him several times, but everything is good now, but he will probably be sore. Oh, great! I want to slap her and tell her to do a better job. She explains that since this protocol calls for so many L.P.'s, the patients back is irritated and swollen and they get more difficult. Awesome. We still have 5 more before we are done. One more this round which should be on Wednesday before we go home. Last time we were home he had numbness in his waist and legs. So today when I'm out walking to Best Buy because I dropped his computer mouse and it broke, I started thinking about all those scary bad things they tell you about lumbar punctures. What comes to mind, but paralysis? So I look this up in the pages they have given me and of course on the web and realize this isn't a "real threat". But still, I think to myself, if he was paralyzed but lived through this cancer, I'd take that any day of the week. Yes, a paralyzed son is better than no son. I would still feel grateful.

Sorry to be such a downer, but this morning was kind of tough. Afterwards, he told me he awoke in the middle and could feel it all. I talked with another oncologist later and asked a ton of questions - we will work to make sure that never happens again. I know many people get this done without sedation, however those people are not usually battling cancer, inpatient in the hospital for days at a time, tired, poked, monitored, questioned about everything, especially pee and poop non-stop, sleep deprived and scared out of their wits. The idea of him doing this twice a week without sedation, or sedation not being adequate is not acceptable.

After we got back, he ate some breakfast while I went to Best Buy, played his guitar, texted with friends and played on his computer. Later after lunch he had a nice long nap which was great, and really perked up after that. Now he seems back to himself after a bad morning and has just begun the cycle again. Zofran, Ativan, Vincristine, Prednisone, Tums, Doxorubicin, Leucovorin, Cyclphosphamide, Filgrastim, Hydrocortisone, Myralax, the list goes on and on. Zero hour is 8 p.m. for him - seems kind of ominous when they refer to it that way, but it is what it is.

Make no mistake however, I am still thankful today, although it may not seem like it. I'm thankful for wonderful phone calls with my hubby today, just passing the time, filling me in about home. A great call with Alison filling me in on the nice family picnic at my Uncle and Aunt's beach house today. I'm sad we couldn't be there, but glad to know everyone got together and had a nice day. I'm grateful that my son is laying in his bed, laughing at his computer screen, eating his yogurt in our quiet room. I'm grateful that you are all taking the time to read my words and keep praying and thinking about my son who is fighting for his life, and is doing so well and being so brave. He is what I'm most grateful for, just like I have been for the past 15 years.

Sweet Dreams from Room 618.

Leslie

JUST FOR ME AND/OR NOT SENT TO MY ENTIRE LIST:

Sent: Sunday, May 19, 2013 10:07 AM
From: Leslie Jermainne
To: Leslie Jermainne
Subject: Just for you re: BRJ

So- people keep saying to me that I should publish the stuff I'm writing every night. I don't really see how they could help someone else. But in thinking about it I realize that although I say a lot in those emails, they are also censored by my mind and therefore not completely me. I've already lost a month of that stuff. Maybe I can re-create it. But in the off chance this might be something to put out there someday - I thought I should record all my thoughts, uncensored. I'm not sure I'll send them all out, or to each of you at different times for varying reasons. But I also feel like someone has to read them, or else they don't actually occur. Hard to explain. Anyway...here was # 1.

Sent: Sunday, May 19, 2013 9:26 AM
From: Leslie Jermainne
To: Leslie Jermainne, Toni, Alison, Brian
Subject: 5/18

Hi!

I'm having a tough time today. Feeling sad, worried and tired. I'm hoping the tired is creating the other two feelings. My big baby boy is asleep right now and his fluid pump keeps up its gentle rhythm. I find that sound comforting.

We had a tough morning today as his 4th lumbar puncture was not as easy as the others. First it was done in the surgery dept. rather than GPAC (no, I don't know what that means). When done in GPAC I get to go in the room with him, which partially freaks me out. I think to myself every time, what if he stops breathing. That is a possibility you know. What if I'm sitting right there 3 feet from his face and he stops breathing. What if

I have to watch them intubate him so he can breathe? What if they can't? Oh my God, what if he dies here right in front of me. My thoughts careen out of control like a car on black ice. But then I think, what if that did happen and I chose NOT to be there. That is even worse. That feels selfish to me. To know I had the choice to be there with him every step of the way and I had taken the coward's way out to avoid some pain or shock. So then I go in, and I sit with a smile on my face so he can see everything is okay while I bite the inside of my cheek to keep the tears at bay. But back to today, I'm not allowed to go in with him in the surgery dept. So I have to sit and wait and pretend like it's all okay and it isn't. None of this is. And it takes a really long time. Then the doctor comes out to say he is in recovery and he's fine, but they had to stick him a few times so he might be sore for a while. WHAT!!! Jesus Christ. I want to punch her in the face. I want to scream at her to do a better job. But instead I say "okay". What else can I do? I will talk about it with them later, but it isn't an option not to have these lumbar punctures. This is what will most likely save him from a relapse. A mother-fucking, God Damn relapse. God Dammit I hate this.

Brian seems fine when I see him, sleepy from the Ketamine. Sad a little with his little bald patch on his head. Small in his big hospital bed with no blanket, sitting up while the back of the bed is down, in his sleeping shorts and t-shirt with plastic tubes coming out the bottom, leading to the ever running pump. I want to sit on the bed and scoop him into my arms and lay him across my legs folded crisscross, like I did when he was little enough to fit there. I want to hold his warm body, kiss his soft head, and comfort him and comfort me in the process. But instead we load into an elevator, making stupid small talk about how the bed barely fits since they added an extender to it because he is so tall. We ride up to the 6th floor and wheel our way around too tight corners and get his bed put back in place. Every nice nurse taking great care of us, as is their daily job, talks about the ins and outs of the procedure, the day, vital signs, fluid bags and such, while we fight to live. It hits me as so absurd sometimes.

I walk to Best Buy about 5 blocks away because earlier I made the mouse to his computer fall and break. He was angry with me, and I promised I would buy him 5 new ones if he isn't mad at me. The time outside is mediocre, although the warm spring breeze feels nice as it swirls around my arms that have hardly seen the sun this spring. I walk the whole way in a little bit of a haze, as I have been lately whenever I'm more than 6 floors away from my son. I just want to be back. I think about the people I see and I want to say, "My son has cancer", to each one so they can feel sympathy for me. Isn't that bizarre? I want them to understand my fear and my pain - and yet most days I don't understand it. Things are going well with treatment, but there is this underlying dread, this base of quicksand that could swallow us up and deliver us to the depths of despair, it seems, at a moment's notice.

Some days I feel I really have my shit together. Some days I even think I could somehow survive if my worst fear comes true. I never think I would feel any joy again, but I might be able to survive - like other's survive a tornado or hurricane, but it would be a tornado every single day of the rest of my God forsaken life. Other days, I know I will not be able to go on. The first full day I was at home with my new born baby boy, I gave him his first bath. A sponge bath on the floor of his neatly painted room, with the heat on very, very warm so he would be comfortable. I had everything I needed and we were finally alone in our home just the two of us. I had lullaby music playing and I had this beautiful little soul who knew nothing of anything and was relying on me to take care of him. In that moment, as I sat on my knees hovering over this little baby boy, I knew and I said out loud, what my purpose in life was. It was to be his mommy. That was it. I recently watched a movie called Guilt Trip with Barbra Streisand and Seth Rogan. At the end of the movie she says to her son "I was meant to marry your father, because if I hadn't I wouldn't have had you. Don't you see, it was always you. You're the love of my life baby. It will always be you. Just remember one thing. If all the boys in the world were lined up and I could only pick one, I'd pick you, every time." She stole my line. Or I'm stealing hers, but it was meant for me.

In recent times I dreaded the fact that my boy was growing up so fast and would soon want to leave me and be on his own. I looked forward to that also, as I've always tried to be present and enjoy every stage of life with my son. But I have felt that our time was coming to an end, and I wished I could keep him young and keep him with me. Well, cancer has really changed all that. Now I pray he will grow up and leave me. Have his own home, car, job, wife, family if that is what he wants. I hope he will come to see me occasionally, call me to say hi. Eat Thanksgiving dinner with me when he can. I wish to know he is out there somewhere, having the life he hoped for and dreamed of. And I will gladly give up my desperate need to be with him all the time, if only I know he is out there somewhere and I will see him again, soon. Because the alternative is too difficult to bear. He asked me the second full day in the hospital as we were crying and holding each other, "what if I'm not alright? What if I die? Will you be alright Mom?" In that moment of despair he was thinking of me. My answer was "No, I won't be alright. I will never be alright again." I couldn't lie to him at that point. I didn't want him to think I would be alright. I want him to know he is the center of my world and always has been since I knew he was inside my tummy. And honestly he always will be, no matter what happens.

Leslie

Sent: Sunday, May 19, 2013 7:21 PM
From: Toni
To: Leslie Jermainne
Subject: Re: Just for you re: BRJ

Just reading this now, in the bathroom with tears streaming down my face. And this is why we connect. Yes, I understand you because we think so much alike. But he will be okay. I know it in my heart. I just do.

Toni

Sent: Sunday, May 19, 2013 8:08 PM
From: Leslie Jermainne
To: My List
Subject: RE: Brian Ross Update 5/19

Wow, the 19th of May already. I seriously cannot comprehend that a month has passed already. It is a blur of tears, appointments, medicine, treatments, worries, bandages, surgeries, hugs, scans, blood draws, kisses, driving, packing, nurses, doctors, temperatures.

Today was a good day. Well, certainly much better than yesterday. Besides some nausea which was controlled with a small extra dose of Ativan this morning, and being very tired, he is still doing well. A chocolate milkshake for breakfast, and three pieces of pizza this afternoon was all he's eaten. This is a change for him. However he just woke up again and wants some spaghetti with butter and parm, so off to Bertucci's I will go in about 5 minutes. He was nauseous again about 45 minutes ago, but the dose of Ativan again did the trick. I think after he eats, he will be off to dream land for the night because he is EXHAUSTED.

Tired and happy since we had such a great visit again with Toni and Christi. Seeing my teenage boy so happy being a teenage boy when Christi is visiting does my heart good. We are so lucky to have friends who make this trip, give him (and me!) support, talks, laughter, understanding and distraction. It feels like today whizzed by instead of dragged. Now we start a new week tomorrow and hopefully will be home Wednesday.

We still have the room to ourselves, which is just such sheer pleasure. I plan on trying to get to sleep a bit earlier tonight too and get maybe an extra hour or two.

Ok - just got back from Bertucci's. Thankfully it is only sprinkling out. Chemo is about to start again for tonight. He is very crabby right now. I dared to look over at his IV pole to see if they did start it and got yelled at. I will keep my eyes forward for now.

Tomorrow and Tuesday will be quiet days, mostly of napping, getting meds and eating when able. We are inching towards Wednesday and getting back home.

I don't think I have much to share tonight but wishes for health and happiness for you all. Please send your prayers to my friend and kinda, sorta family way over the ocean in Bonny Scotland for her family and her Dad who is battling also. I'm wishing nothing but health and a speedy recovery for Lorna's Dad.

Love from Room 618

Leslie

Sent: Sunday, May 19, 2013 9:50 AM
From: Lorna
To: Leslie Jermainne
Subject: Re: Brian Ross Update 5/16

Hi Leslie

Thanks for that. I think Brian is so lucky to have a Mom like you. It's so hard to accept that you can't protect them from everything, but you are there, by his side, fighting in his corner, every step of the way. What more could a son ask for! You are amazing.

L

ANOTHER JUST FOR ME

MAY 20, 2013

Sent: Monday, May 20, 2013 7:20 AM
From: Leslie Jermainne
To: Leslie Jermainne
Subject: Just for you re:BRJ - 2

Hi All,

Last night's update seems pathetic to me when I look at it this morning. Especially for how the night really ended. After finishing my email and thinking about getting some sleep. Brian was awake and restless and said "I want my Mom". Sweeter words I have never heard. I got invited to lay with him in his bed, face to face, holding hands and stroking his back and head. He says to me, as he has before but not for a while now, "I'm sorry Mom". My heart breaks open in one of the barely healed cracks. I then say "No I'm sorry. What if I did something, fed you something, exposed you to something that caused this". It's his body and his fault, he tells me. I ask him if he did this on purpose, if he can control this? Of course his answer is no, and the apologies end. I know the apologies are really us just looking for comfort from the other that it is okay. That everything is okay.

The nurse comes in to change his fluid bag and we are snuggled in bed together whispering and I'm happy someone see's us this way. It is like some sort of weird justification of the love I have for this child of mine. He is sad at first and just keeps saying he wants to go home. I understand completely, but if I'm honest, I don't like hearing this. The repetitiveness of the statement reminds me of visiting Brian's Mom when she was in nursing care for cancer. These words are even hard to write, but she was dying of cancer herself. While visiting a few days before she did pass away, she kept repeating that she wanted to go home. And my heart broke for her to be stuck there. Those words have always stuck with me, and to hear them coming from my son is upsetting. I know he is tired and bored and worried. You don't sleep well here, it isn't comfortable, there are strangers and no cute dogs.

After we talked a bit more, we started to come back to our true selves. Giggling and laughing, processing the people around us in ways only we can. Laughing and snuggling, joking and imitating. He is feeling better and we are happy and I get to be close to his body that is now bigger than mine. I'm happy in my thoughts and thinking how much fun we always have together. Thinking how we have the same sense of humor and that he makes me laugh so much and so hard like no one else. And in this moment of joy the ever present fear rises up, hauls back and slaps me across the face. What if he dies and you don't get to do this anymore? No one else will ever make you laugh again, no one else ever could, like he does. God Dammit!!! Leave me alone for one God forsaken minute cancer!!! PLEASE!!! PLEASE!!! PLEASE!!!

I don't let on to him the sting that slap brings to my face, but keep joking and laughing and I come back to the moment, a red handprint across my face that he can't see in the darkness of our room. Brian wants to play Sims on his computer and wants me to stay sitting with him in his bed and watch. I want to be nowhere else. And I think in my head, "Take that fear. I can take anything you can dish out, as long as I have him here with me. You can kick the crap out of me, but I will take it, and he will not see it, not for one moment." I watch him for the next hour build houses, text Christi, laugh, talk and be as happy as he can be. I doze off, exhausted while sitting side by side with my baby boy. I wake a few times and tell him I should go to bed, but he says "no, stay with me." And I stay. And I'm happy. He wakes me one last time and says "it's okay Mom, you can go to bed now." I kiss his cheek, which I can feel a few manly whiskers poke me, and tell him I love him for probably the twentieth time today and crawl off to my little window seat. Tonight was a great night. Exceptional night. And even though the slap left a mark, I can take it. It is just another badge of honor I have earned being Brian's mother. I will save it like stretch marks, tear stains and broken pieces of my heart. All evidence of my love for my only child. -Leslie

THIS VERSION WAS SENT TO EVERYONE

Sent: Monday, May 20, 2013 8:10 PM
From: Leslie Jermainne
To: My List
Subject: RE: Brian Ross Update 5/20

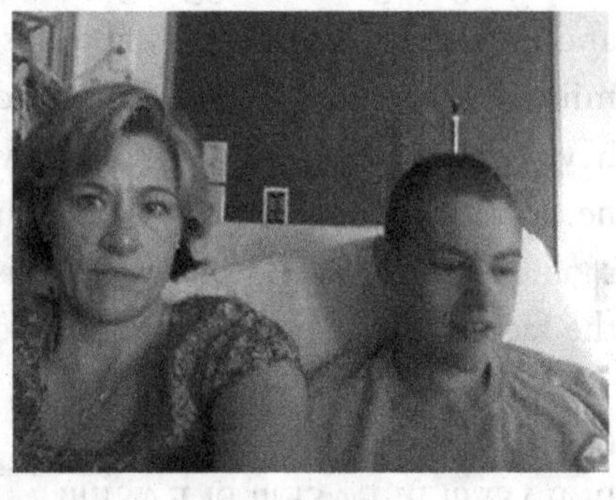

Last night's update seems pathetic to me when I look at it this morning. Especially for how the night really ended. After finishing my email and thinking about getting some sleep. Brian was awake and restless and said "I want my Mom". Sweeter words I have never heard. I got invited to lay with him in his bed, face to face, holding hands and stroking his back and head. He says to me, as he has before but not for a while now, "I'm sorry Mom". My heart breaks open in one of the barely healed cracks. I then say "No I'm sorry. What if I did something, fed you something, exposed you to something that caused this". It's his body and his fault is what he tells me. I ask him if he did this on purpose, if he can control this? Of course his answer is no, and the apologies end. I know the apologies are really us just looking for comfort from the other that it is okay. That everything is okay. The nurse comes in to change his fluid bag and we are snuggled in bed together whispering and I'm happy someone see's us this way. It is like some sort of weird justification of the love I have for this child of mine. He is sad at first and just keeps saying he wants to go home. I understand completely. I know he is tired and bored and worried. You don't sleep well here, it isn't comfortable, there are strangers and no cute dogs.

After we talked a bit more, we started to come back to our true selves. Giggling and laughing, processing the people around us in ways only we can. Laughing and snuggling, joking and imitating. He is feeling better and we are happy and I get to be close to him. I'm happy in my thoughts and thinking how much fun we always have together. Thinking how we have the same sense of humor and that he makes me laugh so much and so hard like no one else. And in this moment of joy the ever present fear rises up, hauls back and slaps me across the face. What if he dies and you don't get to do this anymore. No one else will ever make you laugh again, no one else ever could like he does.

I don't let on to him the sting that slap brings to my face, but keep joking and laughing and I come back to the moment, a red handprint across my face that he can't see in the darkness of our room. Brian wants to play Sims on his computer and wants me to stay sitting with him in his bed and watch. I want to be nowhere else. I think in my head, "take that fear. I can take anything you can dish out, as long as I have him here with me. You can kick the crap out of me, but I will take it, and he will not see it, not for one moment." I watch him for the next hour build houses, text Christi, laugh, talk and be as happy as he can be. I doze off, exhausted while sitting side by side with my baby boy. I wake a few times and tell him I should go to bed, but he says "no, stay with me." And I stay, happy that he wants me. He wakes me one last time and says "it's okay Mom, you can go to bed now." I kiss his cheek, which I can feel a few manly whiskers poke me, and tell him I love him for probably the twentieth time today and crawl off to my little window seat. Last was a great night. Exceptional night. And even though the slap left a mark, I can take it. It is just another badge of honor I have earned being Brian's mother. I will save it like stretch marks, tear stains and broken pieces of my heart. All evidence of my love for my only child.

Today was a good, but quiet day. Brian slept until 11:00 when he was awoken to his bed surrounded by about 9 people. Our nurse practitioner, the attending, the resident, the pharmacist, the charge nurse, his nurse, some lady observing from Mexico, some other doctor I don't know who she was and me. Poor kid. This is how rounds go. I first go out into the hallway where his condition is reviewed and updated. We discussed again the less than stellar lumbar puncture and what to do on Wednesday when he has the next one. Then after everything is reviewed, everyone piles into the room. Ask Brian how he is feeling, does he have pain, nausea, has he pooped, any questions? Then the attending and the resident listen to his lungs, his heart and check him over. Great start to the day huh? But it is necessary and I'm grateful to have these people saving my son. Of course he didn't sleep right through to 11:00 a.m., with his vitals being taken, fluids changed, meds given, etc. But still...

They day was somewhat quiet after that. I watched him play Sims again, he had gummy bears for breakfast. Then he felt nauseous and they tried a new medication that I haven't learned how to pronounce yet, but that seemed to work. While he rested again I went down to the lobby and had some lunch and then my phone rang and it was him, I answered but he couldn't hear me, or I thought maybe he couldn't talk, because I thought I heard crying. I left my lunch on the table and rushed to the elevator. He called me again, and again I answered but heard nothing but kind of heavy breathing. I about ran into his room and his nurse and him look up at me like I was crazy. I said "I thought something was wrong, I thought you were crying". He said he couldn't hear me on the phone but, he wanted pizza from Bertucci's. OY! So off I went. As I got to the lobby they were announcing over the loud speaker "Code Red in the sub-basement". But everyone seemed to be just going about their business. I thought code red was a heart attack or something. The weird thing was the fire alarms were blinking and beeping. I proceeded out the front door, down the sidewalk to the crosswalk when I notice that 5 or 6 security guards are at the intersection and I see fire trucks coming down the road. The light turns to cross the street and we all cross. As I get down the sidewalk a bit, I look back and the fire trucks are turning into Children's Hospital. I just left my son in a building that is on fire?!?! I quickly call him on the phone and ask what is happening on the floor as I run into Bertucci's grab his pizza and go back, jogging now. He says there is a fire in the sub-basement he heard, but nothing is happening and he doesn't hear any fire alarm anymore. So he had heard it too. By the time we hang up I'm walking back into the hospital and the fire alarms are still sounding in the lobby, but everyone is just walking around like normal. I push the up button for the elevator about 77 times before a door opens and ride up to the 6th floor where all is quiet and peaceful and normal. Let's add a little more stress okay?

After that he enjoyed his pizza, he played Sims and wanted me by his side the whole time. Then he got a little bloody nose, which he has never had happened before and of course is a sign of problems, if his platelets were low, which they are fine. It just scared us a bit. He was blowing his nose, it wasn't just spontaneous, but still...any little thing freaks you out during this, and we'd had enough excitement for one day (lifetime?). It stopped bleeding relatively quickly and he didn't even pass out from the blood - which is a plus. For those of you who don't know, Brian isn't a big fan of even the word blood, but I guess all of this has gotten him to relax a little.

At about 5pm he wanted a milkshake from McDonalds, which I got and then he went to sleep. And that's where we are at right now. I'm going to try to get some sleep early too.

Goodnight from Room 618

Leslie

Sent: Monday, May 20, 2013 9:04 PM
From: Alison
To: Leslie Jermainne
Subject: Re: Just for you re:BRJ - 2

I don't know what to say. I'm sitting her sobbing, wishing I could take all this fear and concern and illness and walk away with it so it doesn't affect either one of you anymore. It KILLS me that you two have to go through this. And I wonder why, why did this have to happen, it isn't fair, it isn't right and if anyone ever again tries to tell me there is a God, I am going to deck them - over and over and over again.

I know you are getting good care at DFCI, but I hate that you have to be so far away, that I can't just jump in the car and be there in a half hour.

But all he really needs right now is you, his Mom, and the love you two share. I know it's hard to see him hurting, and know you can't stop it, but being there for him is what's best. Just know that there are a lot of people here for you too, when you need to vent, to cry, to rail against the sheer madness of this whole thing, and I'll be right behind you when he's cured and you decide you want to bitch-slap whoever the hell decided to drop this in your laps....

Love you both!

Sent: Monday, May 20, 2013 10:42 PM
From: Toni
To: Leslie Jermainne
Subject: Re: Brian Ross Update 5/20

Ugh. You have been through the ringer the last two days. Are you okay? I mean I know you are not, but wish I could help. Hope you get some sleep.

Toni

MAY 21, 2013

Sent: Tuesday, May 21, 2013 7:21 AM
From: Leslie Jermainne
To: Alison
Subject: RE: Just for you re:BRJ - 2

Hi Al,

I sometimes feel guilty sharing my real deep down fears with the few people I love and trust and who I think will understand. But I guess I have to or else they might eat me alive from the inside out. It may be selfish but knowing other people are out there crying and railing against the universe for letting this happen to my baby boy, such a good, good person. I say the same things, it ISN'T fair and it ISN'T right but it isn't fair and it isn't right for anyone, especially any other young person to go through this, so why spare us? I wish we were spared. I wish we were in our little selfish dreamlike life of yesterday, but we aren't and some good is coming from this I know.

I hate we are so far away too, but this is the best place for us. In some respects, I think the quietness of not having too many visitors is a good thing. It gets boring and tedious and visitors do break up your time, but he needs to rest, especially now, and it is hard to say no to the people who love you and who you love. I am so appreciative of you and Toni going way above and beyond to visit us as much as you have, so know that.

I understand your feelings about God, and my son shares your view. I have my beliefs too, which are certainly being tested and causing me to review and fine tune how and what I believe. For me, I no longer see "God" as a single controlling force in the universe who sends hurricanes and tornados, sickness, or blessings. To me "God" is the collective consciousness, a power or force, of all the souls living and in what I call "heaven". I have vacillated in the past about why these things happen. Why do people we love and who are good people get cancer, get in a car accident, become disabled, or out of work, or whatever. I believe now, or I'm working on figuring out my belief that as a soul, we have a plan when we come here - but by coming here, other shit just happens. Everything isn't perfect. Kind of like this example: You come to earth to learn something (by the way, I'm kinda thinking earth is a bit like Hell, just sayin') maybe to be less selfish, or to help others, with the bigger purpose always being love. But then while you're here, you get killed in a car accident. And it is just that, an accident. Cars are dangerous, people aren't always paying attention, roads get ice on them, we speed, text, talk, apply makeup and eat while driving, cars break, etc. Shit happens. It is terrible heart wrenching shit, but it just happens. I don't believe any white bearded guy is sitting on a throne in the clouds while his son who he made from his own body (I think that how it goes) sitting next to him and says "Hmmm, the Jermainne's seem pretty happy and lucky. Let's give their kid cancer just to fuck with them. We'll slap them back into reality that life sucks." Maybe this is just me justifying what is going on, but I've been working on these thoughts before this fucking thing ever happened.

I think the end result is that all the souls, the collective force or consciousness, will finally, eventually realize that love is the answer. And by love I mean acceptance, caring, giving, and plain old love. I think it is way, way, way off - but still, there is hope.

So although I would like to slap the shit out of the world, we are not the only ones suffering this accident, this slight gene mutation. There are many out there way worse off than us. Little babies who die just being born. Adults who get killed just crossing the street. Babies right here on this floor with heart problems, that aren't going to live. We have a chance, and a good one, so we are lucky. That is what I'm focused on 90% of the time. It is just that 10% that knocks me on my ass a couple times of day, but I get back up, dust it off, limp a little as I walk again and I walk it off. Jumpy a little for the next shove, but ready, and I will take it.

Love you tons and tons!

Les

Sent: Tuesday, May 21, 2013 6:10 PM
From: Alison
To: Leslie Jermainne
Subject: Re: Just for you re:BRJ - 2

Don't ever feel guilty about sharing your thoughts and concerns....that is what I (we) are here for. To support you while you support your son. Not that I don't support Brian as well, but I think in a situation like this, he needs his Mom to be strong, and sure, and there.... There have been times when I was hurting, a lot, and I thought to myself, "I want my Mommy". I think that is universal that people look to their Mothers to support them and provide comfort and the assurance that everything will be okay. You do that so well with Brian. And he knows it. That's what is important, not what the rest of us feel, however bad we feel, but that he can count on you to be there and help him, comfort him and assure him that no matter what happens....it will be okay. What the rest of us can do is be there for you. To provide the same comfort and support and a shoulder to cry on, if that's what you need.

I too believe that we all come here with a plan for our lives, that we are here to learn something. I would hate to think that in the grand scheme of things that Brian came here to teach us humility, compassion and empathy for all those who are suffering. But that could very well be the case. That he is an advanced soul who has gone through all his lifetimes and has reached that time in his evolution where his sole purpose is to help the rest of us reach our potentials. If that is the case, then I cannot love him more, for what he has taught me. And I am hoping that this will show me that if you care enough, hope enough and give enough that we can sway the outcome of bad things that "happen" to good people. I'm going with that for now, that if I wish hard enough, he will be cured and his mission in this life will have been fulfilled so that he can enjoy the rest of his time here on this earth. I do believe that you and he and Carl and Mom and Dad have been in my lives before, that you will be again and that we have an eternal connection that will last in eternity....

Sent: Tuesday, May 21, 2013 6:48 AM
From: Leslie Jermainne
To: Toni
Subject: RE: Brian Ross Update 5/20

I'm okay. I think we are both at the end of our rope a little with this stay. I pray we get to go home tomorrow as scheduled. His counts are dropping faster this time, but we are still in range to go. I'll write more later. Not a great end to the night last night.

Thanks as always for your notes. I look for them like a seagull looks for french fries. ;-)

These next few are a series of notes between my brother Andrew, a childhood family friend and classmate of his, and me.

Sent: Monday, May 20, 2013 10:21 PM
From: Kim
To: Andrew
Subject: Leslie and Brian

Ok, I have been faithfully reading Leslie's daily updates. She amazes me with her strength, daily appreciation for what she has and ability to find humor in what she is going through. I get a good cry every night. Please tell me if there is anything I can do. Can I send a care package, can you give me some ideas of video games he plays (or just tell me what he has and I could ask Travis for suggestions). I have asked my nephew to look into guitars. He is working making guitars for the second year, I was thinking it might be cool to have a custom made one for him, but before I did that I would need to know more details about his skill, style...

I feel helpless and want to help. Kim

MAY 21, 2013

Sent: Tuesday, May 21, 2013 6:08 AM
From: Andrew
To: Kim
Subject: Re: Leslie and Brian

Kim:

I, unlike you, lose the ability to communicate effectively after reading some of the heart wrenching communications from my sister (ok, most of the communications from my sister). I spend most of my time looking for reasons, answers, and solutions as it is my want to do. I sit here in my cocoon, making donations to any and all cancer research that I can see may make a difference. I can sit here and do that, but I can't face up to going to see them, knowing that I will be standing there with tears in my eyes feeling impotent in my families fight with cancer.

Helplessness is not something I deal with well. I have always worked through the solutions and not the problems, but I am way out of my element here. My own experiences with doctors and hospitals leave me less than satisfied to the point where I won't even go unless I am forced to. It's difficult for me to reach out to anyone, as my first instinct has always been to deal with things on my own. I am lost here, and with my mother and now Brian.

I am sure that anything you do will be a blessing to us all. The idea of getting a custom made guitar seems beyond belief to me and I am sure it would mean the world to him. If you need money or resources of any kind let me know. If your nephew can't make it happen, maybe he can guide us to someone else that can help. It's hard to say, but I am not sure I know enough about Brian to advise you on anything with respect to style or composition. I am forwarding a copy of your kind offers to Leslie to let her know and discretely ask Brian if he has any preferences.

I need to get my old and tired butt going, and earn another contribution to the Jimmy Fund. We are trying to get a table going for some of the parade circuit this summer to gather contributions for the Jimmy Fund. We are looking into doing some of the local musters, as a booth or table during the festivities. As Brian is part of the drum corps we all grew up in, I thought it would be appropriate and worthwhile to pursue.

Thanks for your kind words and all that you have been doing.

Andrew

Sent: Tuesday, May 21, 2013 at 8:04 AM,
From: Leslie Jermainne
To: Kim & Andy
Subject: Re: Leslie and Brian

Hi Kim & Andy:

Hmmm, this is a great email for me in so many ways. First of all, hello Andy...I knew you must be out there somewhere, but I was wondering. I see your name on the donation for Stacy's bike ride - so very, very generous, and yes that does speak volumes. Your quick email asking about the shirts.

The edible arrangement that we plowed through as soon as it arrived. But this email was what I needed to hear from my long, lost brother.

Life, distance, circumstances and time have sent us all in varying directions, as I guess is normal for most families. It is heartbreaking at times, but the days go on and life flies by and we all create our own smaller families and try to reconnect with the whole of us from time to time. It is these horrible moments that have been too many for our family over the past few years that make you want for more connection, more time, less hardship. But, it is what it is. That has become my motto of late. Not in a defeatist way, but in a realist way. A way of acceptance. Trying to find answers that don't exist, at least not yet does nothing for me but use up precious energy. The answer is to do our very best every day. To take the medicine that is what the doctors think is the right thing to do. Say please and thank you to everyone who enters our room in an effort to help, whether it be to take vital signs, administer medicine, deliver food or clean the room. To talk with the care team about what can be done better or differently and tell them what we need and make it happen. The solutions will hopefully be discovered one day so that no child, no mother, no father and no person will have to hear that they, or even worse, their child has cancer and worry that life will end.

I do understand the fear of coming to visit us. It is scary. Now seeing him with his patchy hair, swollen face, scared and tired eyes isn't easy. The physical manifestations of this fight make it all too present every minute. It isn't easy for him to make small talk with people who aren't so very close to him, as he is still a young man and now he is fragile. It is more stress on him to try to visit and make nice, worry about germs and awkward silences. But notes like the one you wrote, knowing that you are heartbroken for us too. That you are doing what you are able to help us and Mom and all those people fighting this, is amazing. Just knowing that people are out there, outside this tall building, outside this unfamiliar city and they are thinking about us through the day. Wishing for us that we weren't here, doing this, helps so, so much. You feel a bit alone here, as everyone does, but when you hear or see words that people are working on your behalf. That they are sending out thoughts of recovery to the universe, it makes it feel like we just had a nice long visit and a good cleansing cry and that people have got our back.

As a note, I thought my very, very good friend Stacy had found it too hard to deal with us. Maybe she was too far away in Ohio, or knew my son too little to really be involved. I was a little hurt that I wasn't hearing from her more often. And then she pledged to do the bike ride, and is raising money for cancer research. She is going beyond her comfort zone to do so much to help us, that I was ashamed in my thoughts that maybe she didn't really care. I should have known she was out there, trying to find the right way to help that worked for her. Patience is a virtue that I have very little of, but I'm learning. And here I am again, feeling ashamed that I thought maybe this wasn't in the forefront of my brother's mind. And now I know, how much we have been in his thoughts. The idea of raising money for the Jimmy Fund Clinic, especially through the drum corps which has become such a big part of our lives and the people so wonderful in their support, amazes me. What an amazing and wonderful idea. Brian will be so touched, that you are taking on such a mission in his name. That is better than any tear filled visit might be. Honestly. If you are interested, my new found, very good friend and current director of the Junior Colonials, Toni, could definitely and gladly help in any way. Her husband Steve is also in the Mariners, and they have tons of drum corps connections. Really awesome people, who have stepped up to be an amazing support for us. Not to mention her daughter Christi is Brian's first girlfriend now.

My only other thought for you Andy is to keep in touch with Mom and Dad. I know you guys are far away, and conversation can be difficult with them. Especially with Mom's memory issues. But I thought I knew how hard a cancer diagnosis is when Mom was diagnosed. I now know that even then, I didn't really understand. Having these contacts, notes, phone calls from people, even just for a moment in time is hugely helpful. Even leaving a message every other day or so on their answering machine would be like getting a hug. I am not really one to have a lot of people in my life, but those little touches now mean the world to me. My how I have changed.

Now on to Kim...first of all thank you for all your words of support and encouragement, your generous donation to Stacy's ride to show your support and now this possible offer of a custom made guitar is really breathtaking. Secondly, thank you for being such a wonderful friend to my brother, who as he says, keeps a lot inside. Seeing that he has a person to listen to his thoughts is heartwarming for me. Your ability to reach out to him and in turn us, and bring him out to share his feelings and fears is awesome. Bridging a connection for us that I thought might be a little lost or at the least pretty rusty - is probably the greatest gift. So thank you.

The guitar, hmmm...so very exciting just the possibility. We have recently been referred to Make-A-Wish and they called me the other day to verify Brian's diagnosis. They need a sign off from his doctor before the wheels can get turning, but it is exciting for Brian to have something like that a mere possibility and something to think about in the future. When they first told me he is eligible to receive a wish, honestly my heart almost dropped out onto the floor. To me, Make-A-Wish happened for kids who are dying. I wanted to scream "WHAT!?!? NOOOOOO!!!!" I'm sure the look on my face explained it all, and they quickly jumped in to educate me. Make-A-Wish is not a last wish. Many kids go on to recover and live long, full lives. This program is about giving kids something to look forward to. To give them hope and something to look forward to, something to think about. And it has done just that for Brian. We are waiting now, and hope that his Wish Granters will be visiting us soon, to help him determine what his wish may be. He has some ideas, and I tell you this because a custom built guitar was one of those ideas. So it amazes me that this option might have the chance to be fulfilled somewhere else. I too, would be happy to provide funds for this potential project. I'm not sure where your nephew is, but my thought would be that if we could make this happen, that Brian could be involved directly, in the design and whatever (I know very, very little about guitars) is needed. It would be more than owning a guitar that was made just for him. It would be a project, something to concentrate on, look forward too, etc. Something to work on and dream about. Brian wouldn't need to know that funds were being added by his family and friends - because he is very conscious of this and would tailor his Wish to make it "affordable". That is just the kind of kid he is. We could make that happen in the background.

Please understand that if this does not come to reality, I understand completely. Nothing will be said to him, unless it can be accomplished. Just the mere thought is a gift enough to me. Your wish to help us in a way is the gift itself. One that will, believe me, be treasured. When he mentioned the custom guitar from Make-A-Wish I told him to add it to his list. But secretly I want him to find an experience that I probably can't duplicate. I could do a guitar, most likely, but in the end the choice will be his. His other wish so far is to go to Switzerland. His Dad's family is from there, and there are relatives that we could see. I'm not sure if that is a possibility either, but to me, that would be the experience to go for. We shall see.

So - to you both - thank you. This email has done me a world of good and I need that today. Like I said in a previous note, the people who show up and stay are the ones that make this all bearable for us. We hope to be home tomorrow, but will still be emailing and reading responses feverishly.

Have a good day! Leslie

Sent: Tuesday, May 21, 2013 8:43 AM
From: Kim
To: Leslie Jermainne
Subject: Re: Leslie and Brian

Note to self, do not read emails from Leslie or Andy when you get to work - I did get my eyes washed out well! Have you ever thought of writing for a career? You words are touching and give so much meaning to life! Thank you for helping me realize the good in my life. Kim

Sent: Tuesday, May 21, 2013 8:47 AM
From: Frank
To: Leslie Jermainne
Subject: RE: Brian Ross Update 5/20

Thank you for sharing with us Leslie!!!

I'm soo happy that you were there at the exact minute that Brian needed you. As a caregiver - sometimes you wander around in a numb fog thinking thoughts, feeling like you're spinning your wheels, so you move forward doing what you think you should be doing catering to the patient's needs - like getting water, or pizza, or new chargers for your electronics then out of the blue - BAM!!! You are tapped on the shoulder without any warning for support, comfort, and love - and low and behold - you are there to provide exactly what they need Big Time. At that moment in time you are able to give nothing but yourself in a pure soul-to-soul connection that means everything - helping, and making a difference in a way that no other person on this earth can. I'm happy Brian was able to reach out to you and that you were able to be there (as you always are). Sometimes the road to recovery is more than medicine or physical needs.

Not sure if this came out right or reads the way I wanted it too as I'm writing quickly - but you touched me with this email and made me smile deep down inside and also made me feel good about my role as a caregiver, my moments, and the road I've walked.

Your caregiver friend,
Frank

Sent: Tuesday, May 21, 2013 10:01 AM
From: Hoyt
To: Leslie Jermainne
Subject: RE: Brian Ross Update 5/20

Leslie,

You both are in our prayers every day. You are doing everything you can and he is in good hands. HE WILL PULL THROUGH!!!! He is young, and strong and a fine young man. Stay positive as you are. I know it is hard, and I am sure a lot easier to say than do, but he will draw his courage from many places to defeat this disease. Like all children we draw our greatest comfort from our parents regardless of our age. The confidence he sees in you will help him. Yes there will be tears and sorrow but he knows you and Big Brian have his back and he has your unconditional love. That plus the medical care you are receiving is the right ammunition. I am by no means an authority on any of this, but we believe in you and Big and Little Brian.

Semper Fidelis,
Hoyt

Sent: Tuesday, May 21, 2013 7:42 PM
From: Leslie Jermainne
To: My List
Subject: RE: Brian Ross Update 5/21

Well, one night ended really good and last night not so much. Let's just suffice it to say that the Prednisone is back in all its' nasty glory. I shut the lid on his laptop, which he hadn't used for an hour or two, and I was worried about it just sitting there burning into the screen. Well, you would have thought I picked it up and slammed into on the ground shattering it to pieces and then stomped on it a few times after that. I tried not to engage in the hissy fit, but it was tough. I went back to lying on my bed after saying I'm sorry about 5 times. He just kept up the remarks until he poked me one too many times. I got up again and again apologized and tried to justify myself, and told him I learned my lesson, I wouldn't touch anything of his again unless he told me too. He responded by starting to cry saying "I'm the one with cancer". I told him I was well aware of the fact and I stood there crying "I'm doing the best I can". Not my finest moment. Not my worse either - but those all happened prior to cancer when my temper, and yes I have a serious one - got the best of me. Now it just goes straight to tears.

I crawled back to my corner and we sat alone in our thoughts for about half an hour before I got the courage to go back to his bed, apologize again - and he apologized too. I got to give him a kiss goodnight and back to my bed I went. I was reading on my kindle on my phone when I got a text from 10 feet away making a joke. We texted back and forth for about 20 min. being silly, but never talking out loud. Just texting and laughing. Finally I fell asleep first, exhausted but at least not going to bed mad or sad. Maybe a little regretful that I didn't handle it better.

Today has been a quiet and pretty nice day. Last dose of Cyclophosphamide went in this morning. He got to be disconnected from his pump about 1:30 and has been drinking his water since then. I tried to get him to take a shower and get out of the room, but to no avail and I wasn't about to push it after last night. Prednisone taper will start tomorrow night and he will be off it by Friday, and is not scheduled to get it again. A shower and activity can wait.

We laid around in his bed talking a lot today, watched him play Sims, talked with doctors at rounds, picked up Rx for home, did laundry, got Bertucci's pizza which he says makes his stomach feel better. Now that's my kid! He napped this afternoon until just about half an hour ago when he got his next round of nausea meds and ate pop tarts. Again, my kid. Now it is texting and computer. I hope he actually stays up a bit tonight, as his Lumbar Puncture is somewhere between 10-12 tomorrow. He can't eat after midnight tonight, so the longer he can sleep, the less waiting there will be. We have talked it over about the LP tomorrow with the doctors and anesthesia and have decided to try propofol as the anesthetic to make things go a bit smoother for him tomorrow. I hope he will not awake in the middle as he did last time and also will feel no pain.

We are also not scheduled to come back here until Friday June 1st for clinic. If his counts are good enough we will stay and start round 4 then. His counts are already down quite a bit, about where they were at his lowest last time. Chemo is definitely cumulative and this time is going to be harder. Let's just hope and pray he doesn't need a transfusion and doesn't get any fevers. We'll see and I'll be prepared. First thing I do when I get home is repack our bag so we are ready to go at a moment's notice. Our plan in place for any emergent care needed is to call Jimmy Fund, then go to our local hospital to be evaluated, then most likely be transported via ambulance to Boston. Having the plan in place and knowing what will happen, makes me feel more secure.

I had some really great emails today. One especially that really touched me and had me reaching out to say thank you and I understand. Other quick notes offering food and support to us and Big Brian. Words of encouragement and hugs and smiles. Also, our local board of Realtors posted the link to Stacy's bike ride to raise funds for research today. I had sent them info in hopes of our local Realtors who know Brian so well supporting him, Stacy and our son. It was nice to see people already reaching out to Big Brian and making donations to help raise funds.

Well, hopefully tonight will continue to be quiet and restful. I can hardly wait to get packing, get home, see my hubby and my dogs and then my bed.

Watching a thunderstorm over the city from room 618. Goodnight!

Leslie

Sent: Tuesday, May 21, 2013 8:44 PM
From: Toni
To: Leslie Jermainne
Subject: Re: Brian Ross Update 5/21

Oh Leslie, so hard, he doesn't mean it but it doesn't hurt any less. You are both hurting and you are the only person he can lash out so you get it all and he knows you still love him. And still it doesn't hurt any less. Don't beat yourself up about your response. It was understandable.

I see a scared little boy who is stuck inside a man size body. He is being perpetually violated by doctors, nurses, technologists, has no privacy, has no idea what tomorrow will bring, and his mom can't fix it like she always has. He's not angry at you, he is angry at cancer, and his body and his lack of control over everything. We all get angry and frustrated but with both of you raw, it's bound to hurt.

I am so glad you have an outlet, your words. Does he journal? I wonder if he shares his thoughts with anyone. Has he talked to anyone there, independent of you? Thinking it might be good for him. Thinking out loud.

Love hugs and always here to listen.

Toni

MAY 22, 2013

Sent: Wednesday, May 22, 2013 2:44 PM
From: Frank
To: Leslie Jermainne
Subject: RE: Brian Ross Update 5/20

Hey Leslie,

Hope all went well with the LP and the propofol. (I had this med with a recent colonoscopy - very good, no pain, no after effects, and a good bottle of wine kind of feeling). I hope you'll be heading home.

Keep in mind it's OK to get frustrated at times (both Brian and you). It's natural and it's Brian's way of venting or blowing off steam - and he needs too! Think about it this way - he knows you are there for him and he is trusting you to handle these silly but important vents. If he were alone up there - he would keep things to himself and slip into bouts of depression - you are invaluable to him!!! While it's extremely personal - it's not personal if that even makes sense.

PS - not that it'll happen - but don't be surprised if the same venting takes place with you and Big Brian - or your sister's, or anyone......and again it'll be OK (and necessary)! Yeesh! All the good stuff I suppressed for years is coming back to me now. LOL. Sometimes the hospitals, procedures, and chemotherapy is the easy part. :-(

We will be around this weekend - though might have a birthday party for one of the young kids in fenwood Saturday afternoon.

Let us know what works for you - sending positive vibes, Frank

Frank

From: Leslie Jermainne
To: My List
Subject: Re: Brian Ross Update 5/22
Date: Wednesday, May 22, 2013 10:16:20 PM

Hi!

We are home! Exhausted and going to bed. Will write tomorrow. All is well

Sweet dreams from home.

Leslie

MAY 23, 2013

Sent: Thursday, May 23, 2013 6:12 AM
From: Leslie Jermainne
To: Frank
Subject: RE: Brian Ross Update 5/20

Hi Frank,

All did go well, and his oncologist came to do the procedure herself which really boosted our feelings for her (not that they were bad, we just haven't had a whole lot of interaction with her directly).

I know it's okay to get frustrated, it's just frustrating! ;-) Thanks for the reminder about keeping depression at bay. That is possible and important to remember. There hasn't been too much venting with others (I'm assuming you mean me...) except a bit with Big Brian. We are talking and we make a good team which keeps us going. We talked about how we are having a little bit of a disconnect right now - nothing bad - but just that we are each doing our own thing but working as a team to get everything done. The poor guy has taken to getting every possible little chore and some made up ones done at home. I know it is his way of feeling like he is participating in Brian's care, by caring for me and our home. It is nice to see, but I feel like he's killing himself. I wish he'd relax a bit more, but you know Brian - work is his work and his release.

I was thinking Saturday night for a fire, but maybe a bit earlier like 6:30 and only go to 9:00. I'm pretty sure I won't be much use to anyone after that. Let me see how Brian is doing and see what everyone's plans are - I guess the other option would be Sunday, since I'm guessing everyone has Monday off - that might work too if Colin is off. I'll get back to you.

Thank you again for being so willing to share so much with me (us).
~ Leslie

Sent: Thursday, May 23, 2013 6:35 AM
From: Leslie Jermainne
To: My List
Subject: RE: Brian Ross Update 5/22

Hi Everyone,

Well one thing that doesn't change at home is getting up far too early. Yesterday I was awoken at 4 a.m. when it was vitals check and couldn't go back to sleep - today it was 5 a.m. and the birds singing. I'll take the birds over automatic blood pressure cuff any day of the week and twice on Sunday! So yesterday went very well. It was a lot of just waiting. Brian had to wait to have his lumbar puncture until 11:30, but the propofol worked well and Brian's lead oncologist came from the Jimmy Fund Clinic to do the procedure herself. That was a big boost for us, since we haven't had a whole lot of interaction with her directly. She said things went well, that the space where they put the needle in is a little tight, but all was good. It went much faster than the last one, so that made me feel better. He had no side effects from the propofol so all in all a win!

I had already packed our bags and delivered them to the car before going to the LP, so afterward I ran to McDonalds (that is what he wanted I swear) and we ate in the room while waiting and waiting and waiting for discharge papers. Finally at about 2:45 we got released and we all but ran to the car. I got my iPhone in the holder plugged in our home address and away we went. Now...I told you before that the lady who lives in my GPS likes to mess with me - and she got me this time. I thought we had worked out our differences, but apparently she just lulled me into a false sense of security. Once we were on 90 West, I fell into my driving trance, listening to my country music in my single earphone and listening to her shout out directions - most of which are unnecessary. Well, I will admit I was relying on her friendship and understanding that I was up since 4 a.m. exhausted and desperate to get my baby boy home. When I did finally start paying attention, is when I saw on the little screen that the next thing I would need to do would be to get on I-91 South. Yup - you read that right. I have no idea what happened to our prearranged plan to go down I395 like usual on that quiet non-traffic filled back country interstate, but she got me. I tried entering various addresses, thinking for sure we hadn't passed that exit yet and she was just playing me the fool, but I finally had to give up - and come home the long way at about 4:30 p.m. So make matters worse, I thought I'd get off in the highway and do a little scoot across to avoid the Rte 9 backup only there was some sort of detour and we paid big time! We got home at about 7pm. However the happiness to be home overruled the incredible frustration and need to throw my phone on the ground and stomp on it. Next time I will pay attention to that sneaky Witch (with a B).

Once home we had dinner, a big glass of wine, a visit with my parents, meds, some t.v. and cookies and bed. Sweet, comfy, soft, roomy bed. Thank goodness.

Thanks everyone for getting us through round 3. We should be home for about 10 days and then off to round 4. We are over half way done - hopefully! Bri's hair is about gone, he is tired and his blood counts are already lower than they were the whole time we were home after round 2. But he is doing well, the meds are controlling the nausea and we are praying for no fevers and hopefully no need for transfusions. So add those two things to the list of prayers for the next 10 days.

Have a good day - from home.

Leslie

MAY 24, 2013

Sent: Friday, May 24, 2013 10:16 AM
From: Leslie Jermainne
To: My List
Subject: RE: Brian Ross Update 5/23

Hi Again,

Sorry to not update last night - again tired and late before I knew where the day went. Being at home is so much more peaceful and relaxed. Brian is doing well, his nausea meds are keeping it at bay, he is resting and relaxing. Playing the guitar, watching some t.v., always on his computer and cell phone. By the end of the day he was bored, but too tired to do anything. I think that is the hard part. The physical exhaustion but the mind doing cartwheels.

His hair is gone, except a few little patches. Really I couldn't care any less about losing his hair, the thing of it is that it is the outwardly sign of the battle raging inside. It is what makes people think "Oh, I bet he has cancer. He must be so sick". The good thing is that he often keeps his hair buzzed down to 1/8" anyway, so when it starts to come back, it will be a quick grow in time!

As for me, I got our bag repacked and it's ready to go at a moment's notice. Talked with our P.A. and confirmed our appointment time change next Fri 5/31 for 12 noon - which is awesome because we can leave at 8 and have plenty of time, and grab some quick lunch beforehand when we arrive. If his counts are good enough then, we'll be admitted for round 4. If not, then back home for the weekend and keep checking every few days to get back to the right numbers and go again.

Visiting nurse will be here today to access his port and do a blood draw. Tomorrow a.m. we will get the results. Although he is feeling o.k. I seem to have a desperate need to know these numbers. If it were up to me I'd have them drawn daily. Lucky for him, it isn't up to me.

We have some thank you notes to write for all the generous donations to Stacy's bike ride for Brian. Also for some other gifts that people have sent to him. Again, my amazement of the generosity of people. For those that know me the best, you know I'm a worrier. I had been having less and less faith in the goodness of people and the future of the world. Almost a year ago, I gave up watching the news, because I would get so distraught and think "what's the point!" Giving up the news was a good decision for me. But still I waivered. So, another lesson this fight has taught me is that people, most all people, are good and kind and thoughtful and generous. It has certainly reinforced and grown my faith in humankind. It has made me a better person, reaching out to others in need, even while we are consumed with our own battle. Giving is really receiving. And I know for sure the point of this all, the point of our time on this earth. For me that is love. The answer is love. And love is a lot of things. Kindness, helpfulness, laughter, tears, sharing, empathy, generosity, joy and peace.

So I am grateful to be shown these lessons. To have every day I can with my child. Even with giving up the news, you can't avoid hearing what goes on out there every day. This morning I overhead the today show talking about the loss of seven children at an elementary school in OK. Again, it made me realize how precious life is. How uncontrollable the world is. How sacred every day is. You never know what the next moments may bring. A tornado, a cancer diagnosis, a devastating accident - or a sunny day, a laughter shared and hug given and received. I know it is impossible to live in the glow of true appreciation every moment, but if you can find those moments and really see them for the value they bring and file them away for a harder time, then I think that is all we can ask. I'm lucky to have oodles of moments in just the last hardest month of my life. I hope this weekend will keep Brian well, will give us time to share with those we love, and I hope you will all have a moment or two of deep appreciation for someone or something in your life.

Happy unofficial start of summer from home.

Leslie

MAY 25, 2013

Sent: Saturday, May 25, 2013 11:36 AM
From: Robert
To: Leslie Jermainne
Subject: RE: Brian Ross Update 5/22

Leslie--We are back in FL and just read all your emails. Sat here with tears streaming down my face and felt like I was right there with you thru all those days of LP's, meds, ups and downs. Our hearts go out to you, Brian and Big Brian. So very sorry you have had to go thru all this. It is all worth it to defeat the cancer cells. Takes me back 20 yrs. ago to my chemo for breast cancer. Never had to have LP's, just IV chemo every 3 weeks. Remember the nausea and vomiting (they didn't have the good drugs for n/v back then) but had time to recover before the next round. Here I am a survivor and I pray Brian will be, too.

You write beautifully---Brian is so lucky to have you--such a loving Mom. You have loving support from friends and family--so very important to a positive outcome. We pray for you all and will continue as Brian goes thru the rest of his treatments.

Our love to you all,

MAY 27, 2013

Sent: Monday, May 27, 2013 8:17 PM
From: Leslie Jermainne
To: My List
Subject: RE: Brian Ross Update 5/27

Hi Everyone,

Sorry to have sent no updates for the past few days. Everything is fine though. Just taking a break. So let's review...Last Friday the visiting nurse came to draw blood and we got his counts which are holding. The nurse will be back here tomorrow a.m. so we'll get counts on Wednesday and see if he is down again or maybe getting back up a bit so we might get admitted Friday after our clinic visit in Boston and start round 4.

Brian is feeling pretty well. Tired, some nausea that is well controlled w/meds, some eye sensitivity, muscle aches and numbness again, like after the last round (which did go away about 12 days after it started). His appetite has stayed pretty well, and if it drops off, one of the nausea meds also works to stimulate the appetite. We used it a bit in the hospital and once when we got home, but hasn't needed it since then.

Today was such a beautiful day weather wise, which I think we kind of needed to help boost our spirits. Brian had decided to try and march with his drum corps today. We drove just over an hour - hung around with our friends, but just before it was time to march he started to get dizzy and feel like he was going to pass out. After sitting for a bit, he felt better and his color came back, but was not up for marching. He was very disappointed and sad on our way home. Even asking me if I was telling him the truth when I tell him he is doing so well, and will be okay. I know he is just looking for reassurance, which I supplied. I told him I wouldn't ever hide anything from him, so unless the doctors are lying to me, he is doing well. Of course we have no guarantees, but for today thing are good.

Once home, we couldn't get to our house because the parade was going on - so we went to Stop & Shop, picked up some cold cuts, rolls, chips and cookies and waited for our awesome friends the Johnson's to make it back from Westport. Auntie Al & Carlo joined us and we had an impromptu picnic complete with our own fife & drum playing. This certainly made Brian feel a whole lot better and even my Mom and Dad came down to see what all the noise was! The enjoyed hearing the music too!

While in Stop & Shop I ran into Estelle and Frank. It was so great to see their smiling faces and get nice big hugs from our dear friends. We had hoped to have a fire night with them and Sheila and Colin while home, but that will have to wait for next time. I did spend Friday night with my two sisters and hubby and a couple bottles of wine. Lots of tears, mostly on my part, but they joined in too. I think it was some sort of weird purging for me to get so much out. My poor stepdaughter Abby brought me flowers the next day because she was sad I was crying so much. Big Brian told me it was like being in a boxing match for him. He of course doesn't like to see me so upset. I told him I didn't cry the entire time. He said that was when he got a break to sit in the corner of the ring and get some water before the next round. Poor guy. But I want to thank you Alison & Laurie and Brian for letting me vent and cry and release all that pent up...stuff.

We also had a nice visit last Saturday afternoon with Toni & Christi - including lunch and talking and Toni even ran errands with me - she's such a sport. I am learning to be a better friend from her. Time is definitely our most valuable resource, and her willingness to spend it on me and my son is a precious gift. I am forever grateful.

I also just saw an awesome photo on Facebook of my BFF Stacy, her husband Andy, her kids Madi & AJ and her Mom Ella all sporting Team Brian shirts. I again burst into tears when I saw it and poor little Brian came out to the dining room (he had just heard me on the phone with the visiting nurse moments before confirming our appointment for tomorrow) and wanted to know if we had to go back to the hospital. I said no - I'm crying because I'm so touched by their devotion, the shirts and her bike ride. She has raised $2,000.00 and Bath and Body works (her sponsor) will match it so that is $4,000.000 for cancer research. Wow - I'm so touched and thankful to those who have donated!

So overall we are good - I still have scary thoughts lurking in my brain that I hate. But I'm guessing they are going to be there for a long, long time - so I will need to practice more shoving them away. Tonight I'm going to ask you all to say a little prayer for a girl named Sydney and her family. Sydney was diagnosed with Hodgkin's Lymphoma within days of Brian's diagnosis. Her Mom is friends with Toni and we have emailed each other and sent each other support through Facebook. Well last week Sydney had her port installed and the next night ended up in the ER and then admitted due to fever. They are still in the hospital and her counts are down. I've never met them face to face, but tonight I hope you will all send your thoughts to another young person fighting the same fight.

Happy Memorial Day to everyone and thank you to all the Veterans for their service. We are indebted.

Goodnight from home. Leslie

MAY 29, 2013

Sent: Wednesday, May 29, 2013 1:08 PM
From: Leslie Jermainne
To: My List
Subject: RE: Brian Ross Update 5/29

Hi!

Yesterday Brian had a blood draw and right before it, a bad bloody nose. It was upsetting, as this time it just started on its own, but it did stop after about 4-5 minutes. I put a call into Jimmy Fund clinic and was told how to handle it, what to watch for, what not to do etc., until the blood test results come in and see where his platelets are at. It was a long day of waiting. Brian is very, very tired and spent a lot of the afternoon sleeping, and so far today has just gone to lie down for his second nap. Well, blood counts never came last night, but today I got them, and he is very low. He is hovering just above Neutropenia. I am so hoping that he is at his low now and will start to rebound, but we won't know that until Friday's clinic day in Boston - as that is his next scheduled blood draw. So for today and tomorrow we have to lay low, gets lots of rest and monitor even more closely for fever. A fever now at this level is immediate admission to the hospital for IV antibiotics, regardless of waiting for a culture to grow. If this were to happen, we'd go to our local hospital and then be transported to DFCI/BCH via ambulance. I'm praying so hard we don't have to do that. The other thing we were looking at was his platelets, which are low, but not quite enough to transfuse, which I guess is a good thing. No more bloody noses so far.

One good thing they could tell me is that he has 17 monocytes. (Hope I'm spelling that right, but doubtful...) They explained to me that these are baby white cells. Once they mature and release, his WB count will go up exponentially, which is awesome. His platelets however will take longer to rebound. I'm not so optimistic that we will start round 4 on Friday as planned, but you never know what 2 1/2 days can do. We will see, and if not on Friday - then hopefully on Monday or Tuesday of the following week. Never thought I'd want to get admitted to the hospital so much.

So today we are just laying low - he's sleeping, I'm worrying. Pretty much how it goes these days. I would like to tape a thermometer into his mouth, but I know that won't make him feel reassured. I just don't want to miss one little thing. It is amazing how something as simple as a nose bleed can turn your life around in a moment. He even started to cry, just from the stress and worry of it. Not to mention he's not crazy about the sight of blood.

I talked before of seeing and appreciating so much joy and gratitude after the initial shock wore off - and although that is still there, I also feel like I'm in a kind of stupor these days. Waiting, worrying, thinking, guessing, imagining and hoping. I feel like the grateful haze has worn away a little and now I'm just fighting to be positive every day. I am reminded frequently that we are lucky in so many ways. I have seen so many great and inspiring videos, for instance one the other day of a young person with no hands who was playing the guitar and the caption was how they were so inspiring...and don't get me wrong - they are. But that type of thing used to strike me so differently. Before I was in awe of that person who didn't let a disability get them down. Now I think, "Wow - good for them, but regardless if they play the guitar with no hands, or they don't, they still get to live." My perception of the world has changed quite a bit. I worry how Brian's has changed. He hasn't been able to communicate how this is affecting him emotionally too well. I'm not sure he knows even. I will be making more appointments with our social worker on our next visit in. I just want to make sure he has an outlet, other than me. Someone who won't cry. Someone who has been through this with other teenagers, someone who is trained. I hope it will help.

Well, I'm tired and fading quick. While he is napping, I think I will try to grab one too. Pray for rising counts. We need them!

Good afternoon from home. Leslie

MAY 30, 2013

Sent: Thursday, May 30, 2013 9:06 PM
From: Leslie Jermainne
To: My List
Subject: RE: Brian Ross Update 5/30

Hi Again!

It seems to have been a crazy day - Bri and I just finished putting window A/C in the bedrooms. This has been the story with that....so we have always cheaped out in NOT putting in central A/C. We were going to do split units back in January or February before it got warm, but SOMEBODY dragged his feet. Soooo...when all this cancer stuff came about, we felt it imperative to get a split unit for at least the bedrooms (primarily little Brian's room) to keep him comfortable for the summer. The reason we were finally going central is because last year his window unit, as well as ours got really moldy and gross even though I clean them constantly. Well, mold is a major issue for everyone, but for little Brian it could be almost deadly. So...Brian finally contracted with a company to do the units and last week on Tuesday, the day before we were to come home, he informed me that the A/C company would be at our house bright and early Thursday (8:30 early). I nearly fainted. One because we are exhausted when we leave the hospital and our first morning we would have workmen in the house and two because Brian can't be around any construction dust/

debris and/or mold. Big Brian felt it would be fine. I asked the doctors on Wed. at rounds and they were like "Uhhhh, NO!" So we had to put off the install. Well...now it's hot and Big Brian (and little Brian) aren't fans of HOT. I am, but....so - to make a long story longer....on our trip to Home Depot tonight to exchange a cabinet we purchased incorrectly, Big Brian picked up a tiny unit brand new, not moldy for Brian's room to keep him comfy for the next week until the central A/C gets in. AWWWW...what a great Dad. But of course that meant after getting back we had to install them all. Which will all be removed the end of next week. Still...little Brian is pretty psyched.

So there were a lot of other work errands, cleaning the pool, getting ready to go back to the Jimmy Fund Clinic visit tomorrow and maybe be admitted, only around 12:00 I get a call from our Nurse Practitioner saying that we wouldn't be admitted tomorrow, no way his counts will be good enough. And probably not early next week, but next Thursday is the new admit day. I was like "WHHAAATTT"!! Wait, I thought you all said how important it was to go again the minute his counts were up. Burkitt is so aggressive you can't give it a second to breathe. I understand if his counts tomorrow are too low, but wait until Thursday? Anyway...we'll get more info tomorrow. I know I have to relax and listen to these awesome doctors we have and they will explain more tomorrow and we will talk it through. It is just that when any little change happens it breaks free my very tight, white knuckled grip of imaginary control and freaks me out! Little Brian on the other hand is thrilled he gets another week home. We'll see tomorrow.

Ran into an old "new" friend when picking up food at Ideal Protein today. We have a new watcher added to the list. It again amazes me how much people care about us and what we are going through. Thank you Ellen! I haven't seen her in a while, and when I tell this new friend of our story, she starts to tear up. This amazes me, how touched people are by our fight. It certainly brings new meaning to "No One Fights Alone". Ain't that the truth! And yes, I am trying to get myself back on Ideal Protein for a bit, since lately I've been eating pretty much anything that isn't nailed down. I don't want to gain back what I worked to lose.

I again am amazed on all the donations for Stacy's bike ride. The generosity is overwhelming and the best part is the money raised is for cancer research - to help not just Brian, and maybe my Mom, but all others facing this fight today and unfortunately tomorrow, but I'm hoping someday there will be no more tomorrow for cancer. I still find it weird to say the word cancer in relation to my son. It was awful enough when my Mom was diagnosed with multiple myeloma over a year ago, but I know she would agree, this is way worse. I still find that I walk around repeating in my crazy head, "My son has cancer", like all of a sudden I will comprehend the fact and have complete understanding. I don't think that will ever come.

Last night I was trying to read a new trashy novel to go to sleep and I had a magazine on my night stand entitled "Spirituality and Health", which I read regularly and Love. While trying to read my new book, I kept glancing at the magazine until finally I decided that I must need to read something in there. I put down the book, opened the magazine to a random page, which landing on an article about Eckhart Tolle (who I've tried to read before, but seems to be beyond me). I read some words that I posted to my Facebook page today - which really resonated with me, and I knew I had read what I was meant to, and went to sleep for a nice sound 8 hours. Here is what I read: "Life is now. If you are always focused on the future, you miss the reality of now." This made me realize that I need to stop thinking about the thing I fear the most. Stop playing out the awfulness of it in my mind. How will I survive, what if I chose not to, what if I go crazy, what if, what if, what if. Every moment I play "what if" in my mind is a moment I lose today, with my baby boy, here fighting to survive. A moment of laughter, a moment of love, a moment of caring, a moment of anything today is so much better than a moment wasted on something I can't control. I must try to live every day, as we all should, appreciating to the best of our ability, what just this day has to offer us. Today offered me time to sit with my boy and play Splinter Cell while cozied up on his bed. It offered me the chance to hear his laughter, see his smile, give him hugs and exchange I Love You's. Today offered me the chance to talk with friends old and new. It offered me the chance to learn more about his care, arrange for delivery of supplies for next week. It offered me sunshine and warm temperatures, which I love. Today offered me the chance to see my Dad mow my lawn for me, take care of me, help me as he has always done through my life, and with that the smell of fresh cut grass, one of my favorites. Today offered my son a trip to the ice cream shop with his sister, texts and phone calls with friends, food, sleep, and sunshine. It offered us both time with our dogs and being silly. There is no one I love to be silly with, more than my son. Today was a good day. As most of them are, at least if you look for it. And tomorrow will take care of itself.

Tonight, I am stealing a line from my good friend Sarah, who delivered a wonderful care package for Brian yesterday from her and her husband and her sons, Brian's BFF Zack, to close my letter. Sarah is a kindred soul of mine and reminds me often of peace. So...

"Love and Light" from home

Leslie

June 2013

JUNE 1, 2013

Sent: Saturday, June 01, 2013 7:59 AM
From: Leslie Jermainne
To: My List
Subject: RE: Brian Ross Update 6/1

Hello:

I had planned on writing an email last night, but it didn't work out that way, even though I was up until 1:30 a.m. So...here is how our day went.

Up early and left the house at 8:00 to get to Boston for 12:00 p.m. Jimmy Fund Clinic Visit. We pretty much knew we wouldn't be admitted, but we brought our bag just in case. There was no traffic and we only had to make one pit stop so we arrive at 10:40 - a wee bit early. Oh well. Got his EMLA cream on his port (this numbs his skin so when they access his port – [read stick a 1" needle into it] - it doesn't hurt) which takes an hour to work. We went into the Yawkey Center Cafe and had a very early lunch, then to their gift shop to kill some time. We headed up to the clinic about 11:35 and by 11:45 we were already in, got accessed, blood drawn and met with N.P. Anna who we love. We went over the few things that have been an issue over the past 9 days when we were at home, nose bleeds, head pain lifting his head off the pillow or standing up, numbness in waist and feet, watering eyes. Went over the fact that he wasn't taking any anti-nausea meds for the last few days but took off his scopolamine patch that morning (which should have come off the day before). Brian was examined and all is good. Blood tests came back super fast while we were still in the exam room and his counts have shot up since Tues. blood draw. Great news!

We went over the fact however, that we wouldn't be going in that day because we are starting a new phase of the protocol, they want him to have a bit more rest, and they are going to review things over the weekend - and maybe we will go in a bit earlier than planned Thursday next week. We also started talking about what the next steps would be, which I know I wasn't ready to hear before this time. There is really only so much Brian and I can handle at one time. We feel like since we are starting round 4 and the final phase of the protocol that we are nearing the end, so...when are the next scans? What if stuff still shows up? Here is what we learned. Brian will go in Thursday (or maybe earlier) have another ultrasound at the sight under his right arm to make sure things still look clear. He will start chemo on Thursday, probably earlier than his normal 8pm start time, since he'll have no scan dye to clear first. This round takes 7 days to complete, with a lumbar puncture on days 2 and 7 - last time we were able to get out on day 6. Once we go home, we should be home for a minimum of 3 weeks, depending on his counts which could make it longer. Once his counts come up high enough he will go in for a PET scan. This will determine how to proceed. If nothing shows up at all, we do round 5 and then go to maintenance which means watching with breath held. If stuff still shows up on the scan, they need to determine if it is lymphoma cells, or the cells that are recovering in the area from his surgery spots. They explained these cells are very busy trying to heal, so therefore they attract the radioactive sugar that the cancer cells attract and can mask what is actually happening. In order to determine this, he will need more biopsy surgery to make sure. If that is the case, or if they are sure at that point that there are still lymphoma cells active, he will received additional higher dose chemo before getting round 5. Whew...a lot of info there!

Just letting that info into my radar at this point is a bit scary, but we need to know and have to deal with it. I just pray to God, that regardless if that scan shows anything that in the end it is all gone and he can go on to live a normal life. Of course there are scores of "late effects" that can happen, heart damage, lung damage, kidney damage, eye damage, other cancers (yup - you read that right), sterility, this bad thing, that bad thing, blah, blah, blah. I'm not going there yet - I know that stuff is out there, but when you have no other choice you just close your eyes, jump and pray you land upright. I know it's out there, but it is one step I can't get to just yet.

So anyway, back to yesterday. Clinic visit is good - we are feeling great! Jump in the car, get home by 4:15 - go roll back the pool cover so Brian can swim and it's completely cloudy. Run out with water sample - my fault, I turned down the chlorinator when it was so clean and beautiful. Come back with Shock - throw in the pool, go out to fill car with gas which is running on fumes and get Brian's water - he must drink a gallon a day - so he likes to have it bought in the gallon container so he knows each day how much he's had. Get back home with his giant ice tea from Starbucks too, throw the hose in the pool because it's low and do a backwash. He wants Burger King - out I go again, but while I'm taking his order, I notice his right pupil is VERY dilated and his left is normal. Hmmm.... Go get his dinner, come back and check again. Yup - his pupil is huge! Ok - here we go. What now? I page the pediatric oncologist fellow at Dana Farber, get a call back, review his eyes, that he has no other symptoms. No headache, no nausea, no impaired vision, nothing. We get off the phone so she can do some more research, calls back in a minute. We're going to the ER! Off we go to the hospital to get this evaluated. Dana Farber calls ahead, so they know we're coming. Get to ER - I go in to say he's in the car - go back to get him all masked up - in we go. There isn't anyone in the waiting room by the way - so I'm thrilled. I will skip the three hours of waiting and listening to a very belligerent older woman rant and swear and say horrible things to the staff, and tell you this... After a CT scan, which was fine, we all talked and decided it was a reaction to the Scopolamine patch. When you handle that stuff, you have to wash your hands immediately. Which we did that morning, and no, he didn't rub his eye once he handed it to me, but we both washed our hands. He had no other issues, so we all agreed that it was safe to go home. Off we went at 10:30 starving - hit Burger King - got home to our lonely dogs, wolfed down a hamburger - they took showers while I then suffered for eating too much, too late and let's face it, Burger King - hence the 1:30 bed time. I should know better! On the way home though my son figured it out. We couldn't believe we didn't think of this with all the talk about the patch. That morning, Brian removed the patch and handed it to me. It was a day late coming off. I threw it out, we both washed our hands - and headed out. Brian realized last night that he is sure he touched behind his ear where the patch came off, and then probably touched his eye - several times - since as I said they have been watering like crazy! OMG!! I'm sure this is it. So lesson learned? Wash behind your ear when you removed a scopolamine patch.

Oh ya, when I'm trying to get my food to digest, I'm in my PJ's, Brian comes out to the Living Room and says, "Are you doing laundry?" I look at him like "I don't know! Are you insane?" But he tells me the water pressure was really low while he was taking his shower. OH MY GOD!!! The hose I put in the pool...remember. I fly out the front door in my PJ's - actually not that rare for me, sorry neighbors, shut off the hose - run out back and I can't believe it but it didn't over flow. Close...but not quite. So...I wake up at 6:30 today and all I can think about is the G.D. Pool - out I go – it's still cloudy - I pump out tons of water and berate myself again for the cloudy water. I will deal with that soon. And just a note – our local pool care company are awesome people. Just sayin'.

So - that was our day. How was yours? People keep telling me, that our stories are helping them appreciate their lives and loved ones a bit more. And that makes me happy. I'm thinking this long story might have a few people say "why was I complaining about the heat yesterday? Or the long work week? Or the economy? When I could have had that day. I think I will look at today and be grateful I'm healthy (and I hope you all are), my family is healthy (I hope they all are), it's a sunny (maybe very warm day) but it will be a good one. By the way, yesterday by far, hasn't been our worst day. In the scheme of "How is your pain" charts that we see every day in the hospital - and Brian entertained me with his version yesterday - our day was a 2. Which is a tiny smile. I mean, it was long and at times concerning day - but overall - he is here, doing well, the sun is shining and warm - our friends and family are supporting us. So it was a 2 day.

I hope today you all have a 1 day - Big smiles!!!

Light and Love still from home!

Leslie

Sent: Saturday, June 01, 2013 8:19 AM
From: Sarah J.
To: Leslie Jermainne
Subject: RE: Brian Ross Update 6/1

Holy shit, Leslie. Really, just holy shit what a day. Laughing, kind of, about the pool...something I would do even with nothing big to distract me.

S

Sent: Saturday, June 01, 2013 8:37 AM
From: Leslie Jermainne
To: Sarah J.
Subject: RE: Brian Ross Update 6/1

I know! The thing that is bugging me the most is I don't know if he can swim in it like that, and he wants to so much. Will be calling doctor again for that question - they'll probably be like "Woman! Leave us alone!"

Have a "1" kind of day - now that his counts are back up - and depending on when we go back - maybe we can get that visit in after all!

Leslie

Sent: Saturday, June 01, 2013 8:46 PM
From: Rebecca B.
To: Leslie Jermainne
Subject: Re: Brian Ross Update 6/1

I was sharing Brian's thank you note with my mother today at lunch, and I couldn't stop crying. It wasn't because I know things look bleak, but because I know that things are going to be fine. It's just such a long, hot road to get there. I applaud your efforts, you are an amazing mother and woman, and I certainly stand in ovation for Brian's bravery.

G-d bless you and your family.

Love,
Rebecca

JUNE 2, 2013

Sent: Sunday, June 02, 2013 9:40 AM
From: Leslie Jermainne
To: Rebecca B.
Subject: RE: Brian Ross Update 6/1

Thank you Rebecca. You may cry over my words - but yours have the same effect on me. All the notes I get from our supporters, touch me deeply and reinforce my strength to care for our son. I too am very, very hopeful that he will live a long and full life. Thank you for your continued support and encouragement. Keep it coming...it keeps me going.

Love, Leslie

Sent: Sunday, June 02, 2013 10:02 AM
From: Leslie Jermainne
To: My List
Subject: RE: Brian Ross Update 6/2

Happy Sunny Day Everyone!

Isn't it beautiful out! So happy. What a great day we had yesterday. Certainly a turnaround from the day before. Yesterday was spent just living. Doing some simple errands, seeing progress be made on the multi-family property project of ours. Brian's girlfriend Christi got to visit for the whole afternoon. She and Brian went for a walk into town - watched a movie - even did a couple of quick errands with me and got frozen yogurt. All the stuff Brian should be doing. Then Christi's parents came down and we had a nice dinner and evening all visiting out on the patio. So much fun - such great friends. What a perfect day.

I did have a story I wanted to mention from Friday - but forgot with all the other stuff that ended up happening. So here it is: When I went to Stop and Shop to get Brian's water, I went to the checkout line where a young lady from drum corps was cashing people out. It was great to see her and get to say hi and report in on Brian and the good day we had just had at our Jimmy Fund Clinic visit. As she was finishing up with the lady in front of me - who seemed irritated, overwhelmed, dressed to the nines - with two big carts of supplies (down to her beach house I would guess?) Maddie asked her if she would like to donate a dollar to the Jimmy Fund. WHOA! Those words floated to me about as light as a ton of bricks! All those times I was asked that question and my answer was yes, at least 95% of the time, I never even gave it a thought. What was the Jimmy Fund? I mean I've heard of it, see ads, bought tons of these little $1.00 scratch off tickets they sell to raise money, but besides that I never gave it a thought. It didn't affect me. I didn't really need to know what they did there. They helped those poor kids fight cancer. I saw their bald little heads and sometimes sad, sometimes smiling eyes on the posters in the grocery store. But honestly, it didn't really affect me other than thinking "those poor kids". And now BAM!!! That is <u>MY</u> "poor kid". That is my son going to the Jimmy Fund so they can try to save his life. Those dollars are working to find a cure so he can live and be happy, and therefore so can we. Those people are there for us, night and day with questions about swimming in a cloudy pool, blown pupils, fevers, Tylenol for pain, what is the next steps, what if that happens, what if it doesn't? Those are the people who call me and say "How is Brian feeling today. Any pain? Any nausea? Is he going to the bathroom? And by the way, how are you? These are the people who talk with us, plan with us, care for us and give us hope. I now know exactly what the Jimmy Fund does. I know what those little faces on the posters look like up close on 6 North at Boston Children's Hospital. I hear the crying during treatments, the begging "no, no, no, no". I see the tired and sad faces of their parents. I also see the smiles these kids have when they have a good day, or get a stuffed animal or a t-shirt or a piece of pizza at the Friday night pizza party. I see the little guys playing in the play room, and the basket of toys outside the door every night that must be sanitized. I see the teenagers playing Xbox in the Teen room - and have been in there several times myself - even though I'll be 44 this month. I see the delight when they are packing up to go home and I feel their joy when we do the same thing. And this is all for a $1.00. Even if I go to Stop & Shop everyday (which often occurs for me), I could easily give $1.00 every day. I know not everyone is as fortunate as I am. I certainly don't expect everyone to give a $1.00, or to give a $1.00 each time they visit. But if you can, the next time you do visit, just do it once for Brian. I stood there that day and watched this woman say "NO!" kind of rudely. As she piled up her supplies for her vacation at the beach. I'm very grateful for all the other people who said yes, just one time. All those times I said yes, I'm pleased with myself. I didn't know what my dollar did back then, but I certainly do now. I could say I wish I didn't know, and a tiny part of me does wish I didn't know, but actually I'm again going to choose to be grateful that I know what an amazing place the Jimmy Fund Clinic in Boston is.

Yesterday was a "1" day - and I'm hoping for us and all of you it will be a "1" day too.

Thanks again to our landscapers. They are amazing friends, awesome and generous people - and they got so much work done at the house yesterday! Thanks guys!!!

Light and Love from home.

Leslie

Sent: Sunday, June 02, 2013 8:40 PM
From: Leslie Jermainne
To: My List
Subject: RE: Brian Ross Update 6/2

It was a "1" day!!! How about you all? First of all the weather was spectacular. Bri and I played Splinter Cell (new favorite instead of Call of Duty Zombies) then the day was spent doing simple things. Spreading some mulch, laundry, cooking dinner for my parents and Alison and enjoying it on the Patio - we even got some ice cream at Salem which is such a nice ride. That was something we used to do a few times every summer when Bri was littler. Then he didn't care to go anymore, so Big Brian and I would go once a summer. But tonight he wanted to go, and it was so nice.

Other than that, not much. It was a simple, happy, summer day. The kind of day that is now most important. A day to do a bunch of not much of anything with the people I love. So happy.

Love and Light and Love again too from home (for another day or two!)

Leslie

Sent: Sunday, June 02, 2013 9:01 PM
From: Sheila
To: Leslie Jermainne
Subject: Re: Brian Ross Update 6/2

It was a .75 day for me, almost a 1. Best part: Watching each of my kids have their BFF's over to the house, hearing them laugh together, and the friends not wanting it to end. What would have made it better, and this is what I have to remember, live in the moment instead of worrying about what has to get done, AND spending some "do nothing" time with Colin. Again, Leslie, thank you for reminding me what is truly important.

xoxo
Sheila

Sent: Sunday, June 02, 2013 9:14 PM
From: Sheila
To: Leslie Jermainne
Subject: Re: Brian Ross Update 6/2

Crying. The other day I was at Stop & Shop, and the cashier asked me if I wanted to donate to the Jimmy Fund, and I thought in my head, "Brian". And, of course, I always give the $1.00. Devin is a new cashier at Stop and Shop, and I asked him to remember Brian every time he asks for a donation to the Jimmy Fund.

The Jimmy Fund is something I always associate with the Boston Red Sox, so I have heard about it since the 70's. And I thank God that Brian is benefitting from this wonderful clinic in Boston.

God Bless.

Here is Brian's thank you letter to everyone who donated to Stacy's bike ride.

Thank you so much for your generous support of my Mom's friend (and my friend too) Stacy who is riding her bike 25 miles to raise money for cancer research. Since Stacy lives far away in Ohio, this has been her amazing way of helping me and my family while I fight against Burkitt Lymphoma. I am amazed by her generosity and by yours too. All these people who don't really know me, but maybe know my Mom and Dad or Stacy have taken the time to give such a generous gift not only to me, but to all people fighting cancer in the hopes that one day, no one will fight it again.

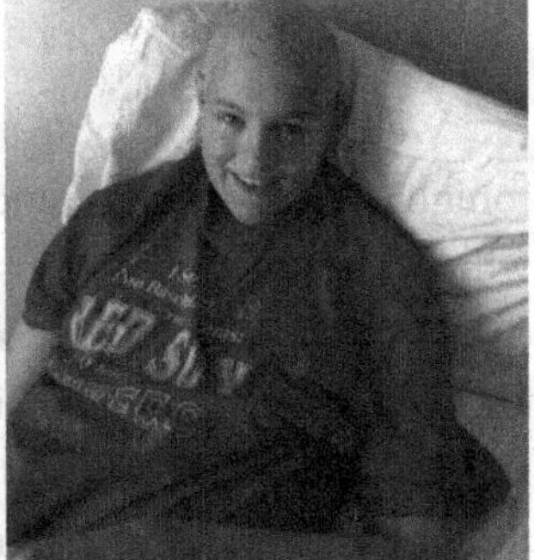

I am home right now recovering from round 3 of my chemo and will re-enter Dana Farber Cancer Institute and Boston Children's Hospital next Thursday 6/6/13 for Round 4. My Mom and I will be there for 7 days and if all goes well, we'll get to come home after day 7 for a 21 day recovery time. During that time, I sleep, a lot! I play video games and get to see my dogs, my Dad and my sister Abby. I get to have some other visitors too, if they are feeling well and haven't been around anyone sick. I'm lucky that it is summer and nice weather, because I can visit with people outdoors and go to outdoor events if I'm feeling up to it without wearing a mask. After Round 4, I hope to have only one more round to go before killing off all the cancer cells and getting into remission and being cured. The last five weeks have been such a shock to me and my family. I wasn't sick, I felt great, I just had a lump under my arm and five days later one appeared in my stomach. I had surgery to remove the lumps and then boom! - cancer. It has been a lot of learning, sitting and waiting, surgeries, blood draws and medicine - but overall I'm doing very well and plan to be completely healthy before the year even comes to an end.

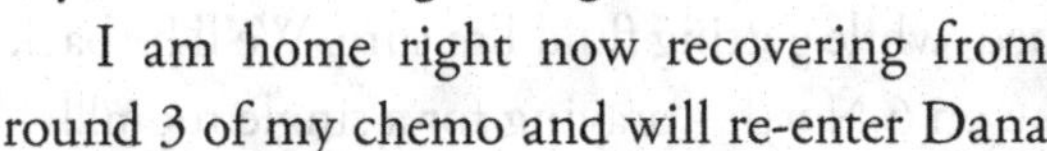

Thank you again for your generosity. I am deeply touched and incredibly grateful.

Sincerely,
Brian Ross Jermainne

JUNE 3, 2013

Sent: Monday, June 03, 2013 7:07 PM
From: Leslie Jermainne
To: My List
Subject: RE: Brian Ross Update 6/3

Hi All!

Well it's only 7 p.m., but I'm planning on getting to sit and relax tonight so I wanted to send a quick update. We found out today that we will be going back to Boston on Wednesday instead of Thursday. His counts are great and they are ready to get going. We'll start Wed. with a 10:15 ultrasound of his right underarm area. Then Jimmy Fund Clinic Visit at 11:30 and then wait for a bed, while getting fluid I'm sure. We'll be back to our home away from home on 6 North - praying for a single room!!!

Today Brian had a blood draw, so we'll get results tomorrow a.m. Also his right cheek is inflamed, and so we had to go see his primary care doctor under the advice of Anna our N.P. at Dana Farber. The thought is it is just irritated from the watery eyes, and wiping them all the time. After a 20 minute wait a CVS, they informed me they don't have the hydrocortisone cream Rx. Went to Walmart, who said they had it - waited another 30 min. and got half the Rx, which is fine - that will get us up to Boston. The clerk at Walmart told me to come back on Thursday for the other half. I said, "Don't fill it, we won't be back, we'll be at Dana Farber." She didn't understand. But I saw the pharmacists head fly up and look and me and she said, "Oh My God". Yup! You can say that again. The clerk said she didn't know how to bill the insurance if they didn't fill the other half. She was quite concerned. Thankfully the pharmacist just looked at me and said, "Just Go! I'll take care of it".

Back at CVS - I picked up tissues for Bri and his watery eyes. The guy who checked me out asked if I wanted to donate a $1.00 to ALS. I really don't know what that is, but I said of course! Thinking of the $1.00 JFC tickets at Stop & Shop. I didn't used to know what they were really for, but I will give. I sort of want to say "See God - I'm happily giving to them too - so give me a check mark to help Brian." Kinda weird I know.

Today I spent 2.5 hours cleaning out the multi-family before Brian even got up - I love it when it works out that way. 7:00 - 9:30 I got a ton of work done - but boy there is a lot to do. We'll do it though. Brian and I are a great team.

So for today, that's it. Tomorrow will be spent catching up on laundry, finishing up loose ends that need to be done before I'm gone for a week and getting one good last night's sleep. I love my bed, have I mentioned that before?

I hope you all have a good couple of days, and I don't expect to write again until we are settled in our new room on Wed. night. Please keep Brian in your thoughts and prayers. We are half way through this ordeal (I hope), but far from the finish line. We need your continued support, and prayers to God that my baby boy comes through this, intact and lives the long and joyful life I hope is in store for him. Thank you all, from the bottom of my Mother's heart.

Love and Light and well wishes from home.

Leslie

NOTE: I just feel like I have to note that every time I hear myself ask for prayers, I cry. I hear my voice of those days, begging God, the universe, our higher power to save my son. I feel like it sounds somewhat light hearted in the emails, but I hear it in my head the sadness, the pleading, the desperation, the heartbreak this time is bringing to me.

JUNE 5, 2013

Sent: Wednesday, June 05, 2013 8:51:06 PM
From: Leslie Jermainne
To: My List
Subject: Brian Ross Update 6/5

Hello!

Brian and I are back at Boston Children's Room 632B and hunkered down for the next 7 days. Before I get into our long day - here's a recap of yesterday. It was pretty stinky. I think Bri and I both had the "going back to the hospital blues". It was such a beautiful day, and yet I feel as though I didn't appreciate it. For some reason I was on the verge of tears if not crying on and off the whole day. I want to chalk it up to hormones or something, but I don't think that was the case. Was it just that we had been home for 13 days, and facing going back? Was it just a new burst of fear? I just don't know. I had a great phone call with Laurie who, listened to my fears and tears and encouraged me to feel whatever it was that was going on. I asked "What do you think I'm supposed to learn from all of this?" - My funny self says - "how many tears the human body can release?" But my sad self says "how much worry and heartache can a mother endure?" And my mad self says "how terrible can the world be?" Laurie had a different answer, which I can't get out of my mind. She asked if maybe Brian and I are the teachers, rather than the students. Hmmmm....interesting. I can't imagine such a noble thought. And I would gladly give up any claim to be able to teach anyone anything, if to just have my son have a long and happy life. I guess time is the only holder of truth.

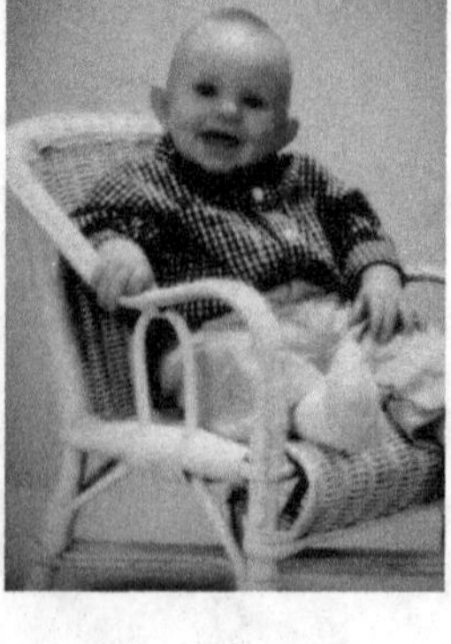

So, after an emotionally cruddy day, a night that ended at 4 a.m., an uneventful drive to Boston @ 6 a.m., a good ultrasound of his underarm area and abdominal area, easy port access, blood draw with good count results and a very long wait and fluid bolster at Jimmy fund Clinic, we finally got placed in our room, and I like it. We have the bigger side of the room - no roommate for at least

tonight - a different view - I have a wall I can lean on while sitting on my little bench, and a wider window sill, which must seem silly, but it my only "table" to put my stuff. I made a trip to CVS to get some snacks, water, and cream for coffee (they always seem to run out in the kitchen). Bri has settled in his bed, gotten his anti-nausea meds and is already getting his first chemo. 6 nights and 6 days left (already counting this one down). Brian got his bed extender installed, so he can stretch his long legs and we are good for the night. I've included a couple of photos this time...something different. There is one of Brian when he was an adorable baby, one of our room and one of our view. Nothing too exciting - except of course my handsome devil of a son. ;-) Well, that's about it from this tired old Mom Tonight.

Needing Love and Light in Room 632B. ~ Leslie

Sent: Wednesday, June 05, 2013 9:11 PM
From: Sheila
To: Leslie Jermainne
Subject: Re: Brian Ross Update 6/5

Funny your sister should say that, since I have known you I have learned many things from you: how to love a dog, how to set boundaries for teen girls, how to build a good fire, how to be a good neighbor, life is to be lived with gratefulness for what you are given, and remember that if you are lucky enough to have married your best friend, then you are so blessed; being a parent is one of the most important jobs you will ever have, AND love is the key to happiness. God bless you and Brian.

xoxo Sheila

Sent: Wednesday, June 05, 2013 10:07 PM
From: Sally
To: Leslie Jermainne
Subject: Re: Brian Ross Update 6/5

Hah! I love the pics, Leslie! It's really nice to be able to picture you and Brian in your temporary digs.

About the emotional day... when I have days/nights like that, which I do probably all too often, I have come to think of them as healing hours. When I'm on top of things and "happy", or upbeat, well... those are good times! That's great! But that's not when most of the healing happens, I think. Some happens then, but not the really hard stuff. Sadness, grief, anger, fear are all legitimate emotions that we need to feel and to come to grips with. I think that for some of us, tears are somehow part of that process. If those times just need to happen, then maybe we should be embracing them instead of regretting them, or hiding them away, or trying to forget about them. I don't want to forget the lessons I've learned during my dark hours. You know what I mean? I don't know. I'm not explaining myself very well tonight. Ah well...

Peace, Leslie. You and your family are always on my mind. The universe is full of positive thoughts and hopeful energy for all of you. I hope it continues to make itself known when you need it the most. And in between those times, too.

~ Sally

Sent: Wednesday, June 05, 2013 10:20 PM
From: Alison
To: Leslie Jermainne
Subject: Re: Brian Ross Update 6/5

I could tell you were not all that chipper when I talked to you earlier today....

I too think that you and Brian are in this world to teach the rest of us something we need to learn in this episode of our lives on earth, and it kills me that it has to bring you guys so much pain. I think you know that

I BELIEVE in reincarnation and learning various lessons until we attain the ultimate spiritual level that we strive towards. We choose our lives each time we are reincarnated based on what the people and events will bring to that particular life in order to learn or relearn a lesson, as the case may be. But I don't want to learn this lesson anymore that you and Brian are teaching....it's too painful.

The only solace I can get from this is that maybe you guys are so far advanced spiritually that you chose this to help me get to your level. But I still hate this lesson!

Lots of tears and wishes for a quick and hopefully uneventful week for you both. We love you and think about you every moment! Me, Carlo and Paisley.

June 6, 2013

Sent: Thursday, June 06, 2013 7:35 AM
From: Leslie Jermainne
To: A very select few….
Subject: What I can't say about BRJ outloud

This was supposed to go out last night (Wed), not sure why it didn't..... I really can't write the things I'm really feeling. I am desperate. I am so scared. I am sick with emotion. I am broken and fragile and so very tired. And I can only imagine how my son must feel. Yesterday was such a really fucking crappy day. I feel like I don't know why, yet I do. I don't know why I feel this horrible ominous feeling, but I do. The week before we found out that Brian had cancer, I was sick with worry and crying myself to sleep at night and I didn't know what was wrong with me. I was overreacting I kept telling myself. And then God Dammit, Mother Fucker, my son has cancer. Did I know? Somewhere deep down in my Mother instincts, did I know this horrible thing was coming? I guess that is what I think. And now I feel this same uncontrollable worry and sadness and it is scaring the ever living shit out of me. Please God, let this just be stress and fear, and not some sick foreboding. I can't take anymore right now. I just really, really can't.

I. Can't. Live. Without. Him. Do you understand that universe? I can't. And I don't want to. And I feel so selfish for even saying those words.

What about him? What about what he is going through? Yesterday in my stupid-ness, I went into his room and laid down with him, and even got a little teary and told him I was scared. I didn't tell him all the crazy shit I'm saying here, just that sometimes I get scared. I am such a fucking asshole! How could I do that to him? He asked me if I was hiding something from him. He asked me if it was worse than I was telling him. I reassured him that was not the case. I told him that it was "Mom worry". That I have worried about him that way for his entire life, which is completely true. He asked me again later if things were worse. I reassured him again, and again I am so mad at myself. It is hard not to share everything with him, because we have shared everything together. But I have to be stronger. I have to be better, for him.

I'm laying here on my little bed, typing this now while he sleeps and his pump ticks as it pumps poison into his body. Should I have looked for alternative medicines? Am I killing him by allowing this to happen? I feel so fucking helpless. I feel like we are trapped. Damned if you do and damned if you don't. And I pray. I pray all day. I beg and promise and barter and offer up my life about 27 times a day. I cry and think and beg and pray some more. I sign more papers giving consent to stick needles in his back, give him more poison, allow more people to listen to him, feel him, poke him and wake him. I am sick with guilt and fear.

I am amazed at my son and how he seems to be handling this. He seems so good. So well adjusted. So accepting. That too makes me afraid. Is he really dealing with this? Can he? Should he? Does he need to talk about it more? Would talking about it more scare him and upset him and do damage to him? Everyone is different and it seems when he talks about it, it upsets him. I don't mean the daily stuff. The "this is the medicine I'm getting today", or "what time is my lumbar puncture tomorrow?" or "my leg hurts, I have a headache, my face stings, my pupil is huge". That is some weird altered state of normal these days.

I don't even know what I'm saying anymore. I'm rambling and exhausted and I should be silently crying myself to sleep instead of going on and on about some strange sense of worry. All I can do is show up and love him. And keep doing that every minute. And I won't stop. I can't stop. It is part of the bargain. I will do anything...anything I can think of...anything asked of me...anything, as long as I don't lose him. I. will. do. ANYTHING.

Goodnight. And sorry for this.

Leslie

Sent: Thursday, June 06, 2013 9:04 AM
From: Laurie
To: Leslie Jermainne
Subject: Re: What I can't say about BRJ outloud

Les...you have nothing to be sorry for and a lot to be feeling blessed about...you have been given the gift of life, love, childbearing, marriage to your best friend, a beautiful, safe place to live, the love and comfort of your extended family, enough to eat, clean water to drink, challenges to solve... you are a beautiful human being who cares deeply, you are a child of the universe and are in touch with its mysteries...I believe we are all spheres of energy and I want you to think about your energy in relation to everything around you. Acknowledge it, protect it, interact with it, and attract all of the positive energy that is out there...YOU did nothing wrong, BRIAN did nothing wrong...perhaps, one day if you are so fortunate while you are here on earth, you will understand the reason, the lesson for all of this. In the meantime, use every ounce of positive energy you possess to love that little boy who is flesh of your flesh...well or ill...that's all any of us have and that is THE most important thing...LOVE...in that you are a champion... the rest is just an illusion...

Sent: Thursday, June 06, 2013 8:22 PM
From: Leslie Jermainne
To: My List
Subject: RE: Brian Ross Update 6/6

Hi Peeps!

Feeling better tonight. Not quite where I was before, but climbing my way out of the pothole I fell into two days ago. Walking through this new life, I got a bit too comfy, took my eyes off the road and fell. I got scraped up a bit, my knees and palms are a bit raw, but I'm standing up, I've dried the tears, wiped off the dirt and I'm walking ahead again, limping a little but keeping my eyes locked on the prize. No matter where this road leads us, I'm going to walk it and I will probably get distracted again by the beauty around me, and bump into something or fall down again, but I will get up and keep going, pulling the little red wagon with my son in it like when he was a little boy, and we will take this walk together.

Last night was not the best. After going to sleep late, Bri woke up with soaked clothes from sweating (the room was 73, so I'm hoping that is why, but relayed the info to his doctors – night sweats is a common question asked), then had a nose bleed. After getting cleaned up, he had a snack at about 2 a.m. since we learned at that time that his lumbar puncture wasn't going to be until 12:30 and he can't eat for 8 hrs. beforehand. He had some chips and water and then it was back to bed. I woke up at 5:30 - usual time, but lazed in bed until 6:10 - WHOA! Got the shower room, dressed, cup of coffee and emails, reading etc.

Rounds was informative. Learned a few things on how this week will go. Talked over all our little adventures at home (ER visit for blown pupil, Doc visit for face rash, bloody noses), and Bri was examined. Bri asked if they could possibly forgo the 4 a.m. vital check, and they agreed! How exciting!!! He is learning to advocate for himself too. I was proud. They agreed to draw blood and take vitals at 12:00 a.m. and then leave him be until 8:00 a.m. - I hope you understand how exciting this is for us. Plus, we still have no roommate, so let's hear it for some sleep!

Brian's lumbar puncture was right on time, and went well. Yes, they agree that he isn't the easiest back to get a needle into, but with the right drugs (propofol), and lots of positioning to get the best shot they can, it's all do-able. Only 3 more lumbar punctures to go, as long as everything stays the same. YA! Again, I didn't even cry when I kissed his bald head goodbye. I'm getting to be a pro.

After LP, we had lunch, then I took a nap, we had some visits from the resource room girls. Lots of good stuff. 1) We're going to have a therapy dog visit tomorrow, which is great. We miss our doggies. 2) He has been invited on a teen retreat at the end of June, for an overnight with other Teen cancer patients. Not sure he wants to do it, but it was nice to get the invite. 3) They have a program called Dec Your Room or something like that for inpatient kids, and they can fill out a form and things are brought in to decorate his room. 4) Bri had a quick Reiki session with one of his nurses, just after he got his next chemo meds started. He was nice and relaxed afterwards, was given a warm blanket and he is off in La-La land now. I love how well he is being cared for. Everyone is wonderful.

Also our social worker and friend Phoebe came in to JFC yesterday to see us, and then came back today. She has asked Brian to help her try out a new program they are working on with biofeedback. He is excited and interested as am I, and I think the idea of "helping her out" is even more exciting. Tomorrow they hope to have a session. Excited!

The next few days are just sitting around and waiting. The Cytarabine drug is a 24/hr 5 day infusion - he can of course walk around with his IV pole, so I hope to try and get him out of his room some. He needed a bit of extra anti-nausea meds today, but nothing too much and it did the job.

Here is another thing I've been wanting to pass along, that I know will seem a bit crazy, but just food for thought. Here it is: hand washing. Yup. Hand washing. I have learned a lot on the subject while being in the hospital and caring for someone with a suppressed immune system. So here's the thing. I've included a little info on hand washing(at the bottom of the page), but here is what I want to say....running water over your hands for about 4 seconds and drying them is NOT hand washing. Using soap and rubbing your hand together for 10 seconds and rinsing and drying is NOT hand washing. Both of those are just a waste of time. Hand washing is soap and water for 20 SECONDS minimum, front back and in between your fingers. EVERY TIME. Hand sanitizers are the next best thing as long as they have at least 60% alcohol. If you know Brian and I, you know we LOVE Purell. Just sayin'.

Anyway, I know this sounds immature or crazy, but to someone who can't fight off just regular old every day germs that most people take for granted, this is huge. If you go to the bathroom and think that you don't need to wash your hands, or that running some cold water over them for a nano-second is fine because you've never gotten sick from doing that before, well this isn't about you. This is about Brian. This is about Brian needing to use the restroom while we are out and about trying to have somewhat of a normal life. Brian has to drink 3 liters of water a day. That makes using the bathroom a real necessity. If he has to use the bathroom at Dunkin Donuts because he can't wait, and has to go in and touch the door knob, the flushing knob, the sink knob, the paper towel knob that have all been touched by people who ran their hands under water for 4 seconds and considered that good enough, he is in real trouble. Don't get me wrong, I know that is what goes on and Brian has always been diligent about washing his hands and using hand sanitizer, but now I've learned a lot. Now I think about all the other people on this floor, in this building, in this city, etc. that I could affect if I don't take 20 seconds after handling food, using the bathroom, picking up after my dogs, after coughing or blowing your nose. Of course, during this time, he doesn't go out and about much, and this is one of the reasons why. Something so simple, so healthful, so helpful to everyone. Okay, I never thought I'd write two paragraphs on hand washing ever in my life! I'm done.

Today I need to thank Laurie, Alison, Brian and Toni, my ever present entourage of cheerleaders who are getting me through the dark stuff. The cheerleader, the listener/rager, the hubby and the information supporter. Without you four I would be locked in the psych ward by now. I need all the stuff you all give me, so thank you. Thank you also to my Mom and Dad who wear their Team Brian shirts in support and who visited with my Mom's oncologist yesterday and got good information that I was glad to have reinforced about Burkitt. It never gets old to hear it is very curable.

So...thank you all for listening, responding, encouraging, praying and thinking about us. Please know how important that is to help us keep going.

Goodnight from Room 632B! Go wash your hands - kidding... kidding...

Leslie

When should you wash your hands?
Before, during, and after preparing food
Before eating food
Before and after caring for someone who is sick
Before and after treating a cut or wound
After using the toilet
After changing diapers or cleaning up a child who has used the toilet
After blowing your nose, coughing, or sneezing
After touching an animal or animal waste
After handling pet food or pet treats
After touching garbage

What is the right way to wash your hands?
Wet your hands with clean, running water (warm or cold) and apply soap.
Rub your hands together to make a lather and scrub them well; be sure to scrub the backs of your hands, between your fingers, and under your nails.
Continue rubbing your hands for at least 20 seconds. Need a timer? Hum the "Happy Birthday" song from beginning to end twice.
Rinse your hands well under running water.
Dry your hands using a clean towel or air dry them

What if I don't have soap and clean, running water?

Washing hands with soap and water is the best way to reduce the number of germs on them. If soap and water are not available, use an alcohol-based hand sanitizer that contains at least 60% alcohol. Alcohol-based hand sanitizers can quickly reduce the number of germs on hands in some situations, but sanitizers do **not** eliminate all types of germs.

Hand sanitizers are not as effective when hands are visibly dirty.

Rub the product over all surfaces of your hands and fingers until your hands are dry.

Sent: Thursday, June 06, 2013 10:17 PM
From: Alison
To: Leslie Jermainne
Subject: Re: Brian Ross Update 6/6

Good to know on the hand washing!!!! Of course I'm sitting here balling my eyes out, sniffing and blowing my nose every two seconds.... so my question is, can I wait until I'm done having my raging crying fit.... or should I get up and wash them after each nose blow???? Just kidding... my attempt at a little bit of humor. I will definitely do a better job than I have in the past, especially understanding better what Brian is up against.

Thank goodness you warned me about your real email, 'cause that was a real tear jerker....but I cannot say I was surprised. I knew this was going on in your head and I figured you would eventually let it out. And you need to do that, a lot. It will help you cope. Did you know that crying for women is how they release all those bad stress chemicals that build up in our bodies until they finally boil over? I don't know the exact terminology, but that's the gist of it. So when you need too, just send me a text....which can read FUCK! FUCK! FUCK!!! and I'll get it. I think swearing also releases the same bad chemicals we tend to build up...just sayin'.

So it looks like we will have Saturday off this weekend, and if you guys are feeling up for a visit, I'll plan on coming up. You can let me know later on if you think it's a good idea or not. If there is anything I can get or bring or whatever that would bring some cheer, let me know. I was going to stop by and see Brian, but to no avail - no car was visible, so I guess he was out working with clients or the new house....I will call him tomorrow and see how he is doing....

I am thinking of you all the time and wishing there was something more I could do to make things easier for you. But I know I can't. He is your son. The idea that you cannot make it better is maddening, that you don't have control over the situation is torture, and the fact that the world is still revolving with other people not knowing the pain you are in (like the bitch at Stop and Shop) is unimaginable. I know that going through this "kind" of thing with my cats is really not the same thing at all, but the same emotions are involved, at least for me since I never had my own children. And it hurts beyond belief when you cannot make them better, or take away their pain. So rail away at the sheer madness of this whole situation anytime you need to, or want to. I get it. I'm here...whatever I can do to help.

Sent: Thursday, June 06, 2013 10:42 PM
From: Leslie Jermainne
To: Alison
Subject: RE: Brian Ross Update 6/6

You can wait until all the nose blowing is done before washing. I know it was probably stupid to talk about it, but it was haunting me so I had to put it out there. You would think with all the tears I've shed and my truck driver mouth I'd be as relaxed as they come. I will pick up the pace on the swearing. Here you go:

Mother Fucker, God Damn Whore, Bitch, Mother Fucking No Good, Shit Fucker Piece of crap this no good fucking cancer can kiss my mother fucking ass!!! ***sniff, sniff*** I hate the God Damn fucker that has taken my life and turned it inside out and upside down and has threatened my son. I will kick its ever-loving, mother fucking ass if I ever get the chance that no good, mother fucking beast of a whore! How's that?

Ok, now I'm smiling. Bri would like this if he was awake.

I know how deeply you care for my son, who I feel is sort of like your son too. And no, it isn't the same with animals, but it's close. I know how difficult it has been for you with your "children". I get it. I used to think how hard it would be to have to put Jackie down someday, and it will be. But it doesn't compare to the thought of losing my precious baby boy. Ok, here come the tears. I know how much you love him and how much you love me. I will never forget the day that Brian and I finally got home from AZ that time we had to go for training for Realty Executives. You had been with Brian overnight, and we arrived at about 7 a.m., after traveling all night. I ran to the door and there was my baby boy in his PJ's with his big toothy smile and you right behind him. I was sobbing because I missed him so much. It had been torture to be away from him. It was physical pain. I scooped him into my arms and he kept asking why I was crying. I looked back and saw your tears at witnessing that kind of love and I saw that you understood. I think of that day often. I think about the sheer joy of seeing him, I can feel his little warm body in my arms and I can see your face. It is a happy memory for me. Somehow when I see people understand, truly and deeply understand how much I love this human being, it is like some weird kind of justification that no mother has ever loved their child like I love mine. That is how I truly feel. I'm assuming most mothers feel the same way as I do, but I think they are all lying. It is me. I'm the winner.

Anyway, I just want you to know that I know how much he is loved by you. And it makes me happy. Saturday visit would be wonderful. Toni and Christi might come on Sunday, but are unsure as of now. It is going to be a long week. Don't tell him, and I've only told Brian so far, but we won't be home on Tuesday. It will be Wednesday because of the timing of the drug administration. Damn it!!!!! I just found out at rounds today, but I asked them not to tell him now. It is too far away and he already wants to go home. He of course always knows that things can change, but if we get closer and then he finds out it will be one more night, I think he'll be able to take it better. If I tell him now, he has all that time to stew and think about it. So....having some distractions will be very helpful. I can't think of anything to bring....but will think on it.

Thank you for being Auntie Pal. We love you.

Les

JUNE 7, 2013

Sent: Friday, June 07, 2013 10:28 PM
From: Leslie Jermainne
To: My List
Subject: RE: Brian Ross Update 6/7

Hi Again,

Not much to say tonight. I guess the hand washing thing didn't go over so big. Only two people had anything to say. I feel better though. ;-)

It was a long and boring, rainy day. Not really much else to say. Brian is doing well. Having chemo, not feeling too many side effects. Thankfully.

Slept through the therapy dog visit time, so that didn't happen. Biofeedback didn't happen either. So it was a big day of nothing. Well, there is sadness, depression, loneliness and fear. But besides that....This darn rain isn't helping.

Tomorrow will be much, much better as Alison is coming for a visit. YAAAA!!!!! We are very much looking forward to this.

So, ummmm....that's it. I have no words of wisdom or even gratitude tonight. Ok, wait - I am grateful we are still enjoying our room with no roommate. So, there you go. A bright little spot in the day, or should I say night. Maybe tomorrow I will have something to share. For now I'm going with the "No News Is Good News" route.

Bored in room 632B, but loving my son is all I need.

Leslie

Rereading the above note of course takes me back to this day. This day had some other stuff in it. Some bad stuff. I realize that since I didn't want to share that stuff, the note was hard to write and therefore short. So, to my best recollection, here is what happened. Brian did sleep through the pet visit. While I was out in the hall trying to figure out what to do to cancel it, so he wouldn't be disturbed, I find Phoebe, our social worker. She is like my Mom in ways, while I'm here. I tell her Brian is sleeping and we won't be having the pet visit. She asks if I'm okay, I guess seeing something in my face. I burst into tears that I can't talk through. She is like "Oh my goodness, let's go find a room and talk". I finally calm down enough and tell her about this foreboding, terrible feelings I'm having. That I had them before he was diagnosed and they are back and freaking me out. That I'm afraid I'm like psychic or something and that I know something horrible is going to happen. And let's be honest, the only real horrible thing at this point is my son's death. She listens, accepts, validates, coaches and consoles. I feel so much better after our talk. She saves me from the brink once again. I know, as I know myself very well, that I couldn't share that info that day because it would be giving voice to the word death. It is a word I don't utter much. If I say it, it gives it power. So I monitor my speech, and try to monitor my thoughts. Every exhausting moment.

JUNE 8, 2013

Sent: Saturday, June 08, 2013 12:04 AM
From: Sally
To: Leslie Jermainne
Subject: Re: Brian Ross Update 6/7

Scotty and I went to see the new Star Trek movie tonight. When I used the bathroom, I counted to 20 while keeping my hands and fingers soapy, and thought about you and Brian up in Boston doing everything you can to kick cancer's ass. Ended up smiling at the mirror like a dope with soapy hands, observed by a gaggle of teenage girls. Glad they have no worries today.

:-) So there. ;-P

~ Sally

Sent: Saturday, June 08, 2013 4:44 PM
From: Leslie Jermainne
To: Sally
Subject: RE: Brian Ross Update 6/7

LOL! Thanks Sally - I can picture it, and it makes me smile. I'm glad they have no worries today too! I hope the movie was good and you both enjoyed yourself. Had a visit from my sister Alison today and really lifted me up. Very thankful to have so much great support from everyone. I was keeping a bit too much inside these past few days - gotta work on that.

Enjoy the sun! Leslie

Sent: Saturday, June 08, 2013 12:24 AM
From: Kim
To: Leslie Jermainne
Subject: In my prayers

You continue to be in my prayers daily. Thank you for your continued updates. What a marathon you are on! I can't believe how much you get done each day.

I understand the hand washing much better now, I just have to get a better song to sing, instead of happy birthday twice! I usually say a prayer, figure it can't hurt and takes the same amount of time. Now I will think of you, Brian, your mom and so many others when I wash my hands.

On the bright side,

1. The rain is washing away the pollen, 2. If you have to be stuck inside, better on a rainy day than a sunny one 3. Your time is well spent taking care of your child 4. You have another day.

Take care of you and your boy, but take care of yourself first and let the doctors and nurses do what they are trained to do.

Kim

Sent: Saturday, June 08, 2013 9:33 PM
From: Leslie Jermainne
To: My List
Subject: RE: Brian Ross Update 6/8

Hi Everyone,

How did it get to be June 8th already? How did we go from "normal" on April 17th (the day before biopsy surgery) to June 8th? Although it seems like an entire lifetime ago too. I've always heard people refer to certain times in their life as a "journey". I hate that saying. This isn't our journey, this is a freakin' nightmare. This is like riding Space Mountain at Disney World when I was 6. By the end of the ride I was on the floor of the ride car crying (safe, huh?) And my Mother was crying too. Only now, I ride it and ride it and ride it.

Anyway...how was today - busy, long, happy, fast, sad, stressful. Why? Well, I slept until just after 8 a.m. - very awesome. It wasn't great sleep, but 8 hours anyway. Awoke with massive headache. After sleeping so late, I couldn't get the shower room, so decided to just take a shower in our bathroom, since we didn't have a roomy. Went into the bathroom, 20 minutes later came out and we had a 2 year old roommate all moved in, complete with parents and newborn sibling. Both kids crying. OMG!!! However, by 2pm they were gone - thankfully. We are back to our peaceful, quiet, dark room.

Auntie Al came for a great visit and it was so good to see him perk up. He hasn't felt so good today, quite a bit of nausea and tiredness. Have all the anti-nausea stuff on board we can get. Has only had saltines today, and fruit punch. Also having some constipation issues, which are serious for cancer patients. We're working on that with meds too. After visiting with Al for a while, he was tired. We set him on the couch in the visitors' room, turned off the light and we went downstairs for lunch. He couldn't sleep in our room do to crying children. Lunch was great and being able to talk and share with Al, by myself, was very, very helpful. After a bit more time with Brian, Al headed out so Bri could rest before Toni and Christi arrived at 5:30. Only rest time didn't happen quite the way we'd hoped. He was so tired, but they decided it was time to clean the room from when the roommate had left. So his 2 1/2 hour nap, was cut back to about 45 min. It was worth it for him to see Christi though. When they left at 8:15, he practically collapsed from exhaustion. He did revive a bit after we cuddled and talked and I listened to him tell me all things he misses at home. His bed, his t.v., his dogs, his Dad, his sister, our street, our home town, sleeping...everything. Every day he likes to repeat in about as sad a voice as I can stand, "I want to go home", over and over. It breaks my heart every time and this goes on throughout the day.

Because of the 24 hr/5day Cytarabine infusion, he can no longer leave the 6th floor, until that is done. He did take two walks around the floor tonight with

Christi, but it is depressing to be unable to leave the floor. Anyway...we just have to live through it. I wish I could find something to entertain him. You would think we would be with all the stuff we have...but the days and the boredom seem endless.

I did hear from more people about the hand washing - every little bit helps. I guess that's about it. Thanks for the notes and phone calls friends. They keep me from feeling like we've been exiled to a foreign country, never to be able to return home again. They help...a lot.

Good night from a very quiet room 632B -Leslie

Sent: Saturday, June 08, 2013 11:42 PM
From: Toni
To: Leslie Jermainne
Subject: Re: Brian Ross Update 6/8

Pretty accurate metaphor. Wish the ride was over and you were firmly planted on the ground and safe from harm both real and that which creeps into your mind. The ride is horrible, and unpredictable, but when you need us, we will be with you to scare away the demons, or beat them off with bass drum sticks.

Toni

JUNE 9, 2013

Sent: Sunday, June 09, 2013 7:37 AM
From: Leslie Jermainne
To: Sarah J.
Subject: RE: Brian Ross Update 6/8

Thank you Sarah - if you can send me info on the pressure points that would be great. Do the reiki for Brian - he needs it. He is getting depressed and not caring. He hasn't showered in 4 days (which is somewhat due to 24 hr. infusion) and I'm working on how to make that happen today. He "doesn't feel himself", he "feels fake". I don't know what these words mean, and I can't get him to explain any better. He told me today when I asked about things, "I just don't care". I'm worried. My next note is to our social worker to tell her what I need of her tomorrow and to our N.P. for tomorrow's visit. I'm hoping today gets better. I was a long worry-filled night.

Leslie

Sent: Sunday, June 09, 2013 8:34 AM
From: Leslie Jermainne
To: Phoebe
Subject: Brian Jermainne

Hi Phoebe,

I am writing because I need two things and I know you can help me.

1.) I need you to forward this to our Nurse Practitioner Anna - I don't have her email or contact info, but I know you do. Here is what I need her and you to know:

I think I understand that Anna will be on rounds tomorrow (Monday) morning. Brian does not know yet that we will have to be staying Tues. night in order for the correct amount of time to pass before he can have his last L.P. and go home - Wednesday. I learned this info on rounds on Thurs., but asked that he not be told. He and therefore I, am having a very difficult time this visit. He is quickly becoming very depressed, which I'll get into in a bit. I couldn't bear to tell him there would be another night here and have him think about it for 7 days, instead opting for the news to come from Anna, who he really, really likes and trusts, and where it can be explained to him why this extra night. Brian also needs to get some real GREAT information, boost, whatever you want to call it. He is struggling and I'm very worried this morning. Brian needs some real reassurance tomorrow, maybe with some results on what is being seen (nothing much) on the ultrasound, that I think you are feeling that the cancer cells are about gone, that although we will do a PET scan in a little over a week or so, you are expecting to see nothing and then there will just be one more round of chemo and that's it! I know this is all subject to change and so does he, but he really needs his spirits to be lifted.

Here is what happened yesterday - He was pretty nauseous in the morning - had all the available drugs, which did help - but not enough to eat more than crackers and fruit punch (his call, not mine). His Aunt came to visit and he perked up and had a great time, but he got tired quickly and took a nap in the conference room as we had a very young roommate yesterday for a few hours, which was upsetting, but ended well for everyone, as they got to go home and we got our room back to quiet. My sister left at 3pm and he tried to nap but the room was being cleaned and then all kinds of people in and out, so he got about 45min. in before his girlfriend and her Mom came at 5:30. He was very tired, but happy to see her. However he just wasn't himself, nor had he been all day. This entire visit he just keeps repeating "I want to go home", about 20 times a day. He hasn't showered since Tues. night at home - although I've requested that Dr. W. give him that job as an assignment today to be completed by 2 pm. I'm not sure how that will work with the infusion, but something must work.

Anyway, after they left at 8:15, things went rapidly downhill. He was exhausted, pale, lethargic, sad and depressed. He finally got off my bed and got into PJs and got into bed, sad and dejected. He just talks of home, all the things he misses, how much he wants to leave. It's gonna kill him to find out he has to stay another night. He played on his computer a bit and then finally wanted to go to sleep, but he kept telling me he felt "terrible". "Not himself". "Fake". "Medical". "The worst I've ever felt". He said he thought the Cytarabine wasn't supposed to be as bad. That rounds 2 & 3 were supposed to be the hardest, but he's never felt so terrible. He can't seem to describe it so that I can understand, what is wrong. I understand nausea, I understand pain, I understand depression - but he can't seem to relay what is going on inside him. I'm very worried. I talked with the nurse, and we agreed to reinstate the 4 a.m. vitals, just in case something was brewing.

Upon waking very early today - just after 6 a.m. when C.A. came to check if there was urine....he said he felt a tiny bit better. But the sadness and depression has really set in. He again said he doesn't feel himself. That something is wrong. He tells me that it's just because we are here, but I'm unsure. He has dealt so much better the times before, why now? We are getting closer to the end. I asked him if he thought it was the Cytarabine, and he said "I don't care". That is what really concerns me. The not caring anymore, the not showering, not brushing his teeth, not eating. What do we do about this...just wait it out? Hope that getting home is the antidote? The thought of spending today, Monday, Tuesday and who knows until when on Wednesday here seems unbearable.

I feel like I no longer know how to console him. While typing this, he just asked me to come over and sit with him. He started crying. He hasn't cried since Saturday April 20th when we were having all the scary lectures at the first hospital and he thought he was going to die. He just repeats, "I want to go home". I'm scared. Maybe more than I should be, but that is all my mother in-law repeated when she was dying of cancer.

Is it the Cytarabine? Is there anything else to take? Is there something anti-depressant wise we should visit? I don't know, but something needs to be done to help him. I talked with his nurse just now and he wants to go to sleep, so we gave him .5 of Adavan to help.

So...I guess what I need is help for him. I need lots of good info tomorrow, I need Anna to explain why we have to stay. I'm hoping Anna can get the LP scheduled very first thing, like crack of dawn for Wed. (or as soon as it can be done) and someone can get us discharged at the earliest possible minute, as I feel it is crucial to get him home. I need to know if there is something we should be doing medically for this sudden onset depression, if it's normal, to tell him it's normal and talk to him about it - maybe some other coping mechanisms for him. Something....

Thank you,

Leslie Jermainne

Sent: Sunday, June 09, 2013 9:24 PM
From: Leslie Jermainne
To: My List
Subject: RE: Brian Ross Update 6/9

Hello,

Ummmm....last night didn't end so well, and this morning wasn't so great either. Things got better a bit late afternoon, but turned back to difficulty tonight. I don't really want to get into it. Brian is doing fine medically, dealing with the nausea and tiredness. He is dealing with the other stuff the best he can, but it is getting harder and harder. We just really, really need to get out of here and get home. Here is still great, everyone is wonderful, no complaints. It is just the being stuck here that is horrible. Brian is having a very hard time dealing with that. Also - it looks like we will not be coming home Tuesday as planned, but Wednesday at some point, I hope. This should all get cleared up tomorrow. That wasn't very good news to help Brian cope.

I'm holding on by a thread to my gratefulness. I had to do some advocating last night and today, which was well responded too - and a minor defending of my decisions, but that was even taken well. Like they keep telling me, they are the experts in cancer treatment, and I'm the expert on my child. They really do listen to me, and I'm grateful for that.

I also want to thank my best friend and husband for being there for me last night, listening to me, trying to comfort me and willing to come up here. I always know he's there for us, even if its 2 1/2 hours away, and I know it is painful for him to be unable to fix things for me and for Brian. But he's doing a great job of being my rock, my support, my partner. I love you Brian.

So, tonight I could really use some prayers for my son to be able to get through the next few days, so he can get home to recuperate physically and emotionally.

Wishing we were out of room 632.

Leslie

Sent: Sunday, June 09, 2013 9:55 PM
From: Brian W.
To: Leslie Jermainne
Subject: Re: Brian Ross Update 6/9

I am praying for you Leslie...to go home, to have strength, to cope and to rest. Thank you for the updates. You all are so strong.

Sent: Sunday, June 09, 2013 11:14 PM
From: Sheila
To: Leslie Jermainne
Subject: Re: Brian Ross Update 6/9

I keep thinking, you can do this, Brian! It will be over soon. Hang in there, both of you, we are praying.

Sent: Sunday, June 09, 2013 11:27 PM
From: Toni
To: Leslie Jermainne
Subject: Re: Brian Ross Update 6/9

Prayers. You got them.

Toni

Another story about Sunday I didn't tell in the daily email.

In the morning, one time that Brian was up using the bathroom, I decided I could quickly change his bed which hadn't been done for a day or more. I scooped up all the sheets and blanket, dumped them in the laundry bin outside our door and grabbed new linens from the cart down the hall. I came back and quickly made the bed and Brian climbed right back in. After an hour or so I asked him why he wasn't on his phone, maybe he could text a friend or something. He didn't know where it was he told me, and he didn't care. He didn't care about his iPhone. His ever present "friend" was missing and he didn't care. I started looking for it and after a long search, calling it several times, it finally dawned on me where it was. In the laundry bin. It had been in his bed, as usual, when I scooped up his sheets. I ran out the door to get his sheets out of the bin, but it was empty. Gone. I went to the nurse's desk and told them what happened. They called the laundry room and explained, gave them the phone number to the phone, and the worker said he'd try calling it and see if they could find it, but it was doubtful. This is Boston Children's Hospital. Do you know the amount of laundry they must have to deal with?

As I walked back down the hall mad at myself, scared to tell Bri, and praying they might find it I was also figuring how I would get him a new phone. When I got back to the room I informed him what I had done and waited for the repercussion. He said he didn't care, that it didn't matter. I promised I would buy him a new phone the next day, somehow, I begged him not to be mad at me. He wasn't. "It's fine." "It doesn't matter." "Phew!" I thought. And I treasured my safety for about 15 min. as I scoured the internet for the nearest AT&T store. Then it started to dawn on me. My teenage son, who slept with his phone, didn't care it was thrown out with the laundry. He didn't care if I got him a new one. He didn't care, at all, about anything it seemed. This is when I started to really panic about how he was feeling. I was so wrapped up in him not being mad at me, I didn't realize at first how important it was that he be mad at me. I started emailing people to help me and help him get through this time. I started getting super worried about his mental health and when I now reread my update late that night, I am brought right back to that room and my heart gets so heavy again. My voice in my head, reading my thoughts of that time, rings slow and low and exhausted, dejected and frightened. I feel like the life is being sucked out of my son, slowly, drip by drip, beep by beep and I am desperate about what to do. I didn't know the mental side of this disease was going to strike, secretly, when we were watching all the medical side. It is a learning curve, sharp and steep, every single day.

JUNE 10, 2013

Sent: Monday, June 10, 2013 8:10 AM
From: Leslie Jermainne
To: Dawne
Subject: RE: Brian Ross Update 6/9

Thanks for all your thoughts and prayers and hard work for us. This has been a very difficult week psychologically, but today we will be working with our great team to figure out how to best help Brian get through this. I am so thankful that we are here, with these wonderful people who are healing my son - and more than just his cancer. It is going to be a longer road than I guess I thought, but I was unable to see the whole path in the beginning - and there are still bends in the road I can't see around, but I will deal with them best I can when we get there. All our friends are certainly a great help - lining the road.

Have a good day!

Leslie

Sent: Monday, June 10, 2013 9:20 PM
From: Leslie Jermainne
To: My List
Subject: RE: Brian Ross Update 6/10

Hi!

What a difference 24 hours can make in life, huh? Today was so much better. It wasn't all roses and sunshine, but still - much better. Rounds went well and our N.P. Anna was here today, as was Dr. W. who was helping me and Brian over the weekend - make it through. We discussed that we will not be going home until Wednesday and Brian took it somewhat okay. We had a long visit in the morning with Phoebe our social worker and that really helped to process things and turn stuff around. She came back later in the day and spent about an hour with Brian doing biofeedback with a new computer they have. He did awesome!

We spent a lot of time talking and cuddling today, which is a big bonus for me. I tried to nap as did he, but we were pretty unsuccessful at that. Too much coming and going, housekeeping, vital taking, medicine giving, etc., etc., etc.

At 6:30-ish his last bag of Cytarabine was hung - so in 24 hours from then, the chemo will be done for this round, except the chemo given during the LP on Wed. We still don't know the schedule for that, but should know by tomorrow lunchtime. Once he is recovered from that (1-2 hours) we are outta here! The car will be packed and ready to roll. We won't be able to get home fast enough.

Next Tues. we will be back for our clinic visit, PET scan and CT Scan. This will be a very big day, as the tests will show if we finish the plan with round 5 of chemo in 3 weeks - or if we need to revisit some other meds and add a few rounds. Please God - let these cancer cells be gone and let us finish with round 5. Please let him live a long and happy life with as little long term side effects as possible. Please. Please. Please.

Ugh!

So, I feel like I gave been ungrateful this last week. So here are a few things I have been grateful for now that I have my 20/20 hindsight in focus. 1. We haven't had an overnight roommate. 2. Alison provided us with fun relief on Saturday 3. Toni and Christi made our day Saturday better with their visit 4. Phoebe really helped us turn a corner today with her interest and caring and support 5. My husband has been working like a crazy man (crazier than usual) at home to make everything nice for our return, and great at our investment property. 6. Abby and her friend are doing a fundraiser for cancer research and selling raffle tickets where they work. 7. All the people who have emailed, texted, message, and called me this week offering advice, support and encouragement. 8. Anna our NP has been a tremendous support and advocate in Brian's treatment and a real friend that we can talk to. 9. I have gotten a bit more sleep this visit. 10. And most importantly Brian seems to have turned the corner and come out of the shadow a bit and had returned somewhat to himself. His laughter, sounds even sweeter to his mother's ears.

Feeling Better in room 632.

Leslie

Sent: Monday, June 10, 2013 10:45 PM
From: Frank
To: Leslie Jermainne
Subject: RE: Brian Ross Update 6/10

Hey Leslie,

Sorry it's been a while, but I've been over busy dealing with work, my god parents estate, little league, and the year of backyard projects. I hate even telling you that I'm busy as I know you are longing for the days to get back to normal mundane tasks and chores. Boring and time consuming maybe, but not stressful as compared to the stuff you guys are going through. I remember sitting in the hospital rooms or even at home and going through every single one of my friends and family and think to myself that not one of them was in a situation that was worse or more serious ours. I would even hear the people talk about money or cars or school or wives, or girlfriends and just think – I wish life was back to being that easy and that we didn't have this monster black cloud looming over us. It wasn't spiteful or anything – just my way of having my own little private pity party.

You never have to worry about feeling ungrateful to this crowd. Everyone on this string is pulling for all of you and your family. We are all honored that you have chosen to share with us. We hang on every word of every email and pray that Brian is not too uncomfortable while he is plowing forward or that he is simply able to relax for a few minutes and forget about the insanity of the current situation. We are also reading to find out how our friend is coping. You are genuine and real with your recaps which I'm sure is nothing but positive for you. As I've said before, hearing you tell your story helps me reaffirm my own sanity.

Hang in there,
Frank

PS – I really got the hand washing. Did you ever wonder coming to our house why Anna put out paper towels in the bathroom for guests to use instead of towels. LOL. You never know who will be doing what – I try not to dwell on that stuff so you trudge forward doing the best you can to protect yourselves. You can get pretty ones with flowers or coastal scenes at Bed Bath and Beyond very cheap.

JUNE 11, 2013

Sent: Tuesday, June 11, 2013 8:36 PM
From: Leslie Jermainne
To: My List
Subject: RE: Brian Ross Update 6/11

WOOHOO!!

11.5 hours until lumbar puncture and then home! I am almost giddy right now. Anesthesiology just came for our pre-LP talk as usual. We have never been so happy to talk about Propofol, breathing, positioning, etc. Neither Brian or I could sign the consent fast enough (we are kinda pro's at it now), and it was confirmed he will be the first case in the morning at 8:30. So, so happy.

The rest of our day - well it was S...L....O.......W. But we made it. He finished his chemo med at about 7:00 and was able to be unhooked from the IV machine that he has been attached to non-stop for the last 6 days. Usually he had been unhooked for a bit for a shower. Usually he could take the IV pole with him to move around the hospital if he wanted, but none of that was allowed for the last 6 days. Plus...the pump this time is Huge! It is a big unit that barely fits in the teeny tiny bathroom in our room that he gets to use. So - he was unhooked, had a shower, change of sheets, clean PJ's and is relaxing, unhooked until a bit later when he will start fluids again to keep in hydrated overnight in preparation for the LP.

Today his mood was still pretty good. Not quite as good as we got to yesterday, but still way better than over the weekend. He is having headaches on and off, and nausea on and off, but everything is controlled with meds. We did discover, we think, that the Ativan was contributing to the sadness and crying over the weekend, so we've switched one of the anti-nausea meds to Marinol. Not sure if that is what is making the difference, but we're sticking with it.

I don't have to much more to report - I'm doing laundry, starting to gather up our stuff, thinking about the morning and how to get us on the road the quickest. I can hardly wait, it feels like Christmas Eve.

Bri still needs your prayers, but I'd like to add to the list of people needing them tonight. I heard today that the Dad of an old friend from high school is suffering with what I'm told is an inoperable brain tumor. So, please, for me - give them a positive thought for love and light tonight.

Best to you all from an excited, soon to be home from Room 632.

Leslie

Sent: Tuesday, June 11, 2013 9:41 PM
From: Alison
To: Leslie Jermainne
Subject: Re: Brian Ross Update 6/10

I can't wait for you guys to be home. Life just isn't the same when I know you are stuck up there and I cannot make you two feel better. This sucks the big one: truly, deeply, madly.....

I can hear his voice saying he wants to go home, and I can feel the madness that sets in when you are stuck somewhere you don't want to be and unable to do anything about it.

Carlo insists that things will get better. He has a "good feeling" about the outcome of all this. I am trusting his feeling and doubling it with my own. This experience has been a really tough one, but it will improve and it will get better. You will be home shortly with good news from the PET scan and a good long stay in the place that you love and where everyone loves you.

Good night from someplace missing you a lot!!!!!!

JUNE 12, 2013

Sent: Wednesday, June 12, 2013 8:53 PM
From: Robert
To: Leslie Jermainne
Subject: RE: Brian Ross Update 6/10

Leslie--Thank you for sending all your up-dates on Brian's care--Bob and I have read every word and cried and rejoiced with you. Bob's eyesight has gotten so poor that I read it to him and we feel like we are right there with you. Thank God for your sense of humor--that will get you through a lot. We are so sorry this is happening to Brian and your family--we can just pray for all of you. I love that you can still be grateful for little things--like no roommate and sleep!!! You mentioned that Abby was doing a fundraiser for cancer research--is there any way we can contribute to this or perhaps to the Jimmy Fund Clinic? Please let us know--we feel the need to help. Stay strong--you are amazing!!! Love to you, Brian and big Brian

JUNE 13, 2013

Sent: Thursday, June 13, 2013 3:30 PM
From: Leslie Jermainne
To: Robert
Subject: RE: Brian Ross Update 6/10

Hi!,

Thank you for your nice note and words encouragement. This last round was very difficult psychologically for Brian - and therefore me. We are so happy to be home, but even that takes a bit of adjusting. Next Tues. will be a very big day for us, as Brian will have his next PET scan and CT scan and this will determine if there is No Evidence of Disease, and we can finish our protocol as planned with round 5 of chemo, or if things have to be changed. I'm scared to death to go. No news is good news seems to be floating around in my head, which is stupid I know, but this is all just so overwhelming. I feel like if there is still evidence of Burkitt

Lymphoma then it will be like being re-diagnosed. Of course it isn't, but it feels that way.

I have included a link to a fundraiser that my very good friend Stacy Lightfoot is doing in honor of Brian. Stacy lives in Ohio now, but grew up with me in Old Lyme. We had lost touch for about 9 years after high school, but reconnected like we never missed a day about the time Brian was 1. I took Brian to visit her when he was almost 2, and she has been here to visit us several times. She too is a Realtor, in Ohio. Anyway, you can read her info and what she is doing to raise money for cancer research at the link. You can also donate directly to the Jimmy Fund. The Jimmy Fund is the children's clinic run by Dana Farber. This is the program that runs Brian's treatment, even though we stay at Boston Children's Hospital.

Thank you for thinking of us and encouraging me. It really, truly helps.

Love,
Les

Sent: Thursday, June 13, 2013 4:16 PM
From: Leslie Jermainne
To: My List
Subject: RE: Brian Ross Update 6/13

Hi!

You probably just got my email from Tues. night...sorry about that. I don't know what I do wrong sometimes - I'm supposed to be the "techy" one. Oh well.

So, yesterday went very well. We got the first spot for Brian's lumbar puncture. It always seems funny when they give him a little "relaxing" medication before going in. The push that through his line, and I'm not kidding, in 30 seconds he giggles and has a big smile on his face. I think I could use some of that stuff sometimes. After a kiss on his bald head, he was off, I went to the waiting room where all the other anxious parents sit and wait for a variety of reasons. I still have the urge to say "my son has cancer", like it is the trump card to win the "who has it the worst" game.

Believe me, I don't have it the worst. I've seen a lot of kids and families dealing with all sorts of issues, and again - there are many times when I'm in the hall, the elevator, the waiting room and think - boy are we lucky.

After the LP - it was back to our room - finish packing, get him some food and wait. Luckily discharge didn't take too long and we left about 12 pm. I had already loaded the car with a bunch of stuff at 6 a.m. - so we carried out last bags out and hit the road. After a few pit stops we got home about 4pm, Bri took a shower and got into bed. I got things organized, vacuumed the pool, threw out the rotten food and rotten flowers, and waited for my hubby to get home for a big glass of wine. The new air conditioning system is great, and Brian will have a healthy (mold free) and comfy room this summer - as will we.

Today so far has been a lot of sleeping and resting for Bri who is very tired. He has a neck ache and wanted to go the chiropractor. This requires a call to his oncologist who said nope! When I told Big Brian, it again hits home how invasive this whole thing is. We must check with his oncologist to do anything. Have a friend over - call. Have a headache - call. Want to go the chiropractor - call. Want your dog to sleep with you - call. Want to know if one pupil should be completely dilated - call. Every. Little. Thing. This is intense. It isn't just stay away from sick people. It's don't eat fruit and veg that comes out of the ground without scrubbing them to death. Be outside if interacting with others. Wear a mask. What's your temperature? Did you poop? What was it like? It is so invasive.

Over the weekend when things got very difficult for Brian to be in the hospital, Dr. W. explained to me that this teenage age group has the most difficult time with a cancer diagnosis. These kids are just getting some real independence. They are trying to find their own way and slowly part from their parents. They are beginning to make their own decisions and plans for life. Then all of a sudden you have cancer and you are forced to be like a 7 year old again, with Mommy doing everything for you. The doctors and adults telling you where to be, what to do, asking you if you have pain, can you touch your chin to your chest, if you pooped (yes, that's a big one), if you can move your legs okay. Two to three doctors all at once, during rounds, are poking your belly, lifting your legs, make you take deep breathes and listen to your lungs and your belly. This poor kids wants to be just that...a kid. Plus teenagers are concerned about their looks, their hair, how they smell, the acne, their clothes. This is important stuff. And now all of a sudden you are living in your pajamas, you can't take a shower because you have a port line that branches off into three other lines, all with some sort of fluid running into you. Saline, chemo, anti-nausea meds. And this last time you couldn't even get unhooked and all wrapped in plastic to have a five minute shower in this teeny bathroom. Every time you have to pee, you have to do it in a urinal bottle so someone can sample it, count it, record it. Record what you have eaten and what you have drank all day. You live in a white, cold, sterile feeling hospital room, with people in and out to take your vitals, empty your garbage, clean your bathroom and bang a mop around to clean the floor. And if you have a roommate - it is a fate worse than just about anything else, and believe me, your roommate isn't so happy you're there either. Your acne explodes thanks to prednisone and your moods go crazy. And meanwhile, just in case you forgot, you are fighting for your life. All those things you thought about doing being a teenager...dating...driving...working... graduating...college...marriage....kids....all that might, never happen. And you have no G.D. control over anything! Hmmm...I wonder why he was feeling so depressed this weekend? And we haven't even gotten to the long term effects of the poison they call "therapy". Chemotherapy.

Okay - enough whining. Let's have something to be grateful for, shall we? Today I'm grateful to be sitting at my kitchen table, with my doggies snoozing in their little beds, my son napping in his bed, I hear my husband's voice on the phone in his office and tonight I get to cook dinner in my kitchen for my family. I will get to sleep in my big, comfy, bed with no one coming in to change a fluid bag, check for full urinals or rip open the Velcro on a blood pressure cuff. I will get to wake up and have coffee made in my French press, take a shower where I don't have to balance my travel size shampoo on the edge of the tub and I can cook myself two eggs, instead of eating cold ones delivered 45 min. after I order them. It will be a good night, and another good morning tomorrow, just like today was because we are home and my baby is with me.

If anyone cares to send me a note with just one thing you are grateful for...and it can't have anything to do with me or Brian. Something ordinary. Something that takes you a minute or two to come up with. Something that without me asking, you wouldn't be conscious of being grateful for. Those are the things....

Until tomorrow from home.

Leslie

Sent: Thursday, June 13, 2013 4:32 PM
From: Sarah J.
To: Leslie Jermainne
Subject: RE: Brian Ross Update 6/13

I feel grateful a lot. But here is something I became aware of just now....I am grateful for the rain. It is filling up my pond and my shallow well. It is soaking the roots of my newly planted fruit trees. It even sounds beautiful coming down and as the cars go by on the wet road. It gave me an excuse to put my feet up and have a cup of tea :-)

Sent: Thursday, June 13, 2013 5:21 PM
From: Sheila
To: Leslie Jermainne
Subject: Re: Brian Ross Update 6/13

I am grateful for my job today, and the privilege to be an educator.

Sent: Thursday, June 13, 2013 5:24 PM
From: Lorna
To: Leslie Jermainne
Subject: Re: Brian Ross Update 6/13

Hi Leslie

Glad you're home. I'm grateful for our wee rescue cat Molly, who is a real cutie and loves sitting on my knee (which is where she is just now) and cuddling up to me. I had a duvet day yesterday, with her snuggled in, as we've had dad's path results and it's confirmed he has pancreatic cancer with involved nodes. Not brilliant news, but they are confident that they have removed all the disease, and it's way better than it being mets from his stomach cancer. He is very upbeat about it all and has made an amazing recovery from his op. I'm grateful for that too.

Sending prayers that the chemo is doing its job for Brian.

Love Lorna x

Sent: Thursday, June 13, 2013 8:50 PM
From: Toni
To: Leslie Jermainne
Subject: Re: Brian Ross Update 6/13

I am grateful to have beaten cancer twice. I am grateful for friends and family who love me, and I love back. I am grateful for my children who are the center of my universe. I am grateful for my crappy job and the roof over my head, Dunkin Donuts Coffee and WINE with my friend:)

Toni

JUNE 14, 2013

Sent: Friday, June 14, 2013 8:55 AM
From: Laurie
To: Leslie Jermainne
Subject: Re: Brian Ross Update 6/13

I am grateful for waking up early (naturally) each morning and seeing the sunrise....the promise of a new day filled with the unknown...

Sent: Friday, June 14, 2013 10:48 AM
From: Brenda
To: Leslie Jermainne
Subject: RE: Brian Ross Update 6/13

He Leslie - first, I cannot let this opportunity slip by without telling you how thankful I am that you and Brian are our friends. I know you didn't want it to have anything to do with you or Brian, but just wanted to let you know how blessed we are that you and Brian are our friends.

The other thing I am thankful for is that we have our front porch to watch the sunset and tell each other that we love each other and still consider ourselves very lucky to have each other in our lives. Regardless of all the health issues over the past two years, we are still very thankful that we have each other.

Last thing (I promise) is knowing that when you "pay it forward" with small acts of kindness towards other people, it has a real impact on their lives and encourages them to "pay it forward". This has happened in my life so many times, and at the end of the day, you understand the impact of your small act of kindness and the happiness it has brought to others, which makes me very happy.

Take care and I hope you have a great weekend. Love you!!

Sent: Friday, June 14, 2013 5:25 PM
From: Leslie Jermainne
To: Brenda
Subject: RE: Brian Ross Update 6/13

You win Brenda! The best gratitude note I got back. And I can't agree more about the pay it forward. I so believe in that. I try to help someone in some little way anytime I can. So many times in the hospital I have helped someone with the elevator, or where they are going, or even the act of holding the door. I always get asked in Stop and Shop to reach stuff off the top shelf - because I'm so tall. I love that one. Have you heard about the study "they" did that says that not only does the person helping, and the person being helped benefit from an act of kindness, but a simple observer of the act benefits too. Everyone benefits from an act of kindness - I like to think our collective consciousness feels it too.

I'm happy you have your front porch - I can picture you two there, ending another day with each other and being in love. What a glorious picture.

I too am happy to have you two as our dear friends. I feel blessed to be traveling the road together. The road to health, and just the road of life.

Love you Both!!!

Leslie

JUNE 15, 2013

Sent: Saturday, June 15, 2013 7:15 AM
From: Leslie Jermainne
To: My List
Subject: RE: Brian Ross Update 6/15

What a beautiful morning!

I get to sit here at my kitchen table, drinking my favorite coffee, with my doggie laying asleep in her bed on the table (don't judge me...she sits on the table), feeling the cool morning air coming in the window, looking at the flowers in my garden and the sun creeping its way across my lawn. My son is asleep in his bed, safe in our home. It is a good morning. It should be a great day with Christi coming for a visit with him - the pool is clean and balanced (not sure they'll use it but still...).

Yesterday was a good day too. A quiet, resting day for Bri. I did detect a slight bump up in his energy. Last night Auntie Al came for dinner and a trip to Salem ice cream at Bri's request and we had a lot of fun and laughs. We also talked with Brian's wish granters from Make-A-Wish. I'm so excited that they will be coming next Wednesday to meet Brian and talk with him about what his wish might be. It really does give him something to think about and look forward to. I had a nice visit with my parents and we plan to have them and Brian's Dad to our house on Sunday for a Father's Day Dinner. Looking forward to it.

So that's about it. I did get several replies to my "what are you grateful for" request. They were all great.

I hope you all have a great day - try to do a little bit of nothing but savoring the moment. I'm gonna try to squeeze some of that in too.

Love and Light from home, Leslie

JUNE 18, 2013

Sent: Tuesday, June 18, 2013 5:23 AM
From: Leslie Jermainne
To: My List
Subject: RE: Brian Ross Update 6/18

I've been lying here in the dark since 4:30. It's about time to get up and get ready to leave at 6:15 for Boston. Today is a big day as you all know. So...I'm asking for extra prayers today for us. I'm praying to have a clear PET and CT scan and hear there is no evidence of disease. Next to hearing "will you marry me", and "you're pregnant", hearing the cancer cells are gone will be the sweetest words. Actually, the sweetest.

I will do my best to send out an update tonight when we get back. Thank you all for your never ending support. Keep it coming. We need it and we need all of you.

Wishing for a super day from home.

Leslie Jermainne

Sent: Tuesday, June 18, 2013 9:19 AM
From: Hoyt
To: Leslie Jermainne
Subject: RE: Brian Ross Update 6/18

Leslie,

We all hope and pray that you all receive good news. Got to have faith. He has made great progress and will continue to. Cross each bridge as you come to it and try to not let your fears take hold. As a team you will help him climb each hill that is placed before him. I know these are clichés, and easy to say, and hard to do but as a Marine who has been in combat I had to compartmentalize my fears so that they would not control me and then focus on my mission. In this case we have only one mission and that is to help him beat the cancer no matter how long it takes or hard it gets. Brian could not ask for a more loving and devoted mother and father. Young

Brian will not quit because he knows his Mom and Dad WILL NEVER QUIT and knowing this will help him stay strong and determined.

I send my best.

Your friend,

Hoyt

Sent: Tuesday, June 18, 2013 9:44 PM
From: Leslie Jermainne
To: My List
Subject: RE: Brian Ross Update 6/18-new update

What a very, very long day. We left the house at 6:15 this morning and returned about 8:50 tonight. Here is as brief a summary as I can. Got to Jimmy Fund Clinic on time 10:15, had his port accessed, blood drawn, then down to Nuclear Medicine for PET scan and CT scan. Lots of time waiting and a bit of arguing with tech over his power port, but in the end all went well. 45 min lunch break at 1:30 then onto appointment with Doctor (oncologist) and Anna our favorite Nurse Practitioner. Here is what we learned today...

We aren't ever going to get NED (no evidence of disease) as an official marker of where we are. Many types of lymphomas don't work that way. What they told us today is this - they are very happy with what they see on the preliminary results for today and all previous scans. The only thing they see "lighting up" is under his arm and they are VERY confident it is from the biopsy and not lymphoma cells at this point. They are 100% sure that the site in his abdomen that is still lighting up slightly is from the removal of the tumor there. All indications and putting all the data together by all the experts says that there is no need for additional rounds of chemo. We are to go onto to complete the protocol as designed with round 5 being our last round. Then we will continue to watch and scan. Once we reach two years, he will be considered "cured".

So - why aren't I jumping up and down for joy? Well, that wasn't what I really wanted to hear. I wanted to hear, "it's all gone!!!" 100% guaranteed gone. "He is safe and perfect and wonderful". And now I know I will never,

ever hear those words. "Our best judgment". "Every indication is that it's gone". "All the signs show". All the signs? All the God Damn signs???? This is my child's life! I don't want "signs" or "judgments". I want guarantees. But I guess that is asking too much. I trust these doctors, this hospital. I really and truly do. But that's all I have to go on, and that concerns me.

We talked only briefly about relapse and this is the scariest part. If there is a relapse, Burkitt is very, very difficult to beat. The prognosis would not be good. Oh my God! I mean, I knew this...sort of. But here we are, facing the "what if's". What if it relapses? Then what. I can't swallow just thinking about it. And I know, I know....here come the... "don't think about it. Everything will be fine. Dr. this person, or my neighbor, or my friend, or my daughter says he's going to be fine". These are the things I hear, and I want to believe and I try to believe, but none of these people know. Our own oncologists don't know. I don't know and Brian doesn't know and yet we have to just plow through the next two years of scans and pray every single time that it will be okay, forever and ever okay.

I love all the support and well wishes and the thinking and praying for us. But nobody knows. And that sucks. Deep down hurts me kind of sucks. And he is tired and scared and asked me on the way home if he was going to die. And I have to say no, I don't believe you will die from Burkitt Lymphoma. And he tells me he doesn't think so either. He reassures me. Inside I am screaming... "I don't know if you will die from this. If you die, I will die." But I can't say any of that. And I can't believe any of it. And I can't really let myself even think any of that. Because it strangles me.

Then, to top off the day - the traffic thanks to the weather, a Red Sox home game and leaving the city at 4:30 was insane! I mean crazy, off the wall insane. It took us over 4 hours to get home. It took us 40 minutes just to get out of the parking garage! I'm exhausted and so is he. So it is probably best I call it a night.

Oh, the other thing is, instead of getting three weeks at home, we will only get two - we'll be going back for round 5 on Tues or Wed of next week. That certainly isn't helping either of our psychological states today. And please...I know it just means we'll be done sooner, home sooner and we're trying to concentrate on that, but it is hard when someone tells you that your three week "vacation" has been cut to two (after only one week) and by vacation I mean recovering from exhaustion, while your body battles poison and oh ya, by the way...his counts are the lowest they have ever been. Still not transfusion low, so that's good, but low. Luckily he is feeling "well".

Hopefully tomorrow will be a brighter day - we have Make-A-Wish coming at 5pm and then we will be driving off to Christi's graduation (Brian's GF). Today wasn't a bad day by the way. I feel like I'm saying it was, and it wasn't. It just didn't live up to my hopes of what I wanted. But I guess I should be and I am grateful that we are not adding extra rounds of chemo. I really did get what we wanted which was onto round 5. I just wanted more definitive results. So....I'm rambling and I should go to bed.

Goodnight all and thank you for all the extra prayers today - they did work!

Yawning from home.

Leslie

Sent: Tuesday, June 18, 2013 10:28 PM
From: Toni
To: Leslie Jermainne
Subject: Sending from work

I am so sorry today was not what you, we all wished for. It's another cancer mind fuck. My doctors never used the words NED or cured. I, to this day get checked every 6 months, and it sucks. It's not the life we had before cancer, we don't have that sense of confidence and there is a distrust in our bodies that won't ever fully go away, but in a way it's good. It keeps us vigilant and aware.

But I promise you, there will come a day when you lay your head on your pillow, and cancer won't have crossed your mind. It will happen.

Terms are what they are but even NED just means no evidence of disease. It doesn't give us a guarantee. It's just an easy definition for those who have not been down the cancer road. There are still treatments and scans, but we get to live. I am so sorry that Bri has to deal with this shit. It's just wrong, and I know your heart breaks at the "what ifs". But try to hold on to the good news, and keep on fighting.

Lots of love, and with you for the long haul.

Toni

Sent: Tuesday, June 18, 2013 10:28 PM
From: Sheila
To: Leslie Jermainne
Subject: Re: Brian Ross Update 6/18-new update

Leslie, it is perfectly ok for you to ramble but more importantly it is okay to be disappointed, angry and scared. I am so glad you are writing about it because I hope it is therapeutic. Because I just have thought every day since this nightmare began that it just sucks for you and your family, but it really sucks for little Brian. At the same time, I am amazed at your strength, little Brian's strength, and the grace with which you are handling this crisis.

All that being said, I am happy to hear that Brian just has one last round of chemo. I hope after that, you guys can get back to your summer and enjoying your life and doing a lot of nothing.

I am praying hard for Brian to beat this lymphoma and for you, a peaceful sleep tonight.

God bless, Sheila

Sent: Tuesday, June 18, 2013 11:04 PM
From: Frank
To: Leslie Jermainne
Subject: RE: Brian Ross Update 6/18-new update

Leslie –

Way to go Brian!!! This was great news. Maybe the best you will get. Not that you should expect bad news, but - unfortunately they will never tell you what you really, really want to hear, and for that I'm sorry. But I do envy your strength and support for little Brian - you have the tough conversations and can provide the re-assurance for him that the doctors will never provide for you - in my mind, this is the most important part of your role.

With remission on your doorstep - you hinted about the next two years. I can confirm they are tough. Just as you should feel elated with a clean scan - ... every scan, test, blood draw, runny nose, or tummy ache will bring you right back to guard duty and the "what ifs?" Remember to stay positive - not ignorant - just positive. I've learned to be a big believer in the conceptual thinking that nothing is wrong until it is wrong. Not sure if that makes sense, but it helped to alleviate a whole lot of my brain from running around in circles.

This is good news overall, though I understand why you are not elated.

Positive vibes still flowing towards you guys from our house, Frank

JUNE 19, 2013

Sent: Wednesday, June 19, 2013 8:33 AM
From: Sarah J.
To: Leslie Jermainne
Subject: RE: Brian Ross Update 6/18-new update

Leslie,

Just the 40 min getting out of the garage sounds like hell! I am so happy for Brian about what is probably the best news you could have gotten!!!!!!!!!! AND I get the part about wanting guarantees. The 100%s, the all clear forevers. The uncertainty of all of life, the fragility of it, takes my breath away sometimes and fear gets a foothold, or a stranglehold. Uncertainty really is our human reality and at the root of so much coping/compensation/addiction/ And here it is in your face having to do with your greatest vulnerability. And you guys have to be deep down exhausted from this chemo marathon. You are so brave. People will say well meaning things that may tweak you while you are experiencing this. They want to be certain too! I think we all desperately want certainty. OK enough of my babble. I hope today is easy on your heart and soul. Sending love and light and prayers for replenishment and soothing of the places that hurt.

Sarah

JUNE 20, 2013

Sent: Thursday, June 20, 2013 8:33 AM
From: Leslie Jermainne
To: Brenda
Subject: RE: Update?

Sorry Brenda - it was a busy day yesterday - did you not get the 6/18 update? Sometimes it seems people get dropped off the list and I have no idea why.

Anyway, yesterday started out tough, but ended up much better. He awoke depressed, into the "why me's", "no one understands" kind of thoughts. It took a while, some talking, some food, some alone time, but he did pull out. We had an okay day, and then at 5pm the Make-A-Wish wish granters came. Things were great. They brought him a little gift and we filled out the paperwork. He wished to go to Pompeii Italy as he is an Ancient history buff. They said they saw no reason why it wouldn't be approved! Wow! He is very happy. I hope it all works out. We might be able to go this fall even...

Then after that we zoomed up to Montville for his girlfriend's 8th grade graduation. They are in drum corps together and if he'd been in public school they'd be a year apart - just saying because most people look at him and say "8th grade!!" Yes, she's 13 and he's 15, but school age wise they are only a year apart. Anyway, so happy for him. Her Mom Toni has become a very good friend and amazing supporter.

So by the end of another long day, he was a pretty happy boy. Today I should get our schedule for our next visit - which will start next week. We expected 3 weeks home, but it will only be 2, which is really dragging on him emotionally. I'm going to look for a therapist in this area with the help of our social worker at Dana Farber and see if he might be interested in having someone to talk with.

I hope you guys are doing well. Have you been enjoying your sunsets

Love you Both!

Leslie

Sent: Thursday, June 20, 2013 11:51 AM
From: Brenda
To: Leslie Jermainne
Subject: RE: Update?

I didn't get the 6/18 update and really got concerned. Thanks so much for the update. That is awesome that the "Make-A-Wish" Foundation may grant his wish to go to Italy. That is so cool!! Will both you and Brian go with him? I hope so! Also, I didn't know he had a girlfriend. How nice!!

Sorry for the bothering you, I just got concerned that we didn't hear from you. We are enjoying our sunsets, every night. And every night we talk about you and Brian and Brian Ross and send special prayers your way. You are always in our thoughts. Just let me know when you have some free time. I understand your schedule is absolutely crazy right now. Hopefully, we will get together real soon. Enjoy the sunshine!!

Sent: Thursday, June 20, 2013 12:09 PM
From: Leslie Jermainne
To: Brenda
Subject: RE: Update?

You are never a bother!! It's actually nice to know you're out there, thinking of us, and looking for the updates. I will resend the 6/18 update. Talk to you soon! Leslie

JUNE 23, 2013

Sent: Sunday, June 23, 2013 9:12 AM
From: Leslie Jermainne
To: My List
Subject: RE: Brian Ross Update 6/23

Hi Everyone!

First of all - Happy Birthday to Me! Yup - 44 today. I didn't write that looking for Happy Birthday's from everyone. I wrote it because of something I realized yesterday. As I was driving to meet my girlfriends for breakfast, I stopped at the drive up window at the bank to cash a check. As I waited, I watched an elderly gentleman make his way out of the bank (no drive up for him! - I'm so lazy!) shuffle to his car and get in slowly. I thought "Ugh! Old Age." Yuck. It's so difficult with the aches and pains, loss of mobility, loss of hearing, eyesight, memory. I thought of the saying "Old age isn't so bad when you consider the alternative". I always thought that was such a stupid thing to say. Until my 15 year old was diagnosed with cancer. I sat there and thought, that elderly man is so lucky. He is lucky to be shuffling to his car, maybe hard of hearing or with cataracts or glaucoma, with back pain or stiff legs. He may feel lucky himself, then again, there is a good chance he doesn't feel so lucky. But I would bet if I was watching this man as Brian who fighting for my life, fighting for my chance to get to the age where everything is harder, stranger, faster but I could watch him with the insight of a 44 year old Mom smack in the middle of the two age wise, I would think he was pretty damn lucky. He has lived a life full of memories, good and bad. Hard days of work and hopefully some weeks filled by vacation. Maybe a long marriage, some kids, some grandkids. A home, friends and family to be loved by and to love in return. And things might seem bleak now for him and worrisome or maybe even lonely. But all those precious years he has lived. That is exactly my birthday wish for my baby boy. I now understand that old age isn't so bad when you consider the alternative. It is actually quite lovely from my point of view. Perspective really is everything.

So - back to Brian. I can't believe I haven't written anything in so many days. We have been relaxing, recovering and planning for our next visit. We will be leaving either late Monday to stay over for 9:00 a.m. appt. at Jimmy Fund on Tues - or getting up and hitting the road at 5:00 a.m. on Tues. I haven't worked that out yet. We will start treatment on Tuesday and will be done the following Tuesday after a 12 pm lumbar puncture. Anna our N.P. has put into place a great schedule for us to lessen the burden and nights in the hospital by arranging for us to stay Tues. night and the following Monday night at a nearby hotel or possibly Ronald McDonald house - and completing some of the treatment as outpatient. This has helped Brian considerably with his thoughts and emotions on going back. I understand and am repeatedly reminded by our support that "This is the last time!" And while yes that is true, and maybe should help him to get through, it is still difficult to face that many days confined to the hospital and specifically 6 north while getting a 5 day 24/hr. infusion, 2 lumbar punctures, high dose methotrexate, tons of fluid, 4 hour vital checks, blah, blah, blah. So…yes! This is our last time, but we still have to just make it through.

We did give him a little something extra to look forward to however. We are going to go away to our favorite place in VT just after we get out (his counts don't fall to the lowest until 7-14 days after treatment) for July 3 & 4th. We are very much looking forward to the three of us being away for two nights and celebrate the end of chemo and get some rest!

Bri has had a great few days, starting with last Wednesday that started on a sour note, but ended very well. Make-A-Wish came and Brian wished to go to Pompeii Italy to see the ruins there. He loves ancient history and according to him, this is one of the most well preserved sites. I'm only slightly embarrassed to reveal I had to ask where Pompeii was. I mean, I knew what it was (sort of) but where it was? No. Let's just say that Ancient and Medieval (I just had to look up how to spell medieval - thinking it was midevil) History in high school was the one class I almost failed. If they'd stop changing the names of everything it would be much easier. Anyway, the wish granters said they see no reason it should not be approved. WOW! And we might be able to go this fall - like maybe late October around 24th would be perfect as that is his 16th birthday. Let's hope we're going to Italy baby!

After we did the paperwork with them, we rushed over to Montville for Christi's graduation and reception at it was a very nice evening. It was so nice to watch Bri meet new people, and be a teenager. Thursday was quiet and Friday brought over Auntie Al and Carl for dinner and a fire and a little ice cream birthday cake for Al - who celebrated her birthday on the 17th. Yesterday was a great day for him (and me) when Christi and her Mom Toni came for a nice long visit poolside with swimming, lunch (dragging Toni with me to let a Realtor into a listing - blah!), ice cream trip and witnessing a raccoon altercation in our woods - Mommy raccoon was teaching one of two babies to behave we think. Why were they out at 4 p.m.? After they left to visit with family, Bri rested up had dinner and then rejoined them for an outdoor screening of JAWS and a fire pit night with their family. How Fun! Bri and I had to wait up until 11:30 for him to return. I'm not complaining - I'm thrilled he had such a great day - as did I. It's just that I go to bed at like 9 - 9:30 and I'm an old lady now. ;-)

So today will be spent once again puttering around, laundry, bills, cleaning - but in my lovely home with my amazing family and with some time napping poolside I hope. Then out to dinner with my hubby and son, my two favorite people in the whole wide world.

I just want to mention that I received a wonderful phone message Friday night from a special person in our lives, wishing us well and praying for us. I was wondering where that person had been, knowing he was out there thinking of us. This has happened several times for me since this has started. I think, wait - I haven't heard from so and so. I wonder why? And then boom - I get an amazing note or call or support and my faith and love is renewed once again, just by someone taking a minute to say "I am here and I'm pulling for you all". So, if you have someone in your life that might need you to reach out for just a minute and say "Hi, I am here. I am thinking of you." Take the time to do it. It will mean the world to them, and probably will mean the world to you also, once done.

Love and love and more love from home for at least one more night.

Leslie

Sent: Monday, June 24, 2013 8:08 AM
From: Frank
To: Leslie Jermainne
Subject: RE: Brian Ross Update 6/23

Leslie - Almost done - Yay !!! I'm proud of you all, and glad to hear you're going to get away to VT and possibly Italy. Wow - that's great. I could have written your first paragraph with regards to the old man you saw at the bank. Must be the cancer caregiver perspective. I often see older people and wonder if they feel lucky. What I can't stand though is the bitter or mean old people - I know everyone has a story and a reason - but when you see your loved ones struggling and fighting for the chance to be old - it's a slap in the face when you see some curmudgeon old person with a poor attitude. That is why, and I'm not proud of it - I stand up to these people at places like stop and shop or wherever.

Anyways - was hoping I hadn't heard anything because all was well - and it sounds like you all had a nice few days.

...and HAPPY BIRTHDAY !!!

Frank

JUNE 24, 2013

Sent: Monday, June 24, 2013 6:29 PM
From: Leslie Jermainne
To: My List
Subject: RE: Brian Ross Update 6/24

We are packing up!

Car is starting to get loaded, laundry is just about done, computer is going to be packed up when I'm done with this note. We will stay here tonight, and roll out of bed early and be on the road by 5 a.m. - my estimated time of departure to arrive between 8:45-9:00 a.m. at the Jimmy Fund Clinic - how do people live with such a huge amount of humanity on a daily basis I do not know.

We had a busy morning. Up and to Lowes to make a return at about 7:00 a.m., Brian working at the new 2 family by then too. Vac the van which we use like a truck, get fueled up (thanks to a generous gas gift card), and home to put EMLA cream to numb his port. Critical Care nurse arrives at 9:00 to access his port, draw blood and be on her way to deliver for STAT results to make sure he meets counts for tomorrow. Bri goes back to bed. Laundry, cleaning, bills and phone calls ensue. Find out we can't get into Longwood Inn Medical tomorrow night, but work quickly to get a room at Ronald McDonald House Boston. WOW!!! All those years of putting change in the bin when we ate at McDonalds, is finally paying off. Ok, I wasn't looking for a payoff, but it amazes me how these "common" places have come to play in our lives. So when you're in McDonalds (if you choose to eat there ever) and see the little bin on the counter for donations for the Ronald McDonald House - it really is a huge help to families traveling and staying for treatment.

I had a nice/quick visit with my parents, to update them on our schedule - ran some errands - and picked up around the house and pool. Bri napped, played video games, his guitar, listened to some music and rested. Mentally he seems much better than the day before our last admit.

Big Brian had a closing today, he's out right now at a CMA appt. and did lots of work at the investment property and his desk. I'm hoping to wait dinner for him, but it will be hard. I did get to swim with "little" Brian and play with Jackie our dog, who has his own pool floaty and loves to jump on it and bark while Bri shoots him with the water gun. These are the moments I cherish. (I don't believe our neighbors do, however.)

So - that's about it. Things sound pretty good, don't they. And they truly are. But as a reminder and a little pity party for me. I woke up in tears today, full of fear for the future of my son. Worries running wild like crazed animals through my brain. It has been days since I cried out of fear, so I guess that is a good thing. Tears are always but a moment away, sometimes they are happy, sometimes they are sad and sometimes they are nonsense driven by unforeseen fears. But they are always there, ready to pop out at a moment's notice. Like the other day when I called to reserve our motel room in VT, the same place we have stayed for years and years and will visit again on Labor Day weekend. The owner lost his wife 2 years ago to kidney cancer - when I tried to explain why we were coming up not only on Labor Day, but on 7/3-7/5 - the choked up voice filled with tears that is almost incomprehensible comes flying out like the evil monkeys in the Wizard of Oz. Some people have the ability to cry and talk at the same time - I don't. The poor guy! He was of course wonderful, and choked up as well. G.D. this cancer - affecting all of us. God Dammit!

Sorry to end on a sour note - but I don't want to forget myself, or have anyone else forget that this isn't all sunshine and roses. This is really hard shit. Really, really hard. But we are getting there. We really, really are getting there.

Peace Out from home - for the last time for the next week.

Love,
Leslie

Sent: Monday, June 24, 2013 6:45 PM
From: Kim
To: Leslie Jermainne
Subject: Extra prayers

I am saying extra prayers for you. You are almost there, stay positive - you have been an amazing inspiration and I believe the two of you will win this battle!

Kim

Sent: Monday, June 24, 2013 8:56 PM
From: Sheila
To: Leslie Jermainne
Subject: Re: Brian Ross Update 6/24

We love you guys. Devin and Meg are thinking of Brian every day even though they don't know how to express it to him. Please know that we are praying HARD for Brian, for you and big Brian.

Safe travels tomorrow. Xoxoxo

Sent: Monday, June 24, 2013 10:19 PM
From: Toni
To: Leslie Jermainne
Subject: Re: Brian Ross Update 6/24

I am so glad you had a good week at home, and hope that those thoughts sustain you over the next week. Keep them in your heart. I know its scary shit, I know it sucks, but you are an incredibly strong woman and Brian is an incredibly strong kid. You will get through this week, and be home before you know it. I am so glad that they are getting Ronald McDonald House for the night.

If you can't sleep or need a shoulder or arm to lean on, you know I am here and I will be up early:)

Hang in there.

Lots of love and never ending support.
Toni

JUNE 25, 2013

Sent: Tuesday, June 25, 2013 9:48 PM
From: Alison
To: Leslie Jermainne
Subject: Re: Brian Ross Update 6/13

Better late than never, right?

Paisley waking me up in the morning by jumping up on the bed and "tapping" me with her paw....a nice cool house to come home to on HHH days because "somebody" put my air conditioners in the windows while I was out.....email......books.....my laptop.......a comfy car with air conditioning.....nector of the gods........a nice cool Tanqueray &Tonic sitting on my back deck in the afternoon watching the hummingbirds flutter up to the feeders on my deck......Mr. Lemley who taught me how to play ancient snare drum......my family, immediate and extended.

Good night from a nice cool comfy home....

Sent: Wednesday, June 26, 2013 6:22 PM
From: Rebecca B.
To: Leslie Jermainne
Subject: Re: Brian Ross Update 6/24

There is a lump in my throat that I remember always having when I wanted to cry but couldn't.

Your pain is so fresh, honest, and loving. There is a blessing inside of sorrow, and your ability to connect is part of that. I know that Little Brian is going to be fine, and I know that you know that too.

The ride sucks...it does, and I know that from watching my little nephew use a walker for the first time and seeing him puke from his cancer medication. Everything is going to be all right, and you will be even more incredible than you are now. Please remember that Sammy was given a few months to live when he was 8 and just finished his second year of college. He was afraid he wouldn't know what to say to your Brian if we decided to have them write, but he said he would love to. That willingness to take a risk like that can only come from angels, and I know you are caring for one now.

G-d bless you and yours too,
Rebecca

JUNE 26, 2013

Sent: Wednesday, June 26, 2013 10:25 PM
From: Leslie Jermainne
To: My List
Subject: RE: Brian Ross Update 6/26

Hi!

Well, we're here. In Boston Children's Hospital, Room 618A, 6 North. The A side is the "small" side. This is the very first spot we ever stayed in when we got moved here via ambulance on April 23rd. Flashback! Bri and I both feel it is better than we remember when we got here that first night @ 9 pm - emotionally exhausted and we entered this little tiny rabbit hutch of room. We had left a big private room at the first hospital that had a big private bath (I'm not allowed to use the bathroom in this room - patients only). A full size cot for me, a couch for visitors and tons of space. Of course nothing else there was good, but still. We walked into this room that first night and I just about cried. But here we are 2 months later on our last round of chemo and we sail into this little side of this room (go request to be moved, which right now they are full, but maybe tomorrow or the next day) and say, "this doesn't look so bad". Of course I just took a picture which I attached and it looks a little scary in the photo. To the side of Brian is his pump and then a curtain that separates us from our roomy. Cozy, huh?

Anyway, let's review. We drove up to Boston yesterday, leaving home at 5 a.m. (Bri slept in his clothes, smart guy!) Traffic that early wasn't that horrendous and we made it to Jimmy Fund in plenty of time. He was accessed (had a hard time drawing back on his port - which means getting blood to come out, but after turning his head, lifting his arm in the air, out it came) and had his blood drawn, vitals done and exam with

Dr. D. We then moved to the infusion area and had a bolus of fluid and 3 hour Methotrexate infusion. He got to sleep about 2 hours of that which was good after only getting 3 hours the night before at home. When that finished we got a hydration pack and we were let loose! A hydration pack is a small backpack with a pump and a huge bag of fluid and he is hooked to it. We also got an extra bag of fluid that needed to be replaced at 2:45 a.m. YA!

We went straight to the Ronald McDonald House which is about 3 blocks away or so and traffic was already getting a bit heavy. We got in there, got our room with two single beds on the third floor, our sheets and towels, a tour and Bri had a bowl of ice cream and a soda. I made up his bed and he pretty much passed out by 5 pm. Besides frequent bathroom runs from all the fluid, he slept until I woke him at 7:30 this morning. During his time asleep I was given a nice dinner cooked and put out by Double Tree Hotel volunteers. It was nice not to have to go out and try to find some food. I had a shower, made up my bed, surfed around on my phone. The house was a great old house, very clean, quiet and nice. It was better than we had anticipated. I finally got to sleep about 9 pm and up at 1:30 to change his fluid- we could change it early since we had plenty of fluid to get us back to JFC at 8:00 today. At about 5:30 a.m. his batteries died in his pump, but they had given us extra and how to change it and we did it all by our little old selves. I was up at that point, so I got ready, took a few things to the car and then had some coffee made by a Dad at the house. It was great to talk to him and exchange our "cancer stories". His daughter has ALL (Acute Lymphoblastic Leukemia) and has been at this fight since December 2011. Oh. My. God. She is just about done recovering from her Bone Marrow Transplant and was back from upstate NY for a checkup. She had been in the hospital for 4 months during her transplant and then 2 months at Ronald McDonald. Unimaginable. I again am feeling blessed.

We went back to JFC at 8:45 and then onto lumbar puncture. As we got ready for that, our nurse tried to draw labs. No draw back from his port. WHAT! You have to understand that any little deviation from our new "norm" is freaky. Did the port fail? OMG! Is he going to have to an IV? We move down to the procedure room and they try again. No good. So the decision is made he needs to be re-accessed. They are sure the port hasn't failed since the fluids go in, but they must be able to draw back to make sure everything is good with the port before getting propofol or chemo. So, out comes the first needle and in goes a new 1" port needle with NO numbing cream. His face is white and eyes are buggy in anticipation. He was a trooper and was so brave. The second access worked! YA! Such a relief. In went the propofol, down closed his eyes, out I walked into the hall and down came the tears. Every little thing is a crisis. Only this time, after 10 seconds of crying, I pulled it together. He was fine, the port was working, all was good. LP went great - first shot. Only one more of those damned things!

After that was done he got to eat (hadn't eaten since ice cream at 4pm the day before) and then more fluids then moved up here at about 11:30 - pretty fast. Chemo started at 1pm so that is our zero hour. That means he will be done with 5 day 24/hr. infusion at 1pm on Monday. So...we are in our tiny little cubby. Our roomy we've been with before, another 16 yr. old tall guy. So at least that is somewhat of a comfort. We are now counting down our days to freedom. Only 6 more days until we're driving home. I. CAN'T. WAIT!

I spent some time at a caregiver group today. I did most of the talking. Anyone surprised? Well, here's the thing. Only two other people were there. One was a grandmother of a patient who has arrived not long ago from Columbia - like Columbia the country - her poor grandson has been fighting for 3 years. There was a language barrier, but she did well and has a lot of love and a lot of faith. The other Mom was young. She was so brave to even come. She didn't even cry once, I don't know how. I would guess from what she had to say, it is because she is in total shock. She has been in this fight 2 weeks with her 18 month old son who has stage IV sarcoma (I think) brain tumor. She has a 4 1/2 yr. old at home. They live 35 minutes (with no traffic) from here. I don't think the prognosis is good. She listened a lot. I hope that I was in some small way of service or help to her with sharing our experience and being the one to talk.

Tonight I am grateful for our diagnosis. As horrible as it is. I've read the saying somewhere that if everyone threw their problems into a pile and you looked at them, you'd probably grab yours back. I feel that way tonight. So, please say a little prayer for this 18 month old child who is fighting to live and for his parents and sister who are fighting to survive.

Love and hope from teeny tiny room 618A

Leslie

Sent: Wednesday, June 26, 2013 10:59 PM
From: Toni
To: Leslie Jermainne
Subject: Re: Brian Ross Update 6/26

Wow came here a few minutes ago thinking there might be a note. And this popped up. Sometimes I really think you do heart thoughts.

Bri missed not much at practice but I missed his sheepish smile. It was a crappy practice. Kids didn't practice, instructors were negative, but still better than getting chemo in a tiny box.

If I can get tickets in the a.m. thinking we will head up for a visit. Can let you know a bit after 10:00 if that works.

Talk tomorrow. Prayers Tonight that these are the last steps in treatment road and that recovery is strong and forever.

Night.

Toni

Sent: Wednesday, June 26, 2013 11:08 PM
From: Sheila
To: Leslie Jermainne
Subject: Re: Brian Ross Update 6/26

Praying for you and them.

JUNE 27, 2013

Sent: Thursday, June 27, 2013 7:19 PM
From: Leslie Jermainne
To: My List
Subject: RE: Brian Ross Update 6/27

Hello:

I feel like I was maybe feeling a bit too comfy yesterday. You see every night before I write this note, I read the one from the night before. Sometimes I cry again just like when I wrote it. Yesterday's was good though. No tears last night and none now. Just a touch of sorrow for all the other families here fighting for their babies.

Well, I hate to sound like this but it is what I'm feeling. Cancer doesn't like you to get comfy or cocky. Like you understand what is going on, or that things are going to be okay. Brian has a fever now. His first one. We were almost there. Almost through this entire protocol with no fevers. Too much to ask I guess. Last fever check was 102.4. Was 103 earlier. Things were good this morning. About lunch I realized he was starting to not feel well. He ate about two bites of food and then went to sleep at 1pm. Christi and Toni were coming and he wanted to rest up. He happened to wake up at 3:00, just when they got here. He didn't look too good. I thought he felt hot, but again...from his perspective, I know not much of anything. And of course he wanted to visit with his guests. We visited for a bit, then Toni and I went downstairs to get some coffee and visit ourselves. Back up to the room to bring Christi her drink and boom. Nurses are there, he has 101.3 fever. SHIT!

Here is what this means for the cancer patient. Blood draw to start cultures to see if anything nasty is really lurking in there. CBC run to check his counts to plan which course of action will be taken. If non-neutropenic meaning his ANC level is above 500 then just one type of IV antibiotic is given. If neutropenic, then two types of broad spectrum IV antibiotics are given. This continues until his fever breaks and stays gone for 24 hours. I don't know if he is neutropenic yet or not, but the one IV antibiotic has already been given. Waiting on CBC. Next comes Nurse

Practitioner visit, full exam, lots of questions. Overall they don't seem overly concerned. Me, I want to scream. Toni and Christi had gone off for a walk to let Bri go through all this and rest. I met them down in the lobby and told them to head home. He was done for the night. Of course Toni can read me like a book, and let me burst into tears and get it out while I was away from Bri. Like I told the group I talked with yesterday, tears are always just below the surface. You might not be able to see them in me, but I can feel them just waiting for a crack so they can burst forth. I came back to reassure him he's going to be okay. This med, Cytarabine, is known for causing fevers. Not usually at this lower dosage, but not completely unlikely either. So that is what we are going with. He is now worried that we will have to stay longer this visit, and all the other underlying worries of course. UGH!

So it is not unusual to get fevers doing this I know. But it is unusual for him. He also didn't clear his methotrexate all the way by hour 24, which he has done every other visit. He was close, but just not quite there. Now he has to say on high fluids until he clears to an even lower level by hour 48 - hopefully. But we were so God Damn close to the end. What the hell! I want this to be done so badly. So deep down gut wrenching badly I can't stand it. It's just too much. He is sleeping now which is a relief. I sent out word for prayers on Facebook and all our supporters are sending them fast and furious. I am so thankful for that. It makes us feel loved and listened to. It makes me feel less alone.

So, I'm done for tonight. Just done. Tomorrow is a new day that will arrive if we are ready or not. I best try to get ready, by sleeping myself. I don't know what this night will bring. I'm hoping sleep and fever going away. I hope, I hope, I hope.

Worry and fear from teeny tiny room 618A

Leslie

Sent: Thursday, June 27, 2013 7:30 PM
From: Leslie Jermainne
To: My List
Subject: RE: Brian Ross Update 6/27-update

Update: ANC is 543 so they are going to double antibiotics. They are ordered and on the way. Damn It!!!

Sent: Thursday, June 27, 2013 9:47 PM
From: Frank
To: Leslie Jermainne
Subject: RE: Brian Ross Update 6/27-update

Leslie - I don't envy these cliffhangers. What I will say is that this is all somewhat expected and they know exactly what to do to get Bri bouncing back and in the car heading home by Monday. I could have wrote the part of your previous email where you said that "tears are always just below the surface. You might not be able to see them in me, but I can feel them just waiting for a crack so they can burst forth". I remember feeling at that point that I was some abnormal emotional wreck. I could hold a conversation with a doctor or nurse, walk down the hall and cry for 30 seconds, and then pop back in with Anna to be her rock with no evidence of what lied underneath. As I look back, these little bursts were my internal vents or pressure relief to help me stay sane. The bad news - I still have tears that stay very shallow for some reason - maybe a thought, seeing Anthony accomplish a minor milestone, or even watching a stupid TV show or commercial will bring them on. (I still feel like a mess from all the Trauma).

Anyway, I know how you must feel alone on an island and scared, but you are not alone. You have your wonderful support network and more importantly you are a rock star caregiver and one hell of a great MOM. Yes, some setbacks this evening, but little Bri will get through this and get home as planned - maybe a day or two late, but who cares in the big picture - your goal is for a long, happy, and healthy life. Tell Bri to be patient - this is no time to rush or panic, trust and go with the new plan and he will have his life back. I haven't said it in a while but I'm proud of you! I can't wait to give you a hug and sit by the fire with a drink.

Love, prayers, and positive vibes from our home.

Frank

JUNE 28, 2013

Sent: Friday, June 28, 2013 5:33 AM
From: Paula
To: Leslie Jermainne
Subject: Re: Brian Ross Update 6/27-update

I am going to be driving and will say prayers on my way to work. Hang in there you just have to get through this week. Picture God holding Brian in his arms. That's what Luca prays.

Love ya,
Paula

Sent: Friday, June 28, 2013 6:08 AM
From: Lorna
To: Leslie Jermainne
Subject: Re: Brian Ross Update 6/27

Hi Leslie

Really hope things get better soon. Hugs and prayers from Fife x

Sent: Friday, June 28, 2013 6:39 AM
From: Ann
To: Leslie Jermainne
Subject: RE: Brian Ross Update 6/27-update

Les,

Hope this morning has brought better news. How is Big Brian right now? Just wondering if he is in OS or up with you. If he is in OS please let me know if he needs anything. I know he won't ask but just remember you can always call Liz, Paula or myself if you think he needs something.

Ann

Sent: Friday, June 28, 2013 12:37 PM
From: Leslie Jermainne
To: Ann
Subject: RE: Brian Ross Update 6/27-update

He's at home. He's worried. Calling a lot more. I'm not sure how he is on food - maybe a little would be good to get him through the weekend. I'm thinking we might be here longer than anticipated.

Sent: Friday, June 28, 2013 7:23 AM
From: Leslie Jermainne
To: Phoebe
Subject: Visit today

If possible can you come see us this morning. Fever started yesterday. 2 rooms (1private) that are open and despite my requests to be moved we are still here. Plus Bri is starting to go downhill a bit with worries. Fever extending stay? Joan told him to get up and walk because she's concerned about blood clots in his legs. That one took me about an hour to calm him down. And our roomy isn't well and when 6 infectious disease docs come in it is unnerving and we start thinking is this a risk? Anyway, your help would be appreciated as always.

Leslie Jermainne

Sent: Friday, June 28, 2013 6:28 PM
From: Leslie Jermainne
To: Frank
Subject: RE: Brian Ross Update 6/27-update

Thanks Frank. Have missed your emails - again they always strike a chord with me. You are right about the pressure release. It has taken me this long to be able to hold it at bay during the conversation - let it go - clean up my act and get back to him. I'm sad for you that you are still feeling the trauma, but maybe it is really the appreciation for life that brings tears so close to the surface.

I know we'll get through, but man it's hard. Thanks for your continued support. I can't wait to see you guys too!

Leslie

Sent: Friday, June 28, 2013 8:56 PM
From: Leslie Jermainne
To: My List
Subject: RE: Brian Ross Update 6/28

UGH!

We are not having a good day. And frankly, I'm just going to give you a "medical" update.

Brian has had a fever all day ranging from 100.8 to 104.2. It seems to respond somewhat to Tylenol, but it is still hanging around. Blood cultures are being run twice a day. He is on two antibiotics as a preventative in case he has a bacterial infection. The other possibilities are viral and chemo reaction. He is on day 3 of 5 Cytarabine 24/hr infusion, which will not be stopped no matter what. Cytarabine is known for causing fevers.

The other concern that has just come up is he had a scheduled ultrasound of his right underarm and abdomen site. While doing the ultrasound the tech seemed to concentrate on one area sort of "lighting up". The tech finished, told us she'd have the doctors check the ultrasound like always. Usually she comes back and says, "All set, looks good". This time she came back with two doctors of radiology who looked some more. They told us they are just taking lots and lots of pictures because this is how he will be followed rather than PET scans. But they kept concentrating on this area. So I asked what was the deal, they said they thought maybe it was a cyst, but since there was blood flow to the area, it wasn't that. But then they said nothing looked "remarkable". I don't even know what to say about this. Brian of course is scared. Burkitt relapse always weighs on our mind, since it is incredibly hard to treat. So every little blip, makes us think about that. I'm waiting for the N.P. on the floor to come talk to me, as I requested. I'm sure she won't have results, but I want to make sure we will get results at rounds tomorrow, or later tomorrow and not wait until Monday. That would be torture. Plus maybe she has some more details. I don't know, I just don't know.

The other not good news is he is officially neutropenic. This means his ANC is below 500. It is 320. This means he is unable to fight infection on his own. A normal white blood cell count is 5,000-10,000. In order for us to get discharged at this point his numbers have to hit bottom and start climbing and he has to be fever free for 24 hours. That seems a daunting task at this point. It is unlikely we will be out on time, meaning Tuesday - but I guess you never know.

The good thing that happened is he finally cleared his Methotrexate. He had always cleared it early or on time, until this time. But it has cleared with no trace so that is great news.

Brian did get out of bed and walk three times today which was good. When his fever is in the lower range he is doing pretty well. When it's up, he tries to sleep.

Anyway, that's all I'm up for Tonight.

Good night from room 618A

Leslie

Sent: Friday, June 28, 2013 10:26 PM
From: Karen
To: Leslie Jermainne
Subject: Re: Brian Ross Update 6/28

Leslie....I'm so sorry today was this rocky. I send hopes and prayers for a much better tomorrow!!! You are doing an amazing job, and Brian is unbelievable - so inspirational! Hang in there and keep the faith! Thinking of you....

Karen

JUNE 29, 2013

Sent: Saturday, June 29, 2013 9:18 PM
From: Leslie Jermainne
To: My List
Subject: RE: Brian Ross Update 6/29

Hi,

Fever has been down all day. Very happy. Stopped Vancomyacin since no cultures grew that you would need that for. Now just waiting on next ANC level. They had dropped even farther down to 150 today. Not happy news. Ultrasound however came back fine - so our fears of something wrong were unfounded, thankfully.

It was a somewhat long day, but with some bright spots. Brian used his computer somewhat and read a little and walked three times and ate a grilled cheese sandwich and a small McFlurry. First real food he's had since Thurs breakfast I think. I'm not sure if it was Wed. or Thurs.

So that's about it for today - not too much to share. I did see an interesting question posed on a website. "What Have Your Hands Done and What Would You Like Them to Do?" Here is what I wrote:

What have your hands done:

My hands have played with Barbies and my dollhouse. They have opened Christmas and Birthday gifts from people who love me. They have built sand castles, swam in the water and played music. They have held onto handle bars and even let go to ride with "no hands". They have petted many dogs and even some cats. They have held the hands of my best girlfriends and some boyfriends. My hands have bounced a ball and waited on tables and run a cash register and fixed my computer and my Dad's computer too. My hands have given and received a ring from my partner in life. They have rubbed my big pregnant belly and scratched my husband's back. They have cradled my baby boys head. My hands have baked every birthday cake for my son and Thanksgiving Turkey for my husband. They have helped build a swing set. They have bathed and dressed my boy and held books that I have read to him. They have cleaned our home and cooked our food and washed our clothes. They have clapped in good times and clenched in times of stress and worry and fear. My hands have given shots to my mother and son when they were recovering and to myself to stay healthy. They have driven the car and filled it with gas while keeping my family safe. They have decorated the Christmas tree, lit fire crackers, raked leaves and shoveled snow. They have pushed the mower and grilled steaks. They have picked flowers and planted herbs. My hands have been cut, stitched and broken. My hands have aged. They have hung up wet clothes, pool towels and photos of my family. My hands have held me up, swung at my side and pointed towards the sky. My hands have made our house a home. They have cared for my son every day for the past 15 years from having a cold to battling cancer. They have wiped away his tears and my tears too. My hands have clasped together in joy and in prayer.

What would you like your hands to do:

I would like my hands to continue the wonderful life they have had so far and continue to care for those I love. I would like them again to point to the sky while viewing the northern lights. I would like them again to swim in the ocean off the coast of Hawaii. I would like my hands to hold the side of a hot air balloon basket while marveling at the sunrise. I would like my hands to continue to age while being intertwined with the aging hands of my husband. I would like my hands to cook and clean and fold. I would like my hands to write a book. I would like my hands to continue to wipe away my tears and the tears of those I love, both happy and sad. I would like my hands to build and sew and decorate more Christmas Trees. I would like my hands to grow food and maybe feed chickens. I would like my hands to arrange more flowers in a vase, mix up more chocolate chip cookies and hold a wine glass while relaxing with my friends. I want my hands to write "Love, Mom" on a birthday card every year until the year I die.

All from little old room 618A - the rabbit hutch.

Leslie

Sent: Saturday, June 29, 2013 11:57 PM
From: Sheila
To: Leslie Jermainne
Subject: Re: Brian Ross Update 6/29

Please write a book.

JUNE 30, 2013

Sent: Sunday, June 30, 2013 8:36 AM
From: Sarah J
To: Leslie Jermainne
Subject: RE: Brian Ross Update 6/29

You made me laugh and cry. That was just beautiful :-) The maybe feed chickens part made me giggle. So relieved about ultrasound and fever.

L+L+ hopes for a peaceful day

Sarah

Sent: Sunday, June 30, 2013 12:30 PM
From: Alison
To: Leslie Jermainne
Subject: RE: Brian Ross Update 6/29

You know, I think the reason your updates make me weepy is that they totally come from your heart, from your inner depths of feeling...and the way you express all your hopes and dreams. It seems like I'm in your head with you and experiencing all those feelings with my own interspersed. Your hands and heart and mind really do need to write a book... you truly have a gift for words and expressing your feelings....

Sent: Sunday, June 30, 2013 4:00 PM
From: Leslie Jermainne
To: Alison
Subject: RE: Brian Ross Update 6/29

Thanks - I don't know if this stuff is book material. Maybe if I had thought that way in the beginning but honestly so much of it - this time, my thoughts are lost to the days. I'm not sure it would help other Moms. I think you are crazy enough in this situation - and every child in here has such a different story and different path. Maybe it would, but I don't know. I'm not sure that I enjoy reading others misery. I went to a parents group on Wed. (I think I said this in one of my updates) anyway the social worker guy asked the group "is there anything in your past, some difficult time that you got through...is there something you did or used during that time to help you?" In my head I was like "What the fuck are you talking about?!?!?" My answer, since nobody else was talking, was "there is nothing in the world that compares to this. There is nothing that even comes remotely close to having your child diagnosed with cancer and being here and fighting for them to live." I couldn't even believe the stupidity of the question. Like you could say, "Oh ya, I lost my job once and that was similar. It was tough but I got a new job and now everything is fine." I mean seriously dude! What. The Fuck. Are you talking about? I wanted to say "do you have children? Have any of them been diagnosed with cancer? Have you spent endless nights and even longer days wondering if they were going to live? Wondering if you could survive if they didn't? Wondering how you would kill yourself if they died? Would your child be mad that if you did kill yourself? That you took for granted the gift of life that they so desperately wanted to receive themselves? Wondering if you fed them something, exposed them to something, did something that you were being paid back for? Have you listened to doctors and nurses tell you about your child. Listened to them talk like your child having cancer isn't the mouth-gaping, most horrific thing you have ever heard. Have you felt completely and utterly helpless day after day after God Damn day, bargaining with God? Pleading with God. Begging God. Even if you don't believe in God? Because if you haven't done these things, then you have no fucking idea what we are going through. So sit down and shut the fuck up."

I think everyone in the room would have been a little upset if I really let them see the real me. Maybe the grandma who couldn't speak English so well would have been okay with it. I guess it did get us (and by us I mean me) talking. Maybe that was the goal. He's lucky the goal wasn't to get kicked in the nuts, because he might have gotten that too!

Anyway - thanks for the nice thoughts. It helps. A. LOT. God I can't wait to get him home.

Love You,
Les

Sent: Sunday, June 30, 2013 7:36 PM
From: Leslie Jermainne
To: My List
Subject: RE: Brian Ross Update 6/30

Hi Again (and again, and again)

Just think - maybe someday soon you won't be getting emails from me about my sons cancer fight. Maybe someday soon, our lives will be back to "normal" whatever that might mean. We might not be talking about ANC levels, ports, methotrexate or Cytarabine. No talk of fevers or hair loss or watering eyes. No blown pupils, steroid anger, no nausea. No biopsies, no lumbar punctures and no propofol. Maybe someday soon we will talk of swimming and drum corps, visits with friends and maybe even a trip to Pompeii. Maybe it will "boring" stuff like rehabbing houses, trips to the grocery store, Labor Day weekend in Vermont with Auntie Al. Maybe it will be heavenly. I just hope it gets here soon.

But for today we are talking about ANC level which dropped again, but only a tiny bit from 150 to 140. WBC count is up very slightly from over the past 3 days from .45 to .52 to .76. Those numbers starting to increase, lead us to believe that ANC will follow in that direction...

eventually. No fever again today! WOOHOO. That is huge. Antibiotics still running and last bag of Cytarabine was hung at 1pm. 1pm tomorrow will be the end of that. On Tuesday his very last chemo will take place during his Lumbar Puncture. Not sure on a time yet, but then that will be it. Done with chemo.

Our plan had been to be discharged tomorrow after 1 pm end time of Cytarabine. Then we have a reservation at the Longwood Inn through the families program at Jimmy Fund. We were supposed to lounge around our hotel room, order room service, get a good night's sleep in our big comfy beds and sleep in late. We were supposed to be at JFC on Tues by 11:00 for his lumbar puncture at 12:00. By 2 pm we'd be in the car on our way home to our little sleepy town. Finished with chemo. This nightmare starting to come to an end. But all that is by the wayside now. At least unless we have a miracle tomorrow and his ANC level goes above 200. If it doesn't, then it's another night in the hospital, then lumbar puncture in the O.R. here on Tuesday (which is a production in itself). And then we wait. We are stuck here until his ANC does go above 200 and begins to climb. I have some arguments under my belt for tomorrow, so we will see what happens when we see Anna at rounds tomorrow. She is wonderful and creative so I'm hoping we can find a way out of here as soon as possible. If it maybe it means staying at Ronald McDonald for a few days or something of that nature. Grasping at straws here.

Meanwhile we are still in our tiny, crappy noise filled room. Last night at about 3:15 a.m. they began trying to place an IV in a young girl in the room next door. I'm going to say about 3 years old. I have never heard such horrible screaming, crying and begging - even in our past visits here. After the nurse tried a few times, she gave up. The child calmed down. Next came the IV team. They tried a few times - again horrible, horrible sounds. They didn't get it either. The child calmed down. Finally someone else came and after a whole lot more screaming, I guess they got it. You can't go back to sleep after that, not to mention it was then 5:30. I'm usually up by 6:00 anyway. Poor Bri has been up since then also. I did manage about a 30 min. nap today - but I can't say it did much. Those little girl's screams will haunt me for a while. All I could think was obviously how bad I felt for her, being violated basically. How horrible it must be for the medical staff, but mostly because I guess I identify most, how absolutely devastating that must be for the Mom. My God. So. Completely. Horrible.

Our poor roommate is so sick too. Fluid around his lungs, fluid around his heart, muscle atrophy so much he fell down today, just trying to stand to get weighed. He is on constant morphine for pain and neuropathy. He sleeps most of the time, except when every medical team is in and out of here all day and all night. I feel very badly for him. He is battling ALL and it isn't looking good to me. Physical therapy is supposed to come and work with him tomorrow. I hope it will help. He is 16 (had his birthday when we were his roommate 3 times ago) and as big as Brian. They still haven't made a connection with each other, mostly due to how sick he is. This whole place is just sad and depressing. Little kids with tubes up their noses, hooked to IV poles 2 times their size. Parents with vacant, red eyes. Visitors that have no idea what they are about to walk in to when they are looking for the right room.

Several times now as I sit in my dark cubby and listen to the nurses voices, day and night, talking in a regular tone and cadence about work stuff, but other stuff too. What they did on the weekend. Where they ate, who they saw, where the shopped. And I think sometimes, how rude to be "normal". To be just working at their job. Laughing or talking or sharing with their coworkers about their ordinary life. But then I think, what if they whispered and looked sad all the time. What if there was no laughter or regular voices or happy tones. Would that make me feel better? And I realize no, it would make me feel worse. So even at 4:15 a.m. when the IV team came to the floor and were standing outside my door getting on their gowns and gloves and masks to go work on that scared little girl and they talked about how they had shopped over the weekend and went up and down every aisle and how great it was, and I'm mad about it (sure it would make me less made at 9 a.m.) I guess I'm going to choose to be grateful that these people do show up here every day and see our sad faces and help children who should be outside playing not fighting for their lives. That they try to be cheerful and respectful and still have a life. How horrible it would be for them if they had to whisper all day and be morose and sad. Does any of that make any sense? I feel like I'm just rambling now.

So tomorrow will be a somewhat big day - or a big letdown. Either way it will arrive and it will end, so we will need to make the best of it.

Thinking and wishing for a good night from Room 618A - our cave as Bri calls it.

Leslie

Sent: Sunday, June 30, 2013 8:47 PM
From: Brian W.
To: Leslie Jermainne
Subject: Re: Brian Ross Update 6/30

That update is emotional Leslie. You ask if your words make sense. Perfect, powerful sense. This post could be the beginning of a novel.

Thank you so much for your exposed, honest emotion.

Sent: Sunday, June 30, 2013 9:22 PM
From: Paula
To: Leslie Jermainne
Subject: Re: Brian Ross Update 6/30

You are so close! Please let this be the best possible night and day tomorrow. I am sad and sick about what you are writing- just can't fathom what all you are going through. Please hang in there, and god bless you and Brian as you get to the finish line.

Sent: Sunday, June 30, 2013 10:31 PM
From: Sheila
To: Leslie Jermainne
Subject: Re: Brian Ross Update 6/30

If I were there with you I would give you the biggest hug. I am so very sorry you are going through this experience and just heartbroken for those other children and their parents. God Bless. Praying for a miracle for the ANC number for Brian.

Xoxoxo Sheila

July 2013

JULY 1, 2013

Sent: Monday, July 01, 2013 11:31 AM
From: Sally
To: Leslie Jermainne
Subject: Re: Brian Ross Update 6/30

I know what you mean about the medical team having their regular conversations. There were moments when that seemed my only connection to the world. At the time, I remember thinking that I'll never be back there. That I'll be living the rest of my life in a hospital-in-my-head. In some ways, that has been the case. Even now, with Matty being 19 years old and quite self-sufficient, I'm always standing right outside the open door to that hospital-in-my-head. I'll hear her stumble to the stairs at 3am, get up and follow her into the kitchen. Find her on the floor grasping the first carbohydrate she could find, grey, shaking. I'm back in the hospital-in-my-head, trying to piece together what happened from her fractured semi-lucid speech. Find a better combination of carbs/fat/protein for the situation, and sit on the kitchen floor with Matty stuffing morsels into her mouth. Still, she doesn't know they're measured, counted, and archived. Like the nurses on rounds, in my head. At 3am, of course. :-/

But hearing the day-to-day discussions of the medical team helped balance the institutional setting and kept that door open too, to the world of streets and beaches and ball fields and concerts-on-the-green. Also, I think it's a good reminder that the wizards of medicine, who know this disease so well, literally from the inside, molecular level, out, well... they are human. They have expertise, they know the treatment protocols for a thousand different scenarios, some have a gift of intuition that is remarkable and beautiful. God given, you'd say. Universe driven, I'd say. Same thing. A connection that goes beyond what they've learned from books and laboratories. I sometimes marvel about that and how, even with that gift, they're still regular people in other parts of their lives. Dealing with broken down cars, kids who sometimes give them trouble, traffic jams. The usual.

It reminds me of that saying about not judging others because you do not know what is going on in their lives. What burden they carry. Can you imagine being "successful", healthy, wealthy, all that goes with that? And in your everyday profession, facing the delicate hold on life of so many of your "customers", watching the difficult battle they fight, ushering some percentage of them to the end of their lives. I know that most of the medical team see the patients as people, not numbers. It has to weigh on them. Given that, it was reassuring to hear them talk about their regular lives. Like a reminder that life is going on and will be there when you're ready. Better than it was before because of the amazing gift of gratitude.

I am so glad you and Brian are approaching the end of this aggressive offense phase of his treatment, Leslie! Next comes healing and rebuilding, and that is going to be positive and life-affirming and awesome!

Sent: Monday, July 01, 2013 7:24 PM
From: Leslie Jermainne
To: My List
Subject: RE: Brian Ross Update 7/1

Hello again for what I hope is our last night in Boston Children's Hospital - ever!

Before I tell you about today, I want to tell you about last night, just moments after sending my email update. One of our nurses, Laura who was taking care of us yesterday came in at shift change last night. She came in to say goodbye because she wouldn't be back until Wednesday and we are all hoping we won't be here then. She was the first face we saw on this floor when we arrived on a Tuesday night, April 23 scared and exhausted after a very long ambulance ride. She showed the ambulance guys where to wheel his gurney to and of course it was this exact same spot room 618A. Brian moved over to his bed, the IV team came and put in two IV's (since he had lost his IV in the ambulance) which wasn't a great part of the night. I tried not to cry at this tiny little spot (I think I've mentioned that before) and reassure myself and Brian that it was going to be okay. That we had come to Dana Farber Cancer Institute and Boston Children's Hospital for the exceptional care and expertise, not the size of the room. We have had Laura help us on several different visits and lots of different shifts. We come in and out of her life, her everyday normal life of being a nurse, but she will not understand fully what she and many of the other nurses have meant to us. But she especially has made an impact on our lives.

As they all have, she has given us comforting looks and listening ears. She has answered questions and got us help. She sat and taught me how to read his blood counts every day and what they meant and what to watch for. She did this on our second night here, as I cried through it. Afraid of what this all meant, that I wouldn't understand or know what to do. Or that he would die. She helped me to prepare the first time we went home and told me I could do it, as I stood there crying through rounds once again. She always had a calm voice that always sounded sure of everything. She has given medicine and fluid and help. Day in and day out. She has watched us succeed and cheer us on. She has been in a way like a Mom to me (even though I'm probably old enough to be hers - almost).

So as I sat on my little bed, behind the curtain and listen to her talk to Bri as he lies in his bed, she tells him that she came to say goodbye. That she wouldn't be back until Wednesday and she hoped she wouldn't see us. She told him how nice it was to have met him and that she hoped he'd come back to visit. I sat in my little chair with my hands covering my mouth, and tears springing out of my eyes as I heard the voice that welcomed us... say goodbye. When she came around the curtain and started to head out the door, she saw me, tears streaming down my face and said the same things to me as I just nodded my head up and down, unable to speak. She said, "Come give me a hug" and I couldn't get there fast enough. I'm not a big hugger as many of you know, but this was one I was happy to give and receive. I tried to squeak out a "Thank you for all you've done for us" and she reassured me she was happy to have helped. Yet, she has no idea what she has actually done for us. At least I would guess she doesn't get it. If she does, what a blessing that must be. What a joy to show up and actually help people every day in the most personal of ways. What a special job to not only help people live, help children live, but to help people live through their time here and doing it with cheerful expertise and providing them with help, respect and dignity. It just dawned on me that I don't even know her last name. I will find out immediately when I'm done writing. And I will let her know how much she has meant to us. And we will come back to visit. That is for sure.

So today started so great! After getting woken up at about 3-ish due to Brian's pump going off twice and having to get up to call the nurse twice since Bri was pretty much dead to the world, I dozed on and off until 6:00 when I got up as usual, showered, dressed, got a cup of coffee and sat back in my little bed perusing great emails from people who I have touched with these updates. They are so nice to see and the first thing in the morning and I always look for peoples responses. They have been so helpful and encouraging to me. Anyway, when Anna came to get me for rounds I crawled out of my 3x7 foot cave and made my way into the hall. I met a bunch of new faces, as usual, and listened to the report on my son. When Anna got to his ANC level of 220 - I thrust my fists in the air and said "YES!!!" Everyone laughed, but they don't truly understand how thrilling that number is. That was the number I asked all the prayers for - and once again it worked!

For a while we thought we'd get discharged today and with our original plan to the Longwood Inn for the night. But that isn't the case. Here is the deal. We stay here tonight, Brian is scheduled for his last lumbar puncture at 8:30 tomorrow morning and as long as his counts stay above 200, we will be discharged late morning (I hope) and on our way home. Oh, please God! We are so excited to get home. Anyway, his Cytarabine ended at 1:00 and he's been unhooked from his IV machine since then. He will have another dose of IV antibiotics shortly and then one at 4 a.m. Hopefully he'll be disconnected all night, as long as he keeps drinking enough water.

So if all goes as planned, we'll be home in less than 36 hours. We won't have to come back for a month - then we'll have just an ultrasound and checkup. I'm so thrilled tonight, that I'm not even going to get into the worries that will start for the next two years. I'll worry about those worries later.

Happy, Happy thoughts from room 618A

Leslie

Sent: Monday, July 01, 2013 9:19 PM
From: Sarah S.
To: Leslie Jermainne
Subject: RE: Brian Ross Update 7/1

Your email tonight was very touching. I really enjoyed the part about the nurse telling you goodbye and how she was such a big part of your life but you were not a big piece of hers. But you're wrong. There are such special nurses who love their job like I do and when their patients are in pain they are too. Just from the many mentions of her I know you both will be a part of her life and history forever. Some patients take a part of your heart when they leave to go home. It happened to me when I finished my internship. I'm so happy Brian is doing well and I want you to know that I think and pray for him every day.

JULY 2, 2013

Sent: Tuesday, July 02, 2013 12:10 AM
From: Sheila
To: Leslie Jermainne
Subject: Re: Brian Ross Update 7/1

Home stretch, Leslie! Amazing, amazing marathon for Brian and for you! These remaining hours are nothing compared to what you've already done!

With love, prayers, and admiration,
Sheila <3

Sent: Tuesday, July 02, 2013 6:35 AM
From: Ann
To: Leslie Jermainne
Subject: RE: Brian Ross Update 7/1

That is a great e mail.

Although I don't save lives I have had occasion when people that I have helped in the past return for a visit. I have had people track down my address 10+ years later and send me a thank you card for changing their lives. I have become friends with someone who lost their arm (they were able to re-attach) who I treated for several years off and on. She tells me often that my encouragement is the reason that she went into the medical field. I can promise you that you have also touched her life and seeing you for the last time in the hospital (for a good reason) made her day. I can also promise you that she will remember you and most likely talk about you fondly to her family and friends.

Hope you guys get home soon

Sent: Tuesday, July 02, 2013 7:00 AM
From: Paula
To: Leslie Jermainne
Subject: Re: Brian Ross Update 7/1

Thank you God!! I am so glad you made it and I can't wait to hear those words that you are home, back in your boring home, with your boring dogs leading your boring lives! Have a safe trip home and can't wait to see you!!

Paula

Sent: Tuesday, July 02, 2013 8:36 AM
From: Laurie
To: Leslie Jermainne
Subject: Re: Brian Ross Update 7/1

Soooo happy for you Les in so many more ways than I can speak...can't wait to see you guys and watch your life unfold AT HOME! Remember that there are people out there who do care but maybe haven't the strength or courage to reach out to you...perhaps they feel like they don't matter, perhaps they don't want to be a bother....there are soooo many good people in the world, I truly believe goodness wins over everything else and thus the world keeps going...love you!

JULY 3, 2013

Sent: Wednesday, July 03, 2013 5:58 AM
From: Leslie Jermainne
To: My List
Subject: RE: Brian Ross Update 7/2

CHEMO IS DONE!!!!!!!!!!

Hi Everyone!

Sorry I didn't write last night like usual, but once getting home - it was just decompress time. But of course I'm up at 4:30, started laundry, talk and snuggle with Jackie Dog (Hollie's still sleeping), threw out old food, unpacked a bag. Then I just couldn't wait to see my emails, see all the "likes" on Facebook - everyone loving Bri's "My Last Chemo" photo. He may not look exactly like himself, but in a few weeks that hair should start coming back in and it won't take long to look like his old self

again since he usually keeps it shaved all summer anyway. I can't wait for that. To see my handsome boy without the only outward physical sign of this nightmare.

So here was our day yesterday. Again, I was awoken at 3:36 by our nurse coming in to hook Bri back up to his pump, administer his antibiotic, draw blood and start fluids. I couldn't go back to sleep. So much was spinning around in my crazy brain. Finally at 5:45 after reading every email and Facebook update I could and playing Candy Crush until I got locked out, I finally just got up. Showered, dressed, came back to our room to get our dirty laundry bag and decided to make the trek across the hospital to use that laundry room, as someone still had the laundry room key from the night before. As I left our room at about 6:15, I see our nurse sitting in the "nurse room" behind the desk. I get her attention and ask her from the darkened hallway, "How long before his CBC is back?" She says "Oh, I left the sheet on your table. 500". I am crying as I type this because the sheer happiness of that number was overwhelming. After several loudly whispered yells of "WOOOOOOO, WOOOOO-HOOOOOO" and a lot of jumping up and down and fist pumping by me, with tears streaming down my face and all the nurses smiling and laughing, I made my way crying in happiness to the laundry room. I sent my three warriors a text that just read "ANC 500!!!!!", as I cried and stuffed dirty clothes into the washer. Bri responded right away, and once knowing he was awake, and I was on my way back from Starbucks across the street - yes an ANC of 500 deserves a celebrational Quad Venti 2 Pump Cinnamon Dolce Latte (yup, that's my drink and in Boston it costs over $6.00 - but if there was ever a time to splurge, this was it)-I called him and cried through the sheer relief of such good news. 500 Baby!!!! 500! Did you hear me world - his ANC was 500! This is the borderline for neutropenia. He was at it and on his way back up. Back up in our room he was turning over in bed and I went to his side to whisper through my tears, "your ANC is 500!!" "YAAAA", he responded followed by "Please don't cry Mom". "These are tears of joy Boo!" And he went back to sleep.

After climbing back into my hole at about 7 (after going back across the hospital to put the clothes in the dryer) I was posting on Facebook for our "village" to see his ANC was 500. I truly, truly in my heart believe that the power of all these people thinking about us, which is what I call praying, and my concentration on him with Reiki (and I think other's out there too - Alison, Sarah) willing his bone marrow to generate white blood cells, is what got his body to respond. Believe it or not, doesn't matter to me, but I know. To have his ANC go from 220 to 500 overnight, and the night before when we all did the same thing and it went from 140 to 220, was nothing short of amazing. Believe me, the doctors thought so too. So again, thank you to everyone who thought about us, said a prayer however it is that you do that, made a wish or what have you. We all did it together.

At about 8:10 our other wonderful nurse Vicky came in and said, "we're going". Which means it's time for the lumbar puncture. Going to the O.R. entails moving him there in his bed, which means rearranging the furniture basically to get him out of the room. But before that happened Joan, the NP came and said to come out into the hall for Rounds - Our last Round might I add. I jumped at the chance, knowing it would take a few minutes to get him ready to go. As I got out our room door and saw the circle of faces standing behind their computers on roll around stands I started pumping my fists in the air again saying "500!!! 500!!! 500!!!" Everyone laughed and had big smiles on their faces, especially Joan. The usual talk started, but with lightness in her voice. "Brian is our 15 year old with stage III Burkitt Lymphoma. He has been afebrile since the 28th....." The talk goes on recounting every CBC number, every chemistry, every number, every option, "From an oncology point of view, from a medical point of view..." After that we were off to LP - which all went well. Only issue was his BP afterwards was 92/30. A little low!!! But they knew he was a little low on fluid from being unhooked all night. After a bolus of fluid it went up to 102/54 and we were good to head back. Once in the room, he got dressed ate his Pop Tarts (his choice) and I started the packing up task. A trip to the car and back and then wait, wait, wait for discharge. Finally at 1:30 (by the way we got back from LP at about 11:00) our discharge papers came through, I signed us out we grabbed our last bags and headed out. There were lots of people waiting for us by the desk, cheering, blowing bubbles, gave Bri an enormous guitar balloon. It was wonderful. Maybe a little embarrassing for the 15 yr. old boy. I felt a bit guilty for the happiness we were causing (remember my post the other night). But as I thought about it over and over on the way home and remembered the nurses and receptionist and resource staff all cheering and clapping for us and their smiles, I think they need those days even more than we do. I mean bubbles or no bubbles we were so thrilled. But it's not many days in there where someone is finished with chemo, feeling pretty good and heading home to get back to life. Maybe the other families were jealous or irritated at the commotion. But maybe, hopefully they were encouraged that their day will come, and I pray it is soon for them all. I know not everyone gets to leave the hospital like we did. I feel so incredibly lucky, grateful and humbled. I have some letter writing to do to the staff there and I'm sure we'll make some visits back to the floor to say hi. But for now, we are free!

The drive home was fine, with hardly any traffic and we got home about 4:30 to our ever excited dogs, beautiful home, pretty flowers and blue pool. I got a visit in with my parents, Laur & Jess (who is going to watch the dogs for us on the 4th/5th while we go to VT), and a nice long phone call with Al. A few glasses of wine and take out on the patio with my hubby and then collapse into bed by 9:15. When we got home Brian took the longest shower in the history of the world, got in fresh PJ's and hit the sack.

We have a blood draw scheduled for Sunday late in the day, and an appointment in Boston in 1 MONTH!!!! We are off to VT today, staying there tonight and Thursday night and back on Friday. Bri wanted to go, and it was something great to focus on this week in Boston. And we get to go! Maybe a mask here and there, lots of hand washing and being smart. A plan in place to Glen Falls, NY hospital if a fever should appear, but we have it under control.

So, we are home. I mean really home. I'm guessing you won't hear from me quite as much now. I still will give updates and maybe share as we actually process all that has happened to us. I'm grateful for many parts of our experience. I read someone saying they wouldn't have changed having the experience and blessings that cancer has brought into their lives. I thought about that for a split second and thought "I would. I would change every damn thing. I would throw this back in a heartbeat." Were there good things to come out of it? Yes. Are we done yet? No. We have at least 2 years until the words "cured" are uttered. And years of worrying. But for these next days - my cares are little and my happiness is huge.

I hope you all have a wonderful 4th of July. Thank you for all your support and love and encouragement and listening and praying and fear and hope. You have all helped us through this in ways you can't imagine. Keep us in your thoughts for Brian's recovery from this round, future scans, blood draws, visits to JFC and years of no long term effects. We will need it all.

Lots and lots of love and happiness from home.

Leslie

Sent: Wednesday, July 03, 2013 6:51 AM
From: Paula
To: Leslie Jermainne
Subject: Re: Brian Ross Update 7/2

You made it!!!! I am crying tears of joy right there with you baby!! You deserve every ounce of happiness you can imagine! Have a fabulous time in VT with your family, getting back to normal. Love and prayers continue, and God bless you all!

Paula

Sent: Wednesday, July 03, 2013 8:02 AM
From: Sheila
To: Leslie Jermainne
Subject: Re: Brian Ross Update 7/2

Tears of joy!!! I needed a good cry this morning. So happy for little Bri, for you, and your family.

Sent: Wednesday, July 03, 2013 12:35 PM
From: Karen
To: Leslie Jermainne
Subject: Re: Brian Ross Update 7/2

Leslie,

I have tears in my eyes writing this...so glad for you all that chemo is over!!!! I so hope that this is the END of illness and that Brian can return to the happy, healthy, normal 15 year old boy stuff that he'd like to do. Thinking of you all and sending hugs and healthy wishes!!!

xo Karen

Sent: Wednesday, July 03, 2013 6:28 PM
From: Rebecca B.
To: Leslie Jermainne
Subject: Re: Brian Ross Update 7/2

This is freedom...

Happy 4th!

Rebecca

JULY 6, 2013

Sent: Saturday, July 06, 2013 8:26 AM
From: Leslie Jermainne
To: My List
Subject: RE: Brian Ross Update 7/6

Wow - 3 days since I've said anything. Miss me? It was probably a relief.

Just wanted to give a quick update. We did go to VT and had a very nice time. We had a few bumps though, as I guess we should expect. But averted a trip to the hospital. On Wed. after we arrived, took a few deep breaths, got the A/C going, we were just laying around on the bed while Big Bri checked his emails. Bri felt warm to me. He said he felt fine, but he let me take his temp. 99.1. WHAT!!! He had a headache he admitted. I called JFC, as you must before you do anything. NO Tylenol for the headache. You can "mask" a developing fever by taking Tylenol. Give him one oxycodone for the headache and then wait and see. "Should I take his temp in an hour?" I ask. No, I'm told. Don't get crazy, and don't drive him crazy. He's 15 and he'll tell you if he feels crappy. YA RIGHT! I try to not do it but honestly, I started taking his temp like it's my full time job. I can't help it. Everything is so freakin' scary. And honestly he wants to know what it is too. Of course his response to potentially going to the hospital is... "I will shoot myself first." Comforting. As we lay around and worry for a bit I am typing away on my phone double checking the distance to Glen Falls NY hospital which I had decided was the closest at 40 min. when I had consulted MapQuest. I officially will never use MapQuest again. As I check the distance on my GPS feature it says something like "1 hour 17 min". Holy Crap! That is too far. It has to be under an hour and preferably under 45 min. I'm panicking. Anyway, his headache goes away and he wants to go to dinner. I'm freaking out. Once at the restaurant I say I have to use the bathroom and I go and call Alison.

Thank God, she is right there for me as I've already texted her a bit. I'm trying hard not to scare my son, but it's tough. I tell her I need her to start looking for the nearest hospital with a cancer center. That I thought Glen Falls was the place we'd go, but now I just don't know. She's on it. I tell her my phone is dying and we are at dinner, so text me the results, but text Big Brian's phone too. She gets working. Back out to dinner, trying to be light and breezy. I have to practically sit on my hand so as not to reach out and feel his head every 20 seconds or so. He doesn't eat much. DAMN IT! We head out to the car when done, and I check my phone - my savior has sent the details. Southern VT Regional Medical Center in Bennington. Phone number, distance, time, address. Perfect. 37 min. That's where we will go. Please send directions for the fastest route I text. I now look over and Big Brian is looking through his phone. He has this weird look on his face. I realize he's gotten the text too, but never knew it was coming. I reach over and squeeze his leg to say "Do not say a word. Brian has no idea I've asked for this information, nor that I'm expecting we will be needing it."

Brian looks at me and says "What was that for!" I give him the big "Shut your mouth eyes". He is not very versed in silent communication. He then announces he has some weird text from a number he doesn't recognize. He recites the number, which of course is Al's cell phone number. Thankfully little Brian isn't really listening. We arrive at the grocery store where we are going to pick up a few things. Little Bri stays in the cool car. Big Brian and I get out. As I round the car I start lecturing him, the poor guy. "What is wrong with you! When I squeeze your leg like that, that means to shut up, not announce what is on your phone." He denies doing any of that.... right honey? Anyway, we end up laughing thankfully, but I give him a short lesson on silent communication, which from my point of view is me saying – 'don't ever talk unless I tell you too.' Poor guy, I don't really know how he puts up with me.

Anyway, we get back to the room and I resume my 15 min. temp taking interval. I can't help it. We hit 100.2 at one point. I start repacking our bags while he takes a shower. Little Brian's and my clothes in one, big Brian's clothes in another. Medicine bag into the bag with my medical notebook, Brian gets directions loaded up on his phone. Brian and I make a plan. I will put EMLA cream on Bri's port because he will get accessed as soon as we get there. We will all drive to the hospital. Once he is hooked up and gets IV antibiotics started, and we've talked with JFC, Brian can go back to the motel. Stay the night, checkout and go home the next day. By that time Brian and I will have been sent via ambulance to Boston. We have our plan in place. Brian comes out of the shower, lays down and falls asleep after one more temp of 99.8 I think. I spend the night popping up every time I hear him move. "Is he hot?" "What's his temp?" "Is he restless?" "Should I wake him and take his temp?" "Will this night ever end?" Well, it does end finally when he wakes up at 9 a.m. with no fever at all. Thank God!! Crisis averted.

We have a very nice morning, go to our favorite breakfast spot, go the VT Country Store, pick up some sandwiches on the way back to our motel. Hang out a bit. He falls asleep about 3-ish. At 5:30 he wakes up but says he's too tired to go to dinner, but please go and bring him back something. We go and as we order our dinner and I order a burger to go for Bri, Big Brian tells the waiter. "Please, this burger has to be perfect. Please wait to cook it until we pay the bill so it will be hot and delicious.

It has to be the best burger ever because it's for my son and he was too tired to come to dinner because he just finished his last round of chemo and he's exhausted." The wonderful waiter asks us questions and tells us he wishes him the best and will keep him in his prayers. He does make sure we get the perfect burger and Bri eats the whole delicious thing when we get back. After the waiter left the table, I look at Bri and I realize he has the same weird feeling of wanting to tell everyone what has happened to our son and our life. It is like some weird compulsion to tell people "My son has cancer". Of course now we get to say "Our son HAD cancer". And I hope it always stays that way. Brian admits he has it too. We smile in understanding that only we get.

Friday we head to breakfast and once delivered Bri takes a bite or two and doesn't feel good. Out to the car he goes. Up pop new intense worry. Although nausea is welcome over fever. I wolf down my food and head to the car as Big Brian waits to pay the check. Once back in our room Bri feels better, we pack up and check out reserving our place for our usual Labor Day weekend trip. We head to the awesome book store and then the little country store on Main St. Then we grab some sandwiches for the ride home and head out of town. A successful trip with a few bumps in the road.

Once home I took a big breath of relief. All that stuff would have happened here I'm sure, but I can't help think I would have worried less being home. It is good to be home. I had a nice email from our social worker Phoebe asking how we were doing and how the transition to being "off active treatment" was going. She is wonderful, but I had to tell her, we haven't even approached that thought yet. I know it's true, but I think it will take a week or two to have that thought set in. But it's a nice prospect anyway. Off treatment. Those are beautiful words.

So today will be spent keeping cool, Brian resting, me cleaning the house up and hopefully swimming a bit and maybe a nap poolside. I hope you all have a wonderful day and weekend and remember to try to do a little bit of nothing.

Happy, happy thoughts from home.

Leslie

JULY 13, 2013

Sent: Saturday, July 13, 2013 11:12 AM
From: Leslie Jermainne
To: My List
Subject: RE: Brian Ross Update 7/13

Hi!

Just a quick note of update. We are doing well. Recovering and resting. Brian is still very tired. He had a blood draw yesterday and the main concern was dropping platelets. Those came back fine. But...his ANC is down again to 850. I thought it would continue to climb. Found out it could be a year or more before that number gets back to normal. GULP! I didn't know that. New questions everywhere. Starting a list for our visit on 7/30/13 to JFC.

We also had a little reminder of our fears. Everything is fine, but a trip to the doctor and tears and fears the night before. This is just all so scary. Starting to see Brian processing a little bit of what has and is happening to him. His fear is just as fresh as mine, he has just kept it under wraps more. But this first little blip brought it right to the surface. We had a good talk and I don't really want to share his thoughts as they are his, but I can share mine. Seeing my child so frightened, so "alone", so stressed is almost unbearable. I am realizing now how hard these next few years are going to be for our psyches. I feel like this wait and watch game is going to be almost more torture than active treatment. Ugh.

I will be seeking council again from our social worker in maybe finding help to get us through. One good point of news however is that we are switching Brian's primary care doctor here to Dr. D. This is the amazing doctor and man who is my father in-laws doctor and who helped me when we were stuck at the other hospital. I was in tears last night after talking with him and him agreeing to take Brian on as his patient. I feel such relief at knowing we will have his amazing oncology knowledge combined with his attention and compassion. I feel a great relief. We will meet with him next Friday for a meeting and I will finally get to meet this angel face to face. I can't wait.

Anyway...we are resting, adjusting, and learning what the future will hold. Slowly, day by day. But each day is a blessing. I saw a great bracelet that I may need to add to my Lymphoma awareness one and my "Life" bracelet that I have worn every day since day 1 at DFCI. It says "BE HERE NOW". Pretty simple. Pretty powerful. Definitely my new goal. Just wish it came in gold. ;-)

I have always asked for prayers from you all in the past, and still I hope for them to come my son's way for continued recovery and health. But today I'd like to add a wish for prayers for my high school friend. I mentioned him a few weeks ago in my note on 6/11/13. I had just found out that his Dad had an inoperable brain tumor. His Dad lost his battle with cancer this week. Just a month after diagnosis. Please send a prayer up to the powers that be for peace for my friend and his family as they say goodbye to their family patriarch.

Love from home.

Leslie

Sent: Saturday, July 13, 2013 1:10 PM
From: Lisa
To: Leslie Jermainne
Subject: Re: Brian Ross Update 7/13

Hi Leslie,

I'm so glad to receive this update. I wanted to talk with you the other night at practice, but I wasn't sure how you felt about discussing Brian's health in person rather than online. Anyway, I'm sorry that this is still so stressful for you and Brian (and I assume big Brian, too). I'm glad you are looking to the social worker for support and guidance.

For what it's worth, I refuse to even consider any other possibility than Brian living a long, healthy life. So if the power of positive thinking is worth anything, there's nothing but positive thoughts coming from our little corner of Westbrook!

Lisa

Sent: Saturday, July 13, 2013 4:15 PM
From: Leslie Jermainne
To: Lisa
Subject: Re: Brian Ross Update 7/13

Hi Lisa,

Thank you for your continued notes of support. I have no problem talking about it, although Brian gets a little upset at times if he overhears me. He isn't upset I'm talking about it, it is just that he wants to move on. But no worries about discussing it in front of others.

The power of positive thinking is worth everything to me. At times I feel like it's all I've got - so the more the merrier. I appreciate all you have done for us - positive thinking, prayers, words of support. It is all greatly appreciated!

Leslie

JULY 15, 2013

Sent: Monday, July 15, 2013 6:42 AM
From: Ann
To: Leslie Jermainne
Subject: RE: Brian Ross Update 7/13

Les,

Know that people are still thinking of you all daily. You may not be getting as many e mails but I know everyone is still wishing you the best. It is ironic that you mention these next two years in some respects will be more difficult than the initial treatment. When we were out on the boat this weekend with Eric and Sharon, Sharon asked me how you were doing. We were talking about how this part of the recovery seems like it would be more difficult; change and decrease in professional support network, and the waiting for that magical two year mark.

Hang in there.

Ann

Sent: Monday, July 15, 2013 5:19 PM
From: Leslie Jermainne
To: Ann
Subject: RE: Brian Ross Update 7/13

Thanks Ann - it is going to be tough. I am still mulling around talking with a therapist myself. I am still on the verge of tears at any given moment (like right now) and it gets exhausting. I am fucking scared to death, anytime I think about relapse, or the future, or appointments, or just about anything to do with this. But it is what it is and I can't change a single thing, except my thoughts, and I'm trying to be positive. It's tough.

Thanks for reaching out so much to me. I really does help getting notes like this, and knowing people are out there and haven't gotten bored with our story or forgotten we are still fighting. It isn't over, and I'm not sure it ever will be.

Love Ya Girlfriend!
Les

JULY 22, 2013

Sent: Monday, July 22, 2013 5:56 AM
From: Leslie Jermainne
To: My List
Subject: RE: Brian Ross Update 7/22

Hi Everyone,

I have been thinking of sending out an update for a few days, and for some reason I couldn't sleep this morning - so now is the perfect time. Things have been really good. It has been over a week since I updated last... what have we been doing?

Brian has been resting and recovering still. His energy is definitely starting to return. As is a little bit of peach fuzz on his head (and face - time to start shaving again?) He has mostly been indoors this past week due to the extreme heat - as I bet a lot of you were.

Last Friday was an awesome day. We went to meet with Dr. D. and he was as fabulous as I expected. Brian, Brian and I spent about an hour talking and Bri had a very quick exam so that Dr. D. would have a baseline to know what his underarm and stomach area feel like. The best part is his encouragement and reassurance that Brian is doing extremely well and it is time for him "to get back to his life". He was so wonderful about empowering Brian that he is a person, not just a patient. That he knows himself and his body and will know if he needs care. To not live in a cancer cage and not rely on everyone else to decide what is right for him to do. He also said to him that "where the mind goes, the body will follow". Boy do I believe that - and I hope he will put more stock in that kind of thinking in the future. It was amazing to hear again that Burkitt Lymphoma is THE most aggressive cancer in humans. The doubling rate for tumors can be 24-48 hours. This is unheard of Dr. D. explained and we are so lucky that Brian caught this early. That he felt these "lumps" and that our doctor, surgeon and we, got on this immediately. Scary, scary stuff.

After our meeting and dinner, Brian and I went to the Deep River Ancient Muster (DRAM) and watched the Tattoo, then Brian played in the jam session until just past 10:30! That was so awesome to see him playing and having fun and being "back to his life". Excellent evening!

Saturday he was so exhausted he was almost near tears to get up at 9:45 and go back to watch the parade. We drove up and he stayed in the car for over half the parade. Then he perked up, watched for a bit and followed his corps to the field. We spent the day there, until about 4:30 when a thunderstorm moved through. I have never been so HOT is my entire life. Seriously. Like I felt sick from the heat. Brian did very well, but I was happy to go home for a break. We both dove in the pool quickly and showered off, ate some dinner before returning to the field for just a bit of jam session - as most people had left.

Here is my amazing story from that day. As I followed my friend Toni to the Mariner's tent for a cold beer - she introduced me to a woman there. This nice woman asked me how I was involved in drum corps and I explained that the corps my brother and sisters grew up playing with is now the corps my son has joined. I explained that he was not participating today because he was recovering from chemo as he had been diagnosed with Non-Hodgkins Lymphoma in April. She replied that her son had just passed his 5 year mark of being cancer free, as he was diagnosed when he was 8. "What kind of Lymphoma?" I asked her. "Oh, it's very rare, you wouldn't have ever heard of it. It's called Burkitt," she replied. "WHAT!!!!!!" I practically yelled in shock. She couldn't believe it either. Her son was pretty sick and had almost a full year of treatment, but is doing great. He is a fifer, but wasn't there that day as he was at basketball camp, but I'm hoping we see them again soon and Brian can meet her son. It was amazing to talk with another Mom - I definitely have to get her email from Toni! *hint, hint*. The poor lady doesn't know what she's in for!

The other great thing we heard on Saturday is more news of Brian's Make-A-Wish. Today, Brian, Brian, Abby and I will be heading to the post office to expedite our passports. We have a tentative schedule to travel to Italy on 10/9-10/16 starting with 3 days in Rome, then a train ride to Sorrento for 3 days where we will have a private tour one day of Pompeii. This is still very tentative and nothing can be booked until passports are in place. Bri was right - we should have gotten on that sooner. But still - super excited. Got to figure out the dog thing - Maybe Jessie??? *hint, hint - again!*

Yesterday was spent recovering from the weekend. Plus dinner with my parents and Auntie Al that entailed a lot of drumming and drum talk. Thank goodness Bri has Auntie Al to play with and talk with as I'm pretty clueless about drums. I should pick up the fife again so I could play with Bri.

Emotionally, I feel a bit better this week. I'm still petrified to go to Boston on the 30th, and it makes me choked up to think about it. The fear pops right back up in front on my face and makes me feel like that wavy heat off the pavement last week. It still completely overwhelms me. The emotions and tears are still just under the surface and pop up in a quick second at any time. Good or bad. Just telling Alison about the trip while watching the parade, brought fresh tears. Anything related to this time, this cancer, this nightmare - even the good stuff - just brings it right back.

Emotionally, I think Bri had a better week - no bumps or lumps or sickness - a touch of swimmers ear, as Dr. D. told us, that brought gut wrenching worry to me - but he was okay with it. Some "crabbiness". Out of sorts. Talking in a not so nice tone of voice, but I'm unsure if it is teenager speak or cancer speak. It could be both. He apologized one day after his snapped retort. He's such a good, brave boy. So much to deal with in his young life. If only I could take it all and free him of this shackle. That would be my wish.

This week should be peaceful and restful with a bit cooler temps, getting ready to camp in NY next weekend, continuing to work on the 2 family house every day from 6:00 am - 9:00 am every day. Ooops! Better get moving, I'm gonna be late!

Thanks for listening. Keep Bri in your prayers. And send some up for my good friends, hairdresser and landscaper, as his Mom is in her own battle with cancer. It just never seems to end now. This person, that person, my Mom, my son, my friends. We are all touched by this nightmare. I am praying for them, and if you can too, I would appreciate it.

Love and Light from home - still!

Leslie

JULY 29, 2013

Sent: Monday, July 29, 2013 2:45:38 PM
From: Leslie Jermainne
To: My List
Subject: RE: Brian Ross Update 7/22

Hi There!

Well it's been another week of life and we are still here doing well. Working hard on the 2 family house. The lower unit is just about done and hopefully we'll get a renter quickly. Then we move to the other unit and get started there. Quite a bit to do.

Last week went well for Bri. Definitely seeing the "chemo brain" set in some more. Forgetfulness, "what was I getting?" "what did you want me to do?" He hasn't said anything yet, and not even sure he realizes it. He has some blond peach fuzz coming in on his head. I can't wait to see it back - will it stay so much lighter than before? It reminds me of his hair as a baby which looked like spun gold.

We had our camping trip muster in NY this weekend. We arrived with a car full of other kids and tons of stuff - thank goodness I have a mini-van. We got set up and all our corps started to arrive. After getting pizza for dinner for everyone, we settled in for the evening, listening to fife & drums all around and the kids went off to the jam session. 11:30 bedtime for me - and I was the first to turn in. Of course I wake up at 5:00 a.m. and always the first to get up. I snuck my car out at 6 a.m. and found the local Dunkin Donuts. Waited around for an hour until Shop Rite opened and brought back stuff for everyones breakfast. The parade and muster went well, and we decided due to showers that might happen overnight to pack up and go home. We got to our house about 8pm. Tired, but happy. Brian marched in his first parade & muster playing the snare drum (he was playing bass before) and did a great job.

So, the big thing is tomorrow. Tomorrow we go back for our first "checkup". We need to arrive at Jimmy Fund Clinic by 10:45 for a blood draw, then go to Boston Children's for an ultrasound, then back to Jimmy Fund at 12 for a visit with Anna our N.P. I'm full of worry. I'm scared to go. I'm scared not to go. I have so much dread and fear it is overwhelming at moments, and the tears come. What if this, what if that...I know it makes no sense to worry about the future, and I'm trying hard to BE HERE NOW, but it is tough at moments. I want so badly for this to be over and never come back. I wish so much this had never, ever happened to my baby boy. This stuff he has been through, his body has endured and mind has wrestled with or blocked out all together is so much. Oh, the joy young people have, who have no cancer or life threatening illness, and they don't even know it. We never knew how lucky we were. How do you go back or forward to being a "normal teenager" again. You don't. And that is sad. But, it is what it is.

So tomorrow, if we cross your minds, send Bri a prayer that all is good, no signs of cancer and welcome home with another month to go before our next checkup.

Thank you all - from home.

Leslie

Sent: Monday, July 29, 2013 2:54 PM
From: Kim
To: Leslie Jermainne
Subject: prayers

Sending prayers your way for you, Brian and your family. It is amazing how far you have come. I know the road is long and you worry about what is normal. Only you can define normal, it is different for each person and I think you have done a fantastic job keeping life normal.

Keep up the good work and I will keep praying for you. I do my praying in the car on my way to and from work - so hopefully you are feeling the love! Kim

Sent: Monday, July 29, 2013 3:49 PM
From: Sheila
To: Leslie Jermainne
Subject: Re: Brian Ross Update 7/22

Prayers and good thoughts for Brian tomorrow (and you). I am training for a half marathon Oct. 12th. Now is as good a time as any. I am dedicating one of my miles to Brian, and one to you.

xoxo Sheila

Sent: Monday, July 29, 2013 8:51 PM
From: Brian W.
To: Leslie Jermainne
Subject: Re: Brian Ross Update 7/22

Just sent you all a prayer and deep thought, Leslie.... so glad he (and you) got to the muster for the weekend. I know that for a fife and drum kid, that can be great therapy regardless of the ailment.

Good luck this week, and I'm thinking of you.

Brian

JULY 30, 2013

Sent: Tuesday, July 30, 2013 8:22 PM
From: Leslie Jermainne
To: My List
Subject: RE: Brian Ross Update 7/30

Hi!

Just a quick note in case you don't see my updates on Facebook - we had a GREAT day today. Preliminary ultrasound results showed all sites looking smaller. His blood counts were awesome! ANC of 4.1, platelets, hemoglobin, hematocrit and WBC all up. Just such an amazing relief from the unbridled fear that had taken hold of me. It was tough at a few times today to keep the tears locked down, both in fear and then in joy. If I show them in joy, then he knows that they were there in fear. We had such a good talk with Phoebe our social worker and of course Anna, our N.P. Lots of restrictions were lifted, and life should return so much to normal - at least in activity.

We should hear about having his port removed in the next two weeks, and then the last remaining restrictions should be lifted. So exciting. Of course the fear will still lurk until a week or so before our next appt on 8/27 when it will pop up and taunt me I'm sure. But until then, I will try my best to practice my new found mantra of "Be Here Now".

Thank you all for the support and words of encouragement for today. They truly, truly helped me and in turn I can help him. So thank you.

Peace, happily from home.

Leslie

Sent: Tuesday, July 30, 2013 8:35 PM
From: Sheila
To: Leslie Jermainne
Subject: Re: Brian Ross Update 7/30

Tears of joy here. Woo-hoo!

August 2013

AUGUST 11, 2013

Sent: Sunday, August 11, 2013 6:02 AM
From: Leslie Jermainne
To: My List
Subject: Brian Ross Update 8/11

Hi!

I planned on sending a quick update last night, but the nice evening on the patio for dinner with my boys and then a movie ("Admission" - so, so) had me distracted. The reason I had wanted to update last night was because an amazing thing took place yesterday. If you all remember my BFF Stacy signed up to ride 25 miles on her bike to raise money for cancer research. Well yesterday was the day! She did it with flying colors. She raised $4,150.00 which was matched by her sponsor Bath and Body Works for a total raised of $8,300.00 all going directly to cancer research. This still makes me cry every time I think of what she has done for my son and for me. She is one of the best!!!!

We have been working on processing this whole mess and recovering at home. We have had some bumps (literally and figuratively) that have made us worried, scared, fearful and sent us to the doctor's office and precipitated phone calls. The worry has been over the scar area on his abdomen. Everyone is in agreement that it is scar tissue. But as it continues to heal it changes in feeling for Brian. Like I've said before, every little "bump" is HUGE! I explained to someone the other day that this whole cancer "thing" has been like not knowing what a tornado is or what it is like, then having no warning system and a tornado came and picked us up. It threw us around for over two months of constant twirling and whirling and fear of dying and then set us back down, gently right in the same spot. But everything is a bit different now. Now we know what a tornado feels like, how scary it is, how it can kill you. And we can't unlearn that. And we keep watching for another tornado even though it may be unlikely to ever hit again.

So...tomorrow will bring a follow up visit to Dr. D. so he can examine Bri's stomach and confirm nothing has changed. Next Thurs. we will be going to Waltham to the medical center there to have Brian's port removed. (Unless something should appear different tomorrow). Then we have changed his next checkup from 8/27 to 8/20. This change is not because anything is a concern, but it's to help alleviate our worries. Brian seems happy about that. We are going to have another nice long talk with our oncologist and nurse practitioner to try and help alleviate our fears of relapse.

So I know it's been awhile, but that is all our news. Brian is doing well, still tired, but all in all doing great. His energy has definitely picked up a lot! He will be marching in the parade and performing on stand at the Westbrook Muster in two weekends and is now playing the snare drum. His hair is coming back - and seems quite a bit lighter. I think he might be a blond for a while. Not seeing curls yet, but it is still just super fine "baby" hair so it's tough to know.

Among all our "good" news, we received some sad news yesterday. My friends, who I reported had his Mom diagnosed with lung cancer just 3 months ago, lost his mother yesterday. She put up the best fight that she could, as they all did. We know No One Fights Alone! So please send my friends prayers for peace as they say goodbye to his Mom.

Peace from home.

Leslie

[This is the email Stacy sent after her bike ride]

Just wanted to take a moment to thank ALL of you. For your donations, your words of encouragement, your prayers for Brian. I thought I would share some information with you that shows just how powerful we are if we all fight together....PELOTONIA: More than 6700 riders. Pelotonia has the most participants of ANY single-event cycling fundraiser in the country. Pelotonia's grand total BEFORE Saturday's Ride was $53.5 Million. Organizers predict that this year's ride will produce a record-breaking $18 Million when they stop collecting donations in October. AMAZING! 100% of that to Cancer Research. So, once again, THANK YOU ALL! No one fights alone.

Love Team Brian!

AUGUST 18, 2013

Sent: Sunday, August 18, 2013 5:31 AM
From: Leslie Jermainne
To: My List
Subject: From Brian Ross Jermainne - Support My Walk to say Thank You

Hi Everyone!

Brian has asked (and we've said yes) that he join his sisters who are walking in his honor at the 25th Annual Boston Marathon Jimmy Fund Walk on Sunday September 8th. I'm not going, as he is asserting his independence and would like to do something without Mom and Dad! Brian had his port removed on 8/15/2013 and on Tuesday 8/20/13 we will be heading to Boston for his next checkup.

Going back up to Boston where we stayed the night before his port removal (since it was a 7:30 a.m. appointment) was a bit of a flashback and made me feel, ummm....uneasy? It felt so much like the time we stayed over at the Longwood Inn @ BCH before entering the hospital for 7 days for round 3. Then having him wheeled off again into surgery and seeing him lying there on the gurney afterwards, asleep and groggy. It was a great day as far as getting the port out is just another sign that he is okay, but it was much harder to take for me than I ever thought it would be.

Anyway...He is signed up to walk and he wants to give back and say thank you to all the amazing people (his doctors, nurse practitioner, nurses, everyone!) who saved his life. So, I'm forwarding his donation page. He needs to raise $300 in the next 3 weeks. I'm hoping there are 30 people in our lives that will make a $10.00 donation to my son and show him your support as you have these long few months. I can't thank you all enough for the support you have given me, that has given me the strength on many days, to give him all my support, love and attention. There is a link below to go to his page.

I will update you all again after our appointment next week, where I pray nothing has changed and he continues to recover from the chemotherapy and all that goes with it.

Thank you!!!

Light & Love from home.
Leslie

AUGUST 20, 2013

Sent: Tuesday, August 20, 2013 8:17 PM
From: Nico
To: Leslie Jermainne
Subject: Lil' Brian

Hello Leslie,

Well, a long belated return note. I am so sorry for the delay. Every time I looked at your note I wanted to call instead of writing but I only wanted to try calling during the daytime during the week so I wouldn't disturb anyone on nights or weekends. I hope Brian is feeling ok and that things are going well. I was quite shocked to get your letter with that info within it. Your journey must have been quite difficult to date...obviously something we see but not something you can ever fully understand (although I try). I hope that the treatments are going as planned without too much interruption because of low WBC counts, side effects, etc. I am glad you found Dana Farber.

It was my pleasure and honor to care for him and get to know the two of you so well over the years. He was always such a nice, kind kid and he has turned out to be such a wonderful young adult. I know that the course over the last 5 months must be tough for him physically but emotionally it certainly can be just as hard (in a sense). I know that the love you always show him will be just as important as his medicines. I guess you have to remain positive and take each challenge head on.

Please give him my best and let him know I have been thinking about him a lot since I got your note--it has been sitting on my desk since.

When time, please send me a line or two on how he is doing.

Be well,
Love
Nico

AUGUST 22, 2013

Sent: Thursday, August 22, 2013 9:58 AM
From: Leslie Jermainne
To: Brenda
Subject: RE: From Brian Ross Jermainne - Support My Walk to say Thank You

Hi Brenda!

So his checkup was really good - we had a good long talk with his team about us not being so worried about relapse (easier said than done), and I think we are getting there. My wonderful son told them when they asked him if he was as worried as his mother was, he said "I'm really just worried For HER." He's such an amazing young man. I am so proud of him. He is so kind and thoughtful and generous.

Anyway - everything was good. We have the next checkup scheduled for 9/24 and he will need an echocardiogram on that visit. They have to watch for heart damage due to one of the chemo drugs. He had a very extensive echo before starting chemo and this will be his first since then to get a baseline being off treatment. So scary. Every little thing just brings up fear after fear after fear. But there is nothing to do about it.

Leslie

AUGUST 21, 2013

Sent: Wednesday, August 21, 2013 6:18 AM
From: Leslie Jermainne
To: Nico
Subject: RE: Lil' Brian

Dear Nico,

What a nice note to wake up to (very early thanks to my dogs). I was kind of wondering what happened. I thought maybe you never got it, but no worries, just great to hear from you. I'm not even sure where in our process I wrote that note so I will try to sum the whole thing up.

On 7/2/13 Brian finished his last chemo. YUP! We are done and he is doing very, very well. He had 5 rounds of chemo at DFCI/JFC/BCH, with each round we were inpatient for 7-8 days followed by up to 13 days at home (usually more like 7-10). It was very intensive treatment. Physically he did so very well. No mouth sores, little nausea (of course all the meds helped with that), didn't lose tons of weight, small bouts of neuropathy which seem to have passed, hair is growing back (blonde like when he was little), he withstood the 11 lumbar punctures (propofol helped). He had no fevers out of the hospital, and only one on his last round of chemo, which broke w/in 24 hrs., he became neutropenic then, but his counts miraculously rose quickly and we got to go home on time (which was huge, emotionally). He had his port removed last Thursday and yesterday we were at Jimmy Fund for our two month checkup (a week early). Everything is fine. He is examined by his doctors and every 3 months he will have an ultrasound under his right arm which appears to be the primary site. He also had a tumor removed from his left abdomen at biopsy by Dr. R. and on his PET scan it showed a smaller area on his right abdomen and right gluteal area. His last PET/CT scan showed all clear. He will not be having anymore PET/CT scans unless they are concerned there is a relapse.

So, that's the physical part and you are right - emotionally is another story. Round 4 & 5 became very difficult emotionally and psychologically. He became somewhat depressed. The caregivers in Boston were amazing. They listened to me, talked with him, and did everything they could to accommodate him, and talk him through this. He is really starting to get back to himself, although we are now realizing that there really is no going back, only forward. I think his biggest difficulty now is how mature he is for his age. I always felt he was an old soul, more mature for his age than many of his peers, being homeschooled and with adults a great deal of the time. But now, having gone through what he has, facing his own mortality in some shape and form has made him all the more older and dare I say wiser. It seems a bit difficult to hang out with his friends his age, as they are concerned with stuff that doesn't seem so important to him now. He wants to get on with life, very quickly these days and with turning 16 in October, it is hard to stop him. But, I guess there are worse things than having a mature, sensitive, smart, funny and kind child. ;-)

As for me, well - I think in some ways this has been the hardest on me. Not physically of course, although those little fold out sleeping chairs in Boston have much to be desired. ;-)

But I still cry at a drop of the hat - even a note like yours. This has all just been so overwhelming. The fear, the worry, the "what if's". But I'm now learning to be much more present every day, and wear a bracelet that say "Be Here Now" to remind me. Today he doesn't have cancer and today is all we have. People say what a blessing cancer can be (or any life threatening condition) because it does make you realize important things like this. I will never say this has been a blessing. It has been a nightmare. And it isn't over. There are years of worry, exams, fears to get through. But I will say it has had some positive effects. Yesterday Brian was asked by his team if he was as worried as me about relapse. His answer was he was worried FOR me. Ugh. The last thing he needs is anymore pressure. I thought I was hiding a lot well, but I guess after us being so close all these years, he knows me so well. Relapse is my greatest fear, because with Burkitt the prognosis on relapse drops, dramatically. But every month, every checkup that we get through, I feel better.

Brian has great things coming up, including his Make-A-Wish being granted. It looks like his wish to go see the ruins at Pompeii, Italy is going to come true in mid-October. Just before his birthday. It's very exciting, as we've not traveled out of the US (and barely in the US for that matter). I'm also allowing him to go to a concert in a few weeks with his sister Abby in Mass., stay overnight, spend the day in Boston doing fun stuff, then staying overnight in Boston and participating in the Jimmy Fund/ Boston Marathon Walk with both his sisters. Here is a link to his page: **http://www.jimmyfundwalk.org/2013/brianrjermainne**. Normally, we wouldn't let him go to a concert at this age, but this changes everything. As long as I know he is as safe as he can be, I trust him and his sister (plus her boyfriend and friend) to be responsible, then I'm choosing to let him experience a concert which is one of the things he wanted to do. And then he turns around and wants to go walk with his sisters to give back to The Jimmy Fund and Dana Farber for saving his life. I've got such an amazing child.

So this was more than a line or two I know, but I've always been a talker, and there is just so much to say about him and going through this battle. I hope all is well with your family and you had a fun summer. I can't believe it is time for school to start already. Last thing I knew it was late April and someone stopped the world from spinning.

Best to you and your wife.

Leslie

AUGUST 22, 2013

Sent: Thursday, August 22, 2013 10:35 PM
From: Nico
To: Leslie Jermainne
Subject: Re: Lil' Brian

Hello Leslie,

What a great story. You do have an amazing child ---mature, not concerned about some of the mundane things kids think of, wanting to give back (Jimmy Fund Walk) so quickly before all his 'wounds have healed'...an old but wonderful soul!!! I have learned a lot about how families deal with this thru work as a resident and in our office and I guess you have to move forward, appreciate the day today and cherish your friends and families. But in retrospect he must be proud how he faced a challenge only a few have faced (even if on occasion he felt depressed, sad, scared) and now is cancer free. I am sure he will have the strength to handle the worries and anxieties when he has his frequent check-ups at DFCI.

Good for him for the walk. We made a small donation to his cause; I am not sure if your family is religious or not but I will say a prayer in church on Sunday for good health for all of you (Greeks are big into that!).

Please give him my best and tell him I am sorry I didn't know that he was dealing with all this until your note;

I am proud of him and really in awe of the clear story you have told me about him.

I hope to see you around town; Safe travels to the concert, the Walk, and most important to Pompeii--how great.

Nico

AUGUST 26, 2013

Sent: Monday, August 26, 2013 6:08 PM
From: Leslie Jermainne
To: My List
Subject: Brian Ross update 8/26/2013

Hi Again!

I never updated you all from our appointment last Tuesday. I guess now is as good a time as any. Everything was good. We met with his NP, and his Oncologist and our beloved social worker, who keeps us sane. Phoebe is leaving the Jimmy Fund Clinic and going to work at the Yawkey Center which is the adult side of Dana Farber Cancer Institute. I don't know what I'll do without her.

We had a long talk about our worries of relapse. We were feeling much better at our appointment than we had 2 weeks earlier when Bri noticed his abdominal scar felt different and we freaked! Was it a new lump? Was it back? But after our wonderful Dr. D. examined him on two occasions, we all agreed it was scar tissue and was changing as it continued to heal. Anyway, while talking in Boston Dr. D asked Brian "Are you as worried about relapse as your Mom?" Brian replied, "I'm more worried ABOUT my mom." This was followed by more "AAAWWWW, you are just the best kid ever!" THAT we have heard before, because frankly he is the best kid ever. I worry that I haven't hidden enough from him however. Not that I want to hide it all, but I don't want him worrying about me. I did read an interesting post on a Burkitt Board I read (although I've stopped because it was too upsetting....for now.) The post was written by a caregiver who felt so badly because she freaked out and cried and cried in front of her husband/ patient with Burkitt. Every response was great and understanding, except for one. That one was so great. It was someone responding that through his cancer his family had been so strong, so courageous, never cried, never let him see their worry. And he felt like maybe they didn't care enough. He felt like if he didn't make it then they would be fine. He talked about seeing tears and worry on his loved ones faces meant they cared. Meant that they too were devastated by what was happening. And when they were upset, it let him comfort them for a change. So the lesson, and it's a true one from my perspective...don't keep it all inside. Don't always show a brave face. Emotions are important, to everyone. Brian worries for me, because strangely enough, during his lifetime, but before I ever thought cancer would be a word that we would become so familiar with, I had told him I wouldn't be able to live without him. That my life would end if his ever did. When we were at the first hospital, on that particularly bad Sunday and he was devastated, he asked me through his tears - "Mom, if I die, will you be okay?" And my answer was "No. I won't. I won't ever be okay." And I wouldn't. I wouldn't want him to ever think I would be okay. I want him to see my tears sometimes, my worries, my love.

Enough of that - things are good. Brian's energy is getting better every day. This past weekend he participated fully in the Westbrook Muster and got a new snare drum! It's beautiful. This coming weekend, we will be going to VT as we always do for Labor Day and we can't wait!!!! Very excited for a relaxing weekend away.

We will be going back to Boston on 9/24/13 for our usual checkup and an echocardiogram that they want to get a baseline after treatment. One of the chemo meds can cause heart damage in years to come, so it's another thing to watch out for. Hopefully everything else will be fine.

Thank you all for your continued support and prayers. I'm hoping to have some photo's after Brian completes his Jimmy Fund walk on 9/8/13.

Lots and lots of love from home.

Leslie

September 2013

Brian and his sisters Abby & Brittany at the JF walk

SEPTEMBER 24, 2013

Sent: Tuesday, September 24, 2013 6:44 PM
From: Leslie Jermainne
To: My List
Subject: RE: Brian Ross update 9/24/2013

Hi Everyone!

We had another appointment at the Jimmy Fund Clinic so I thought it would be a good time to say hello. First of all, nothing but good news.

No lumps or bumps where they shouldn't be. Brian is feeling really good, maybe a bit more tired than the old days but that's it. His hair, eyebrows and eyelashes are all back (much lighter than before) and he looks good!

We had a nice visit with Anna our N.P. and even stopped by 6 North, our old home to say hi. We saw two people who knew us (a nurse and a receptionist) and got to catch up a bit. They all thought he looked taller. I think it's just the hair. After that we went to 6 South and he had an echocardiogram and EKG. Everything seemed fine - but my expertise in reading the Echo isn't what it used to be. No one came rushing in to look at it live, so I'm assuming everything is fine. I know they will let us know if it is not.

We got out of there about 11:00 and headed home getting here by about 2-ish (stopped off for lunch in Pomfret). Bri relaxed and enjoyed the good news for the afternoon - I went to the investment house and spray painted all the kitchen cabinets with Rustoleoum. Never. Again. I will spare you the details, but they are done.

We were so good today, so good at the appointment, feeling so good. I was so happy and so was he. About two weeks ago, while at the other house, I was taking a break, having some coffee and checking email and the ever present Facebook. I see an article from Dana Farber by Dr. D. (she did Brian's first LP - and she was awesome!) about childhood cancer, signs, symptoms, treatments, etc. At the end she wrote where to get good info on the web. I of course had to go look up Burkitt for like the thousandth time. I read through all the details of potential relapse, the averages, the stages whatever. I sat there crying in my folding chair, as Brian breezed through the room with a board or piece of sheetrock and stopped dead and asked "why are you crying now?" "Never mind, I'm fine," I said. He has gotten quite used to it. After reading all this info and trying to figure what box Brian fits into in terms of potential relapse, it finally, finally hit me. THERE IS NO ANSWER. NONE. No matter what, I can't figure it out. Even if he fit into the perfect "what if scenario for relapse", there still is no answer, because it might not happen. And every minute I cry through trying to figure it out is a minute I've wasted living today. It was a very freeing day that day. It doesn't mean I don't worry - but I put it in its place. It doesn't mean I don't think about what we've been through, what might and might not come our way. But I know to put it away, it is doing me no good. If you worry about things that haven't happened yet, and then they do happen, well you have to live through them twice. Once is enough, thank you very much.

So- on a good note - on Monday we are going to have a nice dinner at Penny Lane Pub put on by Make-A-Wish to grant Brian's wish. We will be traveling to Rome, Italy on 10/9 then to Pompeii and back to Rome returning home on 10/16 and we are PSYCHED! I'll fill you all in later.

We have had a nice month, a party at our house last weekend, enjoyed VT very much over Labor Day - and have decided to spend Thanksgiving there as well. I can't wait! We love VT.

So, thanks to all of you that continue to say hi and send us love and prayers and smiles and happy thoughts. We love you all and have never, for one day, lost the idea that you have saved us. In so many, many ways. I am wearing Bri's shirt right now that he got in the hospital and it says it all. Life is Good.

Goodnight from home.

Leslie

October 2013

OCTOBER 18, 2013

Sent: October 18, 2013, 8:43 AM
From: Leslie Jermainne
To: MAW
Subject: Italy Trip

Hi!!!

What an amazing trip. Still recovering from the jet lag a bit, but so worth it. Everything was wonderful. We were so well taken care of, no worries just like you said.

Just to give you a run down, the limo ride down to JFK was great. So nice not to worry about traffic, directions, etc. The car was beautiful and the driver was awesome. We got checked right in with Alitalia and the seats were great. I can't tell you how thankful we were to have a bit of an upgrade on the seats. Being tall and having that bit of extra leg room made such a huge, huge difference. The flight was fine and arrived on time. After getting through security it took a bit of doing to find our driver, but nothing we couldn't handle. He whisked us away and thank goodness we had him. The driving there is insane!

We arrived at Starhotel Metropole which was beautiful. We settled into our rooms, got some food, met with our Monograms tour rep and then napped! The kids were very tired, so they skipped the bus tour around Rome, but Brian and I went and it was great. Dinner every night was wonderful and we tried different spots just steps from our door. Our last dinner in Rome was especially wonderful as we had finally settled in to eating late (8:30 or so) and we sat outside and had a long Italian dinner with lots of discussion of our events and great conversations about life with the kids.

We didn't go the Vatican tour the first morning, we were just too exhausted, but we did do the afternoon tour of the Coliseum, the Forum and more places that were amazing. Brian was eating up every minute! He was teaching us so much stuff. The guides were great and everything went smoothly. Saturday we went on our own to the Pantheon, and then walked to the Trevi Fountain to launch our coins in and then on to the Spanish Steps. It was wonderful to wander through these little alley ways filled with shops and food and culture abound.

Brian, Abby & Me in front of the Pantheon

On Sunday getting to the train station was great and the tour people had everything under control. The train ride was very nice, comfy and we got to see some of the countryside. Again, the tour person waiting in Naples got us all loaded onto the bus and the ride to Sorrento was thankfully driven by someone other than us! It was nice to relax, but those Italian drivers are crazy! The scenery was beautiful and once settled in our new hotel, we got to open the doors and enjoy the amazing view of the Mediterranean and Mt. Vesuvius right from our balconies. Again, the kids were tired so they skipped the walking tour, but Brian and I joined in and

Brian overlooking Sorrento and Mt. Vesuvius from hotel rooma

it was great! We got the lay of the land and returned to wake them up and stroll around town for a dinner spot.

The next day we opted out of the arranged Monograms tour to Pompeii since it would only allow us 2 hours at the site. However the guide helped us to arrange a private driver and we stayed on site about 4 1/2 hours. It was AMAZING! The best part of our trip for sure. Brian was in heaven and it was so completely interesting. Wish we had more time there, but it was outstanding. After a great dinner again that night (you can't have too much pizza over there - YUM!), we had a great day shopping and touring the town before our driver brought us back to Naples and the train back to Rome. Once in Rome, we got a taxi and to our last hotel. It was a crazy busy area of Rome, we had a nice dinner and got to sleep, ready to be up early for our driver (the craziest one yet!) to get us to the airport. Everyone was punctual and helpful and our flight home was great - we even made better time than expected. The limo driver was waiting right there, we loaded up and headed home.

Brian, Abby and Dad at Pompeii

We have so many wonderful stories to share and memories to ponder. I can't thank Make-A-Wish enough for providing this trip for my son and our family. It still brings tears of gratitude to my eyes, even while writing this note. I was so scared the first day in the hospital when Make-A-Wish was mentioned to me. My fear that this was a last wish of my newly diagnosed son. But as I was told, I quickly found out what Make-A-Wish was all about. The days we spent in the hospital, Brian thinking about what his wish could be. Who would he like to meet? Who would he like to be? What would he wish to have? Where would he wish to go? And although there were several other "drafts", once he hit upon Pompeii, he knew it was what he wished for most. He kept telling me while touring all the ancient sites, "I can't believe I'm here. I can't believe I'm really seeing this for myself. I can't believe the history I'm getting to see." The joy and smile on his face was so wonderful. After he met his wish granters, and made his wish, the waiting and wondering, the thinking and dreaming were also great. Then finding out his wish was to be granted and he'd get to indulge his passion of ancient history is one of the most amazing places on earth, was just so amazing.

Make-A-Wish definitely helped Brian and our family to get through the most difficult time in our lives to date. Nothing can prepare you for a cancer diagnosis, especially for us, a cancer diagnosis of a child. Nothing can prepare you for the fear, the sickness, the worry and the unknown. But Make-A-Wish helps so much in getting you through those times. Giving you something to think about other than ports, IV pumps, chemo, pain, fevers, relapse. It gives you a goal, a dream and then the time spent together on the trip, as a family is a priceless gift that can always be treasured.

I thank you all, so much, from the very bottom of my broken heart that is slowly mending as my son is too. You and your organization have given us so much to treasure and we feel so blessed to have been given so much. We will never be the same again, from both the cancer and by the generosity we have received. If we can do anything to help Make-A-Wish in any way, please don't hesitate. We will be lifelong supporters of your amazing foundation.

Sincerely,
Leslie Jermainne

PS - I will forward more photos if you are interested, just let me know!

OCTOBER 29, 2013

Sent: Tuesday, October 29, 2013 6:36 PM
From: Leslie Jermainne
To: My List
Subject: RE: Brian Ross update 10/29/2013

Guess Who?

Yup, it's me. It's been another month. We just returned from Boston about 30 min. ago, and Brian's checkup went great! Here is what we learned today: his blood counts are great! His ANC is 4.7 which is just below "normal" people. Sooo good! All his other numbers are great too.

He had an ultrasound of his abdominal area where the tumor was removed and under his right arm, the original site of the "attack". Everything looks great! I will get official results tomorrow, but the tech spent time talking with us afterwards and told us that the abdominal area is looking great, the fluid has gone away and the area is filling in with scar tissue. The area under his arm looks great too. "Dead" was the word used, but if killing the lymph node that started this is what it takes, I'm all for it. It was great to see our NP Anna - and Bri got to show her photos of Italy.

So...Italy was AWESOME! The flight over was not as bad as anticipated. The driving in Italy is INSANE!!! INSANE!!! INSANE!!! Yes, it requires that many times to explain. Our hotel in Rome was gorgeous. All the sites were amazing, and in particular the Coliseum and the Pantheon. The Trevi fountain was beautiful, and insanely crowded. I'm not sure what all the excitement is about the Spanish Steps, but I now have my very own photo of them. The food - was really good. Okay, don't freak - but besides the pizza, I wouldn't say amazing. Same comment for the wine. My loving husband said it was because I'm such a good cook and we buy better than average wine. I'm going to agree with him. ;-)

However, our favorite night was our last night in Rome before going to Sorrento. We finally got into the Roman way of dining. We went to dinner about 8:30 pm (still a bit early for them), we ate outside at a Ristorante, we had antipasti, lots of wine, and bread and great food. Street peddlers accosted our table every three minutes, but we actually enjoyed it. We purchased several scarves from them. We laughed and talked and enjoyed our evening thoroughly. Brian had his first taste of alcohol, since there really isn't a drinking age, and seriously, the kid has battled cancer. I don't think a beer, or glass of wine, or even a white Russian is out of the question when in Italy. Here, not so much. Anyway, after Rome we traveled by train to Naples (interesting....to watch from a secure window seat), then a bus to Sorrento. Our hotel had us looking out over the olive groves and the Mediterranean Sea and across the bay Mt. Vesuvius! It was beautiful. The next day we hired a driver and went to Pompeii, which was Brian's wish. It was AMAZING! We stayed there for over 4 hours and really could have spent days there. Our last day was spent trying to get cash off our credit card - a story for another time - shopping for gifts and some cream lemoncello to bring home. We then went back to Rome for the night (which was another interesting, sordid tale - but no vacation is as much fun without crazy travel stories) before heading home early on the 16th. Our flight back was uneventful except the guy who coughed every three minutes for 8.5 hours. Our limo ride home was nice and seeing our little doggies even better. We missed them!

Since being home we had another big milestone. Brian turned 16 on October 24th. Or as he called is when he was little "Knocked-over 24th". Don't you love the things little kids say? And to celebrate, like his sisters before him, he received a used car. Now he is ready to drive. We have driven down the road a bit, but now will have to venture out into the real world. We had a nice dinner out and cake afterwards.

As this day approached, I will be honest and say that my anxiety grew and grew. I had one minor panic attack one day while working at the investment property by myself. You see Bri caught a cold, I'm sure from the hacker on the plane, and I was worried. You may remember that every little thing now is scary. So while working there, my mind gets the better of me and I panic. I jump in the car, call Big Bri and ask him to check on Little Brian because I have a "bad feeling" and tell him I'm coming home. Little Brian is of course fine, and after reassuring myself that I am truly crazy, I go back to the house and finish spray painting the porch. My mind does evil things to me on pretty much a daily basis. I think one crazy panic attack over the past 6 months isn't quite so bad...considering. But still, these visits are two edged swords. Worry and joy. Depending on what you get. And according to Forrest Gump (one of our favorites) "Life is like a box of chocolates. You never know what you're gonna get." Hence the reason in my family you poke the bottom of the candy to see if it's what you want and either eat it or put it back in the box for someone else to scoff down.

So, we are "free" until about November 22nd-ish which is when we will go back for the next checkup. Then....we will go 2 months before returning! Holy crap. I'm not sure if I'm excited or panicked about that. Remember when they sent us home the first time and I cried in the hallway with all the doctors at rounds and asked them not to send us home? It isn't that bad, but it does bring up memories. Also, riding in the elevator at Boston Children's Hospital today... the smell...such flashbacks. Somebody should be doing research on smell (okay, I know someone has or did or is, so don't tell me) but truly I think smell might be a bigger trigger than first thought.

Okay, that's probably enough ramblings. Hey! I have a whole month to make up for! Thank you all for keeping us in your prayers. When walking through the Jimmy Fund Clinic to our appointment room today and seeing those families and those children with no hair, trying to choke down some food, the machines beeping, the nurses caring, the doctors planning, and the eyes of each mother looking into mine as I passed by, brought such sadness and such understanding. I wanted to reach out to each and every one of them and say "I know. It's horrible. It's terrifying. I understand, at least a little piece of what you are going through." I made contact this week with a woman who I went to high school with. I think she and her husband were a year behind me. I heard through another alumni they had a child with cancer. I reached out thinking it was a new diagnosis and asking what I could do for them. I found out their son is 19 and they have been dealing with cancer since he was 18 months old. MY GOD! How? How have they coped? I told her I was half horrified at what they must be going through (his tumor is back and growing) and half encouraged by their strength and their 17+ years of knowing how precious every day is. She told me it is still amazing where comfort comes from. She is my new hero. So tonight, instead of us I ask for prayers for them. For her son, her daughter, her husband, their family and friends that have been supporting them through a nightmare for 17 some odd years. It makes me think of my new favorite quote. "You don't know how strong you are, until being strong is your only option." How amazingly true.

Light and Love to you all.

Leslie

Sent: Tuesday, October 29, 2013 7:00 PM
From: Karen
To: Leslie Jermainne
Subject: Re: Brian Ross update 10/29/2013

Thanks for sharing, Leslie....Sooooo happy you got good news in Boston and that you had a fabulous (and well deserved) time in Italy!!!!!

Tears in my eyes reading your last paragraph....so saying prayers for that family tonight, too.

xo Karen

Sent: Tuesday, October 29, 2013 7:20 PM
From: Leslie Jermainne
To: Megan
Subject: FW: Brian Ross update 10/29/2013

Megan....I started emailing a group of people when we were in the hospital. This is my update for today. I thought you might like to know all these people will be saying prayers for you.

Leslie

Sent: Tuesday, October 29, 2013 7:32 PM
From: Megan
To: Leslie Jermainne
Subject: Re: Brian Ross update 10/29/2013

I am speechless.... What a gift you have with words!! The tears are flowing as I write this!! Of joy, understanding and fear. I pray for your whole family each day as I beg God to heal us as well and hold tight to the thought that had gotten me through all these years" I would rather have had him however long God has given him to me then to have not known him, loved him and been loved by him". Each day is a gift even our tough ones. Deep thanks for your kindness and sincerity it's just WHAT was needed just WHEN it was needed. <3

Sent: Tuesday, October 29, 2013 7:47 PM
From: Leslie Jermainne
To: Megan
Subject: RE: Brian Ross update 10/29/2013

I cry still on a daily basis Megan. As I'm sure only another "cancer Mom" can understand. It is instantaneous. I think one thought and BOOM! Here they go. Your words, they are my words. And mine are yours. I hate cancer, and I hate this "journey" as others call it. I call it a nightmare. But, I am the first to admit this nightmare brings certain gifts as side notes. The gift of gratitude, for each and every day and sometimes each minute. The gift of compassion for others suffering in life, not just from cancer. The gift of empathy for the other families who eyes you see and feelings you know. The gift of true sympathy for those who are no longer fighting. And the gift of prayer that we never become those who have lost their babies. I would trade every day of the past 6 months of "gifts" to live in denial and have my son be healthy and never have learned what cancer teaches. That is selfish I'm sure, but true. I would gladly take cancer as my burden and easily give my life in payment for his to be long and well lived. I'm sure you have prayed for the same things, to no avail either.

I have already received several emails in the past few minutes from the friends and family on my list that they are sending you all their prayers for tonight. I know you appreciate them for the gift they are. And I in turn appreciate yours.

Thinking of you all every day.

Leslie

Sent: Tuesday, October 29, 2013 7:51 PM
From: Megan
To: Leslie Jermainne
Subject: Re: Brian Ross update 10/29/2013

It is a nightmare!! And I had such a bad day and then here you are like an angel lifting my spirits and aligning my perspective. WRITE that book, I'll be the first to buy it and I am sure it will soothe, support, and uplift all who read it... You have such a gift, testimony and lesson to share

OCTOBER 30, 2013

Sent: Wednesday, October 30, 2013 1:04 PM
From: Brenda
To: Leslie Jermainne
Subject: RE: Brian Ross update 10/29/2013

Your email made my day. Such great news about Brian and your vacation. Sounds like you had a wonderful time!! My heart sank when I read about the family going through this nightmare for 17+ years. How awful. I don't know how people find the strength to get through these awful issues, but they do. God bless them.

Keep in touch. Talk to you soon.

November 2013

NOVEMBER 3, 2013

Sent: Sunday, November 03, 2013 11:58 AM
From: Leslie Jermainne
To: Leslie Jermainne
Subject: Brian Ross Update 11/3/2013 - **just to me**

Hi Again! I'm Back! So Soon? Yes!

And here's why. We are having a bit of a tough week. Friday night Brian seemed to hit some sort of emotional wall head on. I don't know what happened. It seemed he was happy one minute and depressed the next. Some tears were shed, sadness and grief. He told me his life was "so good before". He doesn't say before cancer. He doesn't ever really say the word cancer, and he doesn't like me to say it either. He was complaining that people treat him differently. That he's tired of people asking "How do you feel?" I tried to say everyone says that... you know "How are you?" But he corrected me and he's right. People say "How are you?" to people all day long. They say "How are you feeling'?" to him. UGH. I explained that these people care about him and want to know, help, be involved. He's sick of it anyway. He just wants to "go back". Ahhh, sadly we can't child. There is no going back. You can't unlearn what it's like to have cancer. Your body can't go back and even if your mind thinks that will make life easier, it is wrong. We have to move forward you and I. It is the only direction to go.

After talking and trying to console and making homemade brownies, which yes I know is not the right thing to do (but it felt and tasted right that's for sure), and talking some more we put it to bed for the night. I did learn some interesting things however, like the fact he doesn't want to be a plumber. We were hopeful but doubtful all along. Basically because of his aversion to dirt and germs. Kinda all over the place in plumbing. So no big news to us, and I'm glad he got that off his chest. Now what will he do? Plenty of time to figure that out.

Well yesterday morning started a bit shaky but better. Until while mowing the lawn he stepped in dog poop. Yup. I've actually written the words Dog Poop. Bet you didn't see that coming...ever. Well, we have dogs and poop happens. I had tried to scour the yard for every last pile, but I missed one and Bri found it. And he was pissed! (I should probably use the word mad here, but it just doesn't do the situation justice.) I told him I was sorry repeatedly. He told me it was my job to clean it up. Now please understand he gets paid to mow. But he is right it's my job to clean the poop. So I pay him for his services and then tell him to forget it from now on, I'll do it myself. I go out and finish up, which isn't much and throw out the shoes. What...just clean them you say. Ha, ha, ha. He will never wear them again I assure you, so I'm going to save myself 20 minutes of picking dog poop out of all the cracks and just heave them in the garbage. Done. When I come back inside he tells me solemnly that he wants to see a therapist. I had brought up the option the night before, but he had once again said no thank you. Well, today is maybe a break through then. I emailed three people who I trust will have the best referrals to offer us and I will begin contacting therapists on Monday. I hope to get him to meet several and make his own choice, give it a go and see if it helps. Please God, let it help.

It is so incredibly frustrating to see my child suffering. It was so hard to see him suffer all those days of treatment, only to get through them and then have his emotional health be so fragile. He looks so good, so strong, so mature, so capable. And he is all those things. But something is amiss, and my "Mommy love" can't seem to fix it. God, how I wish it was me who had cancer, who was a wreck, who had to suffer through this. I mean I have suffered through this too, I know, but I want it all and him to have none.

Of the two people I first told that he was ready to see a therapist, they both told me that I probably need to. Ummm, okay. I'm not against the idea, but I thought I was doing pretty darn good here. I thought this writing was my therapist. Are they seeing something I don't? I'm a little perturbed about it to be honest, but I'm going to file it away in the "look at tomorrow" file and see if they're onto something. I doubt it. ;-}

By the way, we did get a call from our NP Anna, who said the ultrasound results looked so good that they weren't going to order any further ultrasounds. YA! Good news. Brian seemed very happy about this too, which is good.

So, onto another week. Trying to pay attention and appreciate every minute, every hour, every day. I did hear a good thing the other day, thank you Liz for sharing:

"If you are depressed you are living in the past.

If you are anxious you are living in the future.

If you are at peace you are living in the present." - Lao Tzu

I think I'm vacillating between anxiety (worrying about the future of Brian's health/life) and peace. Unfortunately I think Bri might be living in the past a bit. We'll work on that.

Light and Love.
Leslie

The following is a letter I wrote to the surgeon who performed Brian's surgery on 4/18/13 and had the terrible job of telling me my child had cancer.

Dear Dr. R.,

I have been meaning to write you this thank you note for the past six months. Well, that's probably not true, but definitely the last four months. You may not remember me at first, but on April 18, 2013 you performed surgery on my son. You removed what we hoped was going to be a lipoma from his left abdomen and you did a biopsy on the lymph node under his right arm. You were then the catalyst in a chain reaction that has forever changed our lives. Before I go on, my son is doing great!

You came to me in the waiting room. You told he was doing fine, but that the tumor in his abdomen was lymphoma. You asked me if I was alright. I nodded yes and I think squeaked a yes out too. You explained about pathology being sent special courier to pathology and results should be back the next day, with a liberal dose of luck. You asked me again if I was okay. Again, through the ringing in my head I said yes. Then you looked at me and said "Well, I'm not okay," and it looked to me that tears were coming to your eyes, "I've never had this happen with a child before. An adult, yes....but not a child." I write this all out, because I want you to know how much that has meant to me over these months. The fact that Brian wasn't just another surgery to you. The fact that you shared that moment with me, a Mom, whose world was just stopped. It allowed me to know several things that I didn't fully realize at that moment. People were going to care about us. People were going to help us. People knew what they were doing and they were going to do whatever they could to help my son beat this. In some fashion, you knew what lie ahead of us that day. I had no idea. So before I go further, thank you. Thank you for coming into our lives for that brief moment in time and for caring and even more for showing that you cared and it affected you too. People need that. People on the other side of the operating room door need to know that they and their loved ones matter. I hope you share your emotions with other patients and their families as much as you can and still survive your job every day.

I also wanted to send you this note so that you might know what happened to that 15 year old boy you operated on. The boy you told had cancer. A word he no longer wants to hear or say. The first time I heard him say it was in the recovery room at the hospital. Everyone had gone, he was getting dressed and coming out of the sedation fully. "So, it's cancer... right Mom?" "Yes Brian, it's cancer." "Okay," he replied and nodded his head. Those are the worst words I have ever said in my life. But here we are 6 months later and things are good. The day following his surgery, you and I talked on the phone several times and then I was put in contact with a pediatric oncology group that I don't want to really name. We went to the hospital ER that night for a few tests and if all was well, we'd get to go home. Every result of those tests were great, but they never let us go home. We had a very bad experience at that hospital, and five days later I got us moved to Dana Farber Cancer Institute and the Jimmy Fund Clinic in

Boston. I want you to know I'm grateful we went to the first hospital and we had the doctor we did. Even though the experience was very bad, it got us to an amazing facility with amazing people and I couldn't be more grateful.

Brian was officially diagnosed with Burkitt Lymphoma and began his treatment. It took five rounds of chemotherapy inpatient 7 day stays at Boston Children's Hospital. He was amazing. He had NO fevers at home. We never had to go back into the hospital for any problem and on July 2nd he was done with treatment and officially in remission! We go back once a month at this point, but after our November 22nd appointment, we will move to 2 month visits.

It is hard for us to realize and understand fully what we've been through as a family and for Brian to reconcile what he has faced as such a young man. We're working on that part now. Part of what I've learned is to slow down and to take the time to tell people how you feel. So it was time to write you this overdue note. So thank you again for what you do. But thank you more for showing how much you care while doing it.

Very Sincerely,
Leslie Jermainne

NOVEMBER 22, 2013

Sent: Friday, November 22, 2013 5:42 PM
From: Leslie Jermainne
To: My List
Subject: RE: Brian Ross update 11/22/2013

Hi Friends!!

Another month has passed (almost) since you last heard from me. We were up in Boston today and had a great checkup. Everything looks great. A few blood chemistries weren't back before we left, but doubtful anything is amiss. All his other counts were great. ANC 3.7 so down a bit from last month but still really, really good. Brian got to fill Anna in on his "normal teenage life". Learning to drive, girls, upcoming trip to VT, all his curly hair. The only change from last visit is that we learned that we will continue our monthly visits to Boston for a year after treatment. So... until July we will be going every month. Last time, I had reported that after this visit we'd start to go every other month. Well, today I found out that monthly for 1 year is standard protocol, and that is what we will stick too. I think because last time his ultrasound was so great that our NP thought we would push it to 2 months, but not true. Actually, it's fine with me. I like our visits. It is reassuring for me. I'll be much more ready to go less frequently when we get to July. Every month we gain being cancer free is so, incredibly, deeply wonderful. With Burkitt Lymphoma every day we get away from treatment being cancer free is one day so much closer to being "cured". If Burkitt is going to relapse it will be sooner rather than later. And with Brian's great response to treatment, we have nothing but great thoughts for a long and healthy future. (Please God.)

So what else have we been doing this past month? Driving. Driving some more. And then driving a little bit. He is already a great driver. We are still working on the 3 R's. No, I don't mean reduce, reuse and recycle. I mean, rest, recover and recuperate. There are still days....days when my mind takes hold and runs away with a single bad thought, like when you are trying to launch a kite by yourself and you run and run and it just drags along the ground, bumping and ripping and stumbling along until you're out of breath and you can't remember why you thought flying a kite would be fun. I don't have a lot of patience, as some of you out there know. If you do know this, then the next part of that story would be me stomping on the kite, kicking it and then berating myself for getting the stupid thing in the first place. So ya...that happens too. I yell at myself for letting the thought take hold, for playing it out until the only miserable end there can be in my life, and finding myself with tears streaming down my face once more. But...and there is always a but, those days have become so much less than they used to be. Progress right?

I have found a therapist and I think it will be good for me to get this stuff out. Poor woman. She has no idea what she's in for. We've only met once, but it was helpful. And I have a little story to share from that day. As we talked about Brian's cancer diagnosis and it's aftermath of destruction in our lives, she commented how normal it is to try to be so "careful" after something like this. How normal it is to try to control things to keep him safe. And although those sentiments were true when we were in active treatment, I informed her that I've had the opposite reaction. Here is how I look at it. He has survived the most aggressive human cancer there is. How could I try to hold him back from anything from here on out. How unfair would that be? Maybe I would feel differently if he wasn't such an amazing, wonderful and responsible child. Ya, I probably would. Be he isn't like that. And I know now that this is completely his path. And I will walk beside him wherever it takes him, with my arms outstretched trying to catch him if he stumbles, if I'm able, if I'm quick enough. But I will not block his path, or say no, or judge (as best I can). I will only say "yes" and "you can do it" and "Good job". I will probably be biting the inside of my cheek at times, but I will do it nonetheless. I mean, who do I think I am to try and deny him anything - any experience (cliff diving), any path in life (running for President), any moment of joy that I might not share. He has gone to the edge and back again, at age 15. I will support him above all else. My example to the therapist was him learning to drive. As I ride in the car with this very, very new driver (although very good one) I am not in fear. I think to myself, what is the very worst that could happen. We get in a horrible car wreck and die. Well then, so be it. We've looked into those eyes and we know above all else, it's possible. Unlikely, but certainly possible. If something else happens, a smashed car, a broken mirror, a scare - well who cares. We've experienced cancer so bring it world! We are ready!

So next week brings Thanksgiving and our trip to VT. We are so very excited to be going away. Stress free (once we get going), relaxing, clean towels every day. A place we love and find peace. And shopping. (VT Country Store and Northshire Book store). Great food, great wine and great company. We'll miss the rest of our family, but for one year I know they understand and support our need for some peace. Some down time. Some sitting back and saying "Aaaahhhh". I don't have to tell you all what I'm thankful for. I think you know. Okay, I'll say it anyway. Maybe more bluntly than expected but I am most thankful my son is alive. He is happy. He is recovering. He is here. And as a side note, I'm so very thankful so many, many things:

1) My husband for his love, support and cleaning abilities which have grown exponentially over this year and for providing for his

family so that we are safe and secure without all the worry he goes through.

2) The 3 people I call my warriors. You know who you are.
3) My dogs for loving us and greeting us like we've been gone for days when it's only been a few hours.
4) My friends for listening to me be crazy, for letting me be crazy and for loving me anyway.
5) My family for being the brick and mortar that keeps me standing.
6) I'm thankful for all the people who have made their presence known to us throughout this most difficult time in our lives. The emails, texts, cards, meals, phone calls, gifts, donations and shared prayers for my son to be healthy. It has truly and deeply made a difference in our lives. You don't even know.
7) I'm thankful for each and every person at Dana Farber Cancer Institute, the Jimmy Fund Clinic and Boston Children's Hospital that helped us, let us cry, taught us, cared for us, encouraged us, and believed in us. Without them....well, it's too hard to say what "without them" would be like. They are all our angels. Along with the three doctors who helped us figure out what was going on to begin with and where to receive the best treatment.

I'm thankful for so many, many more things that my list could fill the page. I hope you all have a wonderful, joy filled Thanksgiving holiday doing whatever it is that makes you happy on that day. And try to bring that day forward, just for a minute in every day for the rest of the year and remember to be thankful. Life is good.

Happy Thanksgiving.

Love & Thanks!

Leslie

Sent: Friday, November 22, 2013 6:00 PM
From: Paula
To: Leslie Jermainne
Subject: Re: Brian Ross update 11/22/2013

Wooooo hoooooo!!!

And you need a therapist why???? You sound pretty damn fantastic to me- like therapy for me reading all of your blogs. You are amazing!!!!

Love you,
P

NOVEMBER 25, 2013

Sent: Monday, November 25, 2013 12:16 PM
From: Ann
To: Leslie Jermainne
Subject: RE: Brian Ross update 11/22/2013

You always remind us to put things in perspective. You should write a book!!

Ann

December 2013

The following is a letter I wrote and dropped in the box at Macy's for their Make-A-Wish Letter to Santa campaign.

December 3, 2013

Dear Santa,

My son Brian was diagnosed with cancer this year. Well, you already know that don't you? It has been a tough year for us. The worry of possibly losing my only child brings instant tears to my eyes these days. It never goes away. I know that parents always worry about their children from the moment they enter this world, and the fact they might get hurt, or sick or even die. That worry, before it is a real threat, is nothing compared to the real thing.

Brian was treated for Burkitt Lymphoma at the Dana Farber Cancer Institute. They manage The Jimmy Fund Clinic which treats all the pediatric cancer patients. He had his inpatient treatments at Boston Children's Hospital. I mention this because these three places and all the amazing and giving people who work there are a miracle to those of us trying to help our loved ones survive and to survive ourselves. Everyone there from the head honcho to the people who help us park our car when we go back every month for a checkup, are a miracle to us. Not just a Christmas miracle. But an 'everyday, I'm here to help, I've got your back, you can do this' kind of miracle.

Shortly after Brian's inpatient treatments were finished and his cancer in remission, we received another miracle. I know you know, but Make-A-Wish fulfilled Brian's wish to go to Pompeii, Italy. It. Was. Amazing. We got to visit Rome, Sorrento and Pompeii. It was the trip of a lifetime. It was such a joy to spend that week with my son and my husband and my stepdaughter. We were like a normal old family, seeing the sights. Brian's hair had come back by then, so no one knew what he had been through. What he is going through. Recovery doesn't end when they say remission. But life is good.

The people at Make-A-Wish and all the people who support and donate to Make-A-Wish, like Macy's for an example, are a miracle to us Wish Families. After learning my son had cancer and being whisked away to a hospital late on a Friday night, I received a packet of information, and in it was a Make-A-Wish pamphlet. I froze. I didn't know. I thought it was "Make Your Last Wish". I stuffed it into the back of the folder, determined to not let it see the light of day. Awhile later, it was brought to my attention again, and explained to me. I will admit I was still hesitant, but I thought 'if the worst is going to happen, maybe he can have an amazing wish first'. I submitted his name for Make-A-Wish while sitting in our hospital room, overlooking Boston while chemotherapy pumped into my baby boy.

The magic started to happen. I had emails and later phone calls. Yes! They'd love to fulfill Brian's Wish. Tears of joy for a change, filled my eyes. When I told Brian, he was so excited. What would he wish for? This brought about so many times where we talked and dreamed. He thought, gave out suggestions, crossed off a list. What would he want to do most? Or maybe who would he want to meet? What had he always wanted to have? Where would he like to visit?

We visited the Make-A-Wish website, we continued to receive emails and support. Finally our time came to meet with our Wish Granters. They came to our house to meet us, while we were out of the hospital on one of our short breaks. They were so wonderful. They didn't concentrate on Brian's cancer, or our treatment, or my worry. They were bright and uplifting and full of fun and smiles. The time came and with our breath held in, Brian told them his wish. He loves ancient history you see...well you know that Santa. He wished to go to Pompeii, Italy and see the ruins of that most ancient city. They looked at each other, and said "I don't see why not!"

We breathed an excited sigh of relief and couldn't believe it might be a possibility.

Off they went, leaving us with renewed hope and thoughts of normal life. A time when we might not be living in a hospital room for days on end. A time when there would be no port in my son's chest. No PET scans, ultrasounds, echocardiograms. No hospital food, beeping pumps, fluid bags and sleepless nights. There would be hair on his head, fresh air, sleeping in our own beds, home cooked food. There might even be a trip. An amazing trip to a foreign place filled with history and sights and sounds that we've never experienced. It filled us with such hope and excitement.

When we got the word that Make-A-Wish was indeed going to make Brian's wish come true, well...we literally jumped for joy. We couldn't believe it. Someone, lots of someone's, were going to be so generous as to send Brian and his family to Italy to see some of the most amazing ancient historic sites on earth. What a miracle. We bought some books about Italy, Pompeii, speaking Italian. We checked the weather, thought about what to pack and dreamed of what we would see. We got our passports, none of us ever having one before. We waited and dreamed. But we didn't have to worry about a single planning issue. No worries of how to get to the airport, what day to fly, what airline to fly, how to get from the airport to the city of Rome, where to stay, where to eat, what to see. Oh, how wonderful to just sit and wait and dream.

On October 9th, the limo arrived, which was an added treat. We were filled with excitement as we rode to JFK airport, got on our Alitalia flight and flew to Rome. A driver waited for us, took us to our beautiful hotel, we ate, we slept, we met with our tour guide who helped us see the best sites. The Coliseum, the Pantheon, the Trevi Fountain, the Spanish Steps, the Forum. It was spectacular. We hadn't a care in the world as we ate our amazing Italian dinner on the sidewalk of Rome and laughed and talked of our day full of adventures. Then a driver took us to the train station, a guide got us on a train to Naples. Another guide met us, got us on a bus and talked to us the whole way to Sorrento where we stayed overlooking the Mediterranean and Mt. Vesuvius from our balcony. The guide helped us have an amazing day at Pompeii where we were repeatedly amazed at everything we saw. Even the dogs that live there, sleeping in the shade and being fed by guests.

On October 16th we flew out of Rome, back to the U.S. to our awaiting limo ride home. Tired, happy, and filled with love. What an amazing, amazing gift. And I don't just mean the trip Santa. The Wish was the trip, but the gift was all of it. The gift was the people who take the time and money to donate to the Make-A-Wish foundation. The companies who give time, service and money to families like ours. Families who children have a life threatening condition. Families who have been pushed to the limit and then some. Families who know a lot of fear and sadness and who also know great love and strength. The gift is the people at Make-A-Wish who keep things light and talk of fun and laughter, not hospitals and treatments. The gift is the talks about the wish, the anticipation of the wish, the dreaming, the telling of the stories afterwards. The gift is one I remember every day.

So Santa, this year I ask for nothing for Christmas. I already received so many gifts in our very difficult year. My only wish for my son to be healthy and with us, comes true every day. My wish for Christmas is for all the people who have helped us this year and all the families that are struggling to get through their own crisis. My wish is for them all to know peace and joy. To receive whatever it is they need. Whatever it is they want. And for all the families like ours, I ask for their children to receive their Wish. Whatever it may be.

Merry Christmas Santa!

Love Always,
Leslie

DECEMBER 21, 2013

Sent: Saturday, December 21, 2013 8:23 AM
From: Leslie Jermainne
To: My List
Subject: Brian Ross update 12/20/2013

Happy Holidays Everyone!

Yesterday was our recent trip to Boston for Brian's checkup. Everything was great. Still waiting to get his blood test results - as they weren't done before we were, but I'm sure all is good and we would have heard from them if something wasn't good - so all in the clear. Brian has reached the 6 month mark. Well, we really consider the mark to be the day we left the hospital for the last time which was 7/2. So on 1/2 I will consider it a good 6 months. But our NP and Dr. consider it 6 months. Because of that Brian no longer has to take Bactrim 3 times a week. That was our last daily "reminder". We are free! Not sure if that makes sense to everyone else - but to me, well, yes.

We had a nice visit and with Brian delivering a gift card plus a greater gift in his letter to Anna. I wish I had gotten to read it (Mother's curiosity) but he told me about writing her a long note to thank her for all she has done for him. I'm quite sure that will be the treasured part of the gift, rather than the gift card. We also saw Dr. D. our oncologist who was thrilled with his continued recovery. Oh, and we saw Santa, a magician and a mime plus Brian was given a gift card to Target. We stopped at our favorite spot in Pomfret for lunch on the way home. We found it by accident searching for a bathroom months back. It has become our tradition to go there on our way home. Then we drive the "scenic" route looking at the pretty big houses and farmland, Canterbury, etc. down to Norwich. After a quick stop at Target - we even made it home before 3pm. You'd think I would have had time to write last night - but...no. Busy, busy.

So this last month - what have we done? Our Thanksgiving Trip to VT was great! Very low key and relaxing. Although we all did get a bad cold - thanks Carlo! Well, Al and Big Brian didn't get it. But the rest of us are just finally recovered now. I guess it was going around. After

Thanksgiving, we got our selves decorated for Christmas and have been enjoying a relative quiet time.

Last night we were all saying that it doesn't seem possible that Christmas is just 4 days away. How "messed up" our timing feels this year. And of course we all know why. This is the year that kind of wasn't for me. It is the year I kinda WISH wasn't. But it has brought a lot of clarity of what is important. It is hard for me, knowing what I know now, I mean really deep down knowing it, to not regret some of the past with my son. I regret every time I was too busy, too tired, and honestly too wrapped up in what I needed or wanted to do that I said no to doing or playing or watching what he wanted. If I had only known. I thought I did know, I thought I was giving my all to him. But I wasn't. At least not in the way I would have liked to, whether that is even possible or not. Not in the way a parent wants to, who hears the words even if just spoken in their own head, "your child might die."

Now I understand that as adults we have things we have to do. Laundry seems to be a big one for me. Cooking and shopping for food and necessities. Oh ya, and work. That's a big one. And so you can't always say yes to your kids to do everything they want. But I wish we could. The day before yesterday I stopped in Starbucks to pick up some gift cards and a delicious coffee for myself, thank you very much. On my way out I see a Mom with her little boy. He is about three I would say. They are meandering slowly to their car. She sipping her coffee, he in his snow boots and hat and coat is taking the time to kick the little pile of snow on the sidewalk. And she is letting him. And I am thankful. I want to stop and say to her "good job." Take the time, just like you are. Let him kick the snow, or look at a worm in the rain, or touch a flower or tell you a story. Because you never know. I didn't stop her, but I did send her a mental "good job". I have done a lot more of telling people stuff like that. Strangers and friends alike. And that has been one of the gifts I have received this year.

But back to regrets. I then talk myself around and realize that although I have regrets, I have been incredibly, incredibly lucky. I have my one child, and for me, that is the perfect number. I had the fortunate blessing to have a child that wants to be homeschooled and the ability, thanks to my supportive husband to do just that. I have had so much more time during these younger years, before he is off on his own, then maybe other

Mom's get. And I am so very, very grateful. I have such a nice life, amazing husband, wonderful family, the best of friends and warm and loving home. And I used to see a lot of negativity in the world, but now I know how good it is and how good people can be. And all of this was brought about by the worst thing that has ever happened in my life. Life is weird. That I also know is true. It is messy and difficult and confusing. It is tiring and scary and short. But it is what it is and I will take every day with appreciation as best I can, because my son is okay and that is all that matters.

In this season of gifts, I thought it might be interesting to see how many gifts I have gotten this year. And no I don't mean the gift certificate for a facial for my birthday that I still haven't found time to use. But I will!

I have been given the gift of realizing there are no guarantees and today, right now is really the only thing we have, so you better make it count - the best you can.

I have been given the gift of friendship and support from all the expected places and a few new and surprising ones. It has shown me how to be a better friend to others, and I will be from here on out.

I have been given the gift of taking the time to tell people, the best way I can, how I feel about them, or that I appreciate what they do. That means right down to the person who hands me coffee at Dunkin' Donuts. When I say thank you and make sure I say "Have a nice day", I mean it. It is no longer something I just say.

I have been given the gift of saying yes and of saying no. Yes, to help, love, support and time. No, to all the things and people who don't support those things. And having no guilt about it either.

I have been given the gift of being a caregiver. For my son, and for my parents. It isn't always easy, but it is always worth it. I admire doctors and nurses in a way I never understood before. The nurses especially, for they are the ultimate caregivers. And I don't think they even know.

I have been given the gift of realizing my own strength, more than I ever have before. I have gotten through this and I continue to move ahead. I had the strength to advocate for my son and for myself. For me, once I found that strength and confidence, it holds on and moves into the other areas of my life.

I have been given the gift of knowing, for me, what is truly important. I have thought of the line from the movie City Slickers (oldie, but goodie) where Curly says "You know what the secret of life is? One thing. Just one thing. You stick to that and the rest don't mean SHIT!" And Mitch says, "But, what is the 'one thing'?" And Curly replies, "That's what you have to find out." I can't say for me it is just one thing. But now know my 'things' and I'm sticking to it.

Well, there are many, many more gifts that I am discovering and understanding every day. But I don't want to forget, I'm grateful for the Keurig coffee machine. Yes, it's true. Despite my telling my step-daughters over a year ago it was a waste of money, I discovered its wonder and beauty in the hospital. My kind husband has indulged me and we now have a Keurig coffee machine. And I love it. And I appreciate it every day. Several times a day as a matter of fact. But with decaf of course (after cup #1).

I am happy this year is coming to an end. It will be one I never will be able to forget, even if I'd like to. It has changed my life in the way no other time has. I am looking forward to 2014 and hope that it continues to bring me, well...life. My child's life and mine and my families along with it. I hope to continue to realize the gifts we have been given and hope to help others appreciate the gifts they have, as best they can, without them knowing the shear panic and fear that a life threatening condition brings into their world.

I thought I would end this with Happy Holidays and Happy New Year (to encompass whatever your tradition might be at this time of year), but really I want to just say "Happy". I wish you all happiness. Every. Single. Day.

Love & Light,
Leslie

Sent: Saturday, December 21, 2013 10:11 AM
From: Brian W.
To: Leslie Jermainne
Subject: Re: Brian Ross update 12/20/2013

What a beautiful message Les! I'm so happy for you and Brian and Brian. And I'm happy that the tests and trials you all have been through this year have given you a perspective that will guide you toward living your lives with an outlook that you would not have had otherwise. That truly is a gift! That and Brian's health. I am so happy to hear he is well!

You are a remarkably strong and forthcoming person. I've read your messages and updates this year in awe of your honesty, transparency and vulnerability. You are a wonderful Mom and Brian is as lucky to have you as you are to have him. So a good job to you Leslie!

Have a wonderful Christmas, New Year and 2014 and beyond with the Brian's.

Brian W.

Sent: Saturday, December 21, 2013 2:47 PM
From: Sarah J.
To: Leslie Jermainne
Subject: Re: Brian Ross update 12/20/2013

Love and Light back to you, Leslie. Not to sound too over the top but you are a remarkable human being. May I share the middle part of your letter about the little boy with my sister? Happy Holidays.

Warmly,
Sarah

DECEMBER 23, 2013

Sent: Monday, December 23, 2013 9:23 AM
From: Rachel
To: Leslie Jermainne
Subject: RE: Brian Ross update 12/20/2013

Leslie,

Each time I read an update I am amazed. Your insight, honesty, and ability to put into words those things we don't often say or even admit to ourselves is very moving. Thank you for sharing. There is no doubt that these writings must be difficult, but at the same time the clarification of what is important and real is epic. I've been thinking these updates could be put together into a book.

Thank you Leslie, I am so happy that you all are on the other side of this enjoying each moment, time to breathe, and your beautiful son!

Happy! Rachael

Sent: Monday, December 23, 2013 1:07 PM
From: Leslie Jermainne
To: Rachel
Subject: RE: Brian Ross update 12/20/2013

Thanks Rachel. It has been amazing to me how many people have suggested the same things as you. I guess these are just my words, and I'm unsure how they might help someone else. I think I write them because they help me. It is a way I can process what has happened this past year. It was a way to let family and friends know what was happening to Brian as we were so far away. And it was a way for me, while in the hospital, to move forward inch by inch, day by day and get through the nightmare. I still have a lot of processing to do - as does Brian.

I have started to compile all my notes into one "book". I don't know if/when I would do anything with it, but with so many people telling me I should, I thought maybe it would somehow help someone else, some day. We'll see.

Thank you for your support and always kind words. I have been overwhelmed by all the people who have thought of us and loved us through this. My faith in humanity has been restored and is overflowing. It wasn't always that way.

I hope you enjoy a wonderful and peaceful holiday with all the people you love, and take a minute to tell them. You never know.

Happy!

Leslie

DECEMBER 29, 2013

Sent: Sunday, December 29, 2013 7:49 AM
From: Leslie Jermainne
To: Leslie Jermainne
Subject: RE: Brian Ross update 12/29/13 - sent just to me

Hi!

Just having a bit of a rough day here, and unsure why, so I thought I'd write. I guess my thing of the last few days is that I feel like I am not being aware enough anymore. I mean it used to be I thought "My son has cancer" about every other second. Literally. That much. That was followed by a lot of "What if he dies?" And those thoughts spiraled to nowhere good. Then after treatment and he is in remission, it became about "What if it comes back?" "What if he gets another cancer as a side effect from this chemo"? (Yes, that is a real thing.) "What if we have to go through this again", "what if he dies?" And again, that last one leads nowhere good.

But things are good. But I'm feeling weird about it. Not bad, like premonition weird. Like out of sorts. Like how do I acclimate to this new life? Do I think about Brian having gone through this diagnosis? Yes. Every day. And it is reassuring in some sick way. People told me before that I would eventually get to a day where it wouldn't be my <u>first</u> thought of the day - and yes I'm at that point. They told me that some days I wouldn't think of it at all. And that sounded like heaven at the time. And I'm not there yet, but I think about it less and less and I'm realizing these last few days that I don't like it. I feel like I'm letting my guard down, and you should never let your guard down right? Unless you are falling in love, or finding a new friend. Then it's fine. But cancer is no friend. And I can't let my guard down.

What if I get all comfy in our "new normal", which I am still working on figuring out what that is. What if I don't think about it and just like Burkitt, if you give it a break, it sneaks back in, that aggressive little fuck, and takes over your life and makes it a living hell. Even worse than it already is on some days. Kind of dark I know, sorry. Then my newly acquired thoughts come in a rescue me a little. They say, "There are no guarantees, cancer or no cancer. This is it. This is all you've got, and you have no control, you never had any control, and you never will, so deal with it." He could die anyway. Too early. And so could you. He could get killed in a car accident. You could be with him in the car and die too. (And by the way, that is fine. If I don't have to live without him, then I don't mind. I mean I would rather be the one who died in the accident, but if we both go, that's okay). He could get in some other type of accident. There could be a killer storm, flood, hurricane, etc. There could be some other sickness, flu, infection, etc. He could choke, have a heart attack, fall and hit his head, break his neck. Some random act by another could kill him. I mean really, we have no guarantees. Yet every day we all get up and go about life like we have all the time in the world, and I guess that is how you should live so that you don't become paralyzed with fear. But here's the thing. When you lose the "cancer" lottery. All the odds are out the window. Anything really is truly possible and there isn't a good God Damn thing you can do about it. It brings you freedom of sorts to kind of just say "screw it". Because there are no guarantees.

So why am I feeling odd? I guess it is just learning to accept it. That this is the way it is. This is the new normal. I wish I could define our new normal. Maybe that would help me because I am a person of concreteness. (Wow, spell check didn't freak at concreteness, it must be a word.) (Is that a good thought? That if spell check allows it, it is okay?) If I had a definition of what our "new normal" is and maybe a definition of what our "old normal" was, maybe it would help. Let's see if I can try:

Our old normal:

Slight worry that my son could maybe die before me. I thought I worried about it too much. I did. Because any time I lost with that teeny tiny worry was just that, lost. Because the real thing is so much bigger and worse than your pretend little worry, it doesn't much matter whether you ever thought about it or not.

Freedom to think of things years down the road. Would he get married, and would she like me? Would he have babies and love them like I love him? Where would they live? Where would we live? Will I ever have a convertible again? Will I ever learn to knit? Will my mind ever slow down and shut up, for like a second?

We took our health kinda for granted. And I still don't have a handle on that. Too much wine, too many carbs, not enough movement, not the best sleep. But hey, there is always tomorrow to start doing it, right?

We didn't travel to Boston. Like, ever. It was scary and daunting. Drive in the city? Me? No thank you.

I didn't know big words like methotrexate and I didn't know the normal ranges of blood cells and what each little part really did.

I didn't know how many tears I had in me. It's an endless supply by the way.

I didn't know how easily I would give my life for my sons. And I know we all say it as parents, but for me, I had a day and it wasn't the first day of "cancer". I was too busy being in shock to really comprehend it then. It wasn't even until we were at Dana Farber when I had a talk with God and begged Him to give it to me. And I wouldn't fight it. I would just go and leave this world with a smile on my face because I would know that Brian would be alright, and he would live and he wouldn't have to know this thing from the inside out. I realized at that moment how easily I would go. If only God would grant me that wish.

I didn't know how many people cared about us. People who sent messages to me on a daily basis, who cheered me on. Who prayed for my son to beat this beast. Who loved us from afar and became my clan, despite whatever their last name was.

I didn't know that some people who I thought would be there, weren't. At least maybe not how I expected them to be there for me, for us. It was surprising. But in the end, it didn't really matter because of the people who were. They are angels.

I didn't know how much faith I had. By faith, I mean in the collective consciousness in the world. That prayers by so many people could literally change the outcome. And it did, and I will forever be grateful for each and every little thought someone, somewhere sent our way. And I will pay it back, however I can, till the day I die.

I didn't know how wonderful nurses are. I mean really. What a job. And to choose to work with children, who are of course cute, and loving and adorable. But to see them every day and help them when they are suffering so, and still provide a smile and comfort and love to them and their families. Well, I just don't know how they do it. How do you get up every day, eat your breakfast, wash your hair, pay your bills, put on your scrubs and go to help the suffering? Maybe to be vomited on, pooped on, peed on, cause pain when putting needles into people. How can you watch children suffer and maybe die? How can you watch parents break down over and over and watch their pain and their fear, as they care for their children? How can you come in every day with a smile and an air of hope that we need so badly? How? I just don't know. And yet they do. And they do it so very well. And it must hurt them, but they do it anyway. And I am so grateful. Those that care for the suffering are angels on earth. And I didn't even know in my old normal.

I didn't know how strong my son was. How strong he is. I didn't know how strong I was. I didn't know what an inspiration he is to me. What a kind and gentle soul he could be. I mean I did know, but when you are put to this test, I don't think anyone would blame you if you kind of lost it. If maybe you weren't so polite and kind. But he was and is and I love him more every day, just like I always did, and I always will.

Our new normal:

Well, we know a lot more, obviously. We live with this fog that is barely visible, but floats around us, unseen by most. Sometimes we move faster than it and get away for a bit. Sometimes it sneaks up on us and settles in our bones for a bit, reviving old aches from injuries gone by. Even sometimes it creates new damage, but we survive. We go on. We have no choice. Because we know there are no guarantees. And I guess that is the best lesson learned. And I want to hold onto that thought. Every. Single. Minute. Because when I don't, my guard is down and that unnerves me. And I realize now that when I was told there would be a day that I wouldn't think about this at all, and I thought that would be heaven, I was so wrong. They day I don't think about it, I will forget the lesson. I will put away the small gift that came with this demon. So I will remind myself every day, no matter how late in the day, that I am lucky. That there are no guarantees, except for this exact time, so pay attention. Be here now. Focus. This is it.

The words are gone now, the heart is slowed and the mind cleared. All spilled out onto this page. Free from me.

Light & Love,
Leslie

January 2014

JANUARY 15, 2014

Sent: Wednesday, January 15, 2014 7:56 AM
From: Leslie Jermainne
To: Leslie Jermainne
Subject: RE: Brian Ross update 1/14/2014 - **sent just to me**

Hi!

Been a bit of a rough few days again. I'm tired of trying to shake free of this, only to feel like I'm failing at it and keeping it present in our lives (or maybe just my life). One of the things I read first on Facebook today is what I need to focus on. It says "Worrying is like praying for what you don't want. So, got something on your mind? Learn to let go of the things that may be outside of your control and instead, focus on what is – your thoughts. What do you want? What do you want your everyday to feel like? How do you want to feel in yourself? When your mind is struggling to shake those negative thoughts, instead of worrying about what you don't want to happen, try thinking about what you DO want to happen. Fuel the positivity." Seems so simple doesn't it? Just change your thoughts, of course! Why didn't I think of that? It's like when the doctor tells you to eat carrot and celery sticks to lose weight. "Of course, carrots and celery, why didn't I think of that!" But, I guess it's true. I mean not specifically carrots and celery, but veggies, eating healthy. And changing what you think about. The part that says "Worrying is like praying for what you don't want", I was like OMG! Am I praying for cancer to return? Obviously not! But I worry about it and is that the same thing? Holy Shit. I have to never worry about it coming back, ever, ever again. And I do have times like that. Times where I think, 'Why wouldn't he be cured?' I mean the success rate is very, very high. We caught it early. He went through treatment fantastically. He is young and strong and healthy (except for cancer of course - why must that thought always pop into my mind - dagnabit!) So the next part that says, "so, got something on your mind?" Uhhh.... YA! My son having cancer. Him dying. What my life would be after that. How horrible, terrible, gut wrenching. So really am I such a selfish bitch, that all this worry is about me? God I hope not. I mean, I worry about him, a lot. If it came back, what would the treatment be? Would it work? How painful? How long? How destructive to him and his body? Would he survive? Would he even want to fight? What if he didn't? What if he died? What if I had to leave the hospital without him? What if I went there with him, as I would, and stayed there with him every minute, as I would, and what if he died there, as he could, and I had to walk out without him. It makes me want to vomit just thinking about it. But again - that is about me isn't it? I am a selfish, selfish bitch.

Anyway - this is the shit I have to stop doing. When I look back at the quote and it says to learn to let go of the things that may be outside of your control. May be? I know it is outside my control, but I hate it. I know it is all outside my control. Every little bit of this life and of course his, is outside my control. And for a control freak, that is a tough nut to chew. So, I am supposed to focus on what is and what is, is my thoughts. What do I want, the quote asks. What do I want my every day to feel like? How do I want to feel in my self. I need to think about what I want to happen, not what I don't want to happen. I know these lessons already. I mean I read The Secret, I have listened to Wayne Dyer, Depak Chopra, I know that "don't" doesn't work. That if you say "I don't want to be sick", the universe just hears "sick". The universe, God, Higher Power, Collective Consciousness can only create. It can't create "don't", so it has to create "sick". I know this. I know this. I know this. So why do I forget?

So, let's start anew. What do I want? What do I want every day to feel like? How do I want to feel? I'm gonna start a list. Making lists makes me feel in control. ***wink, wink***

1. I want to feel free. Free of worry. Like big worry. Not, I wonder if it will rain while I'm out today kind of worry. The big one. There is really only one worry now. One I can't control. One I need to stop thinking about. Wow, maybe I'm lucky I only have one true worry.

Every morning the possibility of a spectacular sunrise is always there. Maybe that sums up the day, every day, there is always the possibility for it to be spectacular, or just pretty - or some days gray and boring, or stormy - but above the clouds, it is always pretty.

Everyday something tells me to meditate. So why don't I do it? Am I afraid of the amazing life changing results?

[I stopped writing until the 16th, when I added below]

So above is as far as I got yesterday, and now today is worse. I don't even want to explain at this point. And I don't feel I can complete these thoughts.

Over and Out
Leslie

Sent: Wednesday, January 15, 2014 7:09 AM
From: Leslie Jermainne
To: Anna
Subject: Brian Jermainne

Hi Anna,

Sorry to bother you, but.... We are coming to see you on Friday. As of last night my Mom brain has gone into overdrive. Here's why. So when Brian entered treatment he weighed I think about 175. He has grown a bit more, I think he is about 6'1" now. Before being diagnosed, he worked very hard to lose weight. I think his highest was somewhere around 226-230, but I'm not sure. He spent almost a year losing that weight. Approx. Jan 2012 thru November 2012. Of course April 18th was biopsy surgery day and world crashing day. So, during his treatment and then afterwards the "I'm gonna eat what I want" devil got us both and we both ate a lot of "junk". This continued through Christmas. I know you have seen his weight numbers, and they have crept upwards. I think he hit about 215 or so just after Christmas. After that (or maybe it was New Years, but we are just talking a week here) he said "that's it!" He wanted to get this extra weight off and started eating "healthy" again. For him this means no more than 50 -75 carbs a day. He tracks nothing else. That is what worked for him before. Here is an example from yesterday - I don't know what he had for breakfast, besides some decaf coffee as I was at chemo with my Mother. He may have eaten something I don't know. BTW - breakfast was probably somewhere about 11-12 in the morning. I do think he had something, but I don't know what. Later in the day he had a ham/cheese omelet. 2 eggs, 2 oz Canadian bacon, 2 oz or so organic cheddar cheese. For dinner he ate about 7-8 oz steak and a big handful of raw baby carrots. I think he ate 2 chocolate chip cookies later on, which I had brought home for my husband....that was a bit unusual.

Okay - where am I going with this right? Well I have been happy he has lost some weight - I know 215 is a somewhat high. He is thrilled with himself as he is down to 204 now. He comes in and says "Mom I lost 2 more lbs! (that put him at the 204). "Wow - that's awesome!!!" I say. Inside I start to FREAK! He leaves the room and panic sets in. Just before he was diagnosed, he had been adding and adding carbs back into his diet to try to stop the weight loss and get a steady weight at about 180lb. He kept dropping a bit. So now I associate that with the cancer.

He is feeling really good right now. He saw his therapist once a week up until last week and decided he was feeling so much better and didn't need to go back. He says he hardly thinks about having had cancer anymore and that every day is a good day. The therapist did wonders! He has started drivers ed, and is working on his school work and looking for a part time job (sort of). Things are good.

I am certainly going to outwardly do nothing but encourage him, as you know he reads a lot off of me, and I am a worrier. So here is my rational mind talking - He is TRYING to lose weight. He is eating very low carb, he has started to exercise again, a bit and did a 2 hour bike ride around town the other day. He is happy. Sleeping well. His energy seems fine. (You know I worry about him being tired and sleeping a lot, but I actually think things have been a bit better lately). But I worry and worry and worry.

So I'm telling you all this because "Mr. Everything is Great" would never bring up anything, and if I bring up any worry I have he gets very angry and says it makes him feel like he has cancer again. I just want you to be aware for Friday. Know how he is eating. Be looking at every little microscopic part of his blood work, etc. I know I'm crazy, but I'm betting you've run into a crazy Mom or two. I am curious...besides him noticing a swollen lymph gland at any point, would his blood work show something brewing. I know his creatinine being high was our first sign w/his PCP.

I'm sorry to trouble you with this, when I know you have "sick" kids there to help every day. I just want to make sure, of….well, I don't know... honestly...that he is fine and is going to be fine, forever and ever. Not too much to ask right? Please of course don't mention this email on Friday. He would kill me!

Thank you for your understanding and patience with me. See you Friday.

Leslie

JANUARY 17, 2014

Sent: Friday, January 17, 2014 6:09 PM
From: Leslie Jermainne
To: My List
Subject: /RE: Brian Ross update 12/17/2014

Happy 2014 Everyone-

Yes, it's me again. Your local cancer Mom. Just wanted to send an update. We are back from Boston today with another month of nothin' but good news! We had an early appointment today, so Bri and I went up last night and stayed the night at The Elliot Hotel. We have driven by this place every time we come home and Bri has always commented that he'd like to stay there. Well, this was the time. It was a treat for us. And we "rocked" it the way the Jermainne's do. Which means, we check in, check out our room, and stay there. We order room service and movie and go to bed early. That's how we roll.

So, our visit was great. All happy news, good blood counts, no lumps and bumps, scar tissue good, no surprises. And a huge sigh of relief for me.

Why? Well, after calling my therapist, who I had only seen once before the holidays, in a panic on Wed. morning and her kindly fitting me in, we have decided officially that I have PTSD. Let's just say I had a little flashback this week after hearing just a few words out of my son's mouth. A few, simple, great words for that matter. You see he has been working at eating healthy and losing a few pounds that he had put on through this ordeal (yes, not everyone loses weight during chemo, especially with prednisone and a family history of comfort eating, thank you very much). And once again, he sticks to it and has been successful. Well, Tuesday night he came to me happy and says "Mom, I lost another two pounds". "Wow, that's great Brian." And somewhere in my head a ticking bomb goes off. I pray he leaves the room quickly as I want to be supportive, and I don't want to lose it in front of him. You see, from Jan. 2012 through Nov.-ish 2012 Brian worked really hard and lost 60lbs. Yup, he ate healthy, cut out the junk, the carbs, and walked 4 miles a day. And he did it. Unlike me who will do anything to lose weight but eat healthy and exercise. After the holidays 2012, he started to up his carb intake (he was eating no more than 50carbs a day to lose the weight) because he had reached his goal weight. And he evened out, then lost more (a pound or two) then upped his carbs again and evened out a bit (then lost more) and I remember him saying one night at drum corps for some reason, "Hey Mom, I lost 2 more pounds! I don't know why". Well, just a few short weeks after that…BOOM! - cancer. So I guess on Tues. night when he told me this, my brain flipped some sort of crazy switch and went into overdrive. I talked about it with Brian and Toni that night - thanks for the support guys! I called the therapist in tears the next morning and then cried my way through the hour with her. But...I did make headway, she gave me some interesting information and helpful tips and assured me that I was doing the right things (reaching out, getting facts, taking care of myself etc). I also sent an email that morning to Anna our NP so she was prepared for my worries today and addressed them all. She is so wonderful. So - I was feeling so good, so comfortable with everything last month. So positive and so sure. And then a few little words sent me back. And although I feel so reassured today, it takes a while to recover from a shock like that. I find it very weird. And unsettling to say the least.

But - enough already about me, right? It's okay, you can say right - that is how I feel. Our holidays were very nice. Christmas was great - and on New Year's Eve Brian and I celebrated our 17th wedding anniversary. And you know what? I still love that guy - more and more every day! He takes care of me, keeps me loved, comfy and sane. (Well sane might be pushing it, but he tries!)

On January 10th, Brian, Brian, Abby and I went to NBC very early that morning (6 a.m. arrival) and helped Make-A-Wish in their Miles for Smiles Campaign. Brian was interviewed about his trip and we got to meet and talk with such amazing people both working for Make-A-Wish and other volunteers. It was a great, great morning. Our first foray for 2014 in giving back and paying it forward. One of my resolutions for this year is to really step that up!

Brian is feeling great. Like I said, eating healthy, exercising, working on school (now 1/2 way through his JR. year of high school), working for TeamJermainne - helping us get some things done that we let slide last year (by "we" I mean me!) Taking driver's ed and all around feeling so much happier and more grateful for life. He has really turned a big corner and I'm so thrilled. I will get there too, as much as any parent can - as we all worry about our little critters even when nothing is really going on with them.

Thank you all again for sticking by us, listening to my yammering, (holy cow - spell check didn't freak when I wrote yammering), sending us love and prayers. I will be forever, ever grateful. I hope you all have a wonderful, fantastic, healthy and happy 2014.

Love to you All!

Leslie

JANUARY 21, 2014

Sent: Tuesday, January 21, 2014 10:25 AM
From: Kim
To: Leslie Jermainne
Subject: Re: /RE: Brian Ross update 12/17/2014

Leslie, have no doubt you have been paying it forward all through this ordeal. Through your journaling, hopes, fears and love, I have been more able to appreciate each day. I am more thankful for the things I have and more grateful for the other things I haven't had to deal with. You are an amazing woman! I pray for you and Brian every day I drive to work when I get to a certain part of my drive, that is my prayer time for Jermainne family. Everything happens for a reason and I believe you have found yours. I know it will sound weird but I think Brian has been given a special gift for a boy his age, the gift of appreciation which you can only receive by going through an ordeal like he has been through. I bet he is going to be an amazing person (more than he already is). Oh, the places he will go! I will continue to pray for you. Kim

Sent: Tuesday, January 21, 2014 5:27 PM
From: Leslie Jermainne
To: Kim
Subject: RE: /RE: Brian Ross update 12/17/2014

Hi Kim,

It is good to hear from you again. It is funny...after all that intensive writing in the hospital and hearing back from people, it is a bit strange now when I send something out once a month and don't hear much back. I have had more than one person tell me I should put all my emails into a book form, which I'm working on, basically because quite a few people mentioned it. I don't know I'll ever do anything with it, or who it could help, but I guess you never know.

I have had several people like yourself tell me that hearing my words have helped them to have a bit more gratitude in their daily lives. That means the world to me. It certainly was never my expectation to affect others. It was more to keep in touch while we were away, try to explain what we were really, really going through - without me speaking for him, and to not feel so isolated while living in the hospital. It amazes me what sharing hardship with others can do for everyone, but in this case and most especially, me.

I can't tell you how much it means to me that you think and pray for us so often. I learned a lot about prayer and what I like to call collective consciousness through all this. I truly, deep down believe that I have proof that everyone's prayers made a physical change in my child. Remember on our last inpatient he came down with a fever 3 days before going home and his blood counts dropped a lot and we were told that we really wouldn't be able to go home for probably an extra week if not more. I asked everyone for specific prayers, for his WBC count to go up to over 200 which is what they told me we needed to go home, and it did - the very next day! Then when they said "Well, that's probably just a fluke, we need it to continue to go up tomorrow a significant amount in order for you to leave tomorrow", and I asked again for everyone to pray for that. Both those nights I sat in my little chair/bed and imagined his white blood cells growing and multiplying and everyone was praying for him. That next morning so very, very early when they told me that his 4 a.m. blood results were back and he was over 500, well I nearly jumped for joy in the hallway. It brings tears to my eyes now, just remembering. That is my proof - I did it, you did it, he did it, everyone did it. It was one of the most amazing days of my life. And to think that you are still helping us is a wonder to me. So thank you. From Way. Deep. Down. Thank you.

You are right that Brian has gained a special outlook on life after going through this ordeal. He is just now realizing it. It has taken awhile for him to just start to embrace it, but he is doing so and starting to really be healed and move forward with his life. It has been amazing to watch his growth. I'm working on my own, as I think he is ahead of me. As a Mom, especially I'm going to claim, of an only child - this real life, in your face threat of your child dying is catastrophic. My heart bleeds for every mother who has lost a child. I. Can't. Imagine. I find it unbearable to read or watch anything like that. Just to make the point, I don't know if you watch PBS and Downton Abbey, but the new season has just started and the ending of last season was this man Matthew dying in a car crash. Well, the first episode, his mother talks and says "When your only child dies, you are no longer a mother. You are nothing." I had to turn it off and cry for a good long time with that one, because, well - she was right. In a way. But...I am getting better and this nightmare has given me many gifts and that is what I'm choosing to focus on as best I can every day. There is no guarantee's in life - even after beating cancer - all the other risks out there and still present. So every day I have started to ask myself two things that I learned by reading Ram Dass. 1. Where Am I? Here. 2. What Time Is It? Now. Pretty much that sums it up.

I hope you and your family are well and happy and secure. I appreciate your support and prayers and it is wonderful knowing the love you are sending our way. Thank you again and keep in touch.

Leslie

Sent: Saturday, January 25, 2014 8:30 AM
From: Leslie Jermainne
To: Caryn
Subject: Thank you!

Dear Caryn,

I'm not sure if you will remember me, but my son (Brian) and I took a homeschool photography class from you a few years ago. I can't remember how many it has been now....4 maybe? Also my husband Brian and I were the realtors that sold your father in laws house a year or two ago.

Anyway, when my newspaper arrived last night I was immediately drawn to the picture on the front. You see on 4/18/2013 our son was diagnosed with Burkitt lymphoma, a rare form of NHL. He was treated at The Jimmy Fund Clinic in Boston with 5 inpatient stays at Boston Children's Hospital. I'm happy to report that he is currently in remission, almost 7 months now. Treatment is intense, but relatively quick for his type of cancer. You either get it and kill it on the first go around, or else, well....I don't really like to say.

Anyway, I just wanted to thank you for what you are doing. Although I did see info on Flashes of Hope while at Dana Farber, I will admit, I didn't know what it was or take the time to find out. I thought it was some type of photography for the patients to take...and frankly, he wasn't feeling up to snapping photos. Oh, I wish I had known, although I'm not sure he would have participated. But I would have given him the chance. He did have a wonderful Make-A-Wish trip to Pompeii, Italy in October. What a gift that was to us all.

As you can imagine, going through this horrendous nightmare has changed us all, for the better I think, and I now try to pay more attention and reach out more! So that is why I wanted to say hi, and thank you for helping children and their families to get through this ordeal. Any bright spot, even for just a day has wonderful echos throughout treatment time and beyond - as I'm sure you know.

I would love to attend your event, but we have plans for that evening, but I will be sending a donation to the program, thanks to your gift and the awareness it has brought to our community and to me. I hope you have a successful event. If Bri and I find ourselves in Chester soon, we'll stop in and say hello.

Love & Light,
Leslie Jermainne

February 2014

FEBRUARY 22, 2014

Sent: Saturday, February 22, 2014 7:18 AM
From: Leslie Jermainne
To: My List
Subject: RE: Brian Ross update 2/21/2012

Hi All!

Update number....who knows anymore. Brian had his 8th checkup in Boston yesterday and all went well. Scarring from surgeries seems reduced. No lumps and bumps. Feeling good. Has grown taller, lost a little weight that was put on during the "life is short eat what you want last part of the year". Everything was really good. And even better was a wonderful opportunity. Anna (N.P.) asked Brian if he was going on the Teen Trip. "What team trip?" we asked. "The one to spring training for the weekend on March 14th. I'm one of the chaperones," she told us. "Wow that would be great, I'd love to go," answered Brian and of course me! (I'm telling you all this conversation for a reason, so bear with me.) Anna said she'd find out if there were still spaces, apologized for us not knowing about it, our blood results came back just in time - they were awesome by the way - and she said she'd have someone call us. When we got on the elevator, so excited by the potential of this trip for him with other teen patients of The Jimmy Fund going to Spring Training in FL, I finally asked him - "Bri, do you know what Spring Training is?" "No, what?" he said. I KNEW it!

Big Brian follows sports somewhat, but in our family that is about it. So I told him - you're going to get to go to the Red Sox Spring Training for a weekend. How COOL is that??? Even for a non-sports person like Bri. He will get to meet the players, watch a game against the Philly's in the luxury box, hang out and meet other kids, have batting practice, have fun at the hotel which has a pool and rock climbing. Now he says he has to start doing some research and learn about the players and the Red Sox. ;-) What a great, great day.

We went up the night before due to possible icy roads yesterday morning and by the sounds of things, Big Bri made the right call on that. I kept seeing listings of road closings, accidents and warning of icy roads. We stayed at the Longwood Inn which is basically attached to The Jimmy Fund Clinic/DFCI/Boston Children's. We have stayed there before if you remember. Before being admitted. It was a nice break then. Not as much this time. Kinda freaks me out now - too much emotional stuff attached to it. But, it was better than worrying about the ice. It took us a long time to get into the city due to some traffic around Newton (Sheila, is this normal at night?) Got in, ordered dinner, looked at our "tech tools" and then at about 8pm Bri announced it was time for bed. Anybody else seeing some avoidance techniques? Took some Melatonin, lights out. Okay - I made my way around the room by the light of my cell phone doing Mom stuff. Laying out our clothes for the morning, straightening the dirty dishes on the tray, packing the clothes from that day. I then texted Big Brian (instead of calling as planned) and found out Abby wasn't feeling well and was on her way to CCMC. She is fine, will be seen by her cardiologist to evaluate further. When I got home yesterday after what I thought was a difficult drive through constant drizzle and massive fog, I drove her back up to school. Poor Big Bri was swamped with work, and his afternoon appt. had been pushed back. Bri, Ab and I jumped in my car and took her back to Eastern. This drive was progressively worse. But, we made it up there, dropped her off, headed home and things kept deteriorating. On the way home, I could barely see a thing, it got almost pitch black, lightening started, downpour, thunder. It was so weird. I decided to go the back way since we had already seen a bad accident on the highway on the way up and it seemed like people weren't taking this seriously. It was really unnerving. Made it up over the bridge and it was so hard to see, I couldn't even tell if it was safe to move over a lane, so we just got off Exit 1 - wasn't worth the risk. It was not a nice drive.

What was nice was Alison coming to visit us - as Bri had been requesting for the past few weeks. He missed his Auntie Pal. Big Bri joined us for a quick dinner, but went straight back to work. It was nice to sit, have a glass of wine or two, and blow off the pressure that mounts the entire week before a visit. I keep thinking it will get better. And I guess in retrospect it is, but it still freaks me out every time we go. Today, first thing on Facebook, I see Brian's Imerman Angel Sean write that he is going for his CT Scan and is feeling how hard it is to focus on everything - and he is a ways out. And I totally get it. You read everywhere about "scanxiety". How you feel before your checkups. How you feel like it is possible they will rip the rug out from under your life again, only this time it will be worse. This time you know. And although you know you feel fine, and things are going well, your mind starts to play old tapes of how it was, what happened, what it felt like, smelled like, looked like and you are right back there. Then you get your good news, and you pick up and resume your "new normal" and only a few people in your life understand what the last few days were really like. And you are beyond thankful, grateful, elated. You have an emotional bruise or two, but they heal quickly and you get to kinda, sorta pretend you didn't freak a little, until next time - be it is every month for us right now - or every few months for Sean at this point. Today I will be thinking of him and his family and what they have been through and how he has helped my son get through this too. If you have a minute - send a positive thought out into the "field" for Sean today. Thanks.

So - onward and upward for us. Bri is going to Driver's Ed (when it isn't cancelled due to snow), working on his school work and now working for TeamJermainne Real Estate. Future Realtor? Maybe.... Playing his guitar(s) and now wants to build one. Life is good. Today is enough. (That's my new one, trying it out for size.)

Thank you all for your continued support and love and prayers. It really helps to get us through.

I hope you all have a wonderful month - Will update you after next appt. and Spring Training Trip!

Love,
Leslie

March 2014

MARCH 17, 2014

Sent: Monday, March 17, 2014 7:33 AM
From: Leslie Jermainne
To: My List
Subject: RE: Brian Ross update 3/17/2012

Hi Friends!

Well here we are only 3 weeks from my last note. On Friday Brian went to The Jimmy Fund for his checkup a week early this month so that we could coordinate it with him going on the DFCI trip to Red Sox Spring Training in Bonita Springs, FL. First things first. His checkup was great. Believe it or not, I still don't have his blood test results. I know they are fine under the law of "no news is good news", but still I will be calling today to get my copy. I read someone's comment about cancer follow up that said "you know how you dread the yearly physical? Imagine that every month for years. Only every time you go to your physical the doctor might tell you that your biggest fear is true. That cancer is back trying to kill you." That is what every cancer patient goes through, young and old.

One of the nice things about this trip is 'big' Brian came with us. He got to see our routine, meet the famous Anna, Nurse Practitioner - see where we go, what we do.

Anyway - after appointment time, we went and had an early dinner, spent time in the Serenity Garden at the Yawkey Center - here is our selfie.

Now that's a happy boy getting psyched to go to sunny FL.

We went downstairs to the meeting spot for the trip. It was filled with matching bags (everyone gets mailed a rolling duffle from L.L. Bean monogrammed with their first name) excited and maybe nervous teenagers, and excited and definitely nervous parents. There is the usual chaos of organizing a group to travel.

I see the man I met at the Ronald McDonald house, there to deliver his daughter. I got to say hello to this stranger that I shared a cup of coffee with, very early one morning at a Ronald McDonald house kitchen - some place I never thought I'd see the inside of, but thankfully always put my change into the box at the counter in McDonalds. We shared about a 45 min. conversation that morning with talk that included things about our children and their illness that maybe you don't even share with your close knit support group. Because only another parent of a pediatric cancer patient really understands. And walls come down quickly when you are in the presence of someone who knows. Then we said our "nice to meet you. I will pray for your son/daughter/family" and off you go. I have thought of them - said my prayers for that girl and her parents since then, never knowing if I'd meet them again. Anyway I did and I got to stop and say hello and without either of us remembering the others name. We go right to topic number 1 of cancer parents - we question each other on our children's status - "Emily just had her 2 year checkup, all clear" - "Brian is 8 months in remission". It is like reporting your info like the football players during the opening of the game on t.v. "Leslie Jermainne, - my son is Brian, Burkitt Lymphoma, 8 months in remission." He remembered me right away and remembered we were in a bad way at that time. We were staying in Ronald McDonald with the help of JFC to keep Brian out of the hospital for as long as possible due to depression issues. We were entering our last round of chemo that morning, after having one infusion of methotrexate the day before and got to stay there with a hydration pack. And he remembered what was happening with us and I could tell was so genuinely happy to hear the good news of our son. You ask other cancer parents with a wariness, afraid to hear bad news. Afraid to hear the worst.

But Friday was a good day. We got our hugs, watched as the bus drove off. I texted him saying again.... "Have a great trip. I love you." He texted right back "I love you too!!!" I burst into tears in the lobby of Yawkey. Not tears of sadness that he was leaving. Tears of joy that he can. I am so grateful. I'm so happy he was willing to go, step out of his comfort zone. As we had stood in the lobby filled with the budding adults, I looked around and thought about all the parents I was witnessing. I thought how all these people heard the words we heard. "Your child has cancer." All these parents cried themselves to sleep, sat at bedsides, learned a new vocabulary, know how to read a CBC report and decipher what it means. They have watched their vibrant healthy children become ill, without them knowing what was happening. They watched their hair fall out, needles be inserted into their bodies on a daily basis. They listened to pumps beep, and wheeze and pump poison into their kids. Many had to watch as radiation masks were put over faces before getting radiation. We didn't have that, how lucky are we? Very. They prayed and begged and cried and worried. They lost a lot sleep, and they aged. They watch their kids get weak, some using wheelchairs. They watched sickness, fatigue, tears and fears that they can't say "it's going to be fine", because they don't know. They heard good news and felt joy. They heard great words some of them - remission, no evidence of disease, scan is clear - some not yet. And really, for all the parents in that lobby - we are the lucky ones, at least for that weekend because everyone had a child that was well enough to go on this amazing trip. And many times during this ordeal we lived hour to hour, only able to comprehend what had to be done in the next 60 minutes. All of us this weekend were able to go about life at 2 days at a time. I've since learned that going much farther out than that really doesn't matter even in 'normal life'. It's kind of a refreshing way to live.

So off he went. We went home, exhausted. I spent all day Saturday and Sunday until I had to leave at 3pm to head back to Boston for pickup, "refreshing" his bedroom. Touching up paint, deep cleaning, rearranging, etc. It was a nice surprise when he got home last night. He was so happy. So pickup was interesting too. Regular parking was closed, but I was able to park at Brigham & Woman's garage just one block up. As I entered the

Yawkey lobby it was a bit eerie. It was 5:30 - pick up time is 6:30. There are already about 10 parents there. Are we a bunch of worry-warts or what! Everyone was in seats scattered about the lobby, not talking. The air was stressful. We were all wanting our babies back. As I sat reading on my cell phone, holding it about a 1.5ft from my face thanks to forgetting my newly needed reading glasses, a couple came in and the mom sat in the seat next to me. Shortly after another couple walked in and the mom came to talk to mom 1. After catching up like old friends I started to hear the 'cancer talk'. Although I hadn't heard much of the beginning of their conversation, once the words doctor, cancer, treatment, chemo were uttered my hearing had honed in and I couldn't un-tune my ears. I recognized all the fears, the worry, but also the joy for being alive. For their kids being alive. This woman had lost her job while caring for her daughter. Was behind in bills. Was struggling over the past two years with so many other worries besides the worry of her child living. But she was so GRATEFUL. She had a new job, not what she was trained for but a job. And she just picked up a second job cleaning. And she said how she was so grateful "to be able to pay my bills". She was grateful to go to the dentist and have her teeth cleaned, as that was something that wasn't feasible for her before. She said that was the first thing she did when she was able. When was the last time you were grateful for the dentist? I hate going to the dentist. But I will be grateful to go next month, I'll tell you that.

When the buses finally arrived a half hour late, there was a collective sigh of relief as parents jumped up from their seats and stood smiling like fools as they saw their kids coming home, tired, happy, safe. Another hurdle overcome. Life is good.

I have had people tell me to "move on". I have been told not to let the fear of Brian relapsing rule my life. I've been told I use it as an excuse to not reach out to others. I've been told to not focus on Brian's health. I have been told a lot of "well meaning" things by people who have no idea what this it like. People seem to think they know all about having a child with a cancer diagnosis. Especially people with friends or relatives who have a child with active cancer or who had cancer. They think they've 'lived it' with them, and maybe in a way they did - but unless it was their baby, they really didn't. And they mean well, I'm sure. But it isn't helpful. Being in a room full of people who are living this ordeal was amazing. Everyone understands. No one says "I have a feeling, he's going to be just fine." Because they know, that they have no idea. No one says to one another, "Don't focus on this illness", because when your child is diagnosed with cancer there is nothing else to focus on. Nothing. All the other things you do during that time are extraneous time fillers. No one there says "what about me? Can't you give me attention? Can't you understand what I need from you?" Because everyone there knows what it's like, that you have nothing left over to give. It was comforting to be understood. It is however, scary to see your eyes so many times over. It was also amazing to hear all the people and feel all the energy of people with profound gratitude. Not gratitude for a fancy new car, or expensive vacation. Not gratitude that they received jewelry for Christmas or a new electronic device. It is gratitude for another day lived. Another day fought. Another day with their child who has experienced only a small part of what is supposed to be their long lived life. It is gratitude for a hug, a smile, and adventure for their child to go on. It is thankfulness for the doctors and nurses who work so hard so our kids can live. It is thankfulness to go to the dentist. And behind those eyes are so many worries that others can't understand. What if it comes back? What if a new cancer grows? What if he/she can never have a baby? What if their heart is damaged? Their kidneys? Their lungs? Their brains? What if they die? Sorry, if I'm off subject of how great this weekend was for Brian. It was just my first experience being in a room full of parents who know. Just hearing all these words from these two Mom's brings on flashback feelings. I wanted to get up and move honestly, and probably should have, but in a way the words were comforting because they were "mine". I had another not so pleasant flashback at home. PTSD rears its ugly head. I'm saying goodnight to my happy, beautiful son and as he turns his head in his dimly lit room, his face looks a little too thin to me. I flash right back to the week before biopsy, at drum corps practice watching him play and thinking to myself "he looks so tired, so thin, his face gaunt almost" and hoping he was okay. I didn't know then what was coming. What was right there in front of me as I watched him practice. So I go into the bathroom and the fear starts to boil up in my throat. I feel the tears working their way to my eyes and the breathing pick up its pace. But I remember what my therapist said - "reach out and share", so I went into our room and told Brian. He listened as patiently as he always does. He asked me what he could do for me. I told him he already did it by listening. I told him how my worries of Brian dying had really faded over the past few weeks and how well I thought I was doing and I didn't want to backslide. I comforted myself that PTSD is a real thing. My therapist told me I have it. I feel guilty for having it because I feel like I'm comparing myself to a soldier in combat, and I don't want to take anything away from that. I can't imagine what they go through. But as I type this, I wonder what they would say. I wonder if those men and woman would gladly go serve in combat in a trade off to make sure their child never has to face cancer. Hmmmm....I never thought of that before. Well, I know my answer. As frightening and horrible as it would be, I would gladly, happily, eagerly do just that. If God gave me a choice - Either Brian gets diagnosed with cancer and no matter the outcome you and he have to go through it, OR you go serve in combat for ____(fill in length of time you feel happy with - for me it would be forever) and I will take away that diagnosis, and he will never know what he knows now....well I wouldn't even think twice. Choice B please and thank you. I'm not sure if you all believe me, but I assure you it is true. So maybe PTSD is real for me and maybe I shouldn't feel guilty about it. So, I made it through that flashback much better than others I have had. I held back the tears, reached out and shared, made my plan which was to review how lucky I felt that I was getting better and to concentrate on the amazing weekend he had with all those amazing teens. And today, I'm better.

I will go back to the trip. My child hasn't been so happy in so long. He loved it. He was such a teenager, which is amazing. He has new friends now. One's that I think will be lifers. One's that get it. Who live it. One's who know, just like for me - the parents who know. He came home wishing he could have stayed. He came home and said the words that he doesn't usually say - cancer, treatment, lymphoma, brain tumor, chemo, etc. - because it was a new normal. All these other kids had it too, in one form or another. And they know, they understood, and they played golf, drifted in the lazy river, went down the waterslide, tried to hit the baseball, met the players, acted silly, ate the food, slept late, texted on their phones, took photos and made memories too. It was another turning point for him. He can't wait now to find out if he gets accepted to go to a week camp in Montana this summer for teens with a cancer diagnosis. He now knows he will be safe. Accepted. Understood. We should find out by the end of the month. Last week he unexpectedly got invited to go on TV again with Make-A-Wish for the show on channel 3.

I loved what he said about his trip to Pompeii "It was a huge jump from being sick all the time in the hospital to this amazing fun trip that I'm gonna remember for the rest of my life. It really was a huge turning point in my life, not just as a trip." I really feel this trip of only a weekend was as monumentally important because of who he was with, not where he got to go (which was pretty awesome itself!) I hope the trip to camp this summer, if he gets accepted, will be equally as wonderful. His only worry - he can't have his cell phone at camp! Tragic for a teenager, and frankly for me as well. But I'm quite sure we will live through it. ;-)

So that was a lot I'm sure. Please remember to let me know if you no longer want to receive these updates. I do understand that everyone isn't focused on this, and I would never be offended if you want off the list. Just send me an email and I'll take care of it. Seriously. Life it short, be as happy as you can on any given day. I know I'm doing my best and I feel like that is improving every day.

Thank you for listening and loving us through this. You are a bigger help than you know. Have a wonderful day.

Love,
Leslie

Sent: Monday, March 17, 2014 9:20 AM
From: Kim
To: Leslie Jermainne
Subject: Re: Brian Ross update 3/17/2012

Leslie, thank you for sharing and don't stop. Your words of wisdom and what life has thrown at you, helps me to be more grateful for what I have each day. You are amazing and strong and a wonderful mother, wife, sister, aunt, niece, friend and support to others. Keep up the good work. How lucky is Brian to have you helping him along the way. Kim

Sent: Monday, March 17, 2014 9:31 AM
From: Jen
To: Leslie Jermainne
Subject: Re: Brian Ross update 3/17/2012

Oh Leslie, I hope YOU'RE going to be ok. So glad Brian had a great time, he deserves it.

XOXOXO

Jen

Sent: Monday, March 17, 2014 5:14 PM
From: Lisa
To: Leslie Jermainne
Subject: RE: Brian Ross update 3/17/2012

All I can say Leslie is that your strength amazes me. God bless and know I'm thinking of you.

Lisa

April 2014

APRIL 18, 2014

Sent: Friday, April 18, 2014 6:37 PM
From: Leslie Jermainne
To: My List
Subject: RE: Brian Ross update 4/18/2014

One year later....

Well here we are folks, one year to the day that Brian was having surgery to remove a lipoma from his abdomen and an infected lymph node from under his arm and wait....no....it's lymphoma! What a day that was. What a horrible, horrible day. But today....it was a very good day. We were back in Boston, had a wonderful checkup with Anna our NP and our oncologist. All is good! No neuropathy, no fevers, no rashes, no hearing or vision problems, no pain, no lumps and bumps, no learning challenges, his walking and balance are fine. These are all the things they look for every time we go. Not that those are indications of relapse...they are indications of long term issues from chemo. But again, all is good. My boy is a champ!

We then had a quick lunch and met with a big team of genetic researchers, psycho-social, an oncology fellow and we even missed one person due to communication error - but no big deal. We were there because my Mom is battling multiple myeloma and her mother died from leukemia at the age of 57. So is there a genetic link since these three cancers are in the same cancer family? Should I be screened differently? Should his potential future children be screened differently? We learned that as of right now, no. No to all three of those questions because they don't know of any genetic link for these cancers. It may be familial, but not genetic. At least not yet. Anyway, it was all good information. And we made it out of Boston before heavy traffic time.

I did write something very early this morning, to sum up what our last year felt like. I thought I would share since I don't have much more to say other than my son is my hero and my greatest teacher. I have learned so much this past year. About him, about me, about life and what I believe. It has forever changed me, which is a good thing. I am lucky.

So here it is...

One year ago today, I was sent down a path I did not want to travel. I started the trek already exhausted from the fear and worry that the weeks prior had heaped on my mind. I was shoved onto the path landing on my hands and knees, winded and afraid. But I had to move forward, crawling at first, knowing that I could not turn back. I slowly got to my feet, disoriented, angered, fearful and confused. I started to walk through the dark, slowly at first, with thorns ripping at me and branches unseen slapping me in the face. This was no place I had ever been before. Nothing was familiar, there seemed no light ahead, only darkness. The pieces of my heart lay broken and jangling in my chest causing my breath to catch in pain and anguish. But I walked and I started to learn. I listened, straining to hear with my whole body. I watched with my eyes and I felt with my broken heart - the only things I had to help me at first. I learned that other things were going to reach out and grab me. That I would startle and cringe. That I would cry and cry and cry some more. I had no choice. No one asked me if I wanted to go this way. No one offered a way off the path.

And when the light started to break and I could start to see ahead just enough to move a bit faster, I felt like I wasn't alone. I would turn and look and I would catch a glimpse of people I knew and some I didn't. They were following me, at a distance. They were cheering me on, telling me I could do it. They too didn't know how to get off the path. They didn't understand what it was like to walk it every day. But they stayed and they offered support. Some just stood and watched me, quietly from a distance. Some tried to catch up, even wished they could take the lead for me, to ease my pain and let my wounds heal a bit before going on, but they couldn't take the lead. I loved their willingness to try. They stayed on my heels and kept me going, showing me I wasn't alone. And other people showed up along the side, giving me direction, giving me hope, giving me confidence. They told me what I already knew, that I couldn't turn back. They told me they would help me, and they did. They had seen so many others walk this path before, all essentially the same. Only some of those people never got to the end. And they had no guarantees I would either, but they would do everything they possibly could and then some, to try to get me there. I did what they said. I trusted them. I feared not reaching the end more than any other single thing. I prayed and begged and I agreed I would walk this road and I would not complain. I never asked "why me?" "Why not me?" was the answer I gave to others who asked that question for me. No one should take this path. No one. Ever. And especially no one should walk it carrying their child in their arms. Their sick child. Their scared child. Protecting their child the best they can. Telling their child it will be okay, and that they'll find a way out of the forest, when they really had no idea if that was true. While branches slash, and roots tripped, and tears slid down my tired and dirty face.

And when the sun rose finally over the horizon, I could see a fair distance in front of me and I got my second wind. I couldn't see the end. I didn't know what other bends and hills and obstacles might be before me. But I could see and I could see the eyes of my child looking to me, weary and exhausted. And I smiled at his beautiful face. My strength was renewed and I knew I could carry him the rest of the way. Bends in the road did come my way and I took them, slowing down for a time. I did get too confident some days and I would stumble and even fall, while holding my child tight and keeping him safe. I would get up, shake off the pain and keep moving, one foot in front of the other. Hills came and the walk would slow. Sometimes I had to call out and ask for support, because I was needy and needed even more than I was getting. And all those people who had stuck by me and had continued to follow me gave me even more. They helped the sun move up into the sky, they made my arms stronger to keep carrying my boy. They braced my back and gave strength to my legs. And in the times it got quiet, I could hear less of the broken pieces of my heart jingling in my chest. Some of the pieces had grown back together. Fragile and scarred, but healing ever so slowly.

And now a whole year later, I am still walking. I no longer carry my child, but walk with him as we used to when he was younger. Only now we hold hands again, knowing as only us two know, how scary the dark was, how bumpy the path felt, how evil the instigator really is. We heard others along the way, on their own path, over in the dark, struggling to find a way. We would yell out to them, try to encourage them, never too tired to answer their call. And they would answer ours. Sometimes they didn't make it. And we cried. Sometimes now we catch a glimpse of some through the trees walking fast towards the end, towards freedom, just like us. We watch warily, afraid to take our eyes off the ground - afraid they too will get distracted and fall down again. But we have learned so many, many things while walking.

I have learned you never know what path you will have to walk, but you will have no choice but to walk it. And while you do, remember everyone else is on their path and they don't know what mine feels like, just like I don't know theirs. I have learned that we are loved and listened to by people we know and even some people we don't. I have learned the world and life are good, even when it is terribly difficult. I have learned that people will surprise us, in good ways and sometimes in bad. But even that is okay, because it brings clarity. I have learned what is really important. I mean really learned it. I think we all say it, but there is a big difference between thinking you know what is truly important and instead really having knowledge of it.

This time has brought life into sharp focus. It has brought me acceptance of time and faith in the unknown. It has taken awhile but it has brought me peace in knowing I have no control, I have no answers, but I have today and just today to love. It has brought me deep appreciation for those who have loved me and I have learned to be a better person, a better friend because of them. It has brought me the ability to be here now, and deal with the next obstacle when I get to it, if I get to it.

I am still walking. I don't know where the end is anymore. I thought there was one. I thought I knew what it would look like, feel like, sound like. But I now know, that I don't know. I'm not sure there even is an end, or that I *want* to find it. Because the horrible, rocky, dark path has turned into a hike that has strengthened my heart, deepened my love, cleared my mind and opened my soul. And I'm walking it, everyday - whether I am tired, or achy, fearful or happy. It is my trek. My trip. My path. And I don't walk it alone, ever. Even if I go first - taking the scrapes, and the scratches, worrying about the rocks and the roots, I share it with the true hero of this walk. I share it with the one who never looked around, the one who looked into my eyes for strength, unknowing that he was the one who gave it to me. "You never know how strong you are, until being strong is the only choice you have" is my new understanding. He was strong enough for the both of us. He is my greatest teacher and he has made me a seeker. He has always brought me joy, even in the darkest of hours. I cherish every moment we spend walking this walk and I will keep going, full of pride when I watch him move ahead of me, strong and happy blazing his own path, whichever way it goes.

Talk to you all again in month! Love you all! Happily one year later from home.

Leslie

APRIL 19, 2014

Sent: Saturday, April 19, 2014 3:23 PM
From: Toni
To: Leslie Jermainne
Subject: Re: Brian Ross update 4/18/2014

You amaze me my friend. You are stronger and wiser than you can even imagine. So enjoyed our breakfast and some catching up.

Take some time over the next few days to find your inner peace. It's a beautiful time of awakening, and rebirth.

XXOO
Toni

Sent: Saturday, April 19, 2014 7:52 PM
From: Carlo
To: Leslie Jermainne
Subject: Re: Brian Ross update 4/18/2014

You should write a book "How to Walk In The Dark" really! You have so much love inside you for your son, and every time I read of your journeys I feel sad at times but also good, for all is still well and I am kind of his Uncle,...love you. me

APRIL 21, 2014

Sent: Monday, April 21, 2014 7:23 AM
From: Ann
To: Leslie Jermainne
Subject: RE: Brian Ross update 4/18/2014

You NEED to write a book. You are a very talented writer!!

Ann

APRIL 24, 2014

Sent: Thursday, April 24, 2014 4:25 PM
From: Brenda
To: Leslie Jermainne
Subject: RE: Brian Ross update 4/18/2014

Hi Leslie – it is definitely a celebration with this recent update on Brian. You are correct – Brian is a champ – but so are you. You are his champ – his hero. Don't ever lose sight of that.

Thank you for sharing the summary below. I could actually visualize your struggle in the forest, the support you received from your family and friends who love you and Brian so very much. I could see how you protected Brian. I can imagine the exhaustion in his eyes that you saw back then.

And today - the love and strength in his eyes. You are a wonderful, strong, inspiring, loving person. I applaud your strength and determination. You are incredible!

We wish you, Brian and Brian Ross love and continued support. You are always in our prayers. Continue to rock on and move forward and always know that we are here for you.

Love to all of you – Brenda and Mark

May 2014

MAY 17, 2014

Sent: Saturday, May 17, 2014 8:57 AM
From: Leslie Jermainne
To: My List
Subject: RE: Brian Ross update 5/16/2014

Hi Everyone,

We've had another checkup - yesterday on the 16th. Everything was good. CBC counts were fine. All the questions were good. Maybe some seasonal allergies afoot, but nothing to be concerned about. I really wasn't going to write anything. I thought I was done with updates maybe. But...I reread my note from last month, and the responses I had gotten and I decided to keep updating, maybe until we get to July - that will be one year of remission. Hmmmm....I haven't written those words before, or not regularly. I often feel compelled to not count on the future, but not in a bad way. Well maybe a bad way. You see, I feel like if I plan for the future, it will reach back into my current day and slap me for being cocky about it. Like it is a given and I take it for granted. And the only way for life to hurt me, is to hurt my child. So I constantly censor my words, to make sure they stay in the present, as best I can. And I think it is a good thing. A good lesson. Something I needed to learn and that I continue to learn because I'm a planner and planners don't live in today. I find myself always saying things like "when I get this finished...." or "I just have to get this thing done and then I can relax (or substitute: enjoy, sleep, read)". "When this happens, then we can do that and I'll be happier." Sad, really. Today is all we have.

Some days when the fears of relapse sneak back in my mind and start eating away at it a little bit, I have to actually say these words, "he doesn't have cancer today. Today he is healthy and feels good." Of course I just went through a few days of that, leading up to checkup time. This past week was harder than the past two months had been on the lead up week to Boston. I don't know why. Well, I do, but it's stupid. You see he complained his legs were hurting one day. He also has had a blood shot eye about 3 times in the past 2 weeks. And he was tired. And he lost 8 lbs over the past month. And my Cancer Mom brain loves to find any little thing, that before seemed so....mundane....and build it up into a huge mountain that blocks out the sun. So, I have to talk myself through it. Leg pain - he is still growing. He mowed two lawns right before saying that (although he does that every week now, so why that day?) Why was his eye blood shot? Were his eyes being affected by the chemo? Yes, it can happen. Is it likely? Nope. Not at all. Why is he tired? Ummm, maybe because he's a teenager. Maybe because he stays up really late. Maybe because two days in a row, after being up really late, he had to get up really early. Duh! And why did he lose 8 lbs. Oh ya, he has been trying to. He has been eating healthy. Giving up all the white stuff, eating meat and veg and fruit and that's it. And he is at a healthy weight, not underweight. But again - it's a trigger for me.

So we go to Boston and my big 6'1" 190lb. baby sits on the little exam table, his long legs hanging over and he smiles and talks and feels good. I flash back to so many doctor's appointments throughout his life. Watched as he has grown from the times I laid his little body on the baby scale, to sitting him on the table and staying there so he wouldn't fall off. Watching as he grew and could climb up on the table himself to the point he went off to his exam by himself, overpowering the small table in the pediatrician's office. And I felt like I could see that little face still, in this almost grown one. This one that shaves now. But those same sparkly, blue eyes and smiling mouth remind me that he is and always will be my little baby. He has his mouth checked (throat looks a little red), ears checked (a bit of clear fluid), eyes checked (blood shot) and seasonal allergies is addressed. Of course! I latch onto that like it's a life jacket thrown out to rescue me. The seas calm down. Every lymph node is felt, nothing out of place. Scars are examined- under his arm, his port scar, his abdomen. All feel better - scar tissue only and even that has broken down more. Yay! Can you get up and walk? Looks good. Any trouble with rashes, balance, eyesight, sleep, thoughts, worries, lumps, bumps? No. No. No. No. No. No. No. No. I'm not sure he would say yes, but still - I like the "no's". We talk over long term stuff, as I finally finished reading his survivorship notebook. Echocardiograms. Liver Function. Hormone development. Blood Tests. Growth Charts. Doxirubicin. Methotrexate. Cyclophosphimide. Cytarabine. Long term effects. Blah, blah, blah. Again - looking into the crystal ball of the future and nothing can be seen anyway.

So homeward bound we went, which is always a relief and headed right to DMV to get his driver's license!!! Yay! He passed his test on Wed. through AAA. So we had to wait 48 hours to actually get his license. After just over an hour wait - it was in his hand. Arrive home and he hops in his car and drives off by himself. Just down the road to the music store and it wasn't as hard as I thought it would be. He was back in just a few minutes. Went out later to Stop and Shop. And again a bit later to do an errand for me. Returning safe and sound each time. I have thoughts like - "Cancer or no cancer, life holds no guarantees. He could get hurt or killed in a car accident." Sounds like a bad thing to think right? But really, it's the truth and it reminds me that cancer shouldn't be the focus. Neither should being killed in a car accident - but that never has been my focus. So it just reminds me that there are no guarantees and today, right now, he doesn't have cancer and he is a safe driver in a safe car and he is alive and happy and that's all I have. That's all any of us have.

So it's been a hard week, but it's done and we have great things to look forward to. Brian is going on a teen program overnight in June in Boston with The Jimmy Fund – to see a comedy show, see a Red Sox game from the box seats, meet players, have fun, see friends. It will be great. We should open our pool...sometime. The leaves and flowers are out and the weather is warming - albeit slowly. And we have another month to adjust. We will go back in June and then again in July and then they will start to push our appointments out a bit more, maybe 2-3 moths. Gulp. I'll be ready. I have no choice anyway. Besides - that is a long, long, long way away when you live in the present. No need to worry about it now.

I hope this next month brings all of you peace and happiness. And for us too. I am still struggling with where life has taken me and where I feel it wants me to go. I'm in a holding pattern right now, for reasons beyond my control. Like I have any control! HAH! So many things will change in these next few years and I am so acutely aware of it every day. And it is a struggle to stay present, but that is the theme of this note and of my current life. Stay present. Just today. Don't worry. Be Happy. (Good song). It is a hard task for a worrier like me. But it is my current lesson and I'm trying to master it. My son tells me that I make life too difficult. And the wisdom of youth is often right. Although we like to think as adults that we have all the lessons learned and we are teaching the younger generation. Sometimes, it is best to listen. He has taught me so much. So much of what I wish life were still like, and could be like, if I got out of my own way. Working on it. Working on it.

Have Fun. Lots of love from home.

Leslie

Sent: Saturday, May 17, 2014 11:57 AM
From: Karen
To: Leslie Jermainne
Subject: Re: Brian Ross update 5/16/2014

Leslie, I'm so glad to hear everything went well at Brian's check-up!!!! Yay!!!!! I can only imagine how scary it must be each time you take him for a checkup....And I'd be right there with you looking at every "change" as a threat. I remember my mom saying that we don't know what the words "worry" or "guilt" mean until we have kids...and I think she was absolutely right. We moms worry so much...and I think you are amazing in how you handle this, and I also think it's healthy that you are able to so eloquently express the emotional reality of having a child who has been on this journey. Thank you for the update. Thank God he's in remission!!!! I pray that he will be healthy always.

xo
Karen

MAY 18, 2014

Sent: Sunday, May 18, 2014 6:21 AM
From: Leslie Jermainne
To: Karen
Subject: RE: Brian Ross update 5/16/2014

Thank you Karen. Your mom was a wise woman! The fear and guilt are overwhelming at times, but I'm working on it. Thank you always for your kind words of support and encouragement. Friends like you will never understand the impact they have had on me during this time, just by sending prayers and a quick note. Truly they are what have gotten me through. Hope to see you guys this summer! Enjoy!

Leslie

MAY 21, 2014

This is a copy of a note I sent out to Laura T.: (you'll understand what this is about when you read it.)

5/21/14

Hi Laura, today I received your thank you note for my small donation to your huge walk. It made me cry. As a lot of things do these days. I will admit at first I wasn't sure who/what it was about. I have supported so many people/things etc. as much as I can since my life halted to a stop 4/18/13. When I found you on Facebook and saw Sarah B. as a mutual friend I remembered right away. She had messaged me about this incredible woman she met and I was so taken by what you are doing. Your letter is so appreciated and your commitment to the hiking an inspiration. I find it amazing that some people truly realize that these kids don't have a choice. They can't decide on a too hard day to not have chemo. Or not have their 10th lumbar puncture, or not get sick and feel exhausted. They have to do it anyway, or else not live. And I was so incredibly saddened by the piece of news about 'Donna' and her daughter. My God. Her daughter and their family fought from age 18 months to 4 1/2 years and won. And to lose her at age 20, from the long term effects of chemo is so completely and utterly unfair. This now is one of my biggest worries. Brian is now 10 months in remission and I am certainly still worried about relapse, although each day farther away makes it a tiny bit easier. But the new worries start now. He was treated with a chemo drug that can cause heart damage. So this scares me tremendously. Even when you think it's over and you've made it, it's never over. Never, ever. It is so incredibly heartbreaking at times. Both my parents are battling cancer right now. My mother has multiple myeloma and my father prostate cancer. And although I take both of them now to chemo once a week, it is so very much easier, as weird as that may sound. They are both 82. They have had their turn. They have had love and a family and a home and a long and happy life. Cancer is unfair and mean at age 82, but....for a child - it is just so deeply and incredibly worse. I tell you all this, because I want you to know how much people like you, mean to families like mine and for Giulia and Madeline and for all those other adorable faces we see at clinic or in the hospital. Knowing that people care and are willing to be cold, wet, uncomfortable, tired and maybe even sore because they are willing to reach out and help. They are making a difference in not just the lives of those they know well, but those they have never met. What you do restores our faith in the world, when the world it seems, has been so unkind to our babies. So thank you for putting yourself out there to help all of those little people who have no choice, and for their families who would gladly take their cancer themselves, but can't. Your gift is so very much appreciated. Leslie Jermainne

MAY 28, 2014

5/28/14 – received from Laura T.

Leslie, I need to apologize for the delay in my response. I read your message just before leaving work last week and got caught in my tracks. I didn't know how to respond. It provoked so many emotions, I wasn't sure what to do with them. But there was one immediate and obvious response - to share your message with my teammates. I had shared with them the unfolding of the day I met Sarah which led to your donation and how much that meant, and how a simple homemade sign on my back could bring awareness to so many people. I copied your message into an email, reminded them of the story I had previously shared and off it went. Your message touched each and every one of my teammates, and I want you to know that. On the tough days, the tough moments, I want you to know that there is a Team of us out there supporting you. I'm not sure how to use words to respond to everything else you have shared - the fear for your son's future, the cancer that continues to affect your family. This is one of those moments that all I can do is listen, let you know you can reach out any time for anything, and wish that I could give you a hug. I feel like this still isn't enough of a response, but know that I'm thinking of you and your family and praying for strength and healing for everyone.

Laura

5/28/14

It is enough Laura. It is way more than enough. Thank you. Thank you and your team so very, very much.

Here is information from Laura about the fundraising event: "Last year, the Hike team of 26 people raised a total of $142,946 for the Leukemia and Lymphoma Society. We trained for 16 weeks, hiking all over the area. Hikes gradually increased in length and intensity, beginning with a +3 mile hike and getting all the way up to a +12 mile training hike. Once in Yosemite, hikers trekked along their trail of choice, which ranged from 8-9 miles to 17 miles, all in one day. I hiked the 17 miles!"

June 2014

JUNE 10, 2014

Sent: Tuesday, June 10, 2014 5:38 PM
From: Leslie Jermainne
To: My List
Subject: RE: Brian Ross update 6/10/2014

Hi Everyone,

I kinda tricked you with the subject line - this isn't really an update about Brian. It's about me. I'm asking you all for your help once again. I have committed today to raising money for childhood cancer research. And how am I doing this you ask? By asking for donations in order to sponsor me to SHAVE MY HEAD! Yup! Here's the flyer I just made up:

46 Momma's Shave For The Brave 2014

My name is Leslie Jermainne and I'm going to ***SHAVE MY HEAD*** to raise money for Childhood Cancer Research with the 46 Momma's Shave For The Brave 2014!!

Why would I do this? In honor of my son Brian Jermainne who is a survivor, and for all the other Mom's who have heard these words: "Your Child Has Cancer."

On 4/18/13 I heard those exact words. Our world came to a screeching halt. My son was 15 and healthy, except two lumps that he had felt, one under his arm and one in his abdomen. After surgery we knew... Lymphoma. Final diagnosis was Stage III Burkitt Lymphoma, a rare type of very aggressive Non-Hodgkin's Lymphoma.

We are so thankful to the amazing doctors, nurses and staff at Dana Farber Cancer Institute in Boston which runs The Jimmy Fund and treats pediatric cancer inpatient at Boston Children's Hospital. Our son underwent 5 very aggressive rounds of chemo-therapy. By the end of treatment on 7/2/13, Brian's cancer was gone! We are so very lucky.

But every weekday 46 Momma's around our country hear those terrible words: "Your Child Has Cancer." And my heart breaks for them too. So I'm joining the **46 Momma's Shave For The Brave 2014** event on July 27th in Boston, MA to support these children, their families and my son.

I stayed in my hometown area, where my husband and I own TeamJermainne Real Estate Services. This is our home, our community. So many people have supported us this past year as we battled cancer with our son. I'm asking one more time for your support. Help me raise money to help fund childhood cancer research. Here are some quick facts:

* All types of childhood cancers combined receive only 4% of U.S. Federal Funding for cancer research.
* About 60% of all funding for drug development in adult cancers comes from pharmaceutical companies. For kids? Almost none, because childhood cancer drugs are not profitable.

I'm scared to shave my head, I won't say I'm not. I watched my son lose his hair during treatment. I'm sure I will look a little goofy, but I don't care. I wanted to make sure if I was going to do this that the money I raise will go where it's needed. After researching St. Baldrick's Foundation, I was confident and happy at their ability to donate funds directly to childhood cancer research.

I'm a little late to the game though - taking a long time to consider this. But I want to honor my son, my personal hero. When I saw this event was being held in Boston this year, the city we lived in during treatment and where we visit every month for checkups and when I knew it would be in July the month of my son's first "cancerversary", and my 45th birthday on June 23, a personal milestone - well...I felt it was calling my name. So I'm gonna do it! But I need your support. I only have a little over a month to raise money and I want this to really count. It's gonna take well over a year to grow my hair back to my current length. Please - if you can spare anything to help me raise as much money as I can in just one month, I would be grateful. Just to know that our children and my son has your support in searching for a cure for childhood cancer would mean the world to us.

Here is a link to my fundraising page: http://www.stbaldricks.org/teams/TeamBrian

10/2012 7/2/2013 9/2013 11/2013 6/2014

So.....what do you all think? You are all my peeps! The people who have listened to me these past 14 months. You have prayed for my son, sent me special gifts, prayer shawls, cards, food and notes of encouragement. All of them treasures to me. So, this is a big one for me. I'm shaving my head. So, can I tap into this well one more time and ask for some big support. Or little. Anything really. I have a goal of raising $1,000.00. And I'll share my bald head photos when I'm done! Please use the link above if you will donate to help childhood cancer research. Also - please share this message or my Facebook post about this if you feel so inclined. I'd really, really appreciate it.

Love,
Leslie

JUNE 16, 2014

Sent: Monday, June 16, 2014 7:34 AM
From: Leslie Jermainne
To: My List
Subject: RE: Brian Ross update 6/13/2014

Hi Everyone,

Don't worry, this really is an update about Brian. On Friday, Brian had his monthly checkup at The Jimmy Fund. He wasn't scheduled to go until next Friday the 20th, but when his photography class scheduled for Friday night was cancelled and Big Brian suggested I call them and see if they could see him that day and then we stay over because Brian was going to the Teen Program weekend trip, we could save ourselves another trip to Boston on the 20th. Our oncologist said sure! So, we threw stuff in a bag, got a room at the Long Warf Marriott and headed straight up. His checkup was good. Blood counts all good and we got a form to send to camp on July 1st. All the questions they ask him had good answers. We are one month away (actually only 16 days now) to his one year in remission date - his "cancerversary" - of July 2nd. Not sure I like that word. I think 4/18/13 should be his cancervesary and July 2nd should be his "remissionversary". On that note, I learned a new term in the cancer world. One that hit me hard. It is "angelversary". The date a loved one died. I learned this through getting to read and email with other members of the 2014-46 Mommas. But more on that in a minute.

So after Brian's checkup was done, we headed over to the hotel, checked in and walked over to Faneuil Hall in the pouring rain, looked in some shops, had some dinner and I bought a hat to cover up my bald head after the shave event. While there we happened to run into, I think it would be, Brian's 3rd cousin, who coincidentally I went to high school with, she is a year or two younger than me, and her son is 4 yrs in remission from Leukemia. It was great to see her and say hello, introduce Brian and hear how well both our boys are doing. Back to the hotel for a movie and dessert we purchased and Bri tried to get to sleep early 8:30, but I couldn't get sleepy. I must admit that staying in a hotel in Boston is always unsettling these days. At 10:30 when I tried to sleep he woke up. At 2:30 I was awake and that was it. He said he slept horrible all night and was exhausted.

We were back at Dana Farber at 9:00 a.m. for him to go on the Teen Trip. We had such a great surprise too. A roommate he had several times when we were inpatient, who I know I mentioned as was VERY ill, was there! And he looked really good. Last time we saw him at clinic he was in a wheelchair, and although doing better, I was still very concerned. But here he was walking, with a cane, but still....he looked so much better and was ready to go on his first teen trip. Brian and he never really got to connect even though we lived in the same little cubicle for so long. He was so ill then and both of the boys spent a lot of time sleeping and hibernating inside their little curtained bed, just to make it through. Brian and he got to know each other on this trip and they had a great time. They went and had a tour of Fenway, lunch, player meet and greet! Here is a photo of Brian with catcher David Ross (excellent name, as a matter of fact Brian's middle name is Ross - seems destined right?...) They watched the game from the box seats, and a box down at the field too, where I guess Stephen King was taking in the game. They went back to the hotel and had a great comedy show, make your own Sundae's and fun time being teenagers. Sunday morning was brunch at The Cheesecake Factory and then I picked him back up at Dana Farber at 12. He was exhausted but full of great stories! What an amazing place The Jimmy Fund is, and what a team The Red Sox are, for making these kids feel like kids and forget all they have faced and continue to deal with, even if just for 48 hrs. We are blessed to be a part of that family.

While he was having fun I came home, got my father's day stuff done and spent a nice evening with my wonderful husband, then back up to Boston on Sunday for pickup and to meet the leader of the 46 Mommas group and get more info. Back home Sunday to sit by the pool for an hour (after cleaning it) with Abby, Brian & Brian and then dinner and sound asleep with my head on Brian's lap on the couch by 8:00. Little Brian and I were exhausted. I climbed into bed at 8:30 and zonked out! He wasn't far behind me.

So now we move on with lots to do this summer. Brian is going to Camp Mak-A-Dream in MT on 7/1. A camp for teens with a cancer diagnosis. Very excited for him. Nervous about him switching planes in Chicago. His nephew Dominic turns 2 on 6/29 and we get to be at his birthday party which is nice. Last year we were in the hospital when he turned one. Brian is going to be on channel 8 on Thursday in the afternoon for Make-A-Wish. They are going to be doing a piece on the a show - so we go Thurs. morning to tape it. Brian is enjoying his new found freedom of driving his own car. He has been playing tennis, taking drives around to work on his photography and jamming on his guitars. I don't know where he gets his musical talent, but it isn't me that's for sure!

Brian is going to come watch me shave my head in July. Of course he is my honor child. And I hope to raise as much money as I can to help St. Baldrick's, who is the number one foundation for funding pediatric cancer research. I'm excited to shave my head. Any time I think how terrible I might look bald, I think of all the cancer patients, children and adults alike that have no choice. I have a choice, and I can raise money to try to help, by giving up my hair for a little while. No big deal. But here is what has hit me over the past few days. As I read the profiles of the amazing Mommas I have learned new words like 'angelversary'. I have read more stories than I care to, about children who are no longer here. One boy in particular who lived 6 months after being diagnosed with Burkitt. But that was all he got. I could practically hyperventilate just typing those words. So it dawned on me over the weekend that I'm going to meet all these families. Some with children in treatment, some with children who are survivors like Brian and some who no longer have their babies to hold. And selfishly, it is terrifying me. What will I say? How will I offer them any comfort? This will be my first time being this deep in the pediatric cancer world. And I want to make sure I say the right things, give the right support, be of help in any way I can, but I feel like I might freeze up and just burst into tears. I'm afraid. I'm afraid because I will be meeting my greatest fear face to face. Moms who have had their children die from cancer. It is sobering for me. I couldn't care less about my hair. That's nothing. But this is another thing

I have to face. I want to feel like all kids make it, even though I know they don't. But I have turned my cheek a little during this last year to the ones who don't. And now I have to turn my head and make eye contact with the sobering reality of pediatric cancer. I can do it, I will do it, but it's gonna hurt. It is probably going to knock me backwards for a little while. Bring up fears that haven't really been laid to rest yet. That really never will. It will be my reminder to pay attention, every day. To make sure I make the most of the next 24 hrs. One day at a time. Every day. And know I'm lucky, because today I get to spend with my son. And I won't waste it. I will do everything I can to appreciate all parts of our world. Doing what I have to do with a grateful heart. I just hope I can give these families something, some sort of support, like you all have given us.

I know now that everything shows up for a reason. Even the bad stuff, the hurtful stuff, the ugly stuff. And I think now, that it shows up at the right time. I guess it is the right time for me to face this side of pediatric cancer. And try to do something about it, in a teeny tiny little way. But if we all do a teeny, tiny little bit - it will add up. And good will prevail, eventually, it always does I believe. So....I will attach what I sent out a few days ago and ask again that you help me help these kids, these survivors, these angels. Anything and everything will help.

Next month we visit Boston for our 1 year visit on July 18th. After that, we will start going every 2-3 months. A bit scary, yes. But I think...I think I'm ready. I know Brian is ready, and that's what this is about.

I hope you all enjoy this next month and I hope summer finally arrives! Thank you all for listening and continuing to support us.

Love & Love & Light.

Leslie

July 2014

JULY 7, 2014

Sent: Monday, July 07, 2014 8:10 AM
From: Leslie Jermainne
To: Liz
Subject: Thank you!!!

Dear Liz,

I can't write these words without starting to cry already. First of all, thank you for your "anonymous" donation. I'm writing this here because of your choice for anonymity. But really our words are too deep for the world to see on Facebook anyway. Please know I appreciate your support in my fight against childhood cancer. Your money will make a difference, you know that.

But what really makes a difference is your love for me and my son and my family. This has been so incredibly hard Liz. These last 14 1/2 months have been so devastatingly sad, terror filled, heart wrenching months. And I am so God Damn lucky. I mean those words deeply. I am lucky because my son is alive and he could have died. He still can, I know that, but every day is so different now, and so am I. I am lucky because his treatment went pretty much to perfection, if there is such a thing for cancer treatment. I am so lucky because he is alive and happy and doing well and moving forward. I am so lucky because I love my husband and he loves me and we are a team, even when not perfectly happy every single day. I am so lucky because I have friends who love me, deeply. Who feel my pain and worry and cry with me and for me. They may not completely understand what it is I've gone through and continue to go through, but the fact that they try, and haven't lost sight of the fact that this isn't over for me, well....I am blessed. I can't say enough how much the support, just little droplets of love sprinkled through the life of a person dealing with a trauma, means to that person and keeps them moving forward. It has amazed me.

I worry that because this event has changed me in many, many ways and probably will continue, that my friends will tire of me and this fight, this trauma. I worry that they will grow weary of me talking about this. I worry that they will become annoyed with my different view on life, and so I sometimes am quieter than I used to be, because I don't want to scare people away. I feel like our "girls" weekend, I was quiet and maybe you all thought I was distant or not doing well in my recovery. But I try now, to keep some of my newly discovered opinions to myself, because my life has gone where I hope none of yours go. I will say it is a blessing now that I've gotten through to this day, and I wish the entire world could see things how I see them now, how I'm changing every day to see them - but of course they would have to go through the dark to get there. And the dark is blindly black, and heart-wrenchingly scary and because of that, I hope you never know it. So if I was quiet and you were concerned it was only me listening to my friends' talk of their lives and their children and their happiness and their worries and complaints. I listened with open ears and quiet mouth, because I am sure I would be so irritating if I tried to keep reminding everyone that their worries for their children are so unneeded. That worries do nothing. Love does everything. That every day, every 24 hours is a gift. That support and love and understanding and time are the only important elements needed in the day and are the gifts to give our babies.

So I worry that everyone will tire of me. That I will sound full of myself. That I will sound lecturing and really I just want to be a friend and to soothe and to say "don't worry, your children and you and your families are doing just fine." I don't want to lecture from a point of - this is how you should be....I want to tell all four of you.... "You all are doing an amazing job raising and loving your babies. Don't worry so much, just love this day you have. They are all going to be fine." But I think it will come out crazy and you all will just be like "she is so different now. No fun. She doesn't drink. She doesn't complain. She seems quiet, maybe sad." And I can't lose my friends. These are the people I need. And you are the number one person. The person on this earth that knows me the very, very best. Knows all the ins and outs of my life. My fears, my faults, my regrets, my mistakes, my joys and my humor and my dreams and my triumphs. You don't judge me, you don't lecture me, you support me and love me. You have known almost every year (except the first four that I barely remember too) of my life. I don't know how I got so lucky to meet you so early in my life, but I'm sure it was my second true blessing (my first being, my mom being my mom.) I mean that. These aren't words for me that I'm writing, these are my heart letting out its feeling.

My heart shattered into a million little pieces the day Brian was diagnosed. It is strength I didn't know I had and love that was given to me, that has put them back together, slowly, piece by jagged piece. Some of the pieces have been too small to get back together and so love fills in the cracks. It is still rebuilding, but people who love me are the ones bringing me back and propelling me forward. I hope I'm not rambling too much. I have missed you, especially these last two weeks or so. I feel a bit disconnected from you and it unsettles my soul. We both have busy lives. We have jobs and husbands and babies and pets and friends and shopping and cleaning and parents and family that take up our days. One day rolls into the next and I miss you. I feel unable to find the time, with you at work and me with my parents and tons of shit, to find the time to just call and say hi, and I regret that. I will do better. I need to do better, because I need you always in my life. No matter the time, the distance, the struggles, I need my longest, dearest, must trusted friend in my life. And I know you are there for me, and I know you have been towing our boat this last year and I appreciate you so much for doing that. I have been so needy and I will continue to be needy for a while, if I'm honest. But I will try to row my side of the boat more and better so you know that I'm still with you, and that I care, and that I want to hear what your life is doing, and be a support to you, like you have been for me.

Life is really good now Liz. I know you worry about me. I have bad days. But everyone does. Mine might have tinges of scary things that most don't know, but overall, things are coming back together even better than before. Some days I don't realize it. It is like the pains of growing legs. It hurts, I don't understand it, I can't control it, but a day or a week later I see that I'm taller and then I understand that those painful days brought me here, to this new height. This has been the hardest, strangest but in some ways the most rewarding and educating year of my life. I feel like I "get it" now. I get the meaning of life. For me anyway. And it is a belief and thought that tries to escape my hands all the time, but I know the feel of it now, and I grasp it at the last second, on days when it slips through my loosened fingers. And I remember, I feel it, pet it, rub it in my hand and remember that love is the answer and I'm here to just experience this fast and fleeting life and that no day holds any guarantees of anything. So every day I wake up now and I remind myself at some point in the day, sometimes several times a day, that I only have this 24 hours. So love my baby, love my peeps, see beauty, be kind and do my best, whatever that level of best is for that day, and forgive myself that some days the best I can do, isn't very good, but that's okay too. Today it is this letter, telling you how much I love you, how important you and our friendship is to me, to let you know I'm not just okay, but good - even if different and to ask you to stick with me, even though I know you have no thoughts of doing anything but.

So thank you for your donation. Your support that way really does mean a lot. But your support all the other ways in my life is my true gift, and for that, I thank you all the more.

Have a good day, my very best friend.

Love you,
Leslie

JULY 19, 2014

Sent: Saturday, July 19, 2014 10:13 AM
From: Leslie Jermainne
To: My List
Subject: Brian Ross update 7/19/2014

Hi!!!

I am almost done with these updates. I am thinking that my head shaving event next weekend is the end of this journey. Obviously not the end, end. But the end of updating everyone. The end of the intensity of a childhood cancer diagnosis stomping on our lives. I am looking at this event next weekend as a marker and a day of empowerment for me. A day when I say "ENOUGH!" to the fear, the worries, the trauma. I'm taking back the power, as best I can and doing it in a positive way, to help raise funds to beat this beast into submission.

So, yesterday was Brian's official one year visit at the Jimmy Fund. We had a nice ride up - seeing the "Happy Friday" guy at the ticket booth when we get on the Mass Pike. There is this guy that we always seem to be lucky enough to get our ticket from. And every time he says "Happy Friday" and we drive off and high five each other because we got the Happy Friday guy and we know it's gonna be a good day. So this time, on our last monthly visit - we gave Happy Friday guy a card and thanked him for being a part of journey. How happy he had made us and how he contributed to our success. We gave him a handcrafted beautiful Thank You card crafted by my sister Alison, with a quick story of how he has affected us and a small gift. You should have seen the look on his face as we yelled "Bye, Happy Friday" and drove off. I hope it made his day! It sure made ours.

Our checkup was great as we got to see Brian's friend Lynn and her parents also there for her checkup. We got to see Anna our NP (last time we only saw our oncologist) and Brian got to tell her his story about camp. Or should I say not going to camp. I'll keep my rendition brief. On 7/1/14 Brian was up and ready to leave the house before I even got out of bed at 3:50 a.m. We hit the road at 4 a.m., got to Bradley, and I sent him off. I got myself a coffee and plunked down to wait until his flight officially left. Then I drove home. About 20 seconds of tears in the car for me, and then just happiness for him. Until....I get a text at about 12:10 that his connecting flight from Chicago to Missoula, MT was cancelled. WHAT!!!! I tell him it will be fine, go to the counter and they will put you on a later flight. I email the camp, and then call United. Once I get someone at the airline they assure me he has been rebooked....on July 4th!!! Ummmm, no! She tells me to calm down. Not the right words to tell me. After I start getting very stern and explain that my 16 year old son is traveling by himself, as an adult since they won't do unaccompanied minor unless it is a non-stop flight, and that he is on his way to MT to a camp for kids with cancer, I burst into tears. This at least gets her cooperation. She starts frantically searching for a way to get him there, but it doesn't work. I tell her FLY HIM HOME! Meanwhile I'm texting with Brian and he is DONE! He just wants to come home too. They get him on a flight leaving Chicago at 1pm flying standby and then that gets delayed by 4 hrs. A wonderful woman working at United and at the gate assures me that she will take care of my baby for the rest of the day. She says "I'm a mother of 4 and today I'm a mother of 5." More tears. He does make it home and Alison comes with me to get him at Bradley that night. He is wiped out, but has quite a story to tell. So....camp didn't happen. And in the scheme of things, it is fine. Nothing like that much matters anymore. Only his health and that he is here and well and happy is important.

So here we are at a new milestone. Our monthly visits to Boston are over. We don't go back until October 15th! Do you know how far away that is? FAR! I'm happy, confident and nervous. No, not nervous really what would be the right word....unsteady, maybe? It is just new, a new chapter. When we go back in October he will have his usual checkup and an updated echocardiogram, always watchful for long term cardiac damage from the chemo. So far it has been good - and I choose to believe it's gonna stay that way.

As far as our summer goes - it is going quickly. We have done a remodel job to convert 1/2 bath into a full (about to go paint) and Bri and I are going to the Sunflower for Wishes event next Monday to help out Make-A-Wish by volunteering our time. We might be there Thurs. too if they need us. Looking forward to it. Then next week it is off to Boston to shave my head. I left my flyer attached below, just...in....case....

I will update you on the head shaving event next week, and then I'm gonna sign off. Say goodbye and thanks for listening. It's time. I know.

Love & Light.

Leslie

August 2014

AUGUST 1, 2014

Sent: Friday, August 01, 2014 1:09 PM
From: Leslie Jermainne
To: My List
Subject: Brian Ross update 8/1/2014

Hi Everyone!

I did it! I shaved my head!! Here is a before and after.

Let me tell you about this experience. It. Was. Awesome. Big Brian and I went to Boston on Saturday. We had such a nice day together, one we both realized we need more of, badly. Then I got to meet all these amazing women. Women like me whose children have survived. Women who are still fighting this battle with their children, hoping for remission. Women who have faced the unthinkable, whose children have been snatched from them and their hearts have been shattered. And yet they come, they fight still, for their angels and for all the children and their families. They raise money and awareness. They shave their heads and then venture out into the world vulnerable, but brave. They are heroic. They are the inspiration. They, like me, understand that 46 more mothers are going to join our ranks today. And 46 more tomorrow. And they know what they are going to face. They know the utter shock, pain and grief they are about to feel. They know the sleepless nights and the never ending days they are about to endure. They understand the vocabulary that these new mothers will learn. We all know, yet we can't stop it from coming. At least not yet. But with the help of great foundations like St. Baldrick's I choose to believe we will get there one day.

I thought I was going to be an emotional mess when they started shaving my head, but honestly, I was happy. I felt freedom and strength. I felt empowered and I still do. So having no hair is awesome, but it is already growing - fast! My morning shower is so fast I sometimes stand there and think, "What did I forget?" I spend no time blow drying my head, which is super nice when it is this warm out. I don't have to deal with my hair blowing in my face when driving, because I prefer to have the window down than air conditioning on. Everything about it is great. I think I would keep it like this, if my family would agree. I kind of doubt I will ever have it long again.

A lot of you have already seen these photos and you have donated to help St. Baldrick's. Thank you so very much. I very deeply appreciate your help and support. In the beginning days of cancer, I felt very alone and completely scared and panicked. I was amazed by all the support, especially from so many people that I didn't even expect to be touched by our story.

I was going to say, "now that I have come full circle", but you know what - I haven't. It is more like a spiral that started with a huge hard center and every day has been along the path of a circle but never back to where it started, always growing, always expanding. Today, Brian has three friends visiting (unfortunately a 4th couldn't make it last minute). Friends he made at The Jimmy Fund teen program. Three friends who know what he's been through, without needing to discuss it in detail. Today I have so many more friends thanks to people in my life who give me never ending support and through the 46 Mommas who understand my spiraling path.

We are lucky. Deeply lucky people. Our son is here, alive, well and thriving. Our marriage is intact and stronger than ever. Our family has tightened and our friendships have grown. I now know that everything happens for a reasons. Everything. And now I am more able to recognize and trust those reasons. Even the really crappy stuff. The life changing, mind altering, heart opening stuff.

So....this is my last "update". You've all had enough and so have I. Brian needs me to move on too, and he is right. He is my greatest teacher. He always has been. I just didn't know it before. I thought I was teaching him. I don't know what our future holds. And really neither do you. I now really live to the best of my ability 24 hours at a time. Sure I plan and worry and think and dream, but then I stop myself and remind myself that today is all I've got. And this **IS** the most important day.

Thank you all for listening. It is great to express yourself, but sometimes you need a listening ear to know you've said anything at all. Thank you for all your prayers and thoughts these past 15 months. Please keep Brian in your mind for continued good health.

All my love.

Leslie

PS I attached something I wrote the day before shaving my head. It was on Facebook so many of you read it already, but not everyone on my list is on Facebook, so this is just in case....

Why I'm Shaving My Head Tomorrow....

July 26, 2014 at 6:14am

Why am I shaving my head? I guess you could say I'm shaving for 3 people. I'm shaving to honor my son who is a one year survivor of Stage III Burkitt Lymphoma. I'm shaving to empower myself, to move forward as best I can and do something big to mark my son's one year in remission date. But in all honesty I'm shaving for a woman I don't know. A woman

I will never meet. I will never know her name or her child's name. But I do know that tomorrow her world is going to come to a crashing halt.

She will have already spent days, weeks or months sick with worry. She will probably have been to see her child's doctor numerous times. She may have already made several emergency room visits with her sick child. Or she may be like me, and her child isn't sick at all. Her baby just has a lump that won't go away.

She will be sitting in some hospital waiting room with too bright lights and a cup of cold coffee somewhere nearby. She will be pretending to read a book or a magazine while she wonders how her baby is doing in surgery. She will see the doctor walk in and she will hear some of the most horrible words of her life. "Your child has cancer."

She may be like me and look at him and try to absorb every word, but in reality her mind has turned down the volume on the world. She will nod her head and try to swallow the rising tide she feels coming. She will strain to hear words she doesn't understand and all the while her mind is thinking of her baby, whether that baby is 15 hours old or 15 years old, make no mistake that is her baby. And someone just told her in a whole bunch of confusing words that her child is sick, but really they told her that her baby might die. They don't say those words, but every word that sounds like lymphoma, sarcoma, myeloma feels like hearing, "dying, death, gone."

She will burst into tears at some point. The doctor who is probably a surgeon, not an oncologist, tries to comfort her. This surgeon is having a lousy day too. He or she will go home that night and when asked the usual question of "How was your day?" The answer will be, "Terrible. I had to tell a mother her child had cancer. You should have seen the look on her face. She was so shocked, so broken, so bewildered and so alone. I tried to comfort her, but how...how do you tell someone that the one thing they love most in this life, is about to start the most horrendous time of their still young life. That honestly it started a while ago and they didn't even know it. And it might end in her child dying. I will never, ever forget her face."

After hearing the quick diagnosis this Mom will be taken to her child who is groggy and sleepy in a recovery room. She will have to pull herself together and act like it is fine. She will pass faces in the waiting room, nurses and doctors and staff in the hall. She will enter a dimly lit room where a nurse is hovering around her child, checking things, reading her computer and listening to the monitor beep.

She will touch her child ever so gently, her innocence as a mother already shattered into tiny little fragments. She will stroke his hair, touch his arm, smile into his face as he opens his drugged up eyes and looks into hers. The doctor will come in and quickly explain that it is lymphoma, or some other dreaded "-oma". And he will leave. And her child, if old enough to understand, will look into her eyes and say "that's cancer, right Mom?" "Yes honey, it's cancer." The nurse listening to this is heartbroken and leaves to get him some water. And then it is the two of them, looking into each other's eyes. The two souls who have shared a body early in life and shared a life since the day they no longer shared a body. There aren't really words to say. She will have no idea what is coming, but she can tell her child the universal words of comfort, "It's going to be okay."

From that point on, everything is weird and different. Everything. She will have this voice in her head that repeats over and over "my child has cancer". It will want to say it out loud to everyone. Every. One. Because life keeps moving and she will have to see people. At the grocery store, pizza place, gas station. She will look shell shocked as she gets her baby home. She won't remember many details of this day, but she will have a highlight reel that she will watch over and over and over in her head for....well....ever. And that movie will grow and grow over the next few weeks and months and maybe years. It will regain color and sound and even smells will be added. New characters will be added to the story and dialogue she thought she would never learn will become words she uses without thought. Big words like cyclophosphamide, doxorubicin and methotrexate. She will watch her baby be wheeled away from her time and time again as he or she is taken to have some procedure. She will sit in the waiting room every single time and cry and pray. She will watch as bags of poison are hung on the pole that stands ever present beside her baby and watch it flow into their port, the chunk of plastic a surgeon put into her babies chest and veins so that the medicine can go in and blood come out without poking his poor little arms every single time. She will learn how to silence a pump alarm, cry in public, exist on coffee and spend hours doing nothing but pouring love into her baby.

She will beg, threaten, plead and cry to the world, to God, to anyone who will listen. She will ask for the cancer to be moved to her and she will promise she won't even fight it. It can have her, but it has to leave her child alone. Forever. She will cry more than she thought possible. She will read and digest more information on a subject she never wanted to know anything about. She will become somewhat of an expert on blood counts, lumbar punctures, nausea control and fevers. She will learn to live in a 8x10 space probably with another mother and child in the 8x10 space next to them, separated by a curtain that can feel like a brick wall or like thin air depending on the day. She will gladly sleep, if you can call it sleep on a rock hard little chair, just so she can be within 2 feet of her baby at all times. She will sometimes leave the room to get coffee, do laundry, get some food or just get some air, the whole time wanting to run back and kiss that little face again and again and again.

She will feel completely alone at times and she will think that if her child dies, she will die too. She will want to die and she will think of ways to make that happen. But every time she thinks those terrible thoughts of being separated from her baby, it is like a painful stab with a hot knife and she will shove it quickly from her mind before it can take over and do even more damage than it did when she thought it 5 minutes ago.

She will smile at her child through all this. She will reassure that it will be okay. She will entertain, snuggle, read and encourage this child like her life depends on it, because it does. She will listen to every test result with a sick stomach hoping for good words. She will find her strength and she will ask a million questions and she will advocate for her child and their needs. She will constantly fear the worst and pray for the best. And small victories will feel like wars won. And big victories feel scary and joyful all at the same time. And if she is lucky to go home with her child on the road of remission, she will know how lucky she is and she will know to never take one single second for granted ever again. She will understand like no other, how precious and delicate and strong life really is. She will think that someday this may be over. But over the next months of being on constant watch for any teeny, tiny sign that something is not okay she will slowly realize this will NEVER. EVER. END. And by "this", I mean her worry. Her praying and begging that her baby be okay. That he won't relapse. That her child will heal. That her child will regain their strength, their energy, their life. That their baby won't develop so many of the long term effects that they were told about in the beginning, but honestly she didn't even listen too, because "long term" was too far away at that point and mostly because they had no other choice. Nobody asked them if they wanted their child to receive chemotherapy or radiation. And this mother will easily, without a second thought, sell her soul to save her baby.

And if she is this lucky to be at home worrying about every too long nap, warm feeling head, lump or bump, she will never, ever forget that some mothers don't get to do this part. That some mothers go home without their babies. And it makes her feel sick to her stomach. Every single time.

She is the person I'm shaving my head for. She is the one that has no idea what's coming tomorrow. She is about to have her life veer off in a direction she doesn't understand at an unstoppable speed and if she makes it through the ride, she will be such a different person than the person she wakes up as tomorrow morning, before the day even starts. And she has no idea. Today she is safe. Her child is sick, but she doesn't really know how much. So by doing this small, tiny act of shaving my head, I hope that one day, there will be a tomorrow that no mother hears some of the worst words of her life: "your child has cancer." I am shaving for her and for the other 45 Mommas that don't know that tomorrow will forever change their lives. I'm shaving for her. And she is me.

Epilogue – written January 2, 2015

(18 months of remission today!!!)

So, I've put this all into a book. I honored and listened to what my friends and family and the universe told me to do. My hope is my story helps another Cancer Mom. Or maybe those people that are supporting that Cancer Mom. Maybe it will help them to understand what she *might* be feeling. That it offers some comfort, some understanding and maybe a little courage. I hope that Mom knows she is not alone.

As I have re-read each and every note, it has been hard to do. I have cried through a lot of it. I have heard my voice and re-lived the worst days of my life. I heard some laughter, some hope, lots of gratitude and a ton of fear. I don't know if my voice translates to others, but here is what my voice sounds like now.

My "new normal" is one of profound gratitude. Especially when reading these words. Right now my son is asleep in his warm and cozy bed, in our lovely house. His car is parked outside, he has just finished his high school homeschool program and working out what he wants to do next. He is thriving in life – and really, nothing else matters.

I have learned more about myself and my beliefs in the past 17 months than I think I would have ever learned in this lifetime had I not gone through this experience. I am not asking anyone to adopt my beliefs nor for anything really. I have only wanted to share my story in hopes it will help someone else. But I thought it would be a good wrap up to tell you what I HAVE LEARNED out of this horrible experience. Some I have said before, and every day it seems I make new realizations and find new questions to ask myself and new thoughts to ponder.

1. I have figured out that there are no guarantees in life. None. I have no "rights". I don't have the right to a long life. And neither do my loved ones. I don't have the right for great health care, or any for that matter. Many people in the world sadly don't have any. I don't have the right to be treated any differently than anyone else. I don't have the right for happiness to be handed to me. It only comes from the inside anyway. I don't have the right to receive love or to give love, but every day I chose to do both. I don't have the right for food or health insurance or shoes or a home. But, I have the ability to have all those things, if I want them, how I want them and it's up to me to figure those things out. Life can be incredibly hard, but no one owes me anything. I owe myself everything.
2. Life really is incredibly simple. Yet I had made it so overwhelmingly complicated. My life is about loving my child, my husband, my family and my friends. And a lot about loving me. That is a big one! Every day will come whether I'm ready or not, whether I have worried about it or planned for it or made a wish about how it will be. Life now is only the next 24 hours. And that is an incredible struggle every damn day. I think I drive my husband a bit nuts now when I tell him "that's too far away to think about". But it is my truth and every day has gotten so much better since I know it's all I have.
3. Health is everything. I used to hear that statement and think, "of course health is everything, without it you'd be dead." Pretty simple to say and understand, right? But I really would like to sleep more and I love chocolate chip cookies and red wine, and its cold outside in New England and I don't want to exercise. Then someone told me my son's body was essentially attacking him and he could die. And I learned for real what "Your Health is Everything" means. Like, for real. I would have given everything in my life, I would have given my own life, for him to have his health back at that moment and from that day on. So today? Well,

I eat much healthier. I think about exercising every day. But for me the biggest reality of that thought is knowing it is true. Health is everything. But you can't control all of it. You can do things to help yourself in your daily life, and you probably should if you choose. But better yet, for me, is to live this 24 hours the best, healthiest, happiest way I can. And never take life or health for granted.

4. I need to trust myself, completely. And trust that, for the most part the world and its' inhabitants are good, and the good will triumph in the long run. Before this terrible experience, I was thinking the world and its' people were 'bad'. War, starvation, illness, violence, destroying the atmosphere, the soil, the water. Don't eat this, don't drink that, don't wear perfume, don't use cleaners, white vinegar can do anything. Exercise for an hour every day, buy organic, take your vitamin, meditate, set goals. For me, it is intense and makes me crazy to listen to everyone else tell me how to live my life. No more. Now I do it my way. I read about what I care about, I never watch the news, read a newspaper or use a news type page as my home page on my computer. I don't want to invite all the negativity into my life about what the rest of the world is doing. I am trusting myself and learning to love myself and even more importantly learning to be kind to myself. I'm a good person and I should give myself more credit and love myself today, just as I am. I have a faith that the world will work it out, and if I do my part by being me, loving people, being kind and putting positive energy into my life every day, it will seep out into the world with all the other positive people and things will work out. They always do.

5. I have learned to trust that everything happens for a reason. Everything. No exceptions. Sometimes the reason is a bad one. But it is a reason. Some reasons I may never know, but I believe they are there. The reason my son had cancer is nothing more than the fact that sometimes people get cancer. The body isn't perfect. The world isn't perfect. It doesn't have to be some big reason, some life changing reason. But sometimes it is, if you choose to look at it that way. They told us that this cancer is a simple mistake. A cell splits and two chromosomes get reversed and set off a chain

reactions of cell growth. The body made a mistake. If I think about it, it amazes me that not every person in the world gets cancer. We all have cancerous cells they say, and our immune system takes care of them, hopefully. So why didn't Brian's immune system\ take care of these cells before they got out of control. I don't know, neither do the doctors – at least right now. Do people get cancer so doctors and researchers can figure it out? Is that the reason? That seems stupid, and heartbreaking, but maybe…

6. We all have a fight we're fighting. I have learned through my own experience that you may see people walking on the street, in the grocery store, at your child's school or sitting at the beach and you have not a single clue what they have going on in their life. It may seem they haven't a care in the world when really they are just trying to get through the grocery store without bursting into tears and coming to a halt, unable to move when the fear takes a grip and won't let go. Maybe they are crabby to the clerk at the donut shop because they just lost their job and don't know how they will support their loved ones. Maybe they seem quiet or distant or angry because their parent is dying and it's hard to watch and understand. Maybe they avoid your eye contact because they just found out their baby has cancer and they can't really talk without bursting into uncontrollable sobs. I look at everyone so differently now, and I wonder what their behavior is really masking. And even if you know that person's troubles, and you've had the same or close, you don't know what they are going through, because everyone is unique, every situation is unique and it is very different for every person. And EVERYONE is fighting and doing the best they can. Period.
7. Reach out. I learned to be such a better friend from this. I learned from some people in my life what support really means. I also learned from others that they have no idea. But they probably did their best. Mostly I learned to reach out. Even small little droplets help the person in crisis. A post on Facebook that says "hang in there" or a voicemail that just says, "I was just thinking of you." A longer note offering encouraging words, but not telling your own story of woe. Not telling the person you understand exactly

what they are going through, and not giving advice. And for me, I didn't like to hear the words "I just know it's going to be okay. He's going to be fine." Because people don't really know and I sort of wanted to shout back in their face that they have no freaking idea if he would be okay. But of course I didn't and of course I knew they were trying to encourage and do the best they could do. So maybe don't say that one. Unless you are psychic and you really, really do know. Just saying "I hear you. I'm thinking (praying) for you. I'm listening..." That is all it takes. And people need that so much. From family, from friends, from acquaintances, from friends of acquaintance's.

8. It is what it is. Such a simple five words, but it has helped me get through so much. Instead of being stuck on the why, I get to skip over that, because usually the why doesn't come until much, much later, if ever. So saying to myself "It is what it is" lets me move on to a solution. Or to work towards a solution or if nothing else, it brings acceptance. I had a few people say to me "why did Brian get cancer? He's such a good kid!" Never once did I say "I know, right!" I never even thought that thought. At the moment they told me he had cancer I was shocked and sad and so very afraid. But I guess I also knew instantly that it was what it was. No child, no person deserves cancer. Kids who maybe someone judges as not being such a "good kid", well...they should never get cancer either.
9. Less is more. Ugh. If only I could go back and not accumulate stuff. Not waste money on things. Oh the time I squandered on material things. Acquiring, housing, cleaning, disposing. All that time I could have spent doing some nothing with my loves. One thing I hope Brian will take away from this is that less is more. Always. We need way less than we think. And I hope for way more time. Time to watch sunrises and sunsets. Time to read and time to sit and talk. Time to nap, time to garden, time to laugh. Time to play and share good food. Just time. It's the most important commodity. And I don't know if you can learn that lesson, without facing the loss of all time.
10. Let go of the idea of control. I am a control freak. Or at least I was. Nothing like a life threatening illness in your child, or a

loved one to show you that you have no control. None. Zip. Zero. Nada. Your only control is over yourself, how you react, how you deal, what you do to move forward. And sometimes, you have no control over that, at least for a little while. And instead of worrying I can't control "it", I have learned that it is pure, sunshiny freedom that accompanies the acceptance of the loss of control. Or honestly the realization you never had it anyway. Of course control freak still lives in me, but I now listen to what she says and then laugh a little, shake my head, and remind myself, that I have no control. So relax, and just deal. The time I spent trying to control the uncontrollable…ugh. Let go and be ready to deal, as best you can. That's it.

This seems like a good place to stop. I am filled with joy at how my life has changed. I wish it never did. Does that make sense? Probably not to everyone. I mean, I wish my son never heard the word cancer. I wish I didn't either, because it sucks. All of it. BUT…if I choose gratitude in my life, which I do, then I am grateful that I learned so many wonderful things from the horribleness that is cancer. My life is better now, because of what I learned – not because of cancer. I have a "new normal" and it is a "better normal" and honestly it isn't "normal" at all. None of our lives are normal and I don't even like that word. My life is my life. And yours is yours. Enjoy it, as best you can, every single day. You never know where it will take you, but eventually I hope you will know why.

Printed in the United States
By Bookmasters

Printed in the United States
By Bookmasters